# RADICAL OR REDUNDANT?

# RADICAL OR REDUNDANT?

## MINOR PARTIES IN IRISH POLITICS

EDITED BY LIAM WEEKS AND ALISTAIR CLARK

The
History
Press
Ireland

First published 2012

The History Press Ireland
119 Lower Baggot Street
Dublin 2
Ireland
www.thehistorypress.ie

British Library Cataloguing in Publication Data.
A catalogue record for this book is available from the British Library.

ISBN 978 1 84588 744 5

Typesetting and origination by The History Press

# Contents

# 1

# The Dog that Failed to Bark: Why Did No New Party Emerge in 2011?

*Liam Weeks*

## Prologue

As the Irish state has changed, so too have the types of minor, or small, parties that have emerged in the political arena. Where once were the farmers of Clann na Talmhan, the liberals of the Progressive Democrats (PDs) and the environmentalists of the Greens, there now sits in the Dáil a range of former left-wing revolutionaries in the guise of Sinn Féin and within the broad unmbrella group, the United Left Alliance. This book looks at this evolution of minor parties in Ireland, in particular their rise and fall and their lasting political impact. Drawing on a range of sources, including interviews with many of the leading protagonists, we detail the fortunes of minor parties, examine the consequences of participation in government and look at why they fail to persist. We assess the reasons for minor parties emerging, their impact on the political system and why voters fall in and out of love so easily with them. One over-riding theme is the reasons for such parties remaining minor, about which this book offers a fresh insight.

Bringing together some of the leading academic authorities on Irish politics, this volume is a combination of comparative and case studies, which also places the Irish experience of minor parties in the international context. With the first-time entry of the Greens into government in 2007, their wipeout in 2011, the termination of the Progressive Democrats in 2009, and the failure of a new party to emerge despite the ongoing financial crisis, the time is ripe for an analysis of minor parties. For anyone interested in Irish politics and political parties, whether it is those looking to form a new party, to vote for such a party, or just to read about them, this work should be of significance. Readers will be able to evaluate the merits of the claim of Michael McDowell, one of the original founders and later leader of the Progressive Democrats, that minor parties need to be radical to avoid redundancy.

## Introduction

For some, the 2011 general election was Ireland's 'earthquake' election.[1] However, although the dominant party of Irish politics, Fianna Fáil, experienced losses of seismic proportions, when the dust settled the three pillars of Irish party politics remained standing. No new party emerged to take their place, and between them Fine Gael, Labour and Fianna Fáil won 133 of the Dáil's 166 seats, the same total won by these parties at the 2002 election.

One to two years before the 2011 election such an outcome might have come as a surprise to some. An increasing level of disillusionment with the political establishment's failure to deal with the economic crisis, and the apparent lack of an alternative choice had motivated talk of a new political party. In many ways the circumstances were similar to that of the mid-1980s, when the Progressive Democrats had emerged in a recession, offering a new political platform and threatening to 'break the mould' of Irish politics. Indeed, an opinion poll in the *Sunday Independent* in June 2010 detected a desire for a new mould-breaker, with a majority of voters agreeing that a new political party was needed.[2] A new political movement, 'Democracy Now', was resultantly established to tap into this sentiment. Its intention was to run a list of high-profile non-political candidates, including media commentators such as soccer pundit and journalist Eamon Dunphy, *The Irish Times* columnist Fintan O'Toole, and economist David McWilliams. With as much as €400,000 pledged to the group in one day and a significant number of voluntary staff and even free campaign offices provided,[3] it seemed as if the group's aim of twenty seats in the new Dáil might not be unrealistic. In the end, however, the aspirations of this movement came to naught, as it decided not to contest the election in the absence of one resource it could not acquire: time.

There were other attempts to create parties in 2010 and 2011, some via the letters column of *The Irish Times*,[4] but most of these did not come to fruition. The new movements that did emerge were more akin to loose umbrella groups than political parties,[5] and in any case none had a notable electoral impact in the 2011 general election. What adds to the puzzle of new party failure is the relative success achieved by independents. Although Ireland has always been exceptional for its number of independent parliamentarians,[6] in 2011 one in three candidates was independent and their combined vote, at 12 per cent, was the highest achieved since June 1927. Including the loose group United Left Alliance, there were nineteen independents and 'others' elected, just one fewer than Fianna Fáil's total. This group of parliamentarians is quite a diverse collection, ranging from building developers-cum-soccer coaches to Harvard-educated management consultants and from former campaigners for the legalisation of cannabis to a range of left-wing TDs, including former members of Militant Labour, the Socialist Workers' Party, Sinn Féin and Democratic Left. The wide spectrum of ideological flavours (which did not stop a majority of them from banding together to form a post-election technical group in parliament) provided by these independents is suggestive of a mood for change amongst a broad section of society. It also suggests that had a new party with a proper organisational structure in place evolved in time for the election, it might have had a successful breakthrough.

In part, this failure to launch a new political party was the motivation for this work. We wanted to examine this non-event in detail, consider what happened in previous crises, both home and abroad, and assess what a new party could hope to achieve. We wanted to look at the experience of other minor parties: when did they emerge; what are the ingredients for a successful new party? As the title suggests, this book is about minor parties in Irish politics. As well as drawing on the analysis of political scientists, this volume also has a number of contributions from TDs from minor parties, both past and present, who provide a unique insight into their lives within such parties. While such a book seems pressing in the absence of a new party on the contemporary political scene, from a historical perspective a study of this area enables a greater understanding of contemporary political events and might prove useful to those taking a keen interest in the evolution of the Irish party system. Such a study also places the events of 2009-12 in context, next to other economic crises. Do they always spawn new parties, or are the latter more likely to be the product of political circumstances? Are we right to link economic change to political change?

Another factor inspiring this volume is the limited scholarly activity on minor parties in the Irish context. This was not the outcome of an apartheid policy on the part of political scientists and historians, but reflected the dominance (and permanence) of Fianna Fáil, Fine Gael and Labour, which together received on average almost nine out of every ten first preference votes cast at general elections between September 1927 and November 1982. However, the challenge to this dominance in recent decades, with minor party and independent candidates now attracting almost one in four votes and being a regular participant in government, demands greater attention. The purpose of this book is to tackle some of the questions about minor parties that have been raised, but gone unanswered, in the Irish context. The dismay of some commentators over the lack of new political parties through which to channel discontent in the economic downturn indicates the valuable, and sometimes underappreciated, role that minor parties can play in the political system. They can act as a safety-valve to release tension, enabling the bodypolitik to vent their frustration within the system, the best opportunity that exists of achieving change. It is in this context that the founder of the Progressive Democrats, Desmond O'Malley, says in his contribution to this book that the emergence of new (which by implication usually means minor) parties is a vital part of an effective political system; without them democracy will suffer and perhaps even die.

The aim of this introductory chapter is twofold: first, to resolve some definitional issues concerning minor parties, and second, to assess why no new party, whether minor or major, has successfully emerged in Ireland in recent years. The first issue concerns what we mean by minor, or perhaps why we call these parties minor. As Coakley notes in his chapter, this concerns identifying two boundaries: the upper boundary separates minor from major while the lower differentiates genuine minor parties from independent candidates. He provides a general discussion on the ambiguity concerning a definition of minor parties, although there is a broader discussion concerning size that is referred to by Clark and McDaid and Rekawek, namely whether minor necessarily implies small. A major party used to attracting a sizeable share of votes and seats might have a poor election, losing the majority of its representation, *à la* Fianna Fáil in 2011 or the Progressive Conservatives in Canada in 1993. Such a party is then small in composition, but is it necessarily a minor actor? In addition, how are we to differentiate between a party on the way up and one on the way down? At the same election in Canada, Bloc Québécois (BQ) won over 13 per cent of the national vote, Reform almost 19 per cent and the Progressive Conservatives (PC) 16 per cent. This was the first election for the BQ, but it constituted a gain of 17 per cent for Reform and a loss of 27 per cent for the Conservatives. Are we to consider all these parties equally? Both BQ and the PC (who won just two federal seats) were small parties, but do their rise and fall constitute the same phenomenon? To resolve this conundrum, both Weeks and Clark in their comparative chapters employ Mair's definition of minor parties[7] that includes those winning between 1.5 and 15 per cent of the national vote on average at more than three elections. For reasons of inclusivity, the lower boundary of this definition is loosened for cases of analysis within the Irish political system. Thus, Coakley, for example, includes all minor parties (and even some groups that have an ambiguous party status) that fall below the 1.5 per cent threshold. To warrant consideration for inclusion in this volume, Weeks ultimately defines the boundaries of interest as the non-permanent (or 'ephemeral') members of the Irish party system, or what Coakley more specifically labels the, 'non-traditional, non-established, and non-mainstream'. This boundary is expanded to include non-party members of the non-establishment, that is, independent candidates. The latter's inclusion reflects the significant role they play as part of the 'others' category outside of the three mainstream parties; it also reflects an ambiguity that can exist between some minor parties and independents.[8]

Of course, it might seem strange to label Labour a 'major' party, as it has only recently become the second largest party in the Dáil, and even then both Fianna Fáil and Sinn Féin have been challenging this position in opinion polls. Consequently, McDaid and Rekawek explore this very issue for Labour, as they examine its fluctuations between major- and minor-party status. The issue of where Labour fits within this work on minor parties was at times troubling. On the one hand, it is obvious that Labour is different to minor parties when we examine its lifespan. All minor parties, with the obvious exceptions of the surviving contemporary examples, have faded into extinction. Labour, in contrast, is the oldest all of Irish parties, in operation since 1912. On the other hand, the electoral performance of Labour pales in significance compared to its social democrat counterparts elsewhere in Europe.[9] At times Labour has occupied a relatively weak position within the party system and seemed on the verge of being relegated to fourth or even fifth place behind other minor challengers. In this context, rather than laying out a diktat for contributors, we encouraged them to provide their own discussion of this issue where necessary. Some, like Clark, have used a comparative measure, borrowed from Mair,[10] to determine whether Labour warrants inclusion (it does for both of them). O'Malley uses his own arbitrary measure, which results in his inclusion of Labour for some elections, but not all. Both Clark and O'Malley interpret 'minor' in terms of size, that is minor parties are small parties. Aside from the relativity of such a definition, we also need to bear in mind that minor captures more than just size. It is related to a mentality both within the party and in terms of attitudes towards it; it is also affected by the nature of party competition. This is why McDaid and Rekawek's chapter is particularly important in understanding how one party can be at times minor, major, or even neither of these statuses.

The universe of non-permanent actors in or on the Irish political landscape is not limited to political parties, but also includes interest groups and independent candidates. As Murphy indicates for the former, and both Hansen and Weeks[11] for the latter, the impact of these actors has been at times considerable. This ranges from independent parliamentarians being the kingmakers in the Dáil to interest groups having an effect on referendum campaigns. The major difficulty for academics concerning these various actors is identifying a clear boundary between all three. When does an interest group become a party? When does an independent become a party? These definitional issues are addressed by Coakley and Murphy. While the differences between a 'major minor' party such as the Progressive Democrats, an interest group (such as the Society for the Protection of the Unborn Child) and an independent candidate are quite considerable, this does not warrant the exclusion of the latter two categories from our analysis. As Murphy indicates, interest groups can constitute a transitory phase for would-be parties and it is important to consider why some morph into political parties. Similarly, an independent position can also constitute a ford-like status for those wishing to cross a river to the opposite bank that is a political party.[12]

When attempting to understand the experience of political parties, sometimes academics can be overly guilty of focusing on esoteric external factors. Those working within parties usually place more emphasis on organisation and strategy. Indeed, most of the contributors in this book refer to the importance of organisation, but Bolleyer, O'Malley and Varley in particular focus on the strategies of minor parties. Bolleyer analyses the transformation of the Greens from an umbrella protest movement to a normal political party, one that became part of the establishment when entering government in 2007. In this light, O'Malley considers what happens to minor parties when they take the ultimate decision to cross the Rubicon and enter government. This is a particularly relevant issue given what happened to the two minor parties in the Fianna Fáil-led government formed in 2007. O'Malley also looks at the actions of the other parties, in particular the manner in which they 'smother' their minor partners in office. Indeed, Walsh and O'Malley in another chapter suggest that this is why Sinn Féin has not suffered a decline comparable to other minor parties – it has never been in government in the south. Varley considers the fortunes of farmers' parties, which were an ever-present up to the 1960s, but disappeared with the emergence of the Irish Farmers' Association and the decline of the agricultural industry. That being said, agriculture is still an important player in Ireland, and if one wonders why this is not reflected in the party system, Varley indicates how the strategies of the various farmers' parties were also culpable for their decline.

What happens within a party might be considered the secret garden of politics, and for this reason the contributions by three past and present minor party politicians are extremely insightful. Desmond O'Malley indicates that the internal struggles within Fianna Fáil could not be kept silent, and from his account it seems that, with hindsight, it was inevitable that some type of breakaway movement would have emerged as a reaction to Haughey's style of leadership. Dan Boyle's account of the internal struggles within the Greens, from its evolution to party status, to the appointment of a leader, to entry into government, indicates the tension between intra-party democracy and centralising efficiencies within minor parties. Catherine Murphy, formerly of the Workers' Party, and later Democratic Left, writes that sometimes such efficiences can result in an over-emphasis on electoral politics, which can distance the party's ideological strands. This theme is also explored by Walsh and O'Malley and Rafter in their respective accounts of the evolution of Sinn Féin and the Workers' Party. Rafter's analysis of the Workers' Party and Democratic Left is a detailed examination of how a party can split and then merge with another.

As Ó Muineacháin discusses, the disappearance of the Progressive Democrats in an economic situation similar to their formation begs the question whether new parties need to be radical to avoid being redundant. While Michael McDowell suggested changing the name of the PDs to the Radical Party in 2000,[13] it is difficult to support the claim that the Irish electorate necessarily want something radical. Certainly they want something different, but the relative weakness of the more ideologically-driven parties suggests that being radical may not be the most rational path for minor parties to follow. The debate over being radical or redundant was not confined to the PDs, as all the minor parties in Ireland inevitably (because almost all of them folded) faced this question. This is a theme that is re-iterated in many of this book's chapters, where it is shown that this is one of the key debating points for minor parties.

So why did no new PDs emerge in 2011? The failure of a new political party to launch in spite of a public appetite for one, not to mention the availability of prospective candidates and campaign resources, indicates the difficulty in getting such a project off the ground. This explains why almost all the new parties that have appeared in the Dáil since 1945 have been related to existing or former parties – they can capitalise on pre-existing structures. Clann na Poblachta and the Green Party are the only genuinely 'new' parties of which we can speak. Why is this the case? With the pre-election period of 2010-11 as the context, the rest of this chapter assesses from a comparative setting why no new party, whether minor or major, successfully emerged in Ireland. Examining the gestation of minor parties is a natural way to begin this book. We examine the various social and political factors that can inhibit would-be parties, as well as the historical reasons for the emergence of new parties in Ireland and its European neighbours. Ireland is not the only country to experience economic and political change in recent years, and placing the country in a comparative context enables an understanding of what really affects new party emergence.

## What is a new party?

Although this book is about minor parties, most new parties begin their political life with a minor status. While there have been exceptions, such as de Valera's Fianna Fáil in 1920s Ireland or Berlusconi's Forza Italia in 1990s Italy, such new major parties tend to be the product of organisational changes in an existing party or a collapse in the old political order.

The ambiguity of concern here, however, is not between that of minor and major parties, but rather between new and old parties. At this point, a classification is usually the preferred technique to distinguish between the various types of minor parties. As Coakley discusses in greater depth elsewhere in this book, the manner of party emergence is one such classification that can be employed. He examines three other dimensions, including electoral, strategic and ideological. Given the thoroughness of Coakley's analysis, there is little need to go into this in more detail; instead the focus here is on the newness of a party and its indicators.

Such indicators are discussed by Barnea and Rahat,[14] who use Key's tripartite conceptualisation of parties[15] – party-in-the-electorate, party-as-organisation, and party-in-government – to distinguish eight criteria of newness, which include party label, ideology, the party's electorate, its formal status on the party register, the party's institutions, its activists, representatives and policies. The reason why so many definitional criteria may be desired is due to the sometimes ambiguous nature of new parties.

Examining this ambiguity in greater detail, the launch of a new organisation at a public event, such as Fianna Fáil at the La Scala theatre in 1926 or the Progressive Democrats at a press conference in 1985, might seem one obvious indicator of new party emergence. However, the line of demarcation between new and old is not necessarily this clear-cut. In these two cases, both parties were breakaway movements, with most of their elite comprising TDs elected for pre-existing parties. To what extent was Fianna Fáil a new party, offering new ideas and new faces? Was it just a re-hash of an increasingly stale brand (that of the anti-Treaty Republicans, who persisted with their refusal to recognise the new state)? Were the Progressive Democrats simply a liberal wing of Fianna Fáil? Was its formation a type of market segmentation, in that it enabled Fianna Fáil to offer an additional product to the electorate?

While these questions are designed to be of a challenging nature, their intention is to indicate that a new name on the market need not necessarily imply a new party. There are numerous examples from the business world of 'new' products, which were simply a redesign, or renaming of pre-existing products. This rebranding is often motivated by a desire to discard a negative image, such as the tobacco company Philip Morris changing its name to Altria in 2003, or closer to home, Anglo Irish Bank being renamed Irish Bank Resolution Corporation Ltd in 2011. This also explains why Fianna Fáil reportedly considered changing its name, and why in the UK in recent years, the Conservatives changed their logo, and Tony Blair repackaged the Labour Party as 'New Labour'.

It may also be the case that in some instances products change in all but name. The Freedom Party in Austria, which in the 1980s under Norbert Steger had moved to the centre, espousing a liberal position similar to that of the Free Democrats in Germany, swung radically to the right in the 1990s under the leadership of Jorg Haider. Although there was not a total transformation in the party's politics, the populism of Haider was markedly different to the centrism pursued by Steger. Similarly, in 2011 Fianna Fáil's new leader, Micheál Martin, talked about new politics. Although this desired level of newness seems to be primarily organisational, what if, to prevent further meltdown, the party had a radical shift in policy, promoting a new message and new people, but retained its party name? Would it be a new party? Or would it simply be, to paraphrase Tony Blair, 'New Fianna Fáil'?

In order to discuss the absence of a new party we need to be clear of its distinguishing features. Further, since the decline and rise of parties is often treated as a measure of party system change, a conceptualisation of party newness is required for any analysis of change.[16] Coakley discusses in more detail the various boundaries between new, major, minor and micro parties. As he indicates, some have employed particularly strict terms, excluding all parties that are related to existing or former parties (Hug, for example, distinguishes between 'genuinely' new and splinter parties)[17]. Rather than an exclusion, Coakley, along with Bochel and Denver[18] and Tavits[19], suggests a division between 'breakaway' and new parties. Others have focused on timelines for definitional purposes, including all parties formed since 1960.[20] While the latter definition is more open and allows for the inclusion of more parties, thus increasing the number of cases for analysis, it begs the question, when does a new party become old? Indeed, for Barnea and Rahat,[21] this is the crucial distinguishing feature of newness, which they see as a relative term; the newness of a party depends on how different it is from old or existing parties. For reasons of inclusivity a liberal approach to such differences is adopted here, as the emergence of new parties is identified by the appearance of organisations that have not contested any previous general elections. This means there is no discrimination against those with previous party ties or incarnations. The only discrimination is against those that do not register the existence of a new party organisation.[22] In other words, any party that changes all but its name (or continues to be registered as an 'old' party) is not treated as a new party.

## What affects new party emergence?

Pedersen proposed that parties pass through four thresholds in their political life. We are here primarily interested in the first three: declaration, authorisation, and representation. The fourth, relevance, refers to the impact such parties can wield, the nature of which is discussed in most of the chapters in this volume. To understand the absence of new parties in Ireland we need to assess the comparative factors that explain their emergence in other contexts. In terms of party emergence, we are dealing with groups that have crossed the first two thresholds and are seeking to cross the third. An analysis of party emergence then really concerns two questions: what is the nature of party formation, and what are the factors that affect its occurrence. Beginning with the first question, as Hug,[23] Keman and Krouwel,[24] and Coakley indicate, there are four processes by which a new party is born: birth – when an entirely new organisation emerges; re(birth) – when a pre-existing party undergoes a radical transformation; marriage – when parties merge; and divorce – when a fission occurs. These processes are analysed in more detail later in this chapter, but for now we are more interested in the second question: the root causes of these developments.

While the circumstances surrounding the emergence of individual parties might initially seem quite particular and idiosyncratic, closer observation reveals some comparative patterns. Although much of the earlier literature on new parties suggests they are a product of new issues neglected by existing parties,[25] more recent work has pointed to a wider set of determinants.[26] Some, such as Hug[27] and Tavits,[28] have suggested new party entry is a strategic decision, whereby potential party entrepreneurs weigh up the costs and benefits of forming a party, and the probability of their having an impact. In general, however, there appear to be five key factors that affect new party emergence: social, political, institutional, events and personalities. In a wide-ranging work, Harmel and Robertson stress the importance of the first three on the formation and success of new parties.[29] They test twelve hypotheses stemming from these factors, which to sum, stated that there should be more new parties in large countries, in plural and heterogeneous societies, where there is more extreme sectionalism, and higher levels of inequality and post-materialism. The political features of such countries more prone to new party emergence include two-party systems, with few cleavage dimensions, a parliamentary system using a proportional representation electoral system with multi-member districts, liberal ballot access laws, and a decentralised form of government.[30]

While Harmel and Robertson rejected a lot of their hypotheses,[31] it is still worth assessing the influence of each for potential new party entrepreneurs. Beginning with social factors, these include the rise of new issues, a conducive political culture, and a heterogeneous society. The rise of new issues can often give rise to new parties, but such issues are more likely to crop up in heterogeneous and diverse societies that have a more tolerant and open political culture.[32] Examples of new issues include post-materialism and environmentalism, which, as discussed later, emerged amidst the social liberalisation of the 1960s, and in part spawned the Green parties of the 1980s. Similarly, the new waves of immigration into Europe in the 1990s resulted in an emergence (or re-emergence in some cases) of new radical right parties.

The political factors include the convergence of parties, the emergence of new voters, and declining party attachment. One reason why the number of new parties in Europe doubled in the 1990s,[33] for example, was because of the available space in terms of electoral competition. As the established parties converged even more on the median voter, they left a vacuum for parties (both old and new) closer to the extremes to exploit. From a historical perspective, the emergence of new voters has had a significant impact on party systems, particularly following the onset of mass suffrage after the First World War, when it resulted in significant electoral breakthroughs for left-wing parties. Similarly, new waves of immigration into a country could over time result in the emergence of a party to represent these communities, à la the presence of ethnic-minority parties, such as the Swedish People's Party in Finland or the South Tyrolean People's Party in Italy. A pool of new voters can also materialise from within the party system, by which we mean the increasing number detaching themselves from the existing parties. This can mean that voters are less likely to maintain a more concrete attachment to their preferred party, but also that they are disillusioned with parties as a whole. Coakley[34] discusses this further, noting the findings from across the literature on the positive impact of declining partisanship on minor party fortunes.

The question of why new parties are established feeds into a wider question on the formation of parties.[35] The two general approaches used to explain the presence of particular parties are the historical-sociological and the institutional.[36] Elsewhere in this book, Coakley discusses many aspects of these approaches, but it is difficult to over-emphasise the importance of institutional factors, or what Lucardie calls 'political opportunity structure'.[37] These are primarily electoral regulations, including ease of party registration and ballot access. As Weeks shows, onerous deposit and signature requirements and limited access to state subsidies are some of the hurdles that put off would-be parties. The nature of the electoral system can also have a considerable influence on parties' estimations of their electoral prospects. While major parties can play around with electoral rules to gain bonus representation, for minor parties (who typically lack the power to do so in any case) it is a different story. As both Duverger[38] and Rae[39] asserted, while electoral systems can act as brakes to halt the development of minor parties, none can accelerate their development. In particular, district magnitude, threshold and ballot structure can all play a role in affecting party emergence. For example, we might imagine that parties are more likely to emerge in the Netherlands or Israel, where the electoral threshold is less than one per cent, than in plurality systems such as in the UK or France, where a party needs to defeat all others in a constituency to win a seat.

The two other factors affecting new party emergence are not as predictable, but no less important. They are events, or 'political conjuncture', and personalities.[40] While some parties are the product of years of planning or are part of developments that form a natural order of evolution,[41] others are spawned by unpredictable events, or crises. Would a new party have been formed in 1980s Ireland had Desmond O'Malley not been expelled from Fianna Fáil? Would all four of the Progress Party's MPs in Denmark have quit the party to form Freedom 2000 had the controversial party founder, Mogens Glistrup, not been re-admitted into the party fold in 1999? Given the stable nature of many political systems, it often takes such crises to bump things off kilter and allow for the arrival of new parties on the scene.

Finally, parties are not unitary actors and some of their actions can best be understood by an analysis of the motivations and incentives of their components, that is the individual politicians within the party. Some new parties are personal vehicle movements, which although not necessarily designed purely to further the interests of one person, are usually dominated by this individual. The Monetary Reform Party of the 1940s had one elected TD, Oliver J. Flanagan, who was the party's central mouthpiece, and it wound up on his decision to join Fine Gael in 1952. Similarly, the Libertas Institute, which played a pivotal role in the defeat of the first referendum on the Lisbon Treaty in 2008, was the brainchild of Declan Ganley, the party's central backer. Following his failure to win a seat at the 2009 European Parliament elections, Ganley announced his departure from Irish politics, and with him, his Libertas Ireland party, which had a brief lifespan of just over six months (although this could be subject to change). Likewise, from a European perspective, we cannot explain the perhaps surprising emergence in the Netherlands of the right-wing populist parties the Pim Fortuyn List (in 2001) and the Party of Freedom (in 2004) without understanding the motives of the parties' respective founders, Pim Fortuyn and Geert Wilders.

## A surfeit of parties?

Of the five factors that breed new party emergence, some have been evident in Irish political life for the past few years. An economic crisis that has undermined the country's sovereignty is obviously the most significant. New issues related to this crisis appeared, including the banking system and the EU/IMF bailout, but also some non-economic matters, such as political reform. The institutional structures are also favourable to minor parties, as it is not terribly difficult to form a party (details of which are outlined by Coakley in his chapter), and a form of proportional representation is used for elections.[42] Indeed, taking these factors into account, Abedi's study of nineteen western democracies found Ireland to be the third least cartelised system, which suggests it offers reasonable access to would-be party entrepreneurs.[43] So, seeing as new parties emerged during previous crises, including Sinn Féin in 1917, Clann na Talmhan and Clann na Poblachta in the 1940s, and the Progressive Democrats in the 1980s, what makes the 2010-11 period any different? The absence of individuals willing to cross the Rubicon into political life is one answer, but we also need to consider the political factors. While there has been some convergence by the political parties in Ireland, it may be that there has not been enough to trigger the emergence of a new competitor. It could simply be the case that, in spite of the disappearance of the Progressive Democrats, there is no room for a new party. New party emergence (or lack of it) cannot be assessed without considering the context of the actors already present in the game and its level of intra-party competitiveness. To do so, we need to compare the Irish party system with other European states, which in part allows us to assess the 'typical' number of parties in a political system.

Counting the raw number of competitive or parliamentary parties is a flawed methodology because it does not take into account the relative size of parties and how they affect party competition. For example, although ten parties were elected to the British House of Commons in 2010, few have described Britain as a true multi-party system. Two parties won almost 90 per cent of seats, while seven others between them won just 4 per cent of seats. To overcome this issue, Laakso and Taagepera devised a measure of the 'effective' number of parties, which takes into account their relative size.[44] Using this methodology, Gallagher, Laver and Mair count the existing number of effective parties in Europe at the elective (for elections) and legislative (in parliament) levels.[45] Using a three-election average (1997-2010), the mean number of elective parties in Europe is almost five; the mean number of legislative parties is four. This figure varies from a low of two legislative parties in Malta to almost eight in Belgium and six in the Netherlands. Ireland is below the European mean, with four elective parties and three at the legislative level. Indeed, of the other European states using PR electoral systems to elect their lower houses of parliament (all bar the United Kingdom and France), only Hungary and the Mediterranean democracies of Greece, Malta, Portugal and Spain have fewer parties than Ireland.

Rather than rushing to conclude that this confirms that Ireland has a low number of parties, we need to consider other explanatory factors. The first is size. Being a small country, perhaps three legislative parties is more than ample. However, Denmark, Finland, Norway and Slovakia, all with populations not much larger than Ireland, have on average two more parties in parliament. Indeed, states with smaller populations than Ireland, such as Estonia, Lithuania and Slovenia, have two more parties in parliament. Of the other small states in Europe (with considerably smaller populations), Cyprus, Iceland and Luxembourg all have more parties than Ireland; Malta is the exception. So it seems that size of population is not a barrier to the emergence of parties. Remaining on the theme of size, perhaps the capacity of parliament is a factor. The smaller the assembly, the fewer parties we should be likely to see, simply because there are fewer seats to go around. If we consider the states in Europe with lower houses of fewer than 300 members[46], the ratio of MPs to legislative parties is 35 to 1; in other words, there is one party per thirty-five MPs. The comparative figure in Western Europe is even lower, at one per twenty-two MPs. In contrast, the ratio in the Dáil is one party per fifty-three TDs, a significant difference from the European average. Size of parliament should therefore not act as a barrier to the emergence of new parties.

It seems that Ireland has too few parties, a level of under-representation that is not the product of a small population or parliament. While this suggests that the Irish political system is due a new party, this question assumes that there is an optimum number of parties for a parliamentary democracy, which ignores the level of fragmentation in society and the number of social cleavages.[47] The reality is that, as already discussed, the more divided and heterogeneous a society, the more parties we are likely to see, and voters are likely to desire, to represent the various interests. In the Irish context, despite the high level of immigration during the years of the Celtic Tiger, Ireland remains a relatively homogenous society, with no real evident social cleavages. In other words, Whyte's description of the party system forty years ago as 'politics without social bases' remains true.[48] This level of homogeneity means that few political parties may be required in Ireland, as is the case in Malta, another homogenous, Catholic island society, where just two parties predominate.

## When do new parties emerge?

Having considered the reasons why parties do not emerge, what are the positive reasons? Under what circumstances do new parties appear? Harmel and Robertson's study of the formation and success of new parties in nineteen industrial democracies between 1960 and 1980 identified 'natural' formation as the most common reason (48 per cent), followed by a split (37 per cent) and merger (12 per cent).[49] Just 3 per cent of cases of new parties they examined comprised the reorganisation of former parties. They also analysed the purpose of party formation, and perhaps surprisingly, found that just one in ten new parties was mobilised on a new issue (half of these were green parties). The most common purpose was to offer an alternative on an old or pre-existing issue, this being the aim of almost half of new parties. With this study as a template, we examine all cases of new party emergence in post-war Western Europe up to 2010. The degrees of party newness were already discussed in an earlier section, following on from which an inclusive definition of a new party is preferable. This includes any party elected to national parliament post-1955 (to allow time for the settling of party systems) or, in the case of late blooming democracies, following two successive democratic elections. The data was sourced from Nohlen and Stöver's *Elections in Europe* and information on the formation of new parties was sourced from the general secondary literature.[50] A post-hoc taxonomy of party emergence was devised and it indicates a number of patterns, which are summarised in Table 1. Confirming the earlier findings of Harmel and Robertson, there are two dominant reasons for the emergence of new parties.[51] The first is organisational: new parties are the product of either a split from an existing party, a merger of parties, or inherit the mantle of a dying or defunct party. The second factor is ideological: new parties are the product of new politics, both on the left and right of the political spectrum. Those on the left have comprised the new left, and more recently, green parties. Those on the right have been the populist and new radical right parties. The new politics represented by these parties revolve around issues that have arisen in European politics since the late 1970s and early 1980s, primarily, but not exclusively, environmentalism and immigration.

To first consider the organisational factors: the most common cause of the emergence of new political parties in Europe is a split in an existing party (26 per cent of all cases). Whether for ideological, personality-driven, or other reasons, splinter parties have formed in most west European states. For example, the previously discussed move to the right of the Austrian Freedom Party under Jörg Haider resulted in the secession in 1993 of five of the party's *Nationalrat* members (MPs) to found a more classically liberal party, the Liberal Forum. Twelve years later, Haider himself broke away from the party he no longer led to form the Alliance for the Future of Austria. Other examples of party splinters include the Norwegian Liberal People's Party, formed when the Liberal Party split over attitudes to membership of the European Economic Community; and the Centre Democrats in the Netherlands, a moderate faction that broke away from the more extreme Centre Party in 1984.

*Table 1: Circumstances of new party emergence in Western Europe, 1950-2010*

| Organisational | Per cent | N |
|---|---|---|
| Split | 26 | 46 |
| Merger | 14 | 24 |
| Replacement | 11 | 19 |
| Personal Vehicles | 4 | 7 |
| **Ideological** | | |
| New Issue | 16 | 28 |
| Regional | 6 | 9 |
| New Politics | 9 | 15 |
| Sectional | 5 | 8 |
| Others | 10 | 18 |
| | | |
| **Total** | **100** | **175** |

Note: This includes all cases of new party emergence in seventeen west-European states (Austria, Belgium, Denmark, Finland, France, Germany, Greece, Ireland, Italy, Luxembourg, Netherlands, Norway, Portugal, Spain, Sweden, Switzerland, and the UK) between 1950 and 2010, or in the case of late democracies, ten years after the first democratic elections.

So too in Ireland, a party split is the most common causal factor in the emergence of new parties. The two main parties, Fianna Fáil and Fine Gael, are the inheritors of a split in the briefly-dominant Sinn Féin over acceptance of the 1921 Anglo-Irish Treaty. Fianna Fáil is the result of another split in 1926, this time within the group that had originally opposed the aforementioned treaty. We have already discussed the case of the Progressive Democrats, which was led by a number of TDs who split from Fianna Fáil. There are a number of other examples of splinter parties in Ireland. National Labour was founded in 1944 after the Irish Transport and General Workers' Union broke away from the Labour Party in protest over what it perceived to be the increasing power of the left within the organisation.[52] Likewise, as Rafter describes in more detail, the Workers' Party came about following a split in Sinn Féin in 1970, which itself split in 1992 when most of the parliamentary party left to form New Agenda (see also the contribution of Catherine Murphy in chapter 4), which was later renamed Democratic Left. Most of the splits in Ireland have occurred within the left, which is further validated by the presence of the Socialist Party, founded in 1996 by a group of militant Trotskyites who had been expelled from Labour in 1989.

The second organisational cause of new party emergence is a merger (14 per cent of cases). The Liberal Democrats in the United Kingdom is the product of a merger in 1988 of the Liberal and Social Democratic Parties, who for the previous seven years (since the foundation of the Social Democrats, a breakaway party from Labour, in 1981) had worked together in an electoral alliance. Likewise, the People of Freedom Party in Italy, founded by Silvio Berlusconi in 2009, is a merger of his Forza Italia with the National Alliance and other minor parties. The National Alliance itself was the product of a merger in 1995 of the neo-fascist Italian Social Movement and parts of the disgraced Christian Democracy. Although there are fewer mergers in Ireland, there are a couple of notable examples, both involving two established parties. The now largest party, Fine Gael, is the product of a merger in 1933 of Cumann na nGaedheal, the National Centre Party and the Army Comrades Association. Although not originally the product of a merger, Labour has merged with several other parties in its 100-year existence, including the National Progressive Democrats in 1963, the Democratic Socialist Party in 1990, and Democratic Left in 1999. Its reunion with National Labour in 1950 may also be considered a merger of sorts. As is the case elsewhere in Europe, it is rare (if not, as Coakley indicates, non-existent) in Ireland that mergers are the product of solely minor parties. They tend to involve one major party, as is the case in Switzerland, with the example of the FDP. The Liberals, in 2009, merged with the Free Democratic Party, one of the major establishment parties of Swiss politics, with its much smaller rival Liberal Party.

The final organisational factor is where new parties fill a vacuum left by a departing, or departed, party. Almost all the examples of this phenomenon in Europe are limited to Belgium, France and Italy. In the latter two cases, this is a reflection of the fluid nature of the party systems in these countries. They include the Italian People's Party, which replaced the discredited Christian Democrats in the mid-1990s, the Democrats of the Left, who in 1998 replaced the old Party of Democratic Socialists, and in the case of France, Liberal Democracy, which replaced the Republican Party in 1997, and the Democratic Movement, which replaced the Union of French Democracy ten years later. Although there are no examples in the modern Irish party system of successor parties, Garvin has traced an organisational link between Parnell's Irish Parliamentary Party (IPP) of the 1880s and the early Fianna Fáil of the late 1920s.[53] Further, such was the dominance of O'Connell's nationalist movement in the 1820s and 1830s, Parnell's IPP, the Home Rule Party in the early twentieth century, and later Sinn Féin, it is not unfeasible to claim that each of these movements filled a vacuum left by their departing predecessor.

The ideological reasons for the emergence of new parties primarily comprise the promotion of new issues or old issues in a new manner. One in four new parties are concerned with 'new politics'. The most prevalent new issue in the 1970s and 1980s was environmentalism, which spawned Green parties in most European states. In more recent times, the spectrum of emergence has swung to the right as populist parties, concerned with immigration, and often quite Eurosceptic, have made significant inroads in some systems. Although the newness of this message may be debatable (particularly the appeal of these parties to nationalistic sentiment), they claim to represent new politics in that many of them are, paradoxically, anti-political.[54] There are also new parties that have a more restrictive focus, often initially mobilised on one key issue, a position that can evolve the longer such parties remain politically competitive. Examples include United Left in Spain, a left-wing coalition formed in 1986 in opposition to Spanish membership of the North Atlantic Treaty Organisation (NATO), and the Party of the Animals in the Netherlands, formed in 2002 to promote animal rights.

Not all new parties are necessarily concerned with new politics; some form to promote regional issues and sectional interests. Both groups comprise approximately 5 per cent of cases of new party emergence. Not surprisingly, the former are confined to states with regional conflicts, which include Belgium, Spain, Italy and the United Kingdom. The most common purpose for the formation of those pursuing sectional interests has been primarily related to rural, agricultural issues. Such parties include Hunting, Fishing, Nature and Tradition in France in 1989, the Coastal Party in Norway in 1999, and the Farmers' Party in the Netherlands in 1959. A different type of sectional party, representing a generational divide, is the recent phenomenon of pensioners' parties. Examples include Union 55+ and the General Elderly Alliance in the Netherlands, the Gil Party in Israel, the National Party of Retirees and Pensioners in Poland, the Croatian Party of Pensioners and the Pensioners' Party in Italy, although not all of these have secured parliamentary representation.

There are some similarities when comparing these patterns to the Irish experience. As Dan Boyle describes in more detail in his contribution, the Green Party somewhat reluctantly emerged from the various environmental organisations that had cropped up in the 1970s. As of yet, no populist party has sprung up as a counter to the Greens.[55] Although an Immigration Control Platform did run candidates at the 2002 and 2007 general election, it made no electoral impact and did not register as a political party. A Eurosceptic streak in the electorate was evident in the impact made by groups such as Libertas at the referendums on the European Treaties of Nice and Lisbon. However, the depth of this streak is questionable given the negligible impact of these parties at parliamentary elections.

Other parties to promote new issues include Oliver Flanagan's Monetary Reform, a reactionary movement in the 1940s against moneyed influences, which took a populist line that at times bordered on anti-Semitism. Given the importance of Catholicism in the country, it is not surprising that new parties formed to pursue a Christian agenda, particularly in the absence of any genuine Christian Democratic party, although surprising perhaps that such parties have been few and their impact negligible. These parties, which include Seán Loftus' Christian Democratic Party of the 1960s, the Christian Democrats (founded as the National Party in 1996), and the Christian Solidarity Party (founded as the Christian Principles Party in

1991), pursued an old issue in a new manner, in that they campaigned for a greater reflection of a Catholic ethos in government policies. Although their electoral appeal has been minimal, as Murphy outlines, some of these groups did have a role to play in the referendums on divorce and abortion.

Although there have been regional parties such as the Donegal People's Party, the South Kerry Independent Alliance, and the Cork Progressive Association, none of these groups are comparable to the Basque or Flemish separatist movements. These former parties happened to have a primarily local organisation or localised policy outlook; partition from the state was not part of their agenda. Of course, there is another regionalist party from a neighbouring jurisdiction, but Sinn Féin could not be called regionalist in the Irish context. Sectional parties have been more prominent; these have ranged from Clann na Talmhan in the 1940s, the Army Wives' Group in the 1980s, to the Blind Men's Party and Business Men's Party of the 1920s.

In total, as Coakley outlines in more detail, since 1955 there have been nine new parties elected to the Dáil. If we extend our focus back to define a new party as any that emerged since 1932, that is, once the party system and state had found its roots, this leaves fourteen new parliamentary parties. These are, in chronological order: National Centre Party, Clann na Talmhan, Monetary Reform, National Labour, Clann na Poblachta, National Progressive Democrats, Socialist Labour Party, Sinn Féin, Democratic Socialist Party, Workers' Party, Green Party, Progressive Democrats, Democratic Left, and the Socialist Party. Of these fourteen parties, three held representation for just one election, two for two elections, and two for three elections. Of these seven parties, six were subsumed into other parties, while the other disbanded. Four others remain in existence, two of whom retain parliamentary representation. The mean number of elections contested by these parties is almost 5 (4.57), although the median is 3.5. The Greens and Sinn Féin are the only parties of the fourteen that failed to win seats at their first election, and it may be no coincidence that these two parties are the longest in continuance as a single organisation. So for most new parties, the first election is their zenith, following which their electoral performance enters a period of steady decline. Of the fourteen, eleven won their highest number of seats at their first election. Only the Greens, Sinn Féin and the Workers' Party broke this trend, again all of which are still in existence, although the latter is electorally competitive at only the local level. Perhaps this says something about the danger of starting with a big bang. Expectations can be set too high, following which the only way is down. It seems that it is far better to begin gradually and build up the organisation from the grass roots.

## Conclusion

Despite the levels of anger and disillusionment with the Irish political system since the onset of the latest recession, at the time of writing no new party has emerged to tap into this sentiment. But perhaps it would be more surprising if a new party did suddenly make a breakthrough. After all, Ireland has consistently had one of the lowest levels of support for new parties. In a ranking of sixteen West European states by the mean aggregate vote for new parties, Ireland was placed fifteenth in the 1960s, twelfth in the 1970s and 1980s, and fourteenth in the 1990s and the 2000s.[56] Only Malta and the United Kingdom have had consistently lower levels of support for new parties. In addition, the comparative experience of economic crises does not suggest that new parties are a political by-product. In the three other euro member states with genuinely suffering economies, no significant new party has emerged. Greece, Portugal and Spain all had elections in the middle of economic crises, with outcomes similar to that of the Dáil elections of 2011 – the governing party suffers considerable losses, with most of the gains made by the established opposition party. Even in the case of Iceland, whose banking system collapsed in 2008-9, no new party won seats at the 2009 elections. A Citizens' Movement (which later evolved into a party) did win four seats, but in a parliament of sixty-three, this was not exactly a major electoral breakthrough.

In this chapter we discussed the issue of identifying new parties, what affects their emergence, and the context of party formation in Europe. Examining the comparative experience, it is possibly unrealistic to expect a wholly new party to emerge in Ireland. More than half of new parties elected to parliament across Europe have links with former or existing parties, be they a splinter, a re-organisation, or the product of a merger. In the Irish case, this pattern is more apparent, with the Greens the only genuinely new party to enter the Dáil in recent decades. If the likely source of a new party is therefore within the existing parties, from where could this materialise? There were rumours in the summer of 2010 about dissident TDs in both Fianna Fáil and Fine Gael leaving to form a new party, with one TD stating, 'What is motivating this is a generational mood, a generation shift. The idea is coming from those who believe that the electorate is sick and tired of the current tweedledum tweedledee politics'.[57] At the same time, these same TDs put their prospects of forming such a party as low as between 5 and 20 per cent, which makes it hardly surprising that this new 'Fianna Gael' party never emerged. A more realistic possibility lies on the political left. Following a record number of seats won by the left in 2011 (approximately sixty-seven, including Labour, Sinn Féin, the United Left Alliance, and seven independents), there was some talk of the more disparate strands pooling their resources. The most obvious such case is the United Left Alliance of the People Before Profit Alliance, the Socialist Party and the Workers' Unemployed and Action Group. However, at the time of writing, such developments remained a work in progress and the ULA has been described as 'an alliance working within an alliance'.[58]

But could a new party come from a political source outside of the Dáil? In Latvia, which experienced a recession worse than most other global economies, former President Valdis Zatlers established Zatler's Reform party in July 2011, winning twenty-two seats in the 100-seat *Saeima* just two months later. This came shortly after he had exercised a never before used power to call a referendum to dissolve parliament, and after he surprisingly failed to be re-elected to the presidency. Such a Zatler-like party is probably unlikely to emerge in Ireland given the party affiliations of the previous and current presidential incumbents. However, maybe some of the defeated candidates from the 2011 presidential election could replicate Zatler's actions. Seán Gallagher, who came from nowhere to poll almost 30 per cent as an independent, is one example that springs to mind.

The individual contributions to this volume provide an important insight into the workings and fortunes of minor parties. They also constitute a significant analysis of the Irish political system and are an invaluable contribution to anyone interested in this area. The experience of minor parties that is outlined indicates that those that have been successful have had a distinctive message, which has not necessarily been radical (although it may have been so in the respective parties' early days). Taking stock of the Irish party system in 2012, the relatively low number of parties means that any new arrival on the political scene would not be redundant. Whether they need a radical message to maintain immunity from redundancy is another matter. Whatever is the future for minor parties, the trend amongst the electorate is towards dealignment rather than realignment, which increases the likelihood of voters switching to new parties. Although this has not yet happened in Ireland, the increasing level of flux means that anything is possible.

# 2

# From Cradle to Grave: The Impact and Evolution of Minor Parties

*Liam Weeks*

## Introduction

The fate of the Progressive Democrats as an electoral force that threatened to break the mould of Irish politics poses a number of questions for our understanding of parties and party competition. Born in one recession, at a time when there was a demand for a new party, it died in the next recession, ironically at a time when sentiment for the emergence of a new political force was again apparent. As one commentator noted, 'they were abolished just when they were needed'.[1] Some of the questions raised by the experience of the Progressive Democrats are discussed by others in this book, but this chapter serves as an introductory exploration of the various themes concerning minor parties, including their influence, their electoral performance and the factors explaining the level of variation in these two areas. The aim of this chapter is fourfold. The first task is to detail the electoral performance of minor parties, as a precursor to Coakley's more detailed analysis in chapter 3. This performance is then placed in comparative perspective against their counterparts in Europe. The second section details the influence of minor parties in Irish politics, primarily by focusing on what they have achieved, be it by entering government or by taking an active role in a referendum campaign. The third section considers why minor parties emerge and disappear, while the fourth section briefly considers the source of their electoral support.

## Minor parties

Minor or small parties have been a persistent feature of political life in most European democracies since the earthquake elections in Scandinavia in the 1970s. They are an important feature of party systems and hence of the study of party systems, because they are often treated as indicators of fragmentation, realignment and volatility. Indeed, the ability of minor parties to break into an established party system is often treated as the symptom of a democracy's openness. On a similar line of thought, minor parties' size means they are especially open to the vagaries of institutional effects. Party registration rules, campaign finance and, of course, electoral systems can have quite an effect on the presence or otherwise of minor parties, the implication being that those who wish to understand such effects would be well advised to look at minor parties' experience, which is detailed in this chapter.

The problem for most minor parties, however, is survival. While many may find it difficult to form in the first place, maintaining a political existence is even more problematic, as ever more pressures to terminate are heaped on such parties. Some of these forces are detailed by Varley and Rafter in chapters 9 and 10, but also by Des O'Malley, Catherine Murphy and Dan Boyle, who provide insightful accounts of life inside, respectively, the Progressive Democrats, Democratic Left, and the Greens. The former two folded, while the third persists despite its wipeout at the 2011 general election. This chapter is a brief comparative analysis of such fortunes of minor parties. It provides an overview of some of the themes addressed in this book, and should be treated as a complement to the more in-depth chapters. The first place to begin such analysis of minor parties is on their electoral impact.

## Electoral performance

Has Ireland been a fertile breeding ground for minor parties? Figures 1, 2 and 3 suggest not to any great extent, as their performance both in terms of votes and seats has constituted a series of ebbs and flows. Indeed, they seem to suggest there have been three waves of support for minor parties: the first was in the 1920s, when the new party system was in a state of flux, and minor parties profited from this volatility. As attachments to the mainstream parties solidified in the 1930s, the first wave of minor parties died out. The second wave emerged in the mid-1940s and experienced a similar pattern: a quick rise in support, following by an equally swift decline. This culminated in the nadir election of 1969 for minor political actors, when Fianna Fáil, Fine Gael and Labour won all bar one of the 144 seats in the Dáil.

The entry of the Workers' Party, the Greens and the Progressive Democrats into parliamentary politics in the 1980s marked the third wave in minor party activity. In addition, the willingness of individuals to run as independent candidates increased.[2] While an average of twenty-six independents contested general elections before 1977, since then this figure has more than trebled to eighty-four, peaking at 183 in 2011.[3] The third wave of minor party growth is different to its predecessors in that support for minor parties has not faded away. Although this most recent crop of minor parties never managed to win more than twenty Dáil seats, support for them has been quite consistent, averaging about one in six voters. With the termination of the Progressive Democrats in

*Figure 1: Percentage of first preference vote for minor parties at Dáil elections, 1922–2011*

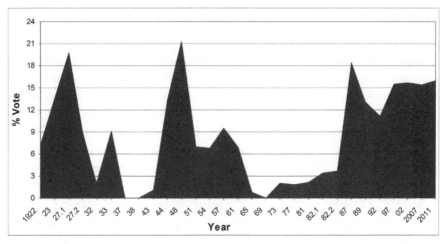

Source: The data for this table, and for all other tables and figures in this chapter – unless otherwise stated – come from various issues of *Election results and transfer of votes for Dáil and by-elections* (Dublin: Stationery Office); B.M. Walker *Parliamentary Election Results in Ireland 1918-1992* (Dublin, Royal Irish Academy, 1993); M. Gallagher *Irish Elections 1922-1944* (Dublin; PSAI, 1994); M. Gallagher *Irish Elections 1948-1977* (London; Routledge, 2009).

*Figure 2: Percentage of seats won by minor parties at Dáil elections, 1922–2011*

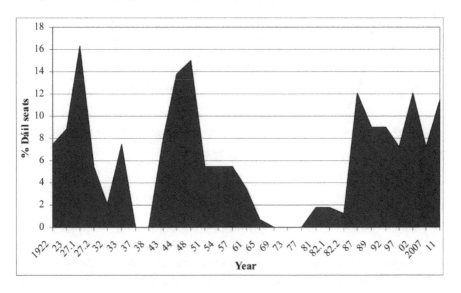

2009 and the obliteration of the Greens in 2011, the largest minor party is now Sinn Féin. One in ten voters gave the party a first preference in 2011, when it won a record high of fourteen Dáil seats.

While the conditions that could account for the fluctuations in the performance of minor parties are examined throughout this book, for now it is worth noting the numbers of candidates running under these labels (see Figure 3). This pattern follows much the same trend as the electoral performance of these groups, which suggests a relationship between the numbers of candidates running and the vote acquired. For example, when minor parties fielded 130 candidates in 1948, they won over 20 per cent of the first preference vote. When they ran thirty-eight candidates three years later their combined vote fell to 7 per cent. Exploring the nature of this relationship a bit further, the correlation between the number of candidates and numbers of seats won by minor parties between 1922 and 20011 is +0.77, quite a strong coefficient (+/- 1 implies a perfect relationship). This tells us that the vote for minor parties is often a product the number of candidates they choose to run. That said, this would not be the case if there was not an available electorate willing to support such parties or candidates.

*Figure 3: Numbers of minor party candidates at Dáil elections, 1922-2011*

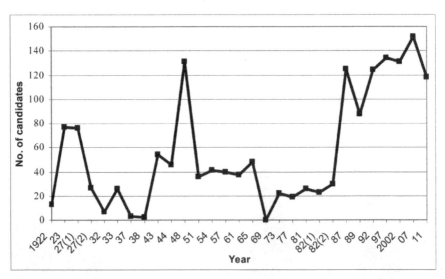

## Comparative presence

To what extent does the outlined performance of minor parties compare to other European countries? For the purpose of comparative analysis, and in line with the methodology of Mair[4] and Clark in chapter 14, minor parties are defined here as those that achieve less than 15 per cent of the national vote but more than 1.5 per cent on average, and which have persisted for more than three elections. Although this excludes some of the Irish minor parties included in Figures 1 to 3, we cannot include every party that received a small share of the vote at a particular election. The countries included for comparison are the sixteen western European democracies that have persisted since the Second World War. Figure 4 indicates the mean vote per decade for minor parties in Western Europe since the 1950s. The only clear pattern is that the level of support for such parties in Ireland has consistently been below the European mean. This divergence began in the 1960s (when minor parties were squeezed out in Ireland), and was particularly striking in the 1970s when some party systems in Europe suffered seismic shocks. Support for minor parties in Ireland did not pick up until the 1980s, since when the trend across Europe has been a steadily increasing vote for these parties (although whether it is more reflective of a declining support base of the major, traditional parties is another matter). It is worth bearing in mind, however, that 'minor' is very much a relative adjective, dependent on the level of support won by other parties within the political system. Despite winning more than 20 per cent of the vote in the UK at recent general elections, the Liberal Democrats remain quite a minor actor. In Belgium, by contrast, no party has attracted 20 per cent support since 1985.

*Figure 4: Mean level of support for minor parties at parliamentary elections, 1940s-2000s*

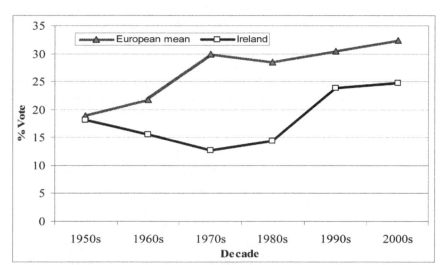

Source: (for Figures 4 and 5): T. Mackie and R. Rose *The International Almanac of Electoral History* (London; Macmillan, 1991); various data yearbooks of *West European Politics* and *European Journal of Political Research*; *Election Resources on the Internet: Western Europe*, available at http://electionresources.org/western.europe.html (accessed January 2012).

Note: The fifteen European states are: Austria, Belgium, Denmark, Finland, France, Germany, Iceland, Italy, Luxembourg, Malta, the Netherlands, Norway, Sweden, Switzerland, United Kingdom.

## Influence of minor parties

While the electoral fortunes of minor parties varies over time, of greater significance is their impact. This is what Pedersen identified as the fourth threshold in
parties' lifespan: that of relevance.[5] There are a number of ways by which parties
can exercise impact, which are discussed in greater detail by the other contributors
to this volume; here we briefly detail these possible areas of influence. The first and
most obvious is participation in government. A considerable number of minor
parties have achieved this goal, including Clann na Talmhan, Clann na Poblachta,
National Labour, the Farmers' Party, the Progressive Democrats, Democratic Left
and the Green Party. With both Fine Gael and Labour, the first three of these parties participated in the interparty government of 1948-51. The lack of a dominant
party within the coalition gave the minor parties a considerable influence. They
had a majority of cabinet seats and Clann na Poblachta's antipathy to the Fine
Gael party leader was a significant factor in his not becoming Taoiseach. Clann
na Talmhan entered government again in 1954, in return for which its leader, Joe
Blowick, was appointed Minister for Lands. Clann na Poblachta was also offered a
ministerial post but it was declined;[6] instead, the party provided external support,
the withdrawal of which in 1957 led to the collapse of the coalition.[7] The next
minor party to enter government was the Progressive Democrats in 1989, an event
that has been described as a watershed in the Irish party system because, amongst
other things, it marked the first time that Fianna Fáil entered coalition.[8] By opening up the party system, it resulted in an increased chance of minor parties gaining
power. No longer were they dependent on Fine Gael. Indeed, apart from the
Fianna Fáil–Labour government formed in 1992, every administration between
1989 and 2011 included a minor party. Being in government is one thing; having
an influence is another. Minor parties often struggle to make their mark on government, a theme that is fleshed out by others in this book, including O'Malley,
Bolleyer, Varley and Rafter (see chapters 5, 6, 9 and 10).

The vast majority of minor parties do not enter government. In other party
systems, particularly consensus democracies such as in Scandinavia, minor parties
can have an influence outside of government. This is generally not the case in
Ireland. The unitary nature of the state and the weak de facto powers of the Dáil
*vis-à-vis* government limit the influence minor parties can have in parliament.
While in some instances the votes of minor parties outside of government have
been crucial to either the formation or survival of a particular administration –
for example, the abstention of Sinn Féin the Workers' Party in the nomination
of Charles Haughey as Taoiseach in 1982 and Labour's supporting the minority
Fianna Fáil government in 1932 – in such cases, there were no *quid pro quo* support
status arrangements in place. In other words, while the votes of minor parties
were crucial, their influence was negligible.

The Dáil is not the sole arena within which to exert influence; where minor
parties have links to interest groups, such networks can be a conduit to shape

policy. Thus, as Varley details in chapter 9, the connections between the various farmers' parties and the farming unions enabled the former to have an influence outside of formal party politics. One recently formed party – Libertas – which contested the European Parliament elections in 2009, began life as an interest group campaigning against the Lisbon Treaty. Indeed, it was the success of Libertas in getting the referendum on this treaty defeated that was a major factor in its decision to become a party (see chapter 8). A further source of influence stems from an existence in another jurisdiction. Some minor parties are all-island entities (examples being the Greens, the Workers' Party and Sinn Féin). The latter is in the particularly unique position of not being in government in the south but having influence because of its significance in another jurisdiction (i.e. Northern Ireland), where it first participated in a power-sharing administration in 1999.

Influence can also come in an indirect manner, in particular how other actors react to the presence of minor parties. Individual independents are unlikely to have an effect on the nature of party competition at the national level, although they may do so in their local constituencies. Examining their emergence in chronological order, the presence of a significant number of minor parties in both the 1920s and '40s threatened to shift Irish party competition away from its duality structure.[9] However, these parties did not survive long enough to seriously alter the mode of party competition which remained Fianna Fáil versus the rest until 1989. Although the arrival on the political scene of the Progressive Democrats in 1985 did not fragment the party system to the extent that some might have predicted, it was their entry into coalition with Fianna Fáil that contributed to fragmentation, particularly since Fianna Fáil became 'just another party'. As Ó Muineacháin outlines in chapter 7, the PDs also captured some middle-class support from Fine Gael; it was no coincidence that during the lifetime of the former Fine Gael failed to go into government after any general election.

The example of the PDs also highlights the manner in which minor parties can have an indirect effect on party competition. The mainstream parties embraced the centre-right economic policies promoted by the PDs (see chapter 7), particularly with the onset of the economic boom that began in the mid-1990s. Similarly, the development of environmental policies by the established parties was undoubtedly a response to the emergence of the Green Party in the 1980s. Likewise, Fianna Fáil has had to re-emphasise its republican roots when different nationalist parties emerged, including Clann na Poblachta in the 1940s, Aontacht Éireann in the 1970s and Sinn Féin in the late 1990s.

The effect on party competition is not limited to a challenge from the outside. Some minor parties, probably due to an acceptance of their limited influence, have sought to pool their resources and merge with other parties. In this fashion, the National Centre Party and the Army Comrades Association merged with Cumann na nGaedheal to form Fine Gael in 1933, the National Progressive Democrats merged with Labour in 1963, the Democratic Socialist Party with

Labour in 1989, Democratic Left with Labour in 1999 and the Progressive Democrats contemplated merging with Fine Gael in 2004.[10] It is difficult to provide a reliable and valid indicator of the influence these minor parties bring to the merged arrangements. However, in cases such as Democratic Left, this party has, since the 1999 merger with Labour, provided two party leaders, one deputy leader and one party president. There have been no examples of the close working relationships/associations with other parties that have arisen in comparative politics, the Conservatives and the Ulster Unionist Party in the United Kingdom, the Christian Social Union and the Christian Democratic Union in Germany and the Liberal Party and National Party in Australia being such examples. This is probably because each of the minor parties in these respective jurisdictions appealed to a distinct electorate, and generally did not face competition from their partner. Such a scenario has not arisen in Ireland, which is possibly a consequence of multi-member electoral districts.

An opportunity for influence can also arise at referendums. This is especially the case when the mainstream parties canvass in favour of a government proposal. The broadcasting laws, requiring equal time for both sides of the argument, afford minor parties an opportunity disproportionate to their size. Thus the Green Party (before its entry into government in 2007) and Sinn Féin have been particularly high-profile in referendum campaigns on EU treaties. This was also evident with the Libertas movement in 2008 when it came from nowhere to lead the no side in the referendum on the Lisbon Treaty. However, running a referendum campaign is an expensive process and interest groups tend to have a greater influence than minor parties (see chapter 8).

## Explaining the emergence and disappearance of minor parties

Weeks' introduction provides a more in-depth analysis of the circumstances of new party emergence, but this section has a greater focus on electoral system effects and on minor party survival. The first question to ask is how many parties have emerged in Ireland compared to elsewhere? Coakley, in chapter 3, details that since 1945 thirty-five minor parties have contested Dáil elections, of which fifteen won seats. For the purposes of consistency and comparative analysis, it is more reliable to retain the definition of minor parties used in the previous section, that is, those winning between 1.5 per cent and 15 per cent of the vote at more than three elections. As we are interested in representation, this definition is widened here to include an additional proviso that such parties must also have won at least one seat in parliament at more than three elections. Applying this definition, seven such parties have emerged in Ireland since 1950. As is detailed in Figure 5, this is slightly above the European average of six, implying neither a paucity nor a surfeit of minor parties in the Dáil. Belgium, the Netherlands and Italy have had the most minor parties in their national parliaments, probably not surprising given (a) the fragmented nature of the Belgian and Italian political systems and (b) the low threshold of representation (less than 1 per cent) in the Dutch parliament. Taking the fragmentation link a step further, three of the top four countries in our chart are federations (a proxy for a divided society). That said, Austria and Germany, both federal systems, have had only five minor parties between them. Other possible hypotheses accounting for the frequency of minor parties are assembly size and choice of electoral system, the latter of which is discussed in a later section. In terms of the former, Malta and Luxembourg, with two of the smallest national assemblies in Europe, have had only a few minor parties. However, as Weeks detailed in the previous chapter, there are other parliaments similar in size to the Dáil with more minor parties. In addition, Germany and Italy, both with over 600 MPs are at the polar ends of the league table, in part because of the electoral threshold of 5 per cent for parliamentary representation in Germany. A correlation between assembly size and the number of minor parties produces a very weak coefficient of -0.03, implying a very weak relationship between the availability of seats and the number of parties making a breakthrough into parliament (admittedly, this low coefficient could be a product of our strict definition as to what constitutes a minor party).

*Figure 5: Number of minor parties elected to parliament in Western Europe, 1950-2011*

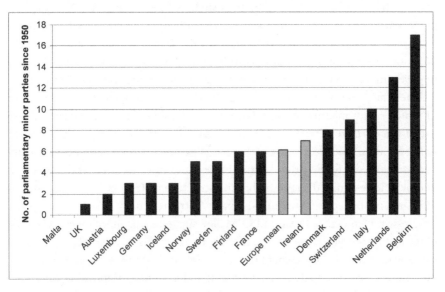

While the previous section detailed the influence minor parties can wield, it is worth bearing in mind that we mentioned only a few of the parties that Coakley lists in his analysis in chapter 3. In other words, a lot of the minor parties have little influence. Why then do they form? Both Weeks and Coakley consider a range of explanations (chaper 1 and 3), with the former focusing primarily on 'social psychological and organisational behavioural factors' and the latter on political and social dynamics. There being little need to repeat the authors' respective arguments, the focus here is on parties' interaction and strategies *vis-à-vis* the different political institutions, primarily in the form of (a) parties as organisations and (b) the electoral rules. All the contributors to this volume make reference to minor parties' organisational weakness as being a contributor to their decline. Indeed, as Coakley tellingly points out in chapter 3, it is this terminal fate that is often identified as the core common feature of these parties. A strong organisation is important for all political parties, but as Boix claims,[11] new parties (which minor parties usually are) only make a breakthrough when their candidates can overcome the 'expectations' advantage' (i.e. about their electoral chances) that existing parties can tap into. To do this, they need a strong organisation, and it needs to be maintained. Most of the minor parties failed to develop adequate national structures, and in many cases, including the two Clanns and the Progressive Democrats, the constituency organisation was often little more than the machine of the local TD. Working in tandem with organisational structure in terms of significance are party finances. In his study of failed minor parties in the UK, Berrington highlighted the importance of finances,[12] which is also a factor for parties in the United States.[13] It is difficult, however, to assess its importance for minor parties in Ireland, especially since there is far less money spent at Irish elections. Indeed, parties such as Libertas and the Natural Law party, two recent examples of minor parties with access to considerable financial resources, struggled to make an impact on the Irish electoral scene. Similarly, donations from its middle-class support base and funding accruing from its tenure in government could not prevent the demise of the Progressive Democrats.

There are a number of aspects to consider concerning electoral rules, most of which Abedi includes in his treatment of anti-establishment parties.[14] These vary from party registration rules to ballot access to deposit requirements to state subsidies.[15] While Coakley (chapter 3) details the requirements to qualify as a party, Abedi's finding that Ireland is the third least cartelised of the nineteen democracies examined suggests that the structure of Irish political institutions offers reasonable access to would-be party entrepreneurs.[16] The founder of the Progressive Democrats, Desmond O'Malley, suggested an alternative hypothesis, claiming that the allocation of state funding to parties on the basis of past electoral performance was an 'impediment to the emergence and survival of new parties'.[17] He claimed that this made it 'very difficult, indeed almost impossible, for a new party to break through in electoral terms'.[18] It is important to point out, however, that the choice for such individuals is not necessarily party or nothing. Rather, the three choices are party, independent or nothing.[19] Therefore, those for whom the party registration process is too onerous a task can still run a quasi-party organisation, but under an independent label. To all intents and purposes, such an organisation could be party in all but name. Such a fate was shared by Neil Blaney's Independent Fianna Fáil and Seán Loftus' Christian Democrat Party.

The primary institution affecting minor parties is the electoral system. There is a general agreement in the literature that plurality systems hinder minor actors, while proportional representation is less of a hindrance. This rule of thumb can be affected by the presence of thresholds in the latter and the dispersal of a party's vote in the former. For instance, if a minor party's vote is concentrated rather than dispersed it can overcome the disadvantages of first-past-the-post. Canada is a prime example of this, where in 2008 Bloc Québéc, with most of its support in the province of Québéc, won 16 per cent of seats in the federal election with 10 per cent of votes. In contrast, the Green Party, whose vote was dispersed throughout the provinces, failed to win any seats with its 7 per cent of votes. In the Irish case, although colloquially referred to as PR, the low district magnitude means that STV is not a strict form of proportional representation. Consequently, minor parties tend to receive a lower share of seats than votes. It was for this same reason that the Liberal and Labour parties colluded in Tasmania (which also uses STV) in the 1990s to reduce constituency size from seven to five, with the aim of making it more difficult for the Greens to elect their candidates (a step that backfired).

Indeed, district magnitude has probably the greatest direct effect of any feature of an electoral system.[20] Put simply, the greater the number of seats available in a constituency, the lower the electoral threshold and the greater the chance minor parties have of winning a seat.[21] Testing this hypothesis is relatively straightforward, and involves an analysis of electoral victories of minor parties by district magnitude. Figure 6 details the ratio of minor party (and independent) seats to the number of constituencies, per constituency size. In 1948, therefore, minor parties (and independents) won eleven seats in the nine four-seat constituencies and eleven seats in the nine five-seat constituencies. This is a ratio of 11:9 or 1.2:1. A score of one or greater in Figure 6 implies that each particular-sized constituency had at least one minor party (or independent) TD on average, which has only happened once since 1948. This was in 2002 when fourteen minor party (and independent) candidates were elected across the fourteen five-seat constituencies. Not surprisingly, minor parties have least success in three-seat constituencies, where the quota to guarantee a seat is 25 per cent, well over our threshold of what defines a minor party. In fact, since the lowest threshold (in a five-seat constituency) is almost 17 per cent, this might suggest that for electoral success, minor parties need to have a 'major status' in specific constituencies to win a seat. The caveat to this is that (a) candidates do not need 17 per cent of first preferences; transfers enable them cross the threshold from minor to major within their constituency, and (b) candidates do not always need to reach a quota to win a seat.

*Figure 6: Ratio of seats to district magnitude for minor parties at Dáil elections, 1948-2011*

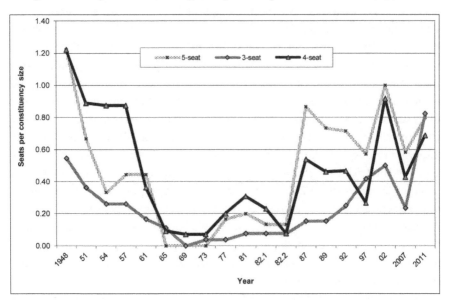

Note: Figures 6-9 and Tables 1 and 2 include all outside of Fianna Fáil, Fine Gael and Labour (independent candidates and 'others' are grouped together with minor parties)

To adequately assess the extent to which district magnitude affects minor parties, we need to consider whether their ratio of percentage seats won to percentage votes won (what Taagepera and Shugart label the 'advantage ratio' (A))[22] is positively correlated with district magnitude. What we find is that since the 1950s, the advantage ratio has been greater than one on only occasion: in three-seat constituencies in 1965. In fact, the average A in the post-war period in three-seat constituencies has been 0.50 and only narrowly greater (0.54) in five-seat constituencies. This implies that minor parties and independents are consistently 'underpaid' for their vote.[23] Not only that, but the overall correlation between district magnitude and A is a very lowly -0.05, an indication of a very weak relationship. While this means that minor parties do not receive a greater 'bang for their buck' the larger the district magnitude, this may be due to the low variation in the magnitude itself. A district magnitude of five or six is generally accepted as the minimum level needed to guarantee relative proportionality in a multiparty system.[24] Because there is little variation in district magnitude in Ireland, and because it is quite low, the best we can therefore say is that the existing district magnitude has little effect on minor parties' seat return from their votes.

In terms of the psychological effects of PR-STV for minor parties, the mechanics of STV should prevent them from losing support to strategic voting (that is, potential voters, wishing to avoid 'wasting' their vote, switching to a candidate with a greater likelihood of winning a seat), as happens in plurality systems. That said, because the mean number of preferences cast in Ireland is between three and four,[25] there may still be an element of irrational strategic voting taking place. The evidence in Figure 8 below does not support this hypothesis. While the overall mean vote for minor parties (an independents) in three-seat constituencies (12 per cent) since 1948 is lower than the equivalent figure in four-seat (17 per cent) or five-seat (15 per cent) constituencies, there is not a great difference in the levels of support from election to election (see Figure 7 below). A small correlation coefficient of +0.11 between district magnitude and minor party vote is further indication of the low level of strategic voting taking place.

*Figure 7: Percentage of the vote for minor parties per district magnitude at Dáil elections, 1948-2011*

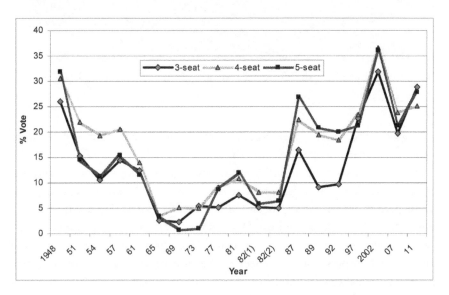

We can also consider the psychological effects of STV for minor parties. It can be reasonably hypothesised that, given the assumption that minor party candidates, *ceteris paribus*, are utility-maximisers, we expect more to run the higher the district magnitude, because the percentage of votes required to win a seat declines accordingly. The evidence in Figure 9 indicates that district magnitude has a positive effect on the number of minor party (and independent) candidates running, as more run in five-seat (3.7 on average) than three-seat (1.3) constituencies (although there is not much difference between the numbers running in four and five-seat districts).

The very factors that affect the emergence of minor political actors can also play a role in their decline. For example, if the social conflict that created a minor party is resolved, the *raison d'être* of the latter may be threatened. The same applies to independents standing on a particular issue. Such a situation could also materialise if the social group that the party represents dwindles in both number

*Figure 8: Number of minor party candidates per district magnitude at Dáil elections, 1948-2011*

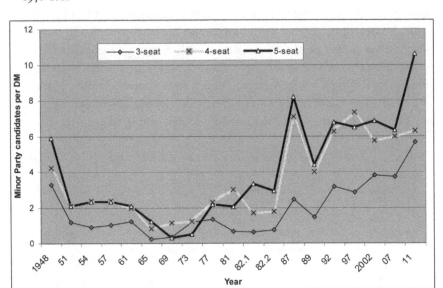

and significance. This in part explains why farmers' parties and independent unionist candidates disappeared after the 1960s.

Other factors to consider outside of the historical-sociological and institutional models are the actions of the minor actors themselves. Where, for example, the minor parties are essentially personal vehicles for particular political actors (both Monetary Reform and the Democratic Socialist Party spring to mind), the emergence and disappearance of such parties can simply be a product of the dominant actors' personal preferences. At the same time, because of their relative size, the personalities and abilities of the leading figures in minor parties can have a disproportionate impact on the parties' performance. Thus, Varley notes in chapter 9 that the decline of the various farmers' parties was due to their lack of prominent national figures. Conversely, McDaid and Rekawek claim that Labour was able to shift from a minor to major status in the 1987-1992 period because of Dick Spring's emergence as a national politician.[26]

The ability of minor parties to manage themselves is another important factor. In the United States, Tamas says that the decline of the Reform Party in the US was a self-inflicted 'implosion'.[27] Minor parties, usually due to a lack of resources, are sometimes run by political amateurs and novices, where infighting and splits are common. For example, the national committee of the Reform Party was so divided over where to stage a party convention, its dispute ended up in the courts. Such implosions occur because of a greater commitment to intra-party democracy on the part of minor parties (but not all; examples of neo-populist parties, which are quite centralised, spring to mind); it is quite difficult for them to fake this.[28] In contrast, major parties can maintain a veneer of democracy while at the same time acting undemocratically as an efficient organisation. This suggests that there are some internal contradictions within minor parties. One of their main selling points to distinguish themselves from the larger parties, is their democratic nature, *à la* the Green movement. At the same time, this emphasis can be the party's downfall if it spills over into internal conflict.

## Who votes for minor parties?

While minor parties may well be different from their major rivals, both organisationally and ideologically, to what extent do they attract a distinctive electorate? Is it the case that there is a pool of potential minor party voters, who because of their anti-establishment views are prepared to vote for any minor party or independent candidate? Or are minor parties in competition with major parties for votes? It is difficult to support the former hypothesis in light of the fluctuating support for minor parties detailed in Figures 1 and 2 above and in Figure 9. So what can we say about minor party voters?[29]

To begin with aggregate data, the vote for minor party (and independent) candidates per province is detailed in Figure 9. It is immediately apparent that the level of support for such candidates follows the same trend across the provinces and that there is a general regional uniformity to minor party support. Two deviations from this trend are worth noting. First, the higher level of support in Connacht-Ulster between 1944 and 1965 is due to the emergence of Clann na Talmhan and Sinn Féin during this era, both of which had concentrated levels of support in this region. Similarly, the higher vote attracted by minor party candidates in Dublin since 1987 was due to the emergence of the Progressive Democrats, the Workers' Party and the Greens in the 1980s, for each of whom Dublin was their respective electoral stronghold.

We can further examine the geographical distribution of support using county-level data (the smallest unit for general elections). Rather than detailing the minor party vote per county per election, a correlation is the preferred method of analysis as this allows us to see the level of variation across elections. Applying this to the distribution of the minor party vote, if there is little variation per constituency across elections we should expect a coefficient close to +1. A coefficient closer to 0 implies that there is little geographical basis to the minor party vote across elections, that is, within constituencies it seems to vary quite significantly from year to year. For the purposes of this analysis, two datasets have been created. The first contains the vote for minor parties and independents (essentially the vote for everyone outside of Fianna Fáil, Fine Gael and Labour) at general elections between 1948 and 1973, while the second contains the same data, but for the 1981-2011 period. The two periods are separated because there were significant boundary alterations in the mid-1970s that do not make comparisons possible. For the same reason, the 1977 election is excluded from our analysis.

*Figure 9: Percentage of First Preference Vote won at Dáil elections by minor parties per province, 1922-2011*

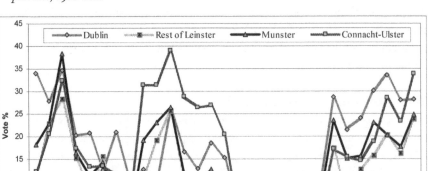

Looking at Tables 1 and 2, it is quite noticeable that the relationship between the levels of minor party support across elections has weakened considerably in recent years, as evidenced by the declining values of the coefficients. For example, there is a stronger relationship between the minor party vote in 1948 and 1973 than the same vote between 2002 and any election preceding it. Although the coefficient for successive elections remains close to +0.60, this weakens considerably after several elections (as evident in the left-hand corner of Table 2), a pattern not so evident in the pre-1980s era. As well as being indicative of the increasing volatility of the Irish voter, it is also reflective of the regional nature of minor party support. As the fortunes of such parties vary per election, it is not always the case that minor party voters switch to or transfer from other minor parties. This data also confirms the national swings that occurred at particular elections permeated to the local level. For example, the increased vote for minor parties and independents in 2002, which motivated talk of a new opposition,[30] explains why the correlations for that year are particularly low. Similarly too, the correlation between November 1982 and 1987 was weaker than other sets of consecutive elections, largely due to the emergence of the Progressive Democrats in the meantime.

While this analysis provides some insight into the national spread of the minor party support base, what do we know about their voters? Here is not the place to discuss those supporting independent candidates, since Weeks devotes a whole paper to this topic.[31] Previous ecological analysis of minor parties' vote by Sinnott and Gallagher found some significant patterns.[32] Gallagher found that support for both the Farmers' Party and the National Centre Party was

*Table 1: Correlation of minor party and independent votes, 1948-1973*

|        | 1973 | 1969 | 1965 | 1961 | 1957 | 1954 | 1951 |
|--------|------|------|------|------|------|------|------|
| 1969   | 0.83 |      |      |      |      |      |      |
| 1965   | 0.84 | 0.89 |      |      |      |      |      |
| 1961   | 0.56 | 0.58 | 0.75 |      |      |      |      |
| 1957   | 0.44 | 0.37 | 0.55 | 0.76 |      |      |      |
| 1954   | 0.40 | 0.37 | 0.54 | 0.77 | 0.87 |      |      |
| 1951   | 0.38 | 0.29 | 0.45 | 0.68 | 0.81 | 0.81 |      |
| 1948   | 0.32 | 0.20 | 0.27 | 0.42 | 0.46 | 0.57 | 0.69 |

N=36 cases. Carlow–Kilkenny, Cavan–Monaghan/Cavan, Clare, Cork City, Cork county, Donegal-Leitrim/Donegal SW, Donegal NE, Dublin North-Central, Dublin North-East, Dublin North-West, Dublin South-Central, Dublin South-East, Dublin South-West, Dublin County, Dun Laoghaire, Galway North-East/East/North, Galway West/South, Kerry North, Kerry South, Kildare, Laois–Offaly, Limerick East, Limerick West, Longford–Westmeath, Louth, Mayo East, Mayo West, Meath, Monaghan, Roscommon–Leitrim, Sligo–Leitrim, Tipperary North, Tipperary South, Waterford, Wexford, Wicklow.

*Table 2: Correlation of minor party and independent votes 1981-2011*

|         | 2011 | 2007 | 2002 | 1997 | 1992 | 1989 | 1987 | 1982(2) | 1982(1) |
|---------|------|------|------|------|------|------|------|---------|---------|
| 2007    | 0.59 |      |      |      |      |      |      |         |         |
| 2002    | 0.51 | 0.64 |      |      |      |      |      |         |         |
| 1997    | 0.50 | 0.58 | 0.31 |      |      |      |      |         |         |
| 1992    | 0.12 | 0.28 | 0.18 | 0.56 |      |      |      |         |         |
| 1989    | 0.04 | 0.25 | 0.10 | 0.46 | 0.85 |      |      |         |         |
| 1987    | 0.07 | 0.21 | 0.20 | 0.48 | 0.76 | 0.85 |      |         |         |
| 1982(2) | 0.15 | 0.15 | 0.14 | 0.42 | 0.64 | 0.69 | 0.57 |         |         |
| 1982(1) | 0.24 | 0.12 | 0.20 | 0.28 | 0.44 | 0.54 | 0.45 | 0.78    |         |
| 1981    | 0.36 | 0.22 | 0.16 | 0.25 | 0.30 | 0.36 | 0.24 | 0.59    | 0.80    |

N=40. Carlow–Kilkenny, Cavan–Monaghan, Clare, Cork East, Cork North-Central, Cork North-West, Cork South-Central, Cork South-West, Donegal North-East, Donegal South-West, Dublin Central, Dublin North, Dublin North-Central, Dublin North-East, Dublin North-West, Dublin South, Dublin South-Central, Dublin South-East, Dublin South-West, Dublin West, Dún Laoghaire, Galway East, Galway West, Kerry North, Kerry South, Kildare, Laois–Offaly, Limerick East, Limerick West, Longford–Westmeath, Louth, Mayo, Meath, Roscommon–South Leitrim/Roscommon, Sligo–N Leitrim/Leitrim, Tipperary North, Tipperary South, Waterford, Wexford, Wicklow.
For the 2002, 2007 and 2011 elections, Dublin Mid-West is merged with Dublin West. Longford–Roscommon and Westmeath are excluded from 2002.

positively related to the proportion of farm labourers in a constituency (that is, where there were more wealthy farmers who could afford to hire labour), while Clann na Talmhan attracted higher levels of support in constituencies with more farmers, particularly amongst those with no labourers (that is, farmers who could not afford to hire help).[33] Support for Sinn Féin was inversely related to the proportion of Protestants and farm labourers and positively associated with the rate of emigration.[34] Clann na Poblachta attracted more support in constituencies with low emigration rates and more farmers, while the vote for independents was stronger in areas with more Protestants, fewer farm labourers and, for a time in the 1950s (when several former Clann na Talmhan TDs ran as independents), more farmers.[35] Sinnott found a positive working-class effect and a negative farmer effect (albeit only at one election) associated with support for the Workers' Party in the 1980s.[36]

At more recent elections, while there has been analysis of individual-level data, this is sometimes limited by the small number of minor party voters included within the selected sample. This makes it especially difficult to reach reliable conclusions about the support base of individual parties. Nevertheless, in three of the more recent volumes of the *How Ireland Voted* series (for the 1997, 2002 and 2007 general elections), there has been sufficient exit-poll data to enable multinomial regression analysis of voters' propensity to support Fianna Fáil or one of the specific minor parties. There were only three socio-economic variables where specific minor party and Fianna Fáil voters differed: sex, class and region. Men were more likely to vote for Sinn Féin, while the middle class and those from rural regions were less likely to do so. Both the Greens and the Progressive Democrats had a distinct middle-class base to their vote, while the latter also received more support from men at the 1997 election. The findings of the Irish National Election Study from 2002 were pretty much in line with these patterns.[37] The Progressive Democrats had a young (under forty), middle-class support base. While Sinn Féin also attracts a youth vote, the Greens do not. Age is the only clear demographic trait of Sinn Féin voters, in contrast to the Greens who have 'the best-defined image of any party',[38] with an urban and better-educated support base. In terms of values, the Greens attract a more ideological voter, with support levels greater amongst those expressing more environmental, egalitarian, secular opinions. They, along with Sinn Féin, also get more support from those on the left and those not as positive about the EU as others. The nationalism dimension was a factor in the Sinn Féin and Progressive Democrat vote, with those slightly nationalist supporting the latter and those strongly nationalist supporting the former. Surprisingly, Progressive Democrat voters were not more pro-business than others. In the absence of the Progressive Democrats and in light of a weakened Green Party, there were fewer options to analyse the minor party vote in 2011. Nevertheless, Marsh and Cunningham found that Sinn Féin attract significantly more support from those in traditional working-class occupations (16 per cent), are still more popular amongst men than women, and are distinctly unpopular with pensioners.[39] What may be a positive development for Sinn Féin is the lessening of the youth slant to its vote, perhaps reflective of fading memories of the troubles.

## Conclusion

It is quite evident that minor parties in Ireland are distinct political actors, both in terms of their identity and in terms of their impact. Indeed, it is because of the latter, particularly in terms of the ability of these actors to acquire a share of the spoils of office, that explains why minor parties will retain an electoral presence, and should they disappear, why others will take their place.[40] One question that was not raised, but was acknowledged in an indirect fashion is to what extent minor parties are explanatory or outcome variables. If the latter, they may well be the product of social change, with the Greens and perhaps the Progressive Democrats testament to this. That said, given the recent level of immigration into Ireland and the authoritarian, intolerant streak in Irish political culture,[41] we may well wonder why there is no radical right party.[42] Of course, we may also ask why there are not more minor parties full stop, given the level of social and economic change in Ireland, the declining level of attachment to parties and a PR electoral system that facilitates such change.[43] On the other hand, parties can often be explanatory variables, and certainly this is something they often profess, particularly when they try to engineer social change. While Fianna Fáil under de Valera may have achieved this,[44] it is an aspiration probably beyond the range of minor parties' abilities.

One aspect of minor parties that makes them especially interesting to study is that a fate common to all discussed here is that they never moved beyond their minor status. However, this is not a destiny set in stone. Fianna Fáil was originally a minority (of the anti-Treaty Republicans) of a minority (of Sinn Féin). Of course the electoral market was arguably more open to competition in the 1920s than the present day. Nevertheless, the experience of Silvio Berlusconi's Forza Italia in Italy in the 1990s is evidence that new parties need not necessarily be confined to minor status (although such an occurrence is quite rare in western democracies – where only seven new parties have won more than 15 per cent at a lower house national election)[45]. In this context, the study of minor parties is useful to those interested in parties of all shapes and sizes and the findings in this book will provide a salutary lesson on party organisation and competition.

# 3

# The Rise and Fall of Minor Parties in Ireland, 1922-2011

*John Coakley*

## Introduction

In assessing the significance of Ireland's 'earthquake' election of 2011, Michael Gallagher lists fifteen records that were broken by the results.[1] One of these was the decline of the two traditionally dominant parties, Fianna Fáil and Fine Gael, which registered their lowest ever collective share of the vote, at 54 per cent. Another was the disposition of voters to abandon traditional voting loyalties, as measured by the level of electoral volatility. In this respect, Irish voters broke with past patterns of stability; the level of volatility in 2011 has been described as 'dramatic even by recent European standards'.[2] Among the beneficiaries of this electoral shake-up was a large, disparate set of minor parties and independent deputies which, indeed, had profited from relatively high levels of volatility since 1987.[3] The smaller parties were in some cases of long standing, and in others had been generated by the economic crisis. Their existence gives rise to important questions about their ideological origins, their electoral profile and their role in the political system – questions on which this chapter focuses.

Although new, minor or 'third' parties have for long fascinated observers in the area of comparative politics, progress in analysing them has been painfully slow. One overview thirty years ago gave four reasons for this: their relative electoral unimportance, difficulties (including linguistic ones) in gaining access to information about them, their limited capacity to influence government policy, and political scientists' distaste for their allegedly dysfunctional role.[4] A decade later, an influential comparative study concluded that 'the role of small parties in western Europe is an area that to date has not been examined in any systematic or comprehensive way'.[5] The literature since then on the appearance, growth, survival and demise of minor parties has still fallen short of producing a real scholarly consensus. This literature, though containing many useful insights, continues to reflect not just an uneven capacity to explain the phenomenon across states, but also a wide range of conflicting implicit political judgements on the contribution of such parties to the political system. As examples, these include acknowledgement of their role in providing a voice for extremists of the right,[6] satisfaction at their success in retaining the engagement of citizens who would otherwise be alienated,[7] and exasperation at their capacity for self-destruction.[8]

This chapter seeks to analyse the phenomenon of Irish minor parties by exploring their long historical evolution, and by seeking to set this in appropriately broad perspective, using comparative insights that help to account for the rise, fall and profile of parties of this kind. The chapter therefore begins by looking at matters of definition: the question of what, exactly, is meant by a 'minor party'. This is followed by an outline of the main approaches to classifying minor parties. The next section generalises about the electoral history of each type in independent Ireland. The last substantive section seeks to place the Irish experience of minor parties in comparative perspective with a view to explaining some of its more distinctive features. A brief description of the parties discussed here is contained in an appendix.

## Defining minor parties

It could not be said that terms such as 'minor party' and its cognates are clearly defined in the political science lexicon. Leaving aside for the moment the lower boundary of this category (that which separates it from independents and other non-party groups), the upper boundary is already sufficiently troublesome. 'Minor parties' have been defined as all except the two largest parties in countries with a plurality electoral system,[9] all except the three largest parties in Ireland[10] and Great Britain,[11] and all except the four largest parties in Scottish local elections.[12]

The related term commonly used in two-party systems, 'third parties', poses even greater problems. This may refer to a national-level challenger that clearly ranks third in an established two-party system, as in US presidential elections;[13] but it may be a pointer to a vaguer third-ranking status, where the 'third party' mobilises against both the government and the main opposition party. In this context, the definition of 'third party' no longer necessarily implies a numerical ranking: a 'third party' may be defined as 'any non-traditional party which has not yet been in power',[14] 'a non-traditional party that has not managed to obtain a minimum of 10 per cent of the votes in each of the previous two elections,'[15] or a 'non-traditional (non-major) party … [which] has not been in office for a relatively long period of time'.[16]

This does not exhaust the set of terms used to describe this kind of phenomenon. The 'minor party' concept is also close to that of the 'new party', which may be seen as coming into existence in four ways: fusion of existing parties, fission or splintering within an existing party, a 'genuinely new' party that appears as a result of autonomous efforts, and the formation of an electoral alliance.[17] Yet another term – though rather narrower – is that of 'niche party', defined as one whose members 'present either an extreme ideology (such as Communist and extreme nationalist parties) or a noncentrist "niche" ideology (i.e., the Greens)'.[18]

While most debate has centred on identifying the upper boundary of the minor party category (that which distinguishes such parties from those identified as major, traditional, established, or mainstream parties), there is also a lower boundary to be taken into account. This presents few difficulties in countries operating proportional representation by means of party lists: in such cases, only formally registered parties are allowed to contest elections. It is true that in exceptional cases provision may be made for what are effectively independent candidacies, but even these must demonstrate rudimentary organisational capacity. In countries where voting is individual-based rather than list-based, though, such as those operating the plurality system, a decision must be made on where the boundary between minor party and truly independent candidates lies. Some analysts resort to a strategy of inclusion: noting the sheer difficulty of distinguishing between the two types, independents may be bundled with minor parties.[19] One alternative would be to acknowledge the porousness of the boundary, while still seeking to distinguish minor parties not just from independents but also from non-party organisations, such as ratepayers', residents' or tenants' associations, or single-issue pressure groups.[20]

The debate in the comparative literature has some implications for the study of Irish minor parties. At first sight, it might appear that the 'third party' label applies precisely to the Labour Party, which until 2011 was always associated with this ranking. But the literature on 'third parties' rests on the assumption of a solid, established two-party system produced by a non-proportional electoral system (typically the plurality system), with alternating parties, against which 'third parties' periodically rebel. In the Irish case, as in that of many other countries using proportional representation, the core is larger – in this case, there was, at least until 2011, a clearly-defined three-party system. Ordinally, then, the phenomenon in which we are interested in Ireland is the 'fourth party', or 'new party', a category that might simply be described as 'minor party': a party that, to use the language of the comparative literature, is non-traditional, non-established, and non-mainstream. We may thus rule out the three 'permanent' members of the Irish party system from this category: the Labour Party is excluded, together with Fianna Fáil and Fine Gael, even though, as it has been pointed out, the Labour Party may at times have matched the image of other parties here seen as 'minor',[21] and it has indeed sometimes so been classified.[22] This leaves a group of relatively distinctive parties corresponding to what were once called 'ephemeral minority parties' – though, in reality, not all were entirely ephemeral.[23]

Since the Irish system of proportional representation rests on voters ranking individual candidates, thus removing the necessity of grouping them into party lists, difficulties arise also at the other boundary of the 'minor party' category —that which distinguishes it from independents. A change in electoral law in 1963, however, which for the first time allowed party names to appear on the ballot paper and provided for the registration of political parties, allows us to introduce a formal criterion for the cut-off point between minor party and independent candidates: for the period since 1963, it is, in general, possible to rely on recognition by the Registrar of Political Parties (a position occupied ex officio by the Clerk of the Dáil). This has the advantage that only groups that satisfy the Registrar that they are 'genuine' political parties organised to contest elections may register, a useful, quasi-objective way of determining the cut-off point.[24] On the other hand, the objectivity of this measure may be compromised by ideological factors. Thus, certain republican groups have from time to time contested elections but without registering as formal parties, since that, in their view, would entail recognition of what they saw as an illegitimate state. To deal with such cases, a more behavioural criterion has been adopted: groups of this kind, provided they conduct themselves like a party, as discussed in the next paragraph, have been included even if they are not officially registered.

It makes sense also to extend this behavioural criterion to the pre-1963 period. Here, it is appropriate to adopt an inclusive (but not all-inclusive) approach. First, the group must be political: it must be oriented towards influencing policy in the country's representative assembly. Second, electoral involvement must form a significant part of its activities (so that the boundary between minor parties and non-party organisations, such as trade unions, professional bodies or pressure groups needs to be defined).[25] Third, it must possess organisational structures with *de facto* power to sanction or to veto electoral candidacies. This comes close to an established minimal definition of a minor party as 'an organization – however loosely or strongly organised – which either presents or nominates candidates for public elections, or which, at least, has the declared intention to do so',[26] and conforms with the approach in an early but definitive account of British minor parties.[27]

## Classifying minor parties

Perhaps because of their standing as a residual category, there is little agreement on criteria for classifying minor parties (this, no doubt, also reflects the same kinds of difficulty as are encountered in the area of definition). We may see classifications as being oriented towards one or more of four dimensions of minor parties: historical, relying on organisational evolution and origin; electoral, referring to the level of political success of the party, especially in respect of support at elections; strategic, based on approach and style in the electoral marketplace; and ideological, focusing on political substance and policy direction. These should not be seen simply as alternative approaches; any party may in principle be classified in respect of each of the four.

The first classification is the most obvious: the manner in which the party has come into existence. The most straightforward categorisation here is a dichotomy. As we have seen, Hug distinguishes between minor parties which have resulted from a split in an existing party, and those which constitute an entirely new formation (he excludes from his analysis two other types, mergers of existing parties and electoral alliances).[28] Tavits follows the same approach.[29] Bochel and Denver make a similar distinction between 'splinter' parties and those formed autonomously, with a further division in the latter category between 'genuine' (longstanding, with a clearly defined policy platform) and 'nascent' (still unproven) parties;[30] they put parties whose appeal is primarily local in a separate category. This suggests a simple classification of parties into two categories. We may ignore a third category, new parties created by mergers of existing parties, since no empirical case occurs among Irish minor parties, though this might be needed in other countries or for larger parties such as Fine Gael. Using the historical criterion, then, we may identify the following types:

- Breakaway parties: parties which have originated in a split within an existing party
- New parties; parties, typically with wholly extra-parliamentary roots, originating quite separately from existing parties.

The second classification principle has to do with the electoral profile of the party over time. A particularly useful framework has been developed by Peter Mair.[31] First casting the net wide, this defines as 'enduring parties' all which have contested at least three elections. Within this, it distinguishes three categories: large parties (which have won at least 15 per cent of electoral support in at least three elections), small parties (which fail to meet this criterion, but have won at least 1 per cent in at least three elections), and ephemeral or micro-parties (which fail to meet even the 1 per cent criterion in at least three elections). In classifying parties in respect of this dimension, we obviously exclude the first category (large parties). It may also be useful to distinguish both in respect of longevity (between ephemeral and enduring, or established, parties), and in respect of size (between minor parties and truly microparties). We thus end up with a four-fold classification on the basis of the electoral criterion, as follows:

- Established minor parties: parties winning at least 1 per cent support in at least three elections
- Ephemeral minor parties: parties winning at least 1 per cent support in fewer than three elections, but in at least one
- Established microparties: parties contesting three or more elections, but never winning more than 1 per cent
- Ephemeral microparties: parties contesting fewer than three elections, and never winning more than 1 per cent

Third, several observers have grouped minor parties in respect of the manner in which they position themselves electorally. Pinard distinguishes between protest parties (based on generalised discontent, possibly of an immediate nature) and radical parties (based on a shared ideology that reflects specific group interests, likely to be long-term and more profoundly held).[32] This overlaps with a second classification. Harmel and Robertson distinguish between 'contender parties', which perceive some prospect of success from electoral competition, and 'promoter parties', which are primarily concerned with articulating a distinctive viewpoint, regardless of their electoral prospects.[33] A third classification follows the same approach, but identifies different categories. Rochon distinguishes between 'challenging parties', which compete with established parties on the basis of existing cleavages, and 'mobilising parties', which seek to mobilise political identities around a new cleavage or a redefinition of an existing cleavage (certain residual parties are placed in a 'personal vehicle' category, essentially a mechanism of convenience for individuals).[34] If we start with Harmel and Robertson's contender-promoter dichotomy, and recognise that all three types identified by Rochon – challenging, mobilising and personal vehicle parties – fall into the former (contender) category, we may identify four types of party by reference to electoral strategy.[35] The strategic criterion thus gives us the following:

- Promoter parties: organisations standing for the defence of distinctive political positions almost regardless of electoral appeal and of the attractions of office, differentiated from mainstream parties by their ideological purity and inflexibility
- Mobilising parties: contender parties arising from a new policy dimension, or from a new position in respect of an existing one, differentiated from mainstream parties by their policy distinctiveness
- Challenging parties: contender parties which compete with existing parties on the basis not of policy but of capacity to deliver, differentiated from mainstream parties by considerations of valence (their self-proclaimed superior competence and integrity in formulating and implementing policy)
- Personal vehicle parties: contender parties created to advance the position of a particular individual, differentiated from mainstream parties by loose structures that virtually reduce them to single-person entities

Fourth, ideological considerations of course matter. As well as looking at historical origins, Tavits distinguishes between minor parties on the basis of their policies (left-libertarian, new right-wing, or regional).[36] Adams *et al.* make a similar distinction between 'niche' parties on the basis of their ideology, with some classed as adherents of an extreme ideology (such as Communist and extreme nationalist parties) and others as following a noncentrist 'niche' ideology (Green parties).[37] We can find further refinements within particular categories. For example, there is a well-established distinction within the right-wing category between fascist-type and 'new right' parties; though sharing authoritarian values, the former are anticapitalist, corporatist and contingently racist, while the latter are procapitalist and inherently racist.[38] Although it does not correspond exactly, this finds echoes in the distinction between the old, traditional extreme right-wing party and the new, post-industrial one,[39] and in the neofascist–populist dichotomy.[40] It is also to be found in the careful carving out for further study of 'populist radical right parties', distinct alike from neofascist parties and other parties of the right.[41]

Mair presents the most comprehensive ideological classification of small parties.[42] As well as a residual category, he distinguishes nine 'party families': the communist, socialist, Christian, liberal, extreme right, conservative right, agrarian, nationalist-regionalist, and ecologist traditions. All of these traditions except the last may easily be located within a well-known, broad classification scheme in which major parties, too, can be accommodated: the Lipset-Rokkan model, whose capacity for adaptability has survived the challenges of several decades, not least in Ireland.[43] This may be used to provide a basis for a classification of Irish minor parties in respect of their ideological orientation. In brief, the model suggests that the party systems of the late twentieth century were generated by political rivalries and alliances generated by four types of conflict: (1) economic conflict between owners and workers, which tends to be reflected in a conservative–socialist division; (2) economic conflict between consumers and producers, reflected in an urban–rural division; (3) cultural conflict between Church and state, reflected in societies with a Catholic tradition in a liberal–Christian democratic division; and (4) conflict between a culturally dominant centre and a subordinate periphery, reflected in a centralist–regionalist division.

In principle, if we dichotomise these four cleavages we have eight types of single-issue positions. But overlapping interests and the limited salience of some of these positions in particular societies normally serve to reduce this number greatly. To simplify the discussion, we confine ourselves here to the Irish case, where we may see two types of party as corresponding to the first of these dimensions, with one pole represented in the case of the other three. We also need to bring back the ecologist tradition – not easily located within the Lipset-Rokkan model, but which may be uncomfortably shoe-horned into the consumer-producer cleavage. The resulting party types on the ideological dimension may be described as follows:

- Left-wing parties, typically challenging parties dissatisfied with the achievements of the mainstream party of the left, but some may be promoter parties, standing for radical positions of principle
- Right-wing parties, typically mobilising parties seeking to occupy what they perceive as new electoral ground; some of these may also be personal vehicle parties

- Agrarian parties, mobilising parties trying to define a new and distinctive policy domain, that of defence of farmers' rights
- Religious parties, mobilising parties seeking to move into ground they see as having been abandoned by the major parties
- Nationalist parties, either challenging parties dissatisfied with the stance of existing parties or promoter parties standing for what they see as the uncompromising values of the nation
- Environmentalist parties, mobilising parties focusing on new global and domestic challenges associated with the degradation of the physical environment

Since in theory all possible combinations of party types may occur, the above four-dimensional framework allows for a total of 192 types (two by four by four by six). As this is many more than the actual number of minor parties in the Irish and most other party systems, it will make sense to use the framework judiciously. As indicated above, there are associations between particular positions across dimensions, and a large number of possible types of parties will simply not occur. This will be clear from the discussion that follows, where, although extensive reference will be made to the first three dimensions, most emphasis will be on the fourth (ideological) one.

## Profiling minor parties
At first sight, the range of minor parties that have existed in Ireland since independence is bewildering. On 29 November 2011, eighteen parties were so classified by the Registrar of Political Parties thirteen to contest Dáil elections (of which all were also registered as eligible to contest local elections, and all but two to contest European elections), four to contest local elections only, and one to contest local and Dáil elections in a particular district only (South Kerry). This compares with 357 parties registered to contest elections in Great Britain on 2 January 2012, and forty in Northern Ireland.[44]

The set of identifiable minor parties which have existed since 1922 is listed in the appendix, where each is described in brief. The approach here is inclusive, extending to some groups whose classification as parties is problematic, and thus resulting in a long list of fifty-one groups. Of these, twenty-three are parties that have been registered since 1963; twenty-five are pre-1963 parties that would have stood a good chance of being accepted by the Registrar had such a system then existed; and three are post-1963 groups that were never formally registered as parties but which played a significant quasi-party role (Independent Fianna Fáil, the H-Blocks Group and the Army Wives' Group).

In this list, each of the frontiers already discussed arises as an issue. First, some parties whose electoral appeal was local have been included: Monetary Reform, for instance, and Independent Fianna Fáil (a particularly problematic case); but parties which are explicitly local in appeal, such as the South Kerry Independent Alliance and the Donegal Progressive Party have been dropped.[45] Second, some pressure groups whose primary arena of activity was not electoral have been included simply because they put candidates forward at general elections: the Irish Association of the Blind, the Irish Housewives' Association and the National Army Spouses' Association, for instance, as well as groups which played a more considerable electoral role, such as the Ratepayers' Association and the Town Tenants' Association. Third, some of the groups included have never actually contested a general election: the National Group (1924-25), for example, and the National Guard (1932-33), each of which played a significant political role, and four contemporary parties, some of which may yet satisfy this criterion.

The overall pattern of support for minor parties since 1922, with peaks in the 1920s and the 1940s, and a strong performance since 1987, has been outlined elsewhere.[46] But how may these parties be described in respect of the four dimensions discussed above? First, as regards origin, most were externally founded. However, sixteen were clearly splinter parties, sometimes from Cumann na nGaedheal (Clann Éireann and the National Group, for example), sometimes from Fianna Fáil (Aontacht Éireann and the Progressive Democrats), and sometimes from the Labour Party (the Dublin Trades Council, National Labour and Socialist Labour, for example). In many cases, though, they appeared as a consequence of fissile tendencies among minor parties on the radical left and militant nationalist fringes.

In respect of their electoral profiles and strategic approaches, the parties also fall into a number of clearly definable groups. First, the great bulk of the 280 deputies returned at general elections from 1922 to 2011 to represent minor parties (78 per cent of the total) came from a small group of nine established minor parties. Some of these (including three manifestations of Sinn Féin and the Socialist Party) were substantially promoter parties; four (the Farmers' Party, Clann na Talmhan, Clann na Poblachta and the Green Party) were mobilising parties; and the remaining one, the Progressive Democrats, was arguably a challenging party (in respect of Fianna Fáil), a category in which, indeed, Clann na Poblachta might also have been accommodated. A second group (accounting for 17 per cent of all minor party TDs elected) comprised ephemeral minor parties: four mobilising parties (the Business Party, the National League, the National Centre Party and the H-Blocks Group) and three challenging ones (the National Labour Party, the National Progressive Democrats and Democratic Left). The next group comprises twelve established micro-parties (5 per cent of all minor party TDs): parties sustained over the years by commitment to a distinctive ideology, by loyalty to a beloved leader, or by commitment to a particular group, even though they were never able to win more than one seat, and more commonly not even that. Here, the most prominent were mobilising parties standing for socialist values (the Socialist Labour Party and, if we are to use this label to refer collectively to the succession of parties occupying this niche since 1922, the Communist Party), each of which was able to win a seat in at least one Dáil election. Others, less prominent and typically mobilising parties, stood for the economic rights of particular aggrieved groups (the Ratepayers' Association, the Town Tenants' Association and Monetary Reform), radical nationalist values (Ailtirí na hAiseirghe and the Irish Republican Socialist Party, though the latter could be more accurately classified as a challenging party), or religious values (the Christian Solidarity Party and the National Party). Finally, the remaining parties were ephemeral microparties, typically contesting only a single election and performing poorly in that. The most noteworthy in this category were two challenging nationalist parties, Clann Éireann and Aontacht Éireann.

*Figure 1: Minor parties by ideological orientation, 1922-2011*

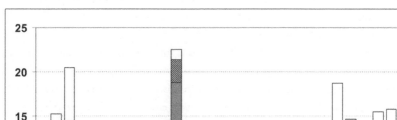

Note: bars refer to share of first preference vote in Dáil elections.

A further question has to do with the political orientation of these parties. Figure 1 breaks the minor parties down into five broad ideological types discussed above (a sixth category, religious parties, is so small that it has been grouped with the right-wing parties). It should be noted that some parties do not fall easily into one category rather than another even at a single point in time; and over time they may move across categories (not just in respect of ideologies, but also in relation to the other classifications discussed above). Sinn Féin the Workers' Party, for example, represented a stage in the transition from the nationalist to the socialist category; and its rival, (Provisional) Sinn Féin, made a transition from promoter party to mobilising party status.

Normally, the ideological orientation of the minor parties discussed here is extremely clear: radical socialist or militant nationalist parties did not mince their words in declaring, for example, that 'the Communist Party of Ireland is guided by the fundamental principles of Marxism-Leninism and its programme and party structure are based on such principles',[47] or that 'Sinn Féin advocates not merely the complete overthrow of English rule in Ireland but also the setting up of a democratic socialist republic based on the proclamation of 1916'.[48] There are times when ideology is less explicitly defined, but it may be inferred from other documents and statements.[49]

As regards overall patterns, the clustering of parties into three phases is clear. In the first two phases, beginning in the 1920s and in the 1940s, the agrarian dimension was very strong, with nationalist parties also making an impact. More recently, however, the issues animating minor parties seem to have changed, with an apparent upsurge in support for the right (as represented in particular by the Progressive Democrats). But this raises significant issues of classification. One perceptive study has suggested that the failure of the 'new right' (on the continental European model) to make any inroads in Ireland may be attributed to the fact that the radical populist terrain associated with this perspective in other countries is occupied in Ireland by a party with many of the external attributes of a new right party, but certainly not its ideology: Sinn Féin.[50] While it would be a misrepresentation of reality to classify Sinn Féin as 'right-wing', this does not mean that it fits comfortably into the 'nationalist' category in which it has been placed in this chapter; in fact, at least in the Republic of Ireland, its profile suggests that it has many of the characteristics of a party of the left. On the other hand, even if the Progressive Democrats lacked the classic features of the new right, their status as a party of the right seems beyond doubt.[51] The most definitive analysis of the social structural and attitudinal support bases of Irish parties in 2002 shows Sinn Féin and Progressive Democrat supporters sharing the characteristic backgrounds and attitudes of left and right respectively – though the difference separating them, and differentiating them from the other parties, was quite small.[52] This is compatible with the results of a survey of expert views in 1997, which showed the Progressive Democrats as lying far to the right of all other parties on the economic policy dimension, that is on matters relating to perceived appropriate levels of taxation and public expenditure.[53]

## Interpreting minor parties

To what extent does the Irish experience of minor parties match that of other European countries? The pattern is rather different from, say, the Netherlands and Switzerland, where small parties have been able to survive across genera-tions, however marginal their political relevance. It is also different from the pattern in France and Italy, where the survival of new parties, especially on the right, has been a big issue, however great their ephemeral political relevance. The Irish pattern bears some similarity to the Nordic model: a relatively stable party system core; the predicable longevity of distinctive promoter parties, such as the Communist Party (to which, in Ireland, we need to add Sinn Féin and its challengers); and near-insurmountable impediments to the survival or even birth of new parties, with environmentalist parties as the big exception.

We may try to generalise about the Irish experience by seeking to relate minor parties to a framework developed to look at stages in their political consolidation. Pedersen has suggested that in their lifespan parties must cross a set of thresholds: (1) declaration, or self-proclamation as a party, (2) authorisation, or formal recognition as an electoral vehicle, (3) representation, or securing at least minimal representation in the national legislature, and (4) relevance, or attainment of a measure of political significance.[54] The meaning of 'relevance' is subjective, but it may help if we go back to an old definition by Sartori,[55] who saw it as reflecting either coalition potential or 'blackmail' potential (the capacity to disrupt other parties' ambitions). More recently, Deschouwer suggested that a fifth stage be added: actual (and not just potential) participation in government.[56]

This offers a useful framework for an overview of Irish minor parties. The number of groups that have proclaimed themselves parties since 1922 is probably greater than sixty. This excludes potential parties which have stopped short of so proclaiming themselves; for instance, the Immigration Control Platform, a right-wing group formed in January 1998, never sought recognition as a party, but nevertheless contested the elections of 2002 and 2007. Of parties which did seek recognition, though, several failed to cross this second threshold. Before 1963 the threshold was a near-invisible one: not even major parties were formally recognised, in the sense of being allowed to use their names on the ballot paper. But even more recently there have been parties which declared themselves as such, but failed to be registered. In May 1997, for instance, the Registrar turned down the application of the Cannabis Legalisation Party, and this decision was upheld by the appeal board on 19 June. Ten years later, the Fathers' Rights–Responsibility Party, formed in February 2007, failed to win registration, but nevertheless contested the 2007 general election without formally using this label.

The third threshold is that of winning parliamentary representation. This acts as a clear filter in reducing the number of parties: twenty-one of those listed in the appendix won at least one seat in a Dáil general election. Although determining which parties crossed the fourth threshold, that of political relevance, is to some degree a matter of subjective judgement, we may identify seven parties which reached this status, and a further two less definite cases. The Farmers' Party, Clann na Talmhan, Clann na Poblachta, National Labour, the Progressive Democrats, Democratic Left and the Green Party all participated in coalition governments (thus definitively reaching the fourth threshold, and indeed satisfying Deschouwer's more demanding criterion of actual government participation). In two remaining cases, it could be argued that the fourth stage was just about reached. The National League was briefly a potential member of a government in 1927, when the prospect of replacing Cumann na nGaedheal by a minority Labour–National League coalition supported by Fianna Fáil arose. Sinn Féin is a more difficult case: its respectable showing in 2002 might have given it some leverage in inter-party negotiations on government formation, but the unwillingness of bigger parties to consider it as a potential partner (mirroring the pariah status of the Italian Social Movement in the Italian party system until the 1990s) undermined its political relevance, and this appeared still to be its status – though less clearly so – in 2007 and 2011.

While the experience of participation in government may have had a 'smothering' effect on some parties, others were undoubtedly able to make a considerable mark on the policy process.[57] Ironically, where minor parties are few and the price they expect for participation is too high, independent deputies may be able to leap-frog them and play a pivotal role, as became clear after the general elections of 1997 and 2007, when Fianna Fáil made substantial concessions to some of them in return for commitments of support.[58]

How are we to explain the emergence, growth and eventual decline of these parties? Here, again, the comparative literature has much to offer. One of the most general explanations is that offered by Tavits,[59] who sees the emergence of new parties as a function of three factors: the cost of entry to the electoral arena, the probability of winning electoral support, and the benefit of holding office. The lower the first of these and the higher the other two, the greater the probability that a new party will appear. The significance of crossing the first threshold (from proclamation to authorisation, in Pedersen's terminology) is obvious: the requirement that any would-be party have minimal organisation, membership, constitution, procedures and funding will rule out 'parties' that exist only on paper, and will play a gatekeeping role in keeping out frivolous or excessively light-weight organisations, thus reducing the universe of formal parties.

There is widespread agreement on the significance of crossing the second threshold (from authorisation to representation). Here, the part played by the electoral system is widely recognised. The role of the plurality system in hindering access by third parties is well established,[60] and, conversely, the role of proportional representation in facilitating minor party entry is well known,[61] though the significance of the electoral system is sometimes questioned.[62] But it has been argued that there are other institutional factors that may play a role: the existence of a two-tiered representative system, as in federal systems, for instance.[63]

Most discussion of the rise of minor parties focuses, however, on social psychological and organisational behavioural factors. While other factors such as community cohesion may be of significance,[64] two stand out as of particular significance: declining partisanship, which frees voters to shift to new parties, and disillusionment with established parties, which provides a more compelling impetus to seek alternatives. The significance of weak partisanship in promoting the rise of 'third parties' has been noted in the USA[65] and Canada.[66] In British local elections, disillusionment with mainstream parties and their declining organisational capacity has been seen as encouraging the entry of new political forces,[67] and the rise of minor parties in Australia and New Zealand has been linked to similar factors.[68] Disillusionment may, of course, be differential. Pinard makes a distinction between the kind of generalised discontent that feeds into protest parties, and the more specific, ideologically driven dissatisfaction with the mainstream that promotes support for specific radical parties.[69] Bélanger, similarly, argues that anti-party sentiment may fuel support for new parties, but notes that this may be directed specifically against the established parties, or against parties more generally (a position that discourages electoral participation of any kind).[70] A more extended literature addresses the issue of disillusionment and the impact of new ideologies on specific types of parties, such as the new right.[71]

To what extent do these insights help in understanding the appearance of minor parties in Ireland? To start with, the electoral system has clearly played a big role: multi-member constituencies lower the barrier for representation significantly, greatly improving the prospects of smaller parties. On the other hand, the fact that the Irish form of proportional representation functions effectively whether organized parties are present or absent may have had the marginal effect of reducing the number of microparties, by giving ambitious individuals a route to a parliamentary career without the encumbrance of a party organisation. The existence of multiple representational tiers no doubt also has an impact: some small parties enjoy their initial success (indeed, perhaps their only success) in securing the election of representatives at local level.[72] They may also sometimes perform exceptionally well at the level of elections to the European Parliament. Thus the Green Party, the Progressive Democrats, Sinn Féin and the Workers' Party have all beaten their Dáil election record (as measured by share of the first preference vote) at European elections. Of course, this is partly due to the fact that it is much easier for minor parties to offer candidates in all European constituencies in Ireland and thus mop up all potential support, since there are only four of these (rather then the much larger number of Dáil constituencies).

Nonetheless, on two occasions minor parties have beaten the Labour Party into fourth position at European elections: in 1989 the Progressive Democrats came in third, and in 2004 Sinn Féin did so. This, and the spectacular success of independent candidates (and of Independent Fianna Fáil) at European elections may be a function of the 'second order' status of such elections (in that they lack the political weight of Dáil elections), but they nevertheless play a vital role in legitimising the efforts of minor parties. Similar considerations are no doubt relevant in respect of presidential elections, where Sinn Féin's Martin McGuinness polled 13.7 per cent of the vote in 2011.

It is difficult to arrive at robust conclusions regarding the extent to which minor parties may have appeared in response to generalised dissatisfaction with the established parties – we simply lack information such as survey data that might shed light on this, except for the contemporary period. It is striking, though, that the rise of Clann na Talmhan and Clann na Poblachta in the 1940s took place at the end of a long period of unbroken Fianna Fáil rule, dating from 1932, and in a context of widespread public criticism of that party. More recently, too, the appearance of new parties in the 1980s and 1990s coincided with a sharp downturn in party attachment: in the late 1970s, more than 60 per cent of survey respondents reported themselves as feeling 'close' to a particular party, but this figure had dropped to about 40 per cent by the late 1980s and to about 30 per cent by the late 1990s.[73]

It may well be the case that this is related to a more general lack of trust in public institutions. Recent survey data show considerable differences between minor parties (collectively) and major parties in their attitudes towards such institutions: in their level of satisfaction with the government or with the way democracy works, for instance, and in their levels of trust in parliament, the legal system, the police, politicians and political parties. Trust in political parties is, of course, of particular importance in seeking to account for the rise of minor parties, and the gap between different types of party in this respect is illustrated in Figure 2. When asked to rate themselves along an eleven-point scale ranging from no trust to complete trust, supporters of the three largest parties in 2006-07 were on average considerably more disposed to trust political parties (in general) than supporters of the three minor parties, suggesting that the same kind of motivations may be present in the Irish case as have been identified elsewhere.[74] It will be noticed, however, that even supporters of the big parties were located in the lower part of this scale, suggesting considerable reluctance all around to trust political parties fully.

There are reasons for looking separately at the appearance of minor parties in the early years of the state. Research on emerging party systems in post-authoritarian or new states suggests that 'founding elections' (a category in which we might place Ireland's general election of 1922) are not followed by a 'shakedown' effect, as the electoral system eliminates smaller parties; rather, parties winning founding elections tend to decline over the following elections, with support for minor parties remaining stable.[75] There is also some evidence of an unusual pattern in relation to new parties. One analysis of post-communist party systems in Central and Eastern Europe concluded that, 'although the number of new entries decreases when democracies mature, the few late entries become more successful'.[76] We see both of these effects in the Irish Free State. The Farmers' Party continued to fly the 'minor party' flag (arguably, from the perspective of the time, alongside the Labour Party), with a big drop after 1923 in the number of new parties contesting elections. On the other hand, when new parties did

Figure 2: *Trust in parties by party size, 2006-7*

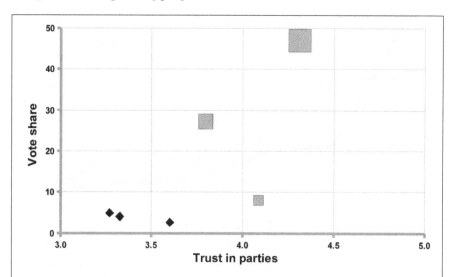

Source: European Social Survey, round 3, 2006-2007.

Note: the horizontal axis refers to level of trust in political parties in general, a scale ranging from 0 (no trust) to 10 (complete trust). Markers represent the mean positions of parties.

appear, as with the National League in 1927 and Clann na Talmhan and Clann na Poblachta later, they were significantly more successful than the earlier parties.

A final question has to do with the life history of minor parties. For some parties, ideological fidelity may guarantee electoral stability. Thus, Adams *et al.* see the survival of 'niche' parties as depending on their remaining faithful to the ideological position with which they were associated in the first place.[77] Nevertheless, as Pedersen has suggested, minor parties tend to follow a definite life cycle, though the pattern itself varies greatly.[78] There is some evidence that new parties may have a big initial impact on the party system, but then lapse into terminal decline. That this may be the case in Ireland is suggested by Figure 3, which profiles the electoral lifespan of the three most significant minor parties in the 1920s and the 1940s (the early Sinn Féin party has been omitted, since it did not contest elections continuously). These do, indeed, appear to have followed a broad pattern of steady decline. More recently, though, a different pattern seems to have asserted itself. This may be seen in Figure 4, which illustrates the support base of the four most important minor parties of the past two decades. It is true that the Progressive Democrats conform to the model of the earlier period, showing a pattern of steady decline (though decline in its level of parliamentary representation was less sharp), and by 2011 the Green Party seemed to have a similar profile. Sinn Féin, however, has been showing a history of steady growth,

*Figure 3: Life cycle of early minor parties*

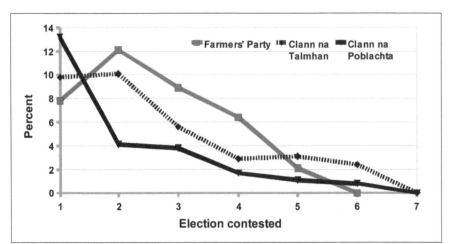

Note: lines refer to share of first preference vote in Dáil elections for Farmers' Party (1922-33), Clann na Talmhan (1943-65) and Clann na Poblachta (1948-69).

*Figure 4: Life cycle of recent minor parties*

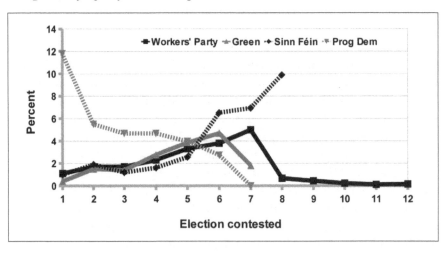

Note: lines refer to share of first preference vote in Dáil elections for Workers' Party (1973-2011), Sinn Féin (1982-2011), Green Party (1987-2011) and Progressive Democrats (1987-2011).

and even though the Workers' Party suffered a big blow with the defection of most of its TDs in 1992, it has refused to count itself out of Irish political life.

Explaining these patterns points us in two directions. First, there is a serious theoretical problem. If minor parties are defined as relatively unsuccessful ones, then it would be tautological to conclude that they all end in failure; failure was, after all, close to being a defining condition for their inclusion. Second, it is possible that in explaining the persistence of individual minor parties we need to look beyond broad ideological orientation, and consider the self-defined 'mission' of the party. If it is a promoter-type party, it is much more likely to survive electoral collapse than if it is, say, a challenging or a mobilising one, open to vigorous competition by long established and better resourced major party rivals.

## Conclusion

As we have seen, then, minor parties in Ireland appear to behave in a way that would be familiar to observers of their counterparts elsewhere. Proportional representation lowered the barrier that they needed to cross to gain political representation, facilitating new party entry; and the personal character of voting (with no formal recognition of parties before 1963) removed the need for formal organisation in earlier elections, allowing parties to self-define their status. The nature of the electoral appeal of each party seems to have had a big impact on its survival, with promoter parties (such as the Communist Party and Sinn Féin) surviving over the decades, mobilising parties (such as the Farmers' Party, Clann na Talmhan and Clann na Poblachta) making a big initial impact, but leaving themselves vulnerable to the theft of their policies by the established parties, and challenging parties (such as the Progressive Democrats) experiencing great difficulty in articulating a separate identity as they matured.

The effects of minor parties on the Irish political system have been considerable. The intrinsic importance of the more durable parties has already been discussed. But such parties may also have a big impact on other parties in the system. It is probably the case that the defection of Cumann na nGaedheal deputies to the National Group and Clann Éireann in the 1920s, and of Fianna Fáil support to Aontacht Éireann and Independent Fianna Fáil in the 1970s, left the parent party rather less nationalist in each case. But challenging parties may have a similar effect. Clann na Poblachta was instrumental in pushing Fine Gael in a more explicitly nationalist direction,[79] and it has been argued that the Progressive Democrats helped to polarise the party system on left-right lines in a new way, and even managed 'to destroy the last vestiges of social democracy in Fine Gael'.[80]

Minor parties have, then, played a distinctive role in Irish politics, one not dissimilar to that of their counterparts in continental Europe, though have had rather less success in gaining a permanent foothold in the party system than the latter. As economic shocks and high levels of disillusionment with established parties escalated in the second decade of the twenty-first century, many expected new forms of electoral rebellion that would breathe new life into minor parties. What has been surprising in the Irish case, however, has been the extent to which deserters from the long-standing dominant party, Fianna Fáil, took refuge not behind the banners of new parties (whether of the right or the left) but by switching to its long-term partners in the Irish political game, Fine Gael and the Labour Party. As these parties are constrained to follow the same policy path as Fianna Fáil, however, it may well be the case that minor and protest parties will gain a new lease of life as economic difficulties push governing parties into ever-harsher remedial policies.

## Appendix: Irish minor parties since 1922

This list includes all minor parties registered to contest Dáil elections since 1963, all de facto minor parties before that date, and three minor groups since 1963 which were not registered but behaved in the manner of political parties. It excludes the following parties registered to contest local elections: Dun Laoghaire Borough Ratepayers' Association (1963-75), Donegal Progressive Party (1967-2009), Dublin Ratepayers' Association (1967-81), Cork City Ratepayers' Party (1967-93), Independent Socialist Party (Sligo-Leitrim) (1991-93), South Kerry Independent Alliance (from 1994; also registered to contest Dáil elections in Kerry South); Workers and Unemployed Action Group (South Tipperary) (from 2008), Letterkenny Residents' Party (from 2008), Seniors Solidarity Party (Dublin) (from 2009), and Éirigí (from 2010). In each case, data on the formal status of the party on the official register of political parties is reported (if applicable), as is its performance in general elections to Dáil Éireann. It should be noted that formal registration and deregistration of parties is recorded on the official register some days after the appearance of a notice regarding the registrar's intentions in the state gazette, *Iris Oifigiúil*.

Sources: Manning, Maurice *Irish Political Parties: An Introduction* (Dublin; Gill & Macmillan, 1972); Gallagher, Michael *Political Parties in the Republic of Ireland* (Dublin; Gill & Macmillan, 1985), pp. 93-120; Gallagher, Michael *Irish Elections 1922-44: Results and Analysis* (Limerick; PSAI Press, 1993); Gallagher, Michael *Irish Elections 1948-77: Results and Analysis* (London; Routledge and PSAI Press, 2009); Barberis, Peter, John McHugh and Mike Tyldesley *Encyclopedia of British and Irish Political Organisations* (London; Pinter, 2000), pp. 196-266; Moss, Warner *Political Parties in the Irish Free State* (New York; Columbia University Press, 1933); O'Sullivan, Donal *The Irish Free State and its Senate: A Study in Contemporary Politics* (London; Faber and Faber, 1940); *Irish Times* 1922-2011; Office of the Registrar of Political Parties, Register of Political Parties, 1963-2011, R1/1-3; and sources mentioned in individual entries.

*Ailtirí na hAiséirghe*
Developed from a branch of the Gaelic League, Craobh na hAiséirghe, in April 1942. It proposed the establishment of a Gaelic, Christian Ireland with a powerful leader, but no political parties, on the model of Salazar's Portugal. Although it won several seats in the local elections of 1942, it fared poorly in the general elections of 1943, 1944 and 1948.[81]

Profile: elections contested: 3 (1943-1948); total candidates: 12; seats: 0; highest vote share: 0.5 per cent.

## Aontacht Éireann

Founded in September 1971 by activists who broke with Fianna Fáil following the 'Arms Crisis' of 1970. Led by Kevin Boland, who resigned from the government at that time, it advocated a more nationalist stance on Northern Ireland. The party fared poorly in the 1973 general election and, following Boland's defeat in a by-election in 1976, he and other leading colleagues withdrew; a motion to disband the party in June 1976 was narrowly defeated, and it survived nominally into the early 1980s.

Profile: initial application for registration as a political party rejected; granted on appeal, 29 October 1971; registered 2 November 1971 to 3 December 1985; elections contested: 1 (1973); total candidates: 13; seats: 0; highest vote share: 0.9 per cent.

## Army Wives' Group

Label used by representatives of the National Army Spouses Asssociation, founded in August 1988. The association was primarily concerned with the issue of soldiers' pay and working conditions. It put forward three candidates in 1989 in constituencies with large garrisons, and is believed to have cost the Fianna Fáil government one seat. Its role was largely taken over by the Permanent Defence Forces Other Ranks Representative Association (PDFORRA), formed in November 1989.

Profile: elections contested: 1 (1989); total candidates: 3; seats: 0; highest vote share: 0.4 per cent.

## Blind Men's Party

Label used by candidates proposed by the Irish Association of the Blind in contesting the June 1927 general election.

Profile: elections contested: 1 (1927-June); total candidates: 2; seats: 0; highest vote share: 0.1 per cent.

## Business Men's Party

Created by the Dublin Chamber of Commerce; it succeeded the Business and Professional Group, which contested the 1922 election in Dublin and Cork, and was similar to the Cork Progressive Association, a pro-Treaty business party in Cork. It aimed to protect business interests, advocating a policy of careful expenditure so that taxation could be reduced; pro-Treaty, but opposed the government's policy of compulsory Irish for the civil service.

Profile: elections contested: 2 (1922-3); total candidates (including Cork Progressive Association): 12; seats: 5; highest vote share: 2.3 per cent.

### Christian Democratic Party

Founded in January 1962 by Sean D. Loftus, who had contested a general election under this label in 1961. Loftus had earlier been involved in National Action and was influenced by American thought on religion and politics. On failing to secure registration of his party, Loftus had continued to contest elections as an independent, working his label onto the ballot paper by changing his name: he contested the 1973 general election as 'Christian Democrat Dublin Bay Loftus, Sean', the 1977 election as 'Dublin Bay Loftus, Sean', and the 1981 election (when he won a seat) as 'Alderman Dublin Bay-Rockall Loftus, Sean'. The other most visible output of the party was a collection of letters to Irish newspapers in 1972–73.[82] Both the party and the name faded out after Loftus's failure to win a seat in the 1973 election.

Profile: applied for registration 26 February 1965; application refused; appeal rejected, 19 March 1965; the party's challenge to the constitutionality of the act failed in the Supreme Court on 11 May 1978. Elections contested: 1 (1961); total candidates: 1; seats: 0; highest vote share: 0.1 per cent.

### Christian Democrats (the National Party)

Founded in January 1996 as the National Party; changed to its current name, 1999. The party has a conservative Catholic agenda, opposed to the liberalisation of laws on abortion and divorce; its headquarters are in Limerick, where the party originated.

Profile: registered since 11 March 1997; elections contested: 1 (1997); total candidates: 16; seats: 0; highest vote share: 1.1 per cent.

### Christian Solidarity Party

Founded in April 1991 as the Christian Principles Party; reorganised in October 1992 as the Christian Centrist Party; further reconstituted in October 1994 as Comhar Críostaí – the Christian Solidarity Party. The party adopted policies covering the whole spectrum of government activity, with a particular emphasis on opposition to abortion and euthanasia, and support for the traditional family.[83] It was one of the groups supporting the candidacy of Rosemary Scallon (Dana) in the 1997 presidential election, when she won 14 per cent of the poll.

Profile: registered since 29 October 1992; elections contested: 5 (1992–2011); total candidates: 52; seats: 0; highest vote share: 0.5 per cent.

### Cine Gael

Appeared in April 1954. It stood for policies of expropriation of land in foreign ownership, and turning of the office of President into an unpaid one. It faded out after the 1954 general election.

Profile: elections contested: 1 (1954); total candidates: 1; seats: 0; highest vote share: 0.0 per cent.

## Clann Éireann

Founded in January 1926 (with the English designation 'People's Party') by former members of Cumann na nGaedheal in protest at the government's accept-ance of the border with Northern Ireland following the failure of the Boundary Commission to transfer predominantly Catholic territory from Northern Ireland in 1925. It had a nationalist agenda, calling for abolition of the oath of allegiance. Following its defeat at the June 1927 election and Fianna Fáil's entry to the Dáil, it transferred its support to that party.

Profile: elections contested: 1 (1927-June); total candidates: 8; seats: 0; highest vote share: 0.5 per cent.

## Clann na Poblachta

Founded in July 1946 and led by former IRA Chief of Staff Seán MacBride. Participated in the first Inter-Party government (1948-51), but never recovered from a major division over the rejection of the 'Mother and Child' welfare scheme brought in by its Health Minister, Noel Browne, and its weak performance in the 1951 election; dissolved itself in July 1965.[84]

Profile: registered 14 December 1963 to 11 November 1965; elections contested: 6 (1948-65); total candidates: 160; seats: 18; highest vote share: 13.2 per cent; held two ministries in the government formed in February 1948.

## Clann na Talmhan

Founded in Athenry in 1939 by farming activists. Its programme emphasised issues of concern to farmers in general but also some points – such as land recla-mation and redistribution – which were of particular interest to smaller farmers.[85] It participated in both Inter-Party governments (1948-51 and 1954-7) but was already in decline from 1948 onwards. Two of its deputies representing Munster constituencies revolted in 1951 and later helped to bring down the government; the party's strength was thereafter confined to Connacht, where it maintained a stronghold until 1965, when it dropped out of political life, though it remained on the register of political parties until 1970.[86]

Profile: registered 14 December 1963 to 27 November 1970; elections contested: 7 (1943-61); total candidates: 122; seats: 43; highest vote share: 10.1 per cent; held one ministry and one junior post (parliamentary secretary) in the government formed in February 1948, and again in the government formed in June 1954.

## Communist Party of Ireland

Orthodox communist movement traditionally taking guidance from Moscow, with successive parties identifiable on the basis of their recognition by the leader-ship in Moscow. The Socialist Party of Ireland, founded in 1909 by James Connolly to succeed his older Irish Socialist Republican Party (1896), was taken over in September 1921 by supporters of the Soviet model and renamed the Communist

Party of Ireland. This first party did not contest elections; it was strongly opposed to the Treaty, but dissolved itself in 1924 on the instruction of the Communist International (Comintern). It was replaced by the 'Irish Worker' League, an orthodox communist group formed in September 1923 and centred around James Larkin's newspaper, *The Irish Worker.* In September 1927 Larkin became the only communist ever to be elected to the Dáil, but he was disqualified on the grounds that he was an undischarged bankrupt. A rival organisation, the Workers' Party of Ireland, founded in May 1926, dissolved itself in late 1927 on the instructions of the Comintern. A Workers' Revolutionary Party, founded in March 1930, was reorganised as Revolutionary Workers' Groups in November 1930 and contested the 1932 general election. From it emerged in June 1933 the Communist Party of Ireland II. Like its successors, it was more a promoter party than a challenging one; it never contested a general election in the south. Its only remaining branch outside Northern Ireland, the Dublin branch, dissolved itself in July 1941, many of its members joining the Labour Party. In November 1948 the Irish Workers' League, a twenty-six-county orthodox communist group, was established; it changed its name in March 1962 to the Irish Workers' Party. Finally, the Communist Party of Ireland III was created as an all-Irish party by a merger of the Communist Party of Northern Ireland and the Irish Workers' Party in March 1970.[87]

Profile: application for registration refused, 27 August 1975; appeal upheld, 11 December 1975; registered since 16 December 1975; elections contested: 15 (September 1927-89); total candidates: 26; seats: 1; highest vote share: 1.1 per cent.

### Community Democrats of Ireland

Name used by Irish affiliates of the European Federation of Liberal and Democratic Parties to contest the 1979 European Parliament elections.

Profile: registered 3 May 1979 to 14 December 1979; did not contest any general election; won 0.3 per cent in the 1979 European election.

### Córas na Poblachta

Founded in March 1940 by republicans dissatisfied with both the IRA and Fianna Fáil; sought formal declaration of a republic and measures to protect employment standards.[88]

Profile: elections contested: 1 (1943); total candidates: 5; seats: 0; highest vote share: 0.3 per cent.

### Democratic Left

Founded as New Agenda in February 1992 by former members of the Workers' Party, including six of its seven TDs; adopted the name Democratic Left at its founding conference in March 1992. Its policy position was similar to that of reformed communist parties elsewhere in Europe, but it was hostile to traditional Irish nationalism. In December 1998 it agreed to merge with the Labour Party.

Profile: registered 8 May 1992 to 27 January 1999; elections contested: 2 (1992-97); total candidates: 33; seats: 8; highest vote share: 2.8 per cent; held one ministry and three junior posts (ministries of state) in the government appointed in December 1994.

### Democratic Socialist Party

Founded in October 1981 by an alliance of independent socialists from Limerick, the Socialist Party of Ireland and elements of the British and Irish Communist Organisation (a small but influential leftist group originally called the Irish Communist Organisation in the 1960s), with former Labour deputy Jim Kemmy (Limerick) as its most prominent representative. It was strongly opposed to traditional nationalism. It merged with the Labour Party in April 1990.

Profile: registered 20 April 1982 to 29 November 1990; elections contested: 3 (November 1982-9); total candidates: 13; seats: 2; highest vote share: 0.6 per cent.

### Dublin Trades Council

Regional part of the labour movement influenced by James Larkin; contested the 1923 election independently of the Labour Party, but in 1926 sought re-affiliation with Labour.[89]

Profile: elections contested: 1 (1923); total candidates: 4; seats: 0; highest vote share: 0.4 per cent.

### Evicted Tenants' Association

Agrarian organisation dating from the late 1880s, active mainly in the south, which contested the 1923 election. Though faring poorly in the election, the association itself survived until the 1930s.

Profile: elections contested: 1 (1923); total candidates: 1; seats: 0; highest vote share: 0.1 per cent.

### Farmers' Union

A federation of county farmers' associations which came together as the Irish Farmers' Union in 1911-12, based on the model of the English National Farmers' Union (founded in 1908). It contested the 1922 election with a good deal of success; generally known as the Farmers' Party. Pro-Treaty in orientation, it supported the Cumann na nGaedheal government; it became in effect the first minor party to enter coalition government when its leader, Michael Heffernan, became a junior minister in the Cumann na nGaedheal-led administration in October 1927; had largely disintegrated by 1932 as an umbrella organisation.[90]

Profile: elections contested: 5 (1922-32); total candidates: 143; seats: 42; highest vote share: 12.1 per cent; held a junior post (parliamentary secretary) in the government formed in October 1927.

## Fís Nua

Founded in June 2010 on a policy of defence of the environment and opposition to political corruption; it opposed the EU-IMF bailout package. It was not officially registered in time for the 2011 general election, at which its five candidates fared poorly. The party, in which former members of the Green Party were active, had difficulty in distinguishing itself from a loose electoral alliance with an identical name in English, New Vision, which was also opposed to the EU-IMF arrangement. Though not claiming to be a party, this group nominated twenty candidates, winning 1.1 per cent of the vote, with one candidate, Luke 'Ming' Flanagan, elected. A similar group, Democracy Now, which brought together several 'celebrity' candidates especially from the world of journalism, disintegrated before the election.

Profile: registered since 8 February 2011; elections contested: 1 (2011); total candidates: 5; seats: 0; highest vote share 0.0 per cent.

## Green Party

Founded in December 1981 as the Ecology Party of Ireland, it changed its name in 1983 to Green Alliance and later added the Irish form as Green Alliance – Comhaontas Glas; in 1987 it adopted the name Green Party. An ecology party, it has a left of centre position on social issues.[91] One of its candidates was elected to the Dáil in 1989, and it steadily built up its Dáil strength; with six TDs after the 2007 election, it was able to negotiate a place for itself in government. The party also fared well in early local and European elections, but suffered a severe reversal in 2009 and in the general election of 2011, where it lost all of its seats.[92]

Profile: registered since 12 April 1984; elections contested: 8 (November 1982–2011); total candidates: 185; seats: 16; highest vote share: 4.7 per cent; fared particularly well in European elections, where its support peaked in 1994 (7.9 per cent; 2 MEPs, Nuala Ahern and Patricia McKenna; these were re-elected in 1999); held two ministries and one junior post (minister of state) in the government appointed in June 2007; acquired a second junior post in March 2010; lost all Dáil seats, 2011.

## H-Blocks Group

Name used to refer to candidates put forward by the National H-Block and Armagh Committee at the 1981 general election. The success of two of its candidates was instrumental in encouraging Sinn Féin down the electoral path.

Profile: elections contested: 1 (1981); total candidates: 9; seats: 2; highest vote share: 2.5 per cent.

## Independent Fianna Fáil

Precipitated by the 'Arms Crisis' of 1970, following the dismissal from the government in 1970 of Neil Blaney, who was expelled from Fianna Fáil in June 1972.

His local organisation broke with the party, performing well in local elections as Independent Fianna Fáil. Following Blaney's election to the European Parliament in 1979 his supporters wished to organise a separate party, but Blaney's reluctance prevented this.[93] Despite speculation in the 1980s on a rapprochement with Fianna Fáil, it was only in July 2006 that the organisation, now led by Blaney's nephew Niall, rejoined Fianna Fáil.

Profile: never sought registration as a political party; elections contested: 7 (1973-89); total candidates: 11; seats: 7; highest vote share: 0.9 per cent; performed well in European elections 1979-89; in the first of these it won 6.1 per cent of the national first preference vote, and its candidate, Neil Blaney, was elected in 1979 and 1989.

### Irish Housewives' Association

Organisation formed in May 1942 to defend the interests of women. Originally mainly Protestant in membership, it later broadened its support base, and contested the 1957 general election on a platform calling for greater involvement of women in politics.[94]

Profile: elections contested: 1 (1957); total candidates: 3; seats: 0; highest vote share: 0.4 per cent.

### Irish National League

Founded in August 1926 by Captain Willie Redmond, independent TD in Waterford and son of John Redmond, leader of the Nationalist Party from 1900 to 1918. It sought to appeal to supporters of the pre-1918 Nationalist Party and such diverse groups as town tenants, publicans and ex-servicemen, and presented itself as a centre party anxious to avoid 'Civil War politics'. It polled sufficiently well in the June 1927 election to win eight seats and to be in a position, with the Labour Party, to threaten the government's parliamentary position; it lost all except two seats in the general election of September 1927. The party dissolved in 1931, with its leader joining Cumann na nGaedheal and its second TD becoming an independent.

Profile: elections contested: 2 (June 1927 - September 1927); total candidates: 36; seats: 10; highest vote share: 7.3 per cent.

### Irish Republican Socialist Party

Broke away from Sinn Féin V in December 1974, alleging that the parent party was merely 'reformist' and had abandoned the struggle for the establishment of a united Irish socialist republic. Its paramilitary ally, the Irish National Liberation Army, maintained sporadic activity until the 1990s.

Profile: registered 22 May 1975 to 3 December 1984; elections contested: 3 (1977 – November 1982); total candidates: 8; seats: 0; highest vote share: 0.2 per cent.

*Libertas Ireland*

Founded in April 2009 under the leadership of Declan Ganley, whose Libertas Institute (established in October 2006) had played a major role in campaigning against the Lisbon Treaty in the referendum of June 2008.

Profile: registered 29 April 2009 to 11 December 2009; failed to win representation in the European election of 2009, though gaining 5.4 per cent of the first preference vote.

*Monetary Reform Party*

Party emanating from the Irish Monetary Reform Association, active in the midlands and influenced by the Monetary Reform Association in Britain (itself part of a wider 'Social Credit' movement that generated parties elsewhere, including most notably in Canada). Its policy reflected a populist response to perceptions of domination by big business; as its programme put it, 'The banks at present create money out of nothing – mere book-keeping. Why cannot the government elected by the people do likewise? ... We demand that money be issued to end unemployment, poverty, debt, and all our present national ills' (*The Irish Times*, 16 June 1943). Following some success in the 1942 local elections, its most prominent member, Oliver J. Flanagan, won a Dáil seat for the party in 1943, 1944 and 1948. The party disappeared with Flanagan's decision to join Fine Gael in 1952.

Profile: elections contested: 3 (1943-48); total candidates: 4; seats: 3; highest vote share: 1.1 per cent.

*Muintir na hÉireann*

Formed in January 1994. It aimed 'to protect the cultural heritage, language and religious traditions of the Irish people', was opposed to abortion and euthanasia and supportive of the traditional family.

Profile: application for registration rejected on 28 October 1994, but upheld on appeal, 12 April 1995; registered 25 April 1995 to 11 May 2000; did not contest any general election.

*National Action*

Founded in the early 1950s. A microparty of corporatist orientation, it claimed not to be a party, but to be based on Catholic social teaching, with the establishment of a Christian state, territorial independence, cultural recovery, economic stability and the 'internal organisation of society' as its goals.

Profile: elections contested: 1 (1954); total candidates: 1; seats: 0; highest vote share: 0.1 per cent.

*National Centre Party*

Evolved from the Agricultural League, founded in January 1932, which formed the basis of the National Farmers' and Ratepayers' League in October 1932;

reconstituted as the National Centre Party, January 1933. Its central organisation sought to replicate the Farmers' Party of the 1920s, but the party also appealed more widely for support. It merged with Cumann na nGaedheal and the National Guard to form Fine Gael in September 1933.

Profile: elections contested: 1 (1933); total candidates: 26; seats: 11; highest vote share: 9.2 per cent.

### National Democratic Party

Small agrarian party founded in April 1922 as the Land League of Unpurchased Tenants; adopted the label National Democratic Party in July 1923 to contest the election. It opposed the security policies of Cumann na nGaedheal and was strongly opposed to the Treaty. Its disappearance in late 1923 may be explained partly by the Land Act of that year, which went far towards meeting many of the demands of the landless population by providing for completion of the land transfer process, and partly by its failure to maintain an identity distinct from that of the Farmers' Party, which tried to play down class differences in the farming community.

Profile: elections contested: 1 (1923); total candidates: 4; seats: 0; highest vote share: 0.5 per cent.

### National Group

Breakaway group of former Cumann na nGaedheal deputies who objected to the government's handling of the 'army mutiny' of March 1924 (an event provoked largely by army demobilisation, but with other nationalist issues in the background). Nine deputies, including a minister, Joseph McGrath, established a separate Dáil group committed to a more nationalist policy line (including maximising Irish independence and seeking to advance the cause of unity more vigorously). They resigned their Dáil seats in October 1924; none was returned in the resulting by-elections in March 1925, though only one member of the group had stood for re-election.

### National Guard

Fascist-type party founded in February 1932 as the Army Comrades Association; reorganised as the National Guard, July 1933; merged with Cumann na nGaedheal and the National Centre Party in September 1933 to form Fine Gael, after which it became a strand known as the Young Ireland Association; this was replaced in 1933 by the League of Youth.[95] Its programme, organisation and public profile resembled its continental European fascist counterparts.[96] Following later disagreements, O'Duffy broke off to found his own National Corporate Party in June 1935, but the party ceased activity following its involvement in the Spanish Civil War in 1936.

### National Labour Party

Breakaway group based on the Irish Transport and General Workers' Union, which disaffiliated from the Labour Party over the allegedly excessive influence of the left and organised a separate party in January 1944. The party was unusual by the standards of the time in largely ignoring the issue of Irish unity.[97] It was one of the five constituent parties of the first inter-party government (1948–51). The sharing of this experience with the parent party, and the abeyance of older personal quarrels, paved the way for the reunion of the two Labour parties in June 1950.[98]

Profile: elections contested: 2 (1944–8); total candidates: 23; seats: 9; highest vote share: 2.7 per cent; held one ministry in the government formed in February 1948.

### National Progressive Democratic Party

Founded in May 1958 by two prominent former Clann na Poblachta deputies, including former minister Noel Browne, with a broadly socialist programme. It merged with the Labour Party in November 1963, having succeeded in securing the return of two members in the 1961 election.[99]

Profile: elections contested: 1 (1961); total candidates: 3; seats: 2; highest vote share: 1.0 per cent.

### Natural Law Party

International movement of the turn of the century advocating transcendental meditation to overcome global problems.

Profile: registered 4 May 1994 to 19 December 2001; elections contested: 1 (1997); total candidates: 10; seats: 0; highest vote share: 0.1 per cent.

### People Before Profit Alliance

Umbrella organisation formed in 2005, with the Socialist Workers' Party as a core element but also including a variety of independent socialists and trade union activists. It became part of a broader United Left Alliance in 2011 (with the Socialist Party and the Tipperary Workers and Unemployed Action Group as its other components).

Profile: registered since 10 July 2007; elections contested: 2 (2007–11); total candidates: 14; seats: 2; highest vote share: 1.0 per cent.

### Progressive Democrats

Founded in December 1985 by Desmond O'Malley, a former Fianna Fáil minister expelled from the party for unspecified 'conduct unbecoming' a member of the party, it made a big impact at its first election in 1987.[100] Almost half of its support initially came from former Fine Gael voters, while former Fianna Fáil voters accounted for less than one third (*The Irish Times*, 10-11 February

1986); one year later these proportions remained almost unaltered.[101] The new party's neo-conservative ideological position, emphasising the need for cuts in taxation and public expenditure, bore some resemblance to that of its similarly-named counterparts in Scandinavia, the Progress parties in Denmark and Norway, but it sought to position itself in the southern European liberal tradition of the right, and affiliated to the Liberal group at European level. In November 2008 it decided to wind itself up.[102]

Profile: registered 25 March 1986 to 11 December 2009; elections contested: 6 (1987-2007); total candidates: 186; seats: 44; highest vote share: 11.8 per cent; outpolled Labour in the European election of 1989, when it won 12.0 per cent of the first preference vote and one seat (its MEP, Pat Cox, was re-elected as an independent in 1994 and 1999 and served as leader of the Liberal Group in the European Parliament, and as President of that body); held two ministries and one junior post (Minister of State) in the government appointed in July 1989; two ministries and two junior posts (Ministries of State) in the governments appointed in June 1997 and May 2002; and one ministry in the government appointed in June 2007. Party leader Mary Harney served as Tánaiste, 1997-2006, and her successor, Michael McDowell, also held this post (2006-7).

*Ratepayers' Association*
Federation of county associations which contested the elections of 1922, 1923 and 1957.

Profile: elections contested: 3 (1922-57); total candidates: 5; seats: 0; highest vote share: 0.4 per cent.

*Sinn Féin IV*
Group which retained control of the party following the secession of de Valera and his supporters to form Fianna Fáil in March 1926; its parent (the 1922-6 party) was labelled the 'Third Sinn Féin' to distinguish it from the 'first' Sinn Féin (1905-17) and the very different 'second' Sinn Féin (1917-22).[103] It was colonised by the IRA following a decision of the IRA's Army Council in 1949 to rescind the ban on members joining political parties, after which it became the IRA's political arm.[104] Prior to this, the IRA had supported other political fronts, such as Comhairle na Poblachta (1929), Saor Éire (1931) and Cumann Poblachta na hÉireann (1936), none of which contested a general election. A similar body, the Republican Congress (1934), absorbed some left-wing republican support but was not supported by the IRA.[105]

Profile: elections contested: 4 (June 1927-61); total candidates: 57; seats: 9; highest vote share: 5.3 per cent.

*Sinn Féin V*
See Workers' Party

## Sinn Féin VI

Founded by activists who withdrew from the 'official' party in January 1970. The initial party leader, Ruairi Ó Brádaigh, was replaced in 1983 by Gerry Adams, in a move that reflected increasing northern influence. In the 1980s it became the main challenger to the SDLP for the nationalist vote in Northern Ireland and established a significant electoral presence in the South. Known originally as Sinn Féin (Kevin Street) from the location of its head office, it was a political ally of the 'Provisional' IRA. It did not take part in electoral politics in the 1970s, but supported 'H-Block' candidates in 1981. Further claimants to the heritage of the party include Republican Sinn Féin (set up in 1986 by a militant group led by Ruairi Ó Brádaigh that broke with the parent party as it moved towards more pragmatic policies), and the Thirty Two County Sovereignty Movement (set up in 1997 by activists opposed to Sinn Féin's involvement in the talks that led to the Good Friday agreement).[106]

Profile: registered since 21 January 1987; elections contested: 8 (February 1982–2011); total candidates: 223; seats: 24; highest vote share: 9.9 per cent; performed well in European elections, beating Labour into fourth position in 2004 (11.3 per cent, 1 MEP, Mary Lou McDonald); its presidential election candidate in 2011, Martin McGuinness, came in third, with a vote share of 13.7 per cent.

## Socialist Labour Party

Founded in October 1977 by radical critics of the Labour Party, with Noel Browne as its parliamentary spokesman; incorporated the Socialist Workers' Movement as a tendency; wound up August 1982.[107]

Profile: registered 18 December 1978 to 6 December 1982; elections contested: 1 (1981); total candidates: 7; seats: 1; highest vote share: 0.4 per cent.

## Socialist Party of Ireland

Name used initially by an organisation founded by James Connolly in 1909; the Socialist Party of Ireland I became the Communist Party of Ireland in 1921. A second such party emerged from workers' groups in Dublin and Belfast in May 1949; this Socialist Party of Ireland II had sister parties of the same name in Australia, Canada, Great Britain and New Zealand, as well as the Workers' Socialist Party USA.[108] The Socialist Party of Ireland III was founded in January 1971 by former members of ('Official') Sinn Féin. It was left-leaning and anti-nationalist in orientation. Its initial application for registration as a political party was refused, but it contested the general election of 1977 through an independent candidate; it later registered and contested the 1981 general election; merged with the Democratic Socialist Party, December 1982.

Profile: initial application for registration refused, and appeal rejected, 15 April 1975; second application successful; registered 18 December 1978 to 20 April 1982; elections contested: 2 (1977-81); total candidates: 3; seats: 0; highest vote share: 0.0 per cent.

*Socialist Party*

Founded in October 1996 by supporters of Militant Labour, a group consisting of the Trotskyite 'Militant Tendency' which had been expelled from the Labour Party in 1989; its best-known member, Joe Higgins, performed well in the Dublin West by-election of 1996, and was first elected to the Dáil in 1997; elected MEP June 2009. It became part of a broader United Left Alliance in 2011 (with the People Before Profit Alliance and the Tipperary Workers and Unemployed Action Group as its other components).

Profile: registered since 18 February 1997; elections contested: 4 (1997-2011); total candidates: 23; seats: 4; highest vote share: 1.2 per cent; Joe Higgins elected MEP in Dublin in European election, 2009.

*Socialist Workers Party*

Left-wing group dating from 1971 as the Socialist Workers' Movement; adopted its present name in 1995; operates also through the People Before Profit Alliance.

Profile: registered since 11 March 1997; elections contested: 2 (1997-2002); total candidates: 11; seats: 0; highest vote share: 0.2 per cent.

*Town Tenants' Association*

Federation of county associations which contested the elections of 1923 and 1927.

Profile: elections contested: 3 (1923-September 1927); total candidates: 4; seats: 0; highest vote share: 0.2 per cent.

*Unpurchased Tenants' Association*

Agrarian organisation established under the auspices of the Farmers' Party. Its main objective was to negotiate completion of the process of land purchase. It presented one candidate at the 1923 election separately from the Farmers' Party, and survived until the late 1920s.

Profile: elections contested: 1 (1923); total candidates: 1; seats: 0; highest vote share: 0.1 per cent.

*Workers' Party*

Continuation of Sinn Féin IV in altered form, following a split in the IRA in December 1969 and in Sinn Féin in January 1970, superficially on the issue of recognition of the parliaments in Dublin, Belfast and Westminster, but with the issues of militancy in Northern Ireland and social radicalism contributing to the division. This Sinn Féin V was known as Sinn Féin (Gardiner Place) from the location of its head office; it was more left-leaning than its rivals on social and economic policy. It moved gradually towards a pro-communist and anti-nationalist position. Its paramilitary ally, the 'Official' IRA, called a ceasefire in 1972. It was renamed Sinn Féin The Workers' Party in 1977, and became simply the Workers' Party in 1982.[109] It was critically damaged by the withdrawal of the reformist Democratic Left group in 1992.

Profile: registered since 23 July 1971; elections contested: 12 (1973–2011); total candidates: 173; seats: 17; highest vote share: 5.0 per cent; its support in European elections peaked in 1989 (7.7 per cent, one MEP).

*Young Ireland Party*

Formed in November 1952. Presenting itself as a party which would protect the interests of middle- and lower-income groups, its policies emphasised the need for a reduction in expenditure and cuts in taxation, as well as decentralisation of industry.

Profile: elections contested: 1 (1954); total candidates: 3; seats: 0; highest vote share: 0.1 per cent.

# 4

# Life in a Minor Party

*Desmond O'Malley, Catherine Murphy and Dan Boyle*

## Desmond O'Malley

*Desmond O'Malley was first elected to the Dáil in 1968 for Fianna Fáil. He was appointed to cabinet in 1970, and went on to hold three different portfolios. He was expelled from the parliamentary party in 1984, and then from the Fianna Fáil party organisation a year later. He went on to become the founder and first leader of the Progressive Democrats in December 1985. He led the party until 1993 and retired from political life in 2002.*

The circumstances of the formation of the Progressive Democrats were such that only limited lessons can be learned from them for the present day. There are of course some obvious and clear parallels, but only some. The most obvious was the economic state of the country and its fiscal position in 1984/5. The imminent possibility of the advent of the IMF in 1985 frightened us. I thought such a thing was truly horrendous because it constituted a loss of national sovereignty, which is, by definition, among the greatest losses an independent state can suffer.

The other circumstances were more unusual and more specific. Fianna Fáil's attitude to Northern Ireland and to unionists annoyed me. It made no sense at the time or since. The party seemed to parrot by rote things that were no longer relevant. Haughey seemed incapable of opposition except in a negative and total form. He was in this sense quite opportunistic. He kept ignoring the merits or reasoning of a policy position if he saw an opportunity to oppose what and whom he disliked, or if there was some political advantage to be gained. To send the unfortunate Brian Lenihan snr to Washington to oppose the Anglo-Irish Agreement was not just crazy – it was bordering on treachery. Earlier he had opposed British defence of the Falkland Islands because, basically, he disliked Britain and Mrs Thatcher (who had rebuffed his earlier attempts to charm her) and because he thought this might play well to some of the greener nationalist elements of Fianna Fáil.

In 1984 a New Ireland Forum Report was signed by all parties, which, as well as proposing three possible solutions to the Northern Ireland problem (a unitary state, a federal/confederal state, and joint British/Irish authority), also indicated that unionism was something that should be respected. Half an hour after signing, Haughey repudiated the kernel of it. When I objected to this I had the parliamentary party whip withdrawn. I was told I was now an independent TD. When I acted as such by refusing to oppose a Family Planning Bill, and saying so in the Dáil, in February 1985 I was expelled from the Fianna Fáil organisation.

These facts are relevant only because my instinct in the early to mid-1980s was to work within the Fianna Fáil party if I could and if others like me could. Fianna Fáil and Fine Gael were large, slightly vague conservative parties that dominated Irish politics and were quasi-coalitions in themselves. One might have hoped to have reformed the party from within as Declan Costello and Garret FitzGerald attempted in Fine Gael in the 1960s, but that proved impossible in Fianna Fáil. It was autocratic rule: '*Uno Duce, Una Voce*'. No dissent was permitted, 'no nibbling at the leader's bum!' So conservative was Irish politics that it was assumed one had to work within the existing structures and framework. There was little or no ideology involved. Office and not policy was the main objective. The reasons for the divisions in the 1920s were irrelevant and long forgotten except for a few well-worn phrases. But the emotions were not. Distrust and loathing were the inheritances of the time. Warped 'core values' became supreme. The 'philosophy' of Pádraig Flynn or Ray Burke became the New Testament.

In 1985 an overspending and sometimes profligate government was being criticised daily by Fianna Fáil for not spending enough! We realised by July or so in 1985 that something had to be done and that could only be done by a new party. I felt this even though Garret FitzGerald offered me a place in his government. A halt had to be called or at least the need for a halt had to be explained and advocated. In Irish politics at the time such an approach was only likely to appeal to a niche market. Populism was the accepted formula. Tweakings of populism amounted to the policy choices – they were of no real value.

Starting the PDs turned out to be easier than expected in the sense that the early volume of support was extraordinary. We were lucky to have formed a team of remarkably talented people. Mary Harney had been, if anything, more anxious to set up a new party, and Michael McDowell offered his immense talents and energies to the project. Others, such as Pat Cox and Stephen O'Byrnes, were recruited and turned out to be top-rate organisers and communicators. In January and February 1986 opinion polls had the party on between 20 and 25 per cent support. That kind of support attracts more support. And with it came money, which was essential for the party to build any sort of foundation. We quickly had a reasonably good geographical spread, even if it was predominantly urban or suburban. Town hall meetings were key to building the organisation throughout the country. These meetings took place as a result of local demand rather than having been centrally organised by us. We would be contacted by someone in a constituency volunteering to organise a meeting. Some of our early 'town hall' -style meetings were attended by 3-4,000 people each, something it is hard to imagine today. In fact, we had many complaints from those who couldn't get in! The first took place in the Marine Hotel in Sutton, and the huge crowds shocked us. Even in other less successful meetings such as in Sligo, Waterford and Kilkenny hundreds turned up. These were possibly the last of what might be regarded as mass political meetings. Today different technologies would be both an obstacle to such meetings and render them obsolete. It was an incredibly exciting time and a special thrill to be part of it.

In these meetings a number of us would speak, setting out our analysis of the current problems and our proposed remedies. Our speeches at the meetings were usually effective, in part because they were unscripted. They were delivered to the members of the audience present, not to the media. They came from the belly and not from the scriptwriter's pen. But it was the beginning of the sound-bite age. Five or ten years later the script was more important than the speech. It did not matter if it left the audience cold, or even if it was never delivered. The script was delivered to the media and that was what mattered. Politics got duller as a result.

That within weeks of being set up the Progressive Democrats had a parliamentary party made a big difference. Bobby Molloy and Pearse Wyse joined Mary Harney and me, as did some senators. Each TD took much of their old organisation with them. This meant that in some constituencies we had ready-made organisations. It also meant we had an immediate presence in the Dáil that the media could not ignore even had it wanted to – though we never had the impression the media wanted to ignore us. To set up a party without parliamentary representation would be much harder and it would have to be organised on a different non-parliamentary basis in the first instance.

Although we were a comparatively well-resourced party for Ireland, we still operated on something of a shoe-string. Many of the staff in the head office worked on a voluntary basis, and TDs had just a secretary. There were no parliamentary assistants, or others such as those available today, to help build up the party.

In our first election in February 1987 we surprised many that we delivered electorally on our early promise in opinion polls. We got fourteen seats, and could have done better. We had nineteen quotas, which managed better would have translated into more seats. Part of the problem was that we sometimes targeted resources in the wrong places, often responding to the demands of the more vocal rather than the more promising. In other cases we wrongly assumed some candidates were unlikely to get elected. In Dublin North, then quite a rural constituency, the candidate, Vincent Gaul, was so young that we thought him a chance for the subsequent election. As a result we didn't give the constituency the attention and resources it deserved. He came within a few hundred votes of taking a seat. With more support he could have taken it.

Opposition from 1987 was wonderful. It was to my mind the best parliamentary party of any party in the history of the state. There were some immensely talented people elected such as McDowell, Geraldine Kennedy, Ann Colley, Máirín Quill and Pat O'Malley, as well as those TDs who had been re-elected. The parliamentary party was big enough that I, as leader, could distribute the portfolios widely and in most cases was confident that they were well taken care of. There are inevitably a few passengers in a front bench, but in this case there were very few. There was a relative freedom from negative constraints, at least in the early days, in leading a small party from formation. It is of course much easier to get agreement on policy matters in the parliamentary party than in the broader membership, where you get the 'debating society' types who join small parties, but for whom discussing policy is more important than actually implementing it.

The party had other problems, however, which threatened it as a political force.

One was not a problem as such but a great compliment to our effectiveness: the new government was basically doing what we had advocated. Haughey, I think, got a fright when he saw the support the Progressive Democrats got at the 1987 election. He had campaigned with the slogan 'Health cuts hurt the old, the sick and the handicapped'. It was a typically populist move, but one that was not sustainable in government. His response was to appoint Ray MacSharry to Finance, to implement the cutbacks that were simply essential for the country to survive. As we had predicted, this policy was successful, and almost immediately confidence returned to the economy. In this context, when Haughey called a snap election many voters may have seen the PDs as no longer essential.

The second problem was that many of our parliamentary party, though immensely talented in legislative matters, failed to take care of their constituencies, despite warnings and urgings. They got little reward for excelling in the mundane, but vitally important, legislative aspect of a TD's work. This work was even more important when there was a minority government. Voters could not see this, because the Dáil, then as now, tends to be covered by the media primarily when there is a shouting match.

In 1989 the party lost many of its most talented TDs and was down to just six seats. We were devastated. We weren't able to lick our wounds because it was also clear that no government would be formed immediately. Haughey again failed to achieve an overall majority. Fine Gael was not going to renew its Tallaght Strategy, particularly after it was not rewarded for it by voters. We were certainly not going to get involved in a pact to support a Fianna Fáil government from the outside. The basic arithmetic was that Fianna Fáil was short six seats and we had six seats. I was on holiday when I got reports that Mary Harney had suggested on radio that a Fianna Fáil-Progressive Democrats coalition might be viable. It made me angry, and evidently made some in Fianna Fáil angrier still. But Harney had been talking to people within Fianna Fáil and it soon became clear that we had to explore this possibility or face another election within weeks from the last. I knew voters had no wish for this and that we would do even worse.

It still took three full days of discussion within the party to agree to start negotiations on a government. We were very wary of supporting a Haughey-led government, especially as most of the surviving parliamentary party had left Fianna Fáil because of Haughey. But there was also huge opposition from within Fianna Fáil. Some such as Flynn, Reynolds and Burke referred to the 'core value' of single-party government. The 'core value' had only ever been a convenient electoral strategy, and I knew Haughey could dispense with it if he needed to.

Government as a leader of a small party was a glorious change from being in a single-party government where the leader and you are at odds. You have a certain independence that gives you a freedom you did not have before. Even though within Fianna Fáil I was a leader of a sort of faction that was much bigger, in formal coalition I regarded myself as the leader of one of two parties in government. Size mattered less. The government ran reasonably well under Haughey, who while he didn't like the situation, knew he had no choice but to accept it. I did not have the advantage of having pre-cabinet meetings with Haughey to iron out potential problems, something that has now become institutionalised.

Things changed under Reynolds. He was always antipathetic to the government, which he had earlier described as a 'temporary little arrangement'. He was true to his word, and appeared to me to do all in his power to undermine the government. He didn't appear to have the intellectual capacity Haughey had to deal with a wide range of policy issues. The Beef Tribunal, something I had fought hard to set up, and which investigated some of Reynolds' actions as minister, was the immediate cause of the collapse, but I'm sure, had he needed to, he would have found another. We had virtually no contact except at cabinet and there Reynolds treated the Progressive Democrats ministers as just two who could be easily outvoted.

In the 1992 election, caused by the collapse of that government, the voters rewarded us for our achievements in government. But the Labour Party was the big winner and it, I thought foolishly, went into government with Reynolds rather than a rainbow coalition with ourselves and Fine Gael.

Government was difficult for us as a small party because it meant you inevitably devote more time to your brief than you can to the party. There were very few advisers and managers, nothing like what became available under recent governments. The advisers I had were primarily policy specialists, filling gaps in the civil service skills. This meant the party became more leadership-based than we should have allowed it.

★★★

Possibly naïvely, we gave no thought to what had happened to parties such as Clann na Poblachta and Clann na Talmhan. They were of a different era and seemed of little relevance in the 1980s. They were comparatively short-lived, at least as important parts of the political system, and had only a brief passing influence. I am not sure that I'm pleased the Progressive Democrats are now classified as just another minor party – we were in government for seventeen of our twenty-five years. At the very least we were relevant, influential and effective, out of all proportion to our size.

There was a need for a new party when the Progressive Democrats was set up, and I suppose it is instructive that around the same time other parties on the left also emerged. The Progressive Democrats responded to the need and were more successful than we could have hoped or expected. Arguably, the need was much greater in 2008–12 but no such party was forthcoming, despite some notable announcements. Why has none emerged?

One of the reasons is money and the laws that have been passed relating to financial contributions to parties and politicians. The establishment parties accepted some years ago that there was a demand for public funding of parties as a result of abuses and corruption, principally by some within Fianna Fáil. They may have also realised that by tightening the rules they could effectively exclude newcomers and guarantee their own primacy. This has had a stultifying effect on Irish democracy. In any democracy the formation of new parties and their encouragement is an essential component of a dynamic system.

If it becomes impossible or very difficult to start and maintain new parties then democracy in such a country will decline and even wither. The preservation of an unattractive status quo will become a primary concern for politicians and the myriad hangers-on: placemen, spin doctors, advisers and other manipulators they currently attract. New parties bring new ideas and force established parties to consider new directions. The outlook for a country that discourages new parties is bleak and potentially dangerous.

One could summarise the current funding situation by saying that public funding has very largely replaced or superseded private funding as a source of political funding. The manner in which public funding is disbursed is based almost entirely on past electoral performance so far as parties are concerned. This means that it is very difficult, indeed almost impossible, for a new party to break through in electoral terms.

The new system means that large parties get the bulk of funding, smaller existing parties get some, but new parties can get none. At the same time, private contributions to parties are so restricted that it becomes difficult to see how a new party could get the funds to challenge the status quo. Allowable private funding is very low. Non-published private funding is even lower – but still some parties can raise large amounts of money without revealing their sources, which in certain cases may be from abroad or as a result of criminal activities. It is no accident that independents are quite generously taken care of – each of them is entitled to a so-called 'Party Leader's allowance' of €41,000. They are free to employ close relatives at public expense as a further subsidy. There is no incentive to start or join a party, even when others of a like mind exist. Their constituency needs were often given priority. It amounts to state-sponsored parochialism.

This active discouragement of new parties has borne fruit. Since the Progressive Democrats in 1985 the Greens were the only new party to make an electoral breakthrough. They are more akin to a global movement than an indigenous Irish party. Democratic Left (DL) also emerged and faded eventually performing a reverse takeover of the Labour Party, but DL was effectively the renaming of the Workers' Party. At the same time public funding for the establishment parties has become so great that some now get several million euro per annum. What electoral prospects has a new party that can avail of none of the public funding and is forbidden from receiving virtually any significant private funding, even if it could obtain it?

If we cannot have any viable new parties in the future, development can only take place as a result of fragmentation. But the financial rules can be tweaked to penalise those who fragment or dissent – which further shores up the status quo.

While some efforts were made in the years before the 2011 general election to form new parties, none succeeded. This was hardly because there was no demand.

Because it is now so difficult to start a new party from scratch, there has to be a real and present danger, given the current loss of sovereignty and the poor economic climate, that when groups are effectively prevented from challenging the status quo through electoral politics, other, perhaps violent and certainly less democratic, methods might be used.

## Catherine Murphy

*Catherine Murphy was first elected in 1998 as a town commissioner for the Workers' Party. When the party split in 1992, she joined the breakaway Democratic Left. Following the merger of Democratic Left and Labour in 1999, she contested and held her council seat at that year's local elections as a Labour candidate. She resigned from Labour in 2003 and was elected to the Dáil as an independent at a by-election in 2005. She lost her seat in 2007, but regained it in 2011, following which she became the chief whip of the technical group in the Dáil.*

I was motivated to get involved in politics because I felt there were a lot of things that needed to change. I've been actively involved for about thirty years; I joined the Workers' Party in the early 1980s – the catalyst was their campaign against water and bin charges, charges that were seen as an excessive burden. They were viewed by me and thousands more as the straw that broke the camel's back: income tax had increased significantly in the late 1970s, resulting in major demonstrations.

It was not enough to be angry and frustrated – I wanted to do something constructive about these and other things I felt strongly about. Campaigns to resist the new charges began to emerge; I got involved in setting one up in Leixlip, where I had moved to from Dublin with my family five or six years earlier. This wasn't my first step into community activism. I was already involved in several community associations at the time, and it was becoming clear to me that rapidly growing areas like Leixlip were not receiving the services they needed. Like other communities around the country, we needed better public transport services, permanent school buildings, better parks and playgrounds, and so much more.

I was invited to join the local branch of the Workers' Party. My own politics were left of centre and while I had no expectation of subscribing 100 per cent to Workers' Party policies I felt the party was the vehicle for change and I was willing to invest time and energy into it. I did not expect when I joined that I would eventually end up contesting elections and becoming a public representative myself. At that time there were four or five branches with an umbrella constituency council organisation in Kildare; the Leixlip branch which I belonged to was the most active. Our branch was small – in total there were fewer than twenty members. Even though we were small, ours was a very enthusiastic and dynamic branch. Unlike the larger parties where membership was something you were nearly born into, the Workers' Party was an organisation you had to commit to. While the party had only minimal representation in the Dáil, there were a number of impressive members who were destined to take seats in the future – some were already (or were about to be) elected at local government level. Members were expected to understand the politics that underpinned our policy positions. It wasn't enough to just carry a membership card: you were expected to be an activist. We were encouraged to join community organisations and associations. By being active and visible, we gave the impression that we were a bigger party than we were. Both our branch and constituency council had monthly meetings, where we planned what work we'd carry out in the intervening weeks. Political education, campaigning, recruiting and fundraising were part of almost every agenda. Every month, usually on a Sunday morning, we'd invite a speaker to talk to us on some topic or other.

As a small party, we faced challenges. Fundraising was tough – most of our money came from a lot of people giving us very little. A fiver would have been a big donation at the time. The rest of our fundraising efforts consisted of church-gate collections, small events in local pubs, parties, raffles, etc. We had a permit to collect door-to-door for six weeks each year. Most of us hated fundraising, but it had to be done. Knocking on doors with a tin box helped fund our campaigns, hire rooms and of course contest elections. The Workers' Party was very definitely anti-establishment, so it was difficult to get articles carried in the mainstream media; as a result we published our own paper, *The Irish People*, and a monthly magazine, *Making Sense*. We sold them in local pubs and door-to-door too.

Circulation was small, but they were a useful way of connecting with people in our own communities on a continuous basis. They also provided a small, but important, source of income.

Big political campaigns, played out at national and local level, often brought in new recruits. The 1985 local election campaign was particularly successful for bringing people into the party. Our main focus continued to be issues relevant to our communities. Our branch managed to bring a new bus service to the area through one of our campaigns; better post office facilities and embarrassing the County Council into filling potholes were other local successes. In 1988, following a long campaign by the Combined Residents' Association (of which I was a member), a nine-member town council was established. The Workers' Party fielded two candidates – me and Seán Purcell – and we were both elected with a surplus. This was a fantastic result for the party. As a further bonus these successes helped our media presence, at least at a local level. Soon after, I was elected to the Ard Comhairle of the party.

In 1989, I contested both the Dáil and European elections. Even though we knew I wouldn't be successful, it was essential towards the future of the party. Funding the campaign was a challenge. We held a major raffle to win exotic holidays, selling tickets door-to-door. They cost £10, which some people paid by instalments. The balance was raised through a bank loan, backed by personal guarantees. It was finally paid off just in time to take out another loan for the 1991 local elections. This time, our campaign was successful, and I took my seat as a member of Kildare County Council. Having been one of the most visible members of the anti-service charges campaign, I wasn't welcomed by the rest of the council with open arms.

As the party became more successful, the media began to look at us more closely. The Workers' Party was an all-Ireland party. While there had always been occasional media interest about links between the Official IRA and the party, we were always assured by party leadership there was no truth in the story. There were also ongoing stories about counterfeit money being used to fund the party. Eventually the strain caused by stories like these became such a liability that it led to a split in the party. A new party, Democratic Left, was founded. It took the bulk of its membership from the Workers' Party membership in the Republic; most members who were in elected positions also opted to join.

The culture of the new partly was quite different; there was more emphasis on electoral politics and less campaigning. Setting up party structures and funding a head office with a small staff was expensive. Separate policy from existing Workers' Party policy had to be developed.

In 1992, just four DL deputies were elected to the Dáil. However, by 1994 we had picked up two additional seats in by-elections. When the Fianna Fáil/Labour government fractured there were now sufficient numbers between Fine Gael/Labour/DL to form a new government. Senior members became totally absorbed with the business of government, and the development of the party, understandably, became a secondary matter.

The general election of 1997 was disappointing. Only four DL deputies were elected. It was time to take stock. An internal party commission was established but there was little appetite from some in senior positions to face into the 1999 local elections with a tired party machine. The close working relationship between and DL and Labour during our time in government laid the groundwork for a merger between the two parties. The idea of a merger, which had obviously been in development for some time, was unveiled after the general election. My initial reaction was one of horror. I had a choice, to join or to become an independent. A few weeks before the merger process started, I decided to join. There is a certain comfort in knowing the party line, in having an organisation to belong to and to be supported by. When I think about it, joining was against my own best judgement. If I learned anything from the experience it was to trust my gut.

The merger allowed for parallel organisations to continue until after the local elections. However, at town and county council level we amalgamated immediately. We did not always vote along the same lines. I particularly remember a proposal about rezoning land within a protected demesne in Celbridge. The person who proposed the rezoning was a fellow Labour member; he did not appreciate my opposing the move. Tensions like these were common. The 1999 local elections were a nightmare, not least because redrawn boundaries meant that there were now three sitting councillors on a Labour ticket in a four-seat electoral area. We worked hard and got more than 50 per cent of the vote, taking two of the four seats. I managed to hold on to mine, despite fierce competition from within my own party. Party rules and regulations bred internal conflict; I had begun to realise that operating in such an environment would mean I had to watch my back. Looking back it was a miserable few years.

I announced my decision to resign from the Labour Party in early 2003, and immediately felt relieved and liberated. I began to focus on getting elected in the upcoming local elections. I was lucky to have a lot of volunteers – some were members of the different parties I had been part of, some were involved in community organisations I had worked with. Some I had campaigned with on issues of mutual interest; in other cases I had assisted with issues on their behalf with the County Council. With their help I won the seat. Later that year it was announced that Charlie McCreevy TD was to take up the position as European Commissioner: a by-election would be called. The core group of volunteers I had worked with on the local elections were quickly assembled, and we began working towards winning the seat.

When I entered the Dáil in March 2005 I was fortunate to attach myself to the Technical Group, formed on the initiative of the late Tony Gregory. In theory it was established to maximise speaking opportunities. In practice, despite the variety of political backgrounds, it ended up being a good support group.

Fianna Fáil did better than expected in the 2007 general election at the expense of most of the independents. I lost my seat. The following year, I returned to my seat in Kildare County Council. I held onto it in 2009 – the large group of volunteers I had assembled helped it become a very successful election for me. They came through for me again in the general election in 2011 – I was returned to Dáil Éireann with the help of more than 250 people. Ironically, I never had that type of assistance while a member of a political party, which dispels some of the myths about party machines.

Once elected, fifteen members and I quickly set up a Technical Group – I act as whip to the group which meets weekly, allocates speaking time, decides on private members' motions, meets with civil society groups, etc. While it is a disparate group, our success has been achieved through accepting difference and co-operating on areas of common ground. While there is an element of specialisation by the independents, we don't have a spokesperson and we generally don't adopt common policy positions – that seems to pose a challenge for some elements of the national media. As time goes by we are becoming a solid resource for each other, while retaining our individual independence. In many ways being an independent is not about being isolated: it's about being liberated.

## Dan Boyle

*Dan Boyle was elected to Cork City Council in 1991 for the Green Party. In 2002 he was elected to the Dáil, where he was the party's chief whip and finance spokesperson. He lost his seat in 2007, but was appointed to the Seanad. He was chair of the Green Party organisation from 2007 to 2011.*

On 3 December 1981 a group of forty or so people met at the Central Hotel in Dublin at the invitation of Christopher Fettes, an English secondary school teacher, who was by then long established in Ireland. The reason these people came together was a shared concern that something was not quite right with the world, and that politics, particularly politics in Ireland, was not dealing with it in any real way.

The previous year a 'green' party had been established in what was then West Germany. Many present at the Dublin meeting wondered whether that was a road that should be travelled in Ireland. Most were reluctant to become politically involved. Some felt that the real challenge was to 'green' other political parties.

The first meeting concluded with an agreement that that option should be examined. Some didn't agree and didn't come to subsequent meetings. The reluctance towards fully fledged political activity even went to an aversion to the word Green. Green in Ireland had another context so instead the new party gave itself a title of the Ecology Party of Ireland. It would be a hard name to explain and a harder name to sell.

In its earliest days the party was stronger in Cork than in Dublin. Built around a nucleus of a well-organised anti-nuclear group, emboldened by the successful Carnsore campaign (successfully stopping a nuclear power station from being constructed) from a few years previously, and informed by many Europeans who had chosen to live especially in West Cork, there seemed a greater enthusiasm in Cork to dip into the murky world of politics.

The February 1982 general election came too quickly for the new party to organise itself. But another election in November of that year saw seven candidates being put forward. The most successful of these was Owen Casey, standing in Cork South Central; a son of a former Labour Party TD and lord mayor, he polled close on 1,300 votes.

The reluctance to engage in conventional politics could be seen in a discussion held by the election team for the Dublin Central by-election in 1983. When qualifying for a televised party political broadcast it was suggested that two minutes of silence in that broadcast would be very 'zen'.

In the 1985 local elections the party put forward a majority of female candidates, most of whom had been persuaded to stand on the basis that there wasn't the slightest hope of being elected.

In subsequent elections political success proved elusive. Most activists realised that introducing a new party to traditional Irish voters would always be a difficult task. In the first eight years of existence, even after a decision to become a Green Party, only a town councillor in Killarney had been elected under a Green banner.

By 1987 the Ecology Party of Ireland had evolved into the Green Alliance/Comhaontas Glas and from there into the Green Party/Comhaontas Glas. Then came the general election of 1989. The media was being informed by the possibility of a breakthrough by the British Green Party. While it didn't break through, the resultant coverage did help elect a first Green TD in Roger Garland. Roger would not have been the expected or preferred person to make this breakthrough, but his election was the bridgehead that the party needed to establish itself.

The local elections of 1991 saw thirteen city and county councillors being elected, largely in the Dublin area. The elections of Trevor Sargent, John Gormley, Ciarán Cuffe, Nuala Ahern and myself, sowed the seeds for future electoral success.

Over a series of elections one TD became two TDs and by 2002 had become six TDs. In 1994 and again in 1999 the Irish political world was stunned to see two Green MEPs, Nuala Ahern and Patricia McKenna, being elected. In 1994 when I was the party's candidate in Cork South Central by-election I won 16 per cent of the vote. The Greens seemed to be well positioned to be the changing force in Irish politics.

During this time the party became more professional. Internal procedures that were difficult for the wider public to understand were changed. The problems of how decisions were made by the party and the lack of a single individual to represent the party to the public were addressed by the selection of Trevor Sargent, first as chief spokesperson and eventually as party leader.

In 2007 the party had the choice of whether it should become part of government. The expectation was that this would be part of a rainbow coalition. The choice that was available was with Fianna Fáil, the party that to many Greens represented much of what was wrong with Irish politics. After twenty-five years on the fringes of political life the opportunity of government was one that the overwhelming number of party members felt should be taken.

The decision to enter government was made knowing that the party's vote support and ability to win seats would be affected in the subsequent election. Part of this would be the swing that naturally occurs against incumbent governments. The secondary factor would be how the junior partner in coalition governments suffers disproportionately. The most damaging factor for the Greens though was the end of being a transfer-friendly party, capable of picking up transfers from across the political spectrum. This ability had been crucial in winning the final seats in constituencies.

While the Greens had been critical of the direction of economic policy before entering government, few had realised how quickly and deeply these policy errors of previous governments would begin to hurt the country. An irony was that the problems that began to surround the Irish economy and then economies in Greece, Portugal, Italy and Spain, were problems that all resulted from the weaknesses inherent in the foundation of the Euro as a currency. In the 1993 Irish referendum on the Treaty of Maastricht, the Green Party was the only party to argue about the dangers that existed with the suggested approach towards creating a single currency.

The party allowed an impression to persist that economics was not part of its wider political agenda. That didn't stop the blame being apportioned when the economy came undone while the party was in government. Neither was any credit forthcoming for attempting to deal with the multiple economic crises.

The parallel narrative fuelled by political opponents was that the Greens were even failing on green issues. Rossport, Tara and Shannon became the mantra of those who wanted to portray the Greens in the worst possible light. No mercy was given to how little change could have been affected in each of these areas, notwithstanding how these issues were magnified to an importance they never really held within the Green Party's policy priorities.

Most of the period of government came to be about economic crisis management, even though despite this, Green ministers fought hard to bring about changes in planning legislation, in increasing renewable energy and insulating thousands of homes, and a significant piece of social legislation in the form of the Civil Partnership Bill.

Important as many of these changes have been, the party, in the general election of 2011, and the circumstances in which it had come about, found itself to be on the wrong side of history. The hope was two seats in Dublin South and North with Eamon Ryan and Trevor Sargent could be held. In the end even this wasn't possible. Worse still was the failure to pass the 2 per cent of the national poll level that would have enabled continued public funding.

Now the party was reduced in the Republic to no more than a dozen local councillors, only three of whom are county councillors. But even at the lowest ebb that the party has found itself there have been significant shafts of light.

As an all-island party, real progress has been made in Northern Ireland. Away from the pressure of being associated with government, the Green Party has succeeded in winning a seat in the Northern Ireland Assembly twice. Brian Wilson in 2007, followed by Stephen Agnew in 2011 in the North Down constituency, were creating a niche in the still difficult sectarian environment of Northern Ireland politics. The election of a number of district councillors there is solidifying a deepening presence.

The first electoral test in the Republic since the general election of 2011 was the Dublin West by-election. For the first time in thirty years the by-election was won by a candidate from a government party. Analysts expressed surprise at the strong performance of the Fianna Fáil candidate. In sixth position, ahead of the independent candidates, was the Green Party candidate Roderic O'Gorman. With 5 per cent of the poll Roderic was never challenging for the seat, but in the aftermath of the Green Party's worst ever general election result, he had succeeded in delivering the best ever Green Party vote for that constituency – a harbinger for the future.

There are many reasons to believe that the Green Party will not go the way of previous minor parties in Irish politics. In the first instance Greens are part of an international political movement that offers support and learning experiences. Green politics continues to be a growing force in European politics. Despite this, many European Greens have also gone through the experience of gaining and then losing a parliamentary presence. In Germany, France, Italy, Sweden, the Czech Republic, Estonia and Belgium, Green parties gained a toehold only subsequently to find themselves out again in the political cold. Many of these parties came back again to gain a greater political strength.

Secondly, the narrative in Irish politics will change. To what extent and by when is still unknown. At some stage the blame attached to the last government will attach to some degree to the new government. Other political parties, still untainted by government, are better positioned to benefit from an ongoing anti-politics mood but that pendulum will also begin to swing back. Some of what is considered now to be strong reasons against supporting the Greens, will be reconsidered in a different light through the prism of time.

The third factor is an unwillingness of members to fold up tents. Membership remains static without people with an enthusiasm to carry things forward. Particularly encouraging is a younger generation of members who want to work to bring a more successful political future into being.

A fourth factor would be a growing desire to go back to the future in the party, to reacquaint itself with its activist roots. In an age of uncertainty, where many citizens have turned away from conventional politics, partly through indifference, partly through distrust, the Green Party, once synonymous with being in the vanguard of non-conventional politics, needs to regain its cache.

If the party was to be sucked into the vortex that has swallowed several dozen minor parties before it, it could indulge in having the opportunity of entering government; of providing two good performing cabinet ministers. In local government the party provided the lord mayor of Dublin and the mayor of Galway, as well the first citizen in several other major urban centres like Dundalk, Bray and Kilkenny. The main reason the Greens will not be as other parties were before it, is that there is an unwillingness by party members to indulge in the past.

As we celebrate our thirtieth anniversary neither we nor the country are where we want it to be. From here we will regroup and reorganise, believing in time the sincerity we showed in government will contrast favourably with those other parties who, at the last election, chose to campaign on policies they knew could not be implemented. The environmental problems of the world have continued and in many ways have worsened. While we live in a time of huge economic uncertainties, the need for a Green Party has never been greater. This is why we will continue to offer voters that alternative, because the need for that alternative has never been greater.

# 5

# Wipeout! Does Governing Kill Small Parties in Ireland?

*Eoin O'Malley*

## Introduction

At the end of November 2010 John Gormley, the leader of the Green Party, likened governing during the economic crisis to wearing a straitjacket and warned opposition leaders that they soon would be entering an asylum.[1] The Greens had been in office during what many felt was one of the most unsuccessful governments in Ireland since independence. It had introduced the Bank Guarantee Scheme, seen by many as having made a difficult situation intolerable for Ireland, and eventually the country suffered the ignominy of having the IMF and the EU introduce a lending programme because Ireland was not seen to be able to borrow on international markets.

The Greens signalled their intention to resign from government not long after the IMF deal, but committed to support yet another austerity budget, seen as crucial to secure the funding Ireland needed to avoid default on its existing borrowing. After an unusually messy break-up, the election held in late February 2011 saw the party lose all six of its Dáil seats. That Fianna Fáil suffered a decline greater than either of the two large parties had ever suffered provided scant consolation for the Greens.

Arguably, the Greens were unlucky to have been in government when one of the largest housing and lending bubbles in economic history burst. But they might also be thought to be the authors of their own downfall. The party, had it analysed the Irish economic situation using its own philosophy, should have known better than most that the property market had grown unsustainable, and that it accounted for a fifth of the economy on some measures. It also witnessed in 2007 the annihilation of the PDs, another small, ideologically driven party. Had the Green Party been in opposition in 2011 it is possible that it would have been one of the parties to have benefited most from the economic crisis. It had been one of the few parties, and the only party that accepted market economics, not to be a cheerleader for the property bubble. Instead the party was wiped out.

While Ireland has had a plethora of minor parties, these tend to rise and fall in relatively short life-cycles. This can be partly explained by the fact that many of these minor parties are personality driven, and cease to exist when the party's sole representative retires or joins a larger party. But other parties, with an ideological identity and organisation that goes well beyond one or two constituencies, have also 'died'. Apart from the Greens, the most obvious recent example is the Progressive Democrats (PDs). Clann na Talmhan, Clann na Poblachta and Democratic Left all died as representative political parties. We see that minor parties tend to come in waves, receding after a time when small parties die (Note: the words small and minor are used interchangeably).

Does participation in government shorten the life-cycle of these parties, or would they have died in any case? Why did some, for instance the PDs, seem to thrive in government at times? Is it the party's size or some other factors that are important in determining the health and longevity of a party in government?

I will outline and consider an argument that government can effectively 'smother' minor parties to the benefit of larger parties by blunting the smaller party's ideological edge. The argument goes like this. Minor parties are, for various reasons, less robust to shocks and so more likely to die. Government puts all parties under electoral pressure, but the weakness of small parties and the nature of compromise in government means that it will have a greater effect on minor parties. These effects are not inevitable. By testing this on aggregate party data since 1927 we see that government is not necessarily bad for small parties. This is not that surprising, otherwise minor parties would not enter government unless they were particularly myopic or office seeking. Small parties are aware of the risks and learn from each other's and their own mistakes. I will conclude that where a party can maintain its own identity, it avoids being 'smothered' and can increase its relevance and support from its experience in government.

## Minor parties and government

Entering government has an impact on any party's relevance, which can in turn have an impact on its vote. This is especially true of small parties whose ideological distinctiveness might be more threatened by the realities of government and who, by virtue of their size, might live constantly on the edge of extinction. The decision to enter government or stay in opposition represents an important junction in paths in a cyclical attempt to remain relevant and regain representation thereby avoiding electoral extinction. A good example of this happening might be the PDs, where government meant association with the larger party in government and arguably led to some voters considering the party redundant. This may have lost it votes and seats, leading the party to decide to dissolve.

## How are minor parties different?

Parties, by their nature, are coalitions of interests. Large parties are coalitions of more diverse views and need mechanisms in place to prevent these divisions disrupting the stability or sound management of the party. At times new issues may arise, challenging the cohesion of this coalition. In these situations new groups can emerge to fill any political vacuum and to respond to political opportunities, for instance the SDP in the UK. However, a minor party's flexibility in being able to respond to new challenges compared to larger, more sluggish parties may be offset by the probability that it will attract more demanding voters and members dissatisfied with the inaction of the larger parties. Therefore minor parties may be more ideological and policy driven than larger parties, who by their nature must tolerate compromise.

But people do not vote for small parties because they are small, and it is only if they offer something distinctive that they can survive. To survive in the long term parties must either have strong social roots or they must retain an electorally attractive policy position to a certain cohort. In many countries small parties have strong social bases, for instance the regionalist/nationalist parties in Spain or the UK (in fact these might be regarded less as small parties but large parties occupying a small territorial space within a country), enabling their long-term existence.

Where minor parties are not rooted in some societal cleavage, they could be more likely to be considered as outsiders to the political system. They may have emerged through a charismatic leader recognising the political opportunity.[2] As such, there could be an over-reliance on such leaders, who may demand policy flexibility and tight control over the organisation and this could cause tensions within a political organisation that has weaker links with its more ideological and demanding members. Those ideological members may demand more control within the party leading to tensions between leaders and members, that while existing in all parties may be more exaggerated in more ideological minor parties. Minor parties may also be less experienced in government and electoral politics. These factors might make minor parties less robust to crises and shocks.

## Smothering hypothesis

If it is reasonable to expect that minor parties are more vulnerable to extinction, and that large parties view minor parties as challengers, we can also expect that 'major parties attempt to destroy them'.[3] However, in the times of flux that minor parties emerge larger parties may also need smaller parties to allow them to make radical policy shifts. The legislative strength of minor parties will affect larger parties' government formation potential. Larger parties need to work with minor parties in order to form governments. This would appear to be advantageous for minor parties. If minor parties need to remain relevant to retain or increase representation, government gives them relevance by giving them access to policy-making power. It will also increase the party's profile. As well as media access, government will also give the party access to state resources – civil service advice, state patronage, and make the party potentially more attractive to donors.

But a minor party entering government assists the larger party in government's development in its life-cycle, by allowing it enter government, enabling it to shift policy and remain relevant, while at the same time reducing the electoral attractiveness of the new competitor. By entering government, the larger party may effectively 'smother' the smaller one. This smothering can occur though a number of mechanisms:

- Government with a smaller party allows the larger party adopt or be associated with the new policies of the smaller party. This will have the effect of removing from the smaller party its *raison d'être* but enables the larger party to be seen to respond to the event that caused the emergence of the minor party, but where it wishes the party may also be able to frame its policy shift as a concession to the smaller party where that it advantageous.
- Government participation makes blunt the policy distinctiveness of the smaller party. Coalition government involves compromise, but government decisions are made collectively and parties in government are prevented from criticising aspects of government policy with which they disagree. As a result one will see that a minor party's radical edge is blunted by the inevitable compromises of government and their inability to express their differences.
- Minor parties' leadership and organisation devotes more time to government than organisation building. By entering government minor party leadership usually assume office and are subject to its day-to-day pressures and the strictures of collective responsibility. Though government affords huge resources in terms of political appointees, the leaders get 'captured', unable to comment or criticise government policy where they might want to and time constraints restrict their ability to build up the party organisation. New parties' organisational vulnerability mean they are more likely to suffer the organisational costs of public office.[4]

If the reason for the demise of small parties in Ireland is 'smothering' by larger parties through government participation we would expect to observe:

- That small parties electorally suffer more as a result of government compared to their larger colleagues and compared to small parties in opposition.
- That the larger party adopts or becomes associated with the smaller party's policies.
- That the smaller party is seen as moderating its ideological views, perhaps causing disquiet among party supporters.
- Leaders grow more distant from the party organisation, weakening party unity.

Of course larger parties can be said to be muffled by government, and have been accused of having been dominated by a smaller party. Coalition also causes disquiet within larger parties. This ideological and organisational smothering will not necessarily happen nor will it be uniform across all minor parties. It may be possible to be seen to deliver policy benefits to one's core constituency. This will be helped if the small party holds a relevant ministry, and if it has clear, achievable policy goals.

## The Irish experience

### Size and Government Policy in Ireland

If small parties enter government they need to ensure they have an impact, thus continuing their relevance and increasing representation. This can be achieved through the apportionment of cabinet posts and other policy relevant or capacity building appointments (including Seanad appointments, junior ministers and EU Commissioners) as well as through the negotiation of the programme for government. The literature on the distribution of cabinet posts in government points out that bargaining power rather than size should determine whether and how well a party does in the government formation process. The psychological attachment to the principle of 'fairness' means that it is difficult to deviate too greatly from proportionality, but we do see some. In particular, we see deviations in favour of the smaller party. In the two post-war coalitions small parties did badly, but since 1973, apart from one exception, smaller parties are over-represented in terms of ministerial posts. In fact, between 1973 and 2007 the ratio of cabinet posts to legislative seats for junior coalition parties is 1.5, so a party with ten per cent of the government's seats in the Dáil can expect to receive 15 per cent of cabinet posts.[5] Smaller parties report that their demands for personnel and portfolio allocation tend to be met, even if publicly the larger party put up a fight.[6] In terms of policy successes there has been a more mixed picture. The large Labour Party was able to draw significant concessions from a weakened Fianna Fáil in 1993, but other small parties have been forced to defend a decision to go into government where few substantial concessions are offered.[7]

One might expect that with large catch-all parties leading a coalition, the smaller party could have strong policy influence. This was the opinion of PD leader, Michael McDowell, who argued '[t]he larger party may lead. The junior party defines the direction'.[8] A systematic study of parties' manifestos and the delivery of policy pledges show a mixed picture in terms of policy delivery. Mansergh and Thomson gathered data from manifestos and estimated the enactment of pledges.[9] They found that for two Fianna Fáil governments formed prior to 1987, almost 80 per cent of pledges were fulfilled, but in the minority and coalition governments that followed this fell to 68 per cent. The other large party, Fine Gael, could only manage a third in its three governments in the 1980s and 1990s. Of the smaller parties the PDs fared best, fulfilling about half its 1989 and

1997 pledges, whereas Labour and Democratic Left achieved just a third of their respective pledges.[10] Work on the 2002-2007 government shows that the PDs at least partially fulfilled two-thirds and Fianna Fáil three-quarters of each party's socio-economic pledges at least partially fulfilled, and of pledges fully enacted the PDs managed 47 per cent to Fianna Fáil's 45 per cent.[11] However, for the years 1977-2002 we can see that opposition parties are not much less likely to achieve their policy pledges – 50 per cent for government and 45 per cent for opposition parties.[12] Nor can these figures control for the significance of certain pledges, so some pledges are more important than others and will affect voters' and party supporters' perceptions of the party in government more than others. As such this data does little to confirm or refute the smothering hypothesis.

## Size and electoral performance in Ireland

As we have seen, there are strong empirical results on the electoral effects of incumbency. Using data from 1927 to 2011 we can immediately see that like other Western European countries, Irish government parties tend to do worse than opposition parties in elections. Parties coming from opposition gain on average over one percentage point and government parties lose on average 2.6 percentage points. Rather than use raw percentage point gains and losses in seat terms Table 1 shows the average relative effect for parties. The 'relative effect' is the change in support as a proportion of the overall initial size of the party. These are percentage changes, not percentage point changes. So if a party goes from forty to thirty seats or from eight to six seats, this represents a 25 per cent fall.

*Table 1: Relative effect of government for parties' proportion of seats*

|  | Type of Party | |
| --- | --- | --- |
| **Opposition or Government** | Mainstream Party | Minor Party |
| Opposition | 4.4 | 43.6 |
| Government | -7.2 | -16.8 |

Note: When parties merge the party that dissolves is coded as missing data.

We see that opposition parties make gains compared to incumbent losses. More interestingly, when one compares the differences between minor and mainstream parties, minor parties are much more badly affected by government participation. Minor parties are much more volatile. On the face of it, this would suggest that government is far more damaging to minor parties, and indicates support for the smothering hypothesis. However, these differences are not statistically significant, even when controlling for ideology. It is therefore useful to look at the experiences of minor parties in a more qualitative way, focussing on the rationale for the emergence of the minor party, the ability of minor parties to achieve and take credit for policy gains, whether the smaller party moderates its policy stance in government, and whether the larger party adopts the policies of the smaller party/parties. I now look at a number of cases of how small parties performed in government, starting with those involved in the 1948-51 and the 1954-7 inter-party governments.

## Clann na Talmhan

As Varley points out in chapter 9, the fact that there has not been a strong farm-ers' party in the history of the state is not as much of a puzzle as perhaps might first seem. Farmers' interests were heterogeneous, so one might find it difficult to unite tillage farmers of the East with the ranchers of the Golden Vale or the small-holders in the West. Clann na Talmhan, founded in 1939, aimed at alleviat-ing the plight of the last group. It did very well in its first general election, and its vote and seats fell only marginally in 1944. Despite this, the party leader resigned his leadership as it did not give him enough time to tend his farm. The party considered the idea of allowing one of the independent farmers take over.[13] This did not happen and support halved in 1948. Part of the reason for this was that it failed to develop beyond being a loose federation of farmers in the west. Indeed, according to Chubb it, 'could only just be called a party at all'.[14]

Clann na Talmhan made no impression when it entered government in 1948. McCullagh reports that a regular attendee at cabinet could not remember a single contribution from its sole cabinet representative, Joseph Blowick, Minister for Lands.[15] In the Dáil, Blowick attracted the derision of those on government benches.[16] Contemporary observers could not identify any achievements – 'there is a growing similarity between the two major parties in government, and no sign of a different view from the third, Clann na Talmhan'.[17] Added to this was the comparative success of James Dillon as Minister for Agriculture in both governments. The alleviation of the problems of the small farmers in rural Ireland' increased Fine Gael's support and reduced the importance of Clann na Talmhan.[18] In its first government the party lost a number of members who resigned and the party was lucky to lose just one seat in the following election. It lost another seat in 1954 and its position in the second coalition did nothing to increase its profile of being little more than a 'sectional and regional interest group'.[19] The party maintained a small Dáil presence until its last remaining TD, Blowick, retired in 1965. Clann's experiences clearly support the smothering hypothesis, where it failed to associate itself with the delivery of policy gains that Fine Gael could take credit for.

## Clann na Poblachta

Led by the dynamic but Quixotic Seán MacBride, Clann na Poblachta burst onto the political scene in 1946 promising to overtake Fianna Fáil as the party of social radicalism and republicanism. It somewhat spectacularly won two by-elections in

1947 giving MacBride a voice in the Dáil, and expected to perform well in the 1948 election. So worried was Fianna Fáil by the threat of Clann na Poblachta that the electoral law was amended, increasing the number of three seat constituencies thus reducing the system's proportionality.[20] De Valera's other tactic, to call an early election, prevented the new party from building an organisation. Its own estimates of overtaking Fianna Fáil meant that it nominated too many candidates and overstretched its weak organisation and scarce resources.[21] So despite gaining a creditable 13.2 per cent of the first preference vote, the party won just ten seats (6.8 per cent).

The decision to enter government immediately caused controversy in the nascent party. Many were against coalition, especially with the conservative Fine Gael party, and the choice of Noël Browne as MacBride's cabinet colleague was also questioned.[22] MacBride also immediately caused discord in the party by using his Senate nominees for two people from Northern Ireland rather than the party's Director of Elections and one of its best-known members who had indicated a desire to be appointed.[23] In government both ministers were highly active and MacBride's interventions in cabinet went well beyond his brief. In the declaration of the Republic in 1949 the party may have been able to claim it had achieved one of its goals. However, this policy probably did more to improve Fine Gael's fortunes by having 'removed the Union Jack which [De Valera] ... had wrapped around [the party] in 1922'.[24] In health Browne made some remarkable achievements, and was moving the country towards a British-style health service. However, the intervention of the medical profession and the Catholic hierarchy caused controversy and division between the minister and the rest of the cabinet. MacBride's decision to allow his party rather than the government to split on the mother-and-child issue allowed the party continue 'drifting into anarchy' and prevented him from arresting 'his waning radical reputation'.[25] Browne and a number of others resigned from the party, which was reduced to two seats in the following election. MacBride struggled on, gaining a seat in 1954, and supported the second coalition government formed in that year. Its withdrawal of support over the budget and the government's reaction to the IRA's border campaign caused the collapse of Costello's second government. MacBride lost his seat in 1957 and despite attempts at a revival, the party never recovered from its part in the first coalition.

Seán Lemass later attributed Clann's demise (effectively in 1951) to its decision to enter government. He pointed out that many supporters would have come from Fianna Fáil and would have returned in disgust at its support of Fine Gael. He also argued that MacBride appeared overly concerned with his own advancement in office.[26] This analysis was shared by Browne, though MacBride pointed out that it would have been difficult not to enter government which would have meant putting Fianna Fáil back in, following an election campaign run on the slogan, 'Put Them Out'.[27]

## National Labour

The smallest of the parties in the first interparty government, National Labour, was a break-away from the Labour Party, caused by a rift over connections to British trade unions, aided by a personality clash.[28] National Labour was more nationalist in outlook and even more antipathetic to socialism. The party had indicated that it favoured Fianna Fáil and asked voters to transfer to that party, though there is evidence that its voters did not share the enthusiasm for Fianna Fáil.[29] As such it was expected to support a Fianna Fáil minority government, but surprised many by entering the coalition against Fianna Fáil. Its entry to government was assisted by the fact that the division between the two Labour parties was a proxy for union rivalry and the rivals were not part of the government. In government the two parties worked well together and soon agreed an amicable merger. Organisationally the Labour Party was loose and rarely received the support of the large trade union membership,[30] and in particular the failure of Labour to support Noël Browne in the mother-and-child controversy increased tension between the party and the unions.[31] More worrying for the party was its inability to draw any major policy successes from the government – the party had increased state pensions, but its Social Welfare Bill was successfully filibustered by Fine Gael.[32] Furthermore, some genuinely progressive measures such as the setting up of the Industrial Development Authority, the nationalisation of the railways and provision of sanatoria for tuberculosis were achieved by ministers from other parties. Added to this was the fact that Labour was the most disciplined of the parties in government and its ministers seldom wandered outside their briefs. In the election of 1951 the reunited party received more or less the same support as the two parties had separately three years earlier. The experiences of the Labour Party in this and the second coalition, where Labour 'left no footprint on government policy', were to set the tone for the debate on coalition up to the early 1990s.[33] Again we see the smaller party is incapable of achieving or claiming credit for even modest policy successes, nor could it offer a distinctive voice in government.

## Labour 1981–2; 1982–7

According to Gallagher, the question of whether Labour should enter coalition has animated the party's, 'passions probably more than any other single subject'.[34] Mair felt that 'the potential for long-term electoral growth was sacrificed in the interest of the short-term advantage of incumbency'.[35] In 1981 Labour was small again, despite having threatened a breakthrough in the 1960s. It had formed part of a stable and reasonably cohesive government with Fine Gael in 1973 having campaigned on that basis. In 1981, led by the enigmatic Michael O'Leary, it formed a short-lived minority government. This fell on the issue of VAT on children's shoes where Labour was forced to compromise and was shown up by a left-wing independent. Labour survived the subsequent election, but lost its leader on the issue of coalition. Dick Spring, aged just thirty-two, took over days before yet another election was called. In that election Fine Gael achieved its best result ever with seventy seats, and Labour managed to gain one seat. Spring convinced his party to enter coalition with Fine Gael, having agreed a programme for government carefully 'designed to maximise support within Labour'.[36]

The government was faced with a number of difficult problems: a recession, poor public finances, a weak currency and low credit-worthiness. Some in Fine Gael (possibly excluding the Taoiseach) took a tough line on the state's fiscal position, but this was not one the Labour Party could support. The need to save money led to the introduction of water charges by Spring as Minister for Environment. This deepened the split in his party and aided the rise of a militant left. Furthermore, the government had agreed to introduce a constitutional ban on abortion, which would have deepened the rift between the liberal, middle class and usually Dublin-based members of the party and the electorally stronger rural TDs. Issues such as water charges allowed the Workers' Party overtake Labour in Dublin in the local elections in 1985. In 1986 the newly appointed General Secretary of the Party described the situation, 'an impecunious party, a demoralised party membership and a divided Parliamentary Party. The Labour ministers seemed more under siege than any set of ministers since the end of the second Inter-Party Government'.[37] Labour's position within the government was further weakened by Fine Gael's use of its majority in cabinet in the discussions for the 1987 budget.[38] Labour left government and both sides tried desperately to disassociate themselves from the other.

Both incumbent parties lost about a quarter of their seats in 1987. Many on the left of the party felt this was due to an unnatural alliance with Fine Gael,[39] though Mair argued that the parties were actually closer than is often thought.[40] Fine Gael's leader was a social democrat and certainly as close to the Labour leader on many issues as either one would have been to many in their respective parties. As well as governing in a deep recession with the hyperactive but inefficient FitzGerald as chairman of government, Fine Gael and Labour were also unfortunate to have well-organised and committed parties challenge each side's flank. So the newly formed Progressive Democrats put Fine Gael under pressure on its right flank and the Workers' Party exerted significant pressure to Labour's left.

Labour evidently felt that it was overshadowed by Fine Gael in that government, and that it failed to deliver or be seen to deliver policies to its constituency. On entering government in 1993, the Labour Party developed extensive institutional structures to maximise the party's policy impact within government.[41] While Fine Gael hardly smothered Labour in 1994-7, Labour did suffer from not being able to offer distinctive policies that its members would have supported. We can also see that Labour when in government with Fianna Fáil and widely regarded as defining policy for that government was doing well in the polls at late 1994.[42]

## Democratic Left 1994–97

As outlined by Murphy and Rafter, Democratic Left (DL) was formed in early 1992 when the leadership and six of the seven Workers' Party (WP) TDs left following a split between traditionalists and modernisers within WP. In DL's first electoral outing in the general election of 1992 it lost two seats. Part of the reason for the loss was that in the WP split 'the head of the party went in one direction … and the body in another'.[43] The new party failed to rebuild the political machine that threatened Labour in 1989. Following the election of 1992 a resurgent Labour chose to coalesce with Fianna Fáil, rejecting a possible deal with Fine Gael and the PDs. By the time that government collapsed DL had gained two seats through by-elections,[44] making Labour's preferred option, a coalition government between Fine Gael, Labour and DL, possible. For Labour it offered to make it the centre party in the government and to protect its left flank from being attacked. For DL it gave the party a chance to set policy and an impetus for possible renewal. As is common with minor parties, DL's support was remarkably volatile, going from 1 per cent to 5 per cent and back down to 2 per cent in opinion polls between August and November 1994.[45]

DL took the social welfare portfolio in a government that was thought to have a centre-left bent. But government participation failed to increase the party's support, which stabilised at 2 per cent up to the election of 1997.[46] At the time, journalist Vincent Browne asked what the point of the party was, and, 'particularly, how, in any substantive respect it differs at all from its "left wing" partner in government, Labour?'[47] Despite governing at a time when the state's finances were improving, the achievements of the party in government were marginal: reform of child benefit, housing regeneration and a Consumer Credit Act, but Pat Rabbitte, a DL minister, admitted failure in attempts to reduce long-term unemployment.[48] Symbolically, one of the last acts of the government was to privatise a state-owned bank. This caused DL to be vulnerable to a new threat from the left, Sinn Féin.

In 1997 DL failed to retain the two seats it had won in by-elections and with just 2.5 per cent of the vote, a weak organisation, and lacking a critical mass to be an effective opposition in the Dáil, it was forced to consider its future as a viable political entity. Such consideration became even more pressing after a disastrous by-election result in 1998. Having had already started its centre-ward shift, even before government, and because the parties had come closer on some of the issues that separated it from Labour, such as Labour's less nationalist position on Northern Ireland, DL decided to enter merger talks with Labour in 1998. These turned out to be successful, as the 'bodiless' DL quickly assumed many of the leadership positions in the stronger Labour Party, for example. The government DL served in was popular but almost certainly blunted the party's more radical edge. It became impossible to differentiate itself from Labour in policy terms.

## Progressive Democrats 1989-92; 1997-2009

From inception the PDs succeeded in redefining economic policy in Ireland. A good performance in its first election in 1987 was followed by a period of Fianna Fáil government in which FF pursued many of the policies the PDs had advocated. Thus we can see that smothering is possible when a party is in opposition. The snap election in 1989 saw its support decline sharply, losing some of the party's most talented TDs, but also provided the opportunity to go in to government. Entering government with Fianna Fáil might have immediately called into question the purpose of the party, but the PDs were seen as a strong partner who would put Fianna Fáil under pressure in a number of policy areas and more controversially in ethical considerations. The party made significant policy gains in taxation policy and was frequently seen as the dominant party in coalition. The PDs were attuned to the need to retain a distinctive identity and from early on it felt that to survive it needed to be radical – the phrase 'radical or redundant', coined by one of its TDs and the theme of this book, gained some currency within the party. As a result, the relationship between the parties in government was always tense – the PDs sought to protect their interests in government and used a defeated TD, Michael McDowell, to act as the guardian of the party's interests.

The election in 1997 seemed set up for the PDs. Fine Gael tying itself to its left-wing partners should have allowed the PDs to position itself as the only proponent of liberal economics, but a disastrous election campaign wiped out all the poll gains the party had made in the previous two years (it had overtaken Labour in late 1996). Reduced to just 4 per cent and four seats, three of whom had been FF TDs, it was given the opportunity to form a minority government with Fianna Fáil. This government was much more cohesive, and with a number of FF ministers sharing the PDs' economic philosophy, the party could point to a number of policy victories particularly in the areas of taxation, growth in the economy and employment, all of which seemed to bear out the party's philosophy. Though there were some tensions between Bertie Ahern and Mary Harney, the two party leaders, Ahern seemed to go out of his way to be conciliatory to his junior partner. The PDs entered the election campaign in 2002 pointing to its achievements and asking for a return of the same government, successfully framing the election as one of between one party government or coalition. The two parties won an overall majority, with the PDs doubling its number of seats to eight. The PDs also got a number of new faces elected, some in constituencies that would not have been considered fertile ground for the party. However, the PDs failed to increase its vote and Fianna Fáil came close to achieving an overall majority and with a number of Fianna Fáil 'gene-pool' independents, it could have governed without the PDs. The weakening of the PDs' bargaining power did not become apparent immediately, but the government, and Fianna Fáil in particular, immediately lost popularity. This caused a change of strategy in Fianna

Fáil. Ahern moved the pro-market Finance Minister, Charlie McCreevy, to Brussels and attempted to reposition the party in the centre. The PDs lost policy disputes, most notably on the deregulation of transport services and a second terminal in Dublin Airport. Harney, who was no longer looking for tax cuts, took on the role of Health and was optimistic in believing that she could reform what had become a money pit for the government. The party remained at 3 or 4 per cent in opinion polls. Continued media coverage and a new leader failed to arrest the party's decline in support, and in the election of 2007 it lost six of its eight TDs. Despite the defeat, the party entered a surplus majority coalition government with FF and the Greens, but this time it was probably due to Mary Harney's personal relationship with Ahern rather than for the stability of the coalition. By the end of 2008 the party leadership, under an unknown senator as leader, decided that it could not continue to viably fight and win elections. That process took over a year to complete after which Mary Harney remained in the cabinet as an independent.

The varied experiences of the PDs in government tell us a great deal about the impact of government on small parties. In its first two governments it was seen as central to setting the direction for government yet maintained a presence that was distinctive from its larger partner. By its third government, though bigger than before, it had lost its bargaining strength and policy battles. Fianna Fáil had already regained its mantle as being a party of business, and the core PD message of tax reductions had been achieved. While it tried to carve out other areas to push its ideology, it failed to sell these clearly either in government or to the public. This loss of relevance in government in its core policy area, the economy, made the party less necessary for voters trying to influence government policy.

## Green Party

Founded in 1981, the Green Party's progression to a party of government was slower than for other minor parties (see chapter 6). As a party it had consistently claimed that it wanted to enter government, but this remained unlikely in the immediate aftermath of the 2007 election. The party had failed to make its promised surge and there were insufficient numbers for a coalition between it, Fine Gael and Labour. Given what the parties had said about each other it may have seemed unlikely that the Greens would have chosen to go into government with Fianna Fáil.[49] Fianna Fáil was pivotal and could choose the type of government it wanted, but indicated that it wished to start negotiations with the Greens. The Greens were much criticised for this, and in agreeing a programme for government the party was forced to concede on a number of issues that might have been considered too important, for instance a motorway extension through a historic monument. Though the programme for government was the Fianna Fáil manifesto with minor adjustments, it was easily passed by a special conference of the party. The opposition parties, however, put down motions that they knew the Greens would find difficult to vote for. With two ministries in key green areas, Environment and Energy, the party may have expected to make key gains. However, their choice of portfolios did not give them the opportunity to deliver real policy outcomes for Irish voters – a portfolio such as transport may have been more useful. From autumn 2008 the party's position in government strengthened. A defection by a FF TD, the withdrawal of support by an independent, the demise of the PDs and some less cohesive voting from Fianna Fáil backbenchers meant the Green's withdrawal could have been fatal. However, by early 2009 the party was not seen to assert its potential influence. This was especially puzzling given that many of its aspirations were cost free.

There were signs that the party may have suffered from its entry to government. In late 2008 one of the party's TDs criticised the government in an email that was made public. Another felt the party was 'getting screwed' by Fianna Fáil.[50] In January 2009 a number of councillors resigned from the party, claiming the party was 'irrelevant and out-of-touch' and one of the Greens' former MEPs described the party as being in 'freefall'.[51] To counteract this, the party used one of its senators, Dan Boyle (who has his own contribution in this volume), as the voice of the party outside government. He would frequently make suggestions as to what the government should do. This enabled the party to maintain its own identity, while adhering to conventions of cabinet government. One of the party's senators resigned in early 2010, citing a consensual style favoured by the Green Party ministers as being ineffective.[52] This was echoed by Dan Boyle who worried that the fact that so many disagreements were internally resolved created a perception that the party was being walked all over.[53] Though the party's support in opinion polls was low but static, the local elections in 2009 were a disaster (it won just three council seats) and caused much misgiving within the party, forcing a renegotiation of the programme for government. The increased power of the party within the government, party leaders felt, was made tell as it extracted some concessions on fox hunting, and other arguably less significant political reforms.[54] However, it was seen as a payoff for supporting the Bank Guarantee Scheme, Nama legislation and budget retrenchment. And some 'achievements', such as including an environmental pillar in social partnership, can reasonably be derided as tokenistic. As well as being forced to compromise on issues that the party may not have wished to, it did not have many easily deliverable policies that voters could see as changing their lives. The party leader, John Gormley was reported to be much more eager to leave government than some of his colleagues. It was only after the IMF/EU funding deal had been announced that the Greens indicated they would leave government, and then it was done ineptly. The Greens had hoped to retain two seats in the election, but the party returned no TDs, making the prospect of rebuilding more difficult. It raises the counterfactual question of what would have happened had the Greens not entered government. As a small party with a distinct ideology, a history of being critical of Fianna Fáil and sceptical of the property boom, one might have expected it to have thrived in the wake of the economic crisis. Instead it became associated with the crisis.

## Discussion

Obviously parties die without ever having entered government, but few parties that gained at least two seats over at least two elections have died except after a time in government. Since the 1930s only Sinn Féin and Workers' Party have had more than two TDs and not entered government. The Workers' Party is effectively dead as a representative organisation. However, the party's death was due to the fact that its leaders formed Democratic Left in response to the failure to achieve the requisite majority to change WP's direction. The eventual death of that political organisation came when it merged with Labour. (Provisional) Sinn Féin has contested Dáil elections since 1987 and achieved representation since 1997. While initial growth was halted in 2007, in 2011 Sinn Féin took advantage of its outsider status in Irish politics and came close to Fianna Fáil – see chapter 12. Whether the party would or could enter government remains unclear, as it was seen as beyond the pale for Fine Gael at least. If it were to enter government one could see immediately that it would face some problems. In most governments its more radical left-wing agenda might have to be compromised, in which cases its young supporters might question it. Contrast this to in Northern Ireland were Sinn Féin is in government as one of the largest parties, but also where the absence of normal rules of government in parliamentary democracies mean that it can maintain its ideological distinctiveness.

While it is evident that government can be difficult for all parties, it poses special challenges for minor parties. If we assume that small parties in Ireland emerge to fill policy vacuums rather than represent any long-existing social cleavage, their existence might only be possible as long as larger parties find it difficult to respond. One response is to adopt the policy concerns expressed through coalition with the minor party. This could have the effect of smothering the smaller party as it will find it harder to maintain a distinct voice and identity, and because they start from a low and volatile electoral position they are especially vulnerable to shocks. There is some evidence of 'smothering' of the minor party's identity, for instance Fine Gael in 1951 and 1997 successfully assumed the mantle of the smaller parties. Minor parties are forced to compromise on key ideological issues, which damages them in the eyes of their target electorate. Parties are acutely aware of this and many disagreements in coalitions emerge as the parties are tempted by electoral imperatives to express different points of view.

But minor parties sometimes increase representation. The minor party can survive and even thrive in government where it delivers on a 'signature' policy and gains credit for having done so. This might happen when the small party is powerful enough within the government to push a radical programme and get away with upsetting coalition colleagues by claiming the credit. While many small parties in government find it difficult to achieve policy gains or stake out a distinct position, some parties have been able to, most especially the PDs between 1989 and 1992 and from 1997 to 2002. The structural aspects of the government and the party system, and each party's position in these seems crucial to a party's ability to survive government. Where parties, either in government, or in opposition, successfully define the structure of policy or party competition or where they find themselves alone on one side of the political cleavage, they will be in a position to benefit electorally. Where previously they had, in their third government the PDs ceased to define the salient policy that voters considered and became irrelevant. The PDs also benefited from the fact that the party never had any challengers to its right. Equally a distinctly left-wing party in opposition to a distinctly right-wing government should be an effective opponent and then benefit. Small parties in Ireland seem to have short lifespans compared to say the German FDP, or the Dutch or Belgian parties. In this chapter we see that government per se does not mean there will be smothering and therefore does not determine a party's short lifespan. And the larger party does not always benefit from the association with the smaller coalition partner, but there does seem to be an association between government and losing one's position in the party system. This is something even a relatively large party, such as Labour in the 2011 coalition with Fine Gael, might find to its cost.

# 6

# The Rise and Decline of the Green Party

*Nicole Bolleyer*

## Introduction

Until recently, the Irish Green Party mirrored the typical transformation of quite a number of Green parties in western democracies. It evolved from a loose protest movement opposed to 'conventional politics' into a party that seemed an established part of the parliamentary party system. After its national breakthrough in 1989 it consolidated electoral support for a longer period and, with it, its parliamentary position, and finally joined national government for the first time in 2007. Unlike most other types of minor parties, the large majority of Green parties in advanced democracies are characterised by a remarkable sustainability. Once making the breakthrough into parliament, they tend to maintain a constant representative presence. This was the case despite the internal strains suffered by many of these parties when entering parliament or participating in government. For hardly any Green party (and even more so for other minor parties), public office – parliamentary or governmental – has been completely without its costs.[1] Nonetheless, the Irish Green Party stands out among the members of its family. Its decision to form a coalition with Fianna Fáil and the Progressive Democrats proved disastrous, as it won just three council seats at the 2009 local elections and lost all its TDs at the 2011 Dáil election.[2] This was a considerable setback for the Green movement, especially since the Irish political system is highly centralized and success in the national arena is crucial for any party's electoral fate. This chapter looks at the Greens' organisational evolution from its foundation in 1981 until the aftermath of the general election in 2011.

Most Green parties are 'newly born' parties. Although they tend to be rooted in social movements, they need to build up a party organisation from scratch. They are usually characterised by a very decentralised infrastructure and dominated by anti-elitist attitudes on behalf of its activists. Initially, no pre-established organisational procedures direct or constrain intra-organisational behaviour. The ideas on which kind of organisation ought to be built in the longer run are likely to be diverse. Even if, ideologically speaking, the founders of a new party agree on one vision of how processes should work, the procedures chosen to generate such processes often work quite differently in practice. Organisation-building of new parties functions usually as a 'trial and error process', with high levels of uncertainty, a process during which the actual effects or unintended side-effects of newly created organisational procedures are explored.

The organisational dimension of Green parties has attracted an increasing interest in the comparative politics literature, particularly after various Green parties in Europe experienced electoral success and some served in government.[3] The fundamental decision to contest elections is often part of the early conflicts over the nature of the organisation as such (whether to become a party or not). Taking over public office creates new organisational tensions and puts particular pressure on inexperienced office-holders, which is taken on a new level once the party takes over government responsibility. The alternative to conventional politics that Green parties present opposes organisational centralisation, bureaucratisation and professionalisation, features dominant in long-established parties. Yet entering public office, be it parliament or government, pushes new parties into the opposite direction and towards 'normalisation', easily alienating and frustrating ideologically driven members strongly attached to ideas of participatory democracy.[4]

This chapter argues that, as in other Green parties, the Irish Greens' evolution as an organisation were shaped by two sources of tension which are closely intertwined: first, to reconcile the decision to run elections (thus to 'normalise' to some extent) with the members' ideological preferences, who tended to oppose conventional politics; second, to overcome internal resistance against the necessary reforms of the initially created party organisation to enable party representatives to effectively operate in public – legislative and governmental – office, without alienating the party base. The following section specifies these two sources of conflict and on this basis, the remainder of the chapter analyses the Green Party's evolution in four periods during which these tensions became particularly visible.

## Challenges of party building and of party reform

A major tension in the Irish Green Party was linked to the question which type of organisation to create. As Dan Boyle discusses in this volume, the Irish Greens started as an anti-establishment party and some of their members were highly sceptical of, even averse to, the party's engagement in conventional politics. While some within the movement still share this sentiment today as interviews indicate, many of them have left, as visible in splits of more radical groups such as the GANG (Green Action Now Group) in 1986 who refused to engage in conventional party politics.[5] As with other Green parties in Europe, the Irish Greens suffered from early conflicts between ideologues (refusing an engagement in normal electoral politics) and pragmatists over the nature of their organisation. This conflict was won by the latter, a first push towards the 'normalisation' of the party and an acceptance of the need for serious engagement in electoral politics. Yet even if the decision in favour of running elections has been made, parties still need to build an organisational structure from scratch able to effectively participate in elections. As is discussed in a later section, since the Irish Greens tried to ensure equal influence of members on internal decisions by inclusive deliberations, consensus decision making seemed initially the only acceptable option. Facing frequent blockade, however, the shift to majority voting was unavoidable. Such reforms were triggered by internal functional needs of a party organisation and highlight the tension between the party's original anti-establishment credentials and participatory ideals on the one hand, and its activities in the electoral arena on the other.

Party building is crucial to run elections, while running elections can secure the access to resources to build a party. Public funding and media attention for instance, tend to require successful participation in elections. The co-existence of multiple arenas is particularly important here since the Irish Greens (as other new parties) tend to find more electoral support at the European level than either the national or local level. Their mean vote (5.2 per cent) over the last four European elections is twice that achieved at local elections (2.7 per cent). Similar to the local results, the results at general elections for the same period are below their European performance with a mean vote of 2.1 per cent (see Table 1). Elections are crucial windows of opportunity, especially for a relatively unknown and under-resourced party to access public resources such as secretarial support, donations from office-holders' salaries or media access.[6] This is all the more so for new parties with a limited and often quite volatile membership, who tend to be heavily dependent on such (direct and indirect) state resources. The decline of the Greens' vote in 2009 and its collapse in 2011 (see Table 1) is particularly dramatic since it left the party not only without the resources attached to parliamentary seats but also without state funding, as the threshold for eligibility is 2 per cent of the national vote.

Running elections is one crucial step in Green parties' evolution. Having public representatives is another, which leads to the second fundamental tension mentioned earlier. Once a Green party successfully participates in electoral politics, theories of party change predict the empowerment of a party's public office-holders and of professional staff at costs of party activists constituting and maintaining the membership organisation.[7] This changing intra-organisational balance generates an increasing distance between the two arms of the party, which pursue partially different and conflicting interests. The tension between the desire to maintain bottom-up structures (implying slow and responsive internal decision-making) and the need to make compromises in government and decide

Table 1: Electoral performance of the Greens, 1982-2011

| Year of Election | Dáil vote % | Dáil seats | EP vote % | Local elections vote % |
|---|---|---|---|---|
| 1982 (Nov) | 0.2 | 0 | – | – |
| 1984 | – | – | 0.5 | – |
| 1985 | – | – | – | 0.5 |
| 1987 | 0.4 | 0 | – | – |
| 1989 | 1.5 | 1 | 3.7 | – |
| 1991 | – | – | – | 2.0 |
| 1992 | 1.4 | 1 | – | – |
| 1994 | – | – | 7.9 | – |
| 1997 | 2.8 | 2 | – | – |
| 1999 | – | – | 6.7 | 2.5 |
| 2002 | 3.8 | 6 | – | – |
| 2004 | – | – | 4.3 | 3.9 |
| 2007 | 4.8 | 6 | – | – |
| 2009 | – | – | 1.9 | 2.3 |
| 2011 | 1.8 | 0 | – | – |
| **Mean** | 2.1 | – | 5.2 | 2.7 |

Sources: Coakley, John and Michael Gallagher *Politics in the Republic of Ireland*, 4th edition (London; PSAI Press/Routledge, 2005), p. 466-7; Boyle, Dan *A Journey to Change: 25 Years of the Green Party in Irish Politics* (Dublin; Nonsuch, 2006), p. 40; http://www.rte.ie/news/elections2007; http://www.rte.ie/news/election2011/ipad/index.html

on a wide range of issues quickly (if necessary without any member consultation) is particularly pronounced for parties with strong grass-root traditions (such as the Irish Greens) and tends to intensify the more successful a party becomes.

## Sources and methods

To analyse the organisational responses of the Irish Greens at various stages of their history, I draw on primary material (e.g. party publications, reports by working groups and memos of internal meetings provided by the party's main office in Dublin)[8] as well as fifteen semi-structured, face-to-face interviews with office-holders (TDs, former MEPs and Senators), party staff and activists (i.e. parliamentary assistants, party secretaries, party spokespersons, some of whom were active since the party's foundation) as well as academic experts. The combination of distinct types of sources as well as the different perspectives of interviewees allows for the triangulation of information. While one goal is to identify major organisational shifts, another one is to capture the underlying dynamics and motives. This primary analysis is complemented by the existing case study literature and newspaper reports to capture more recent events.

## The Irish Greens: From protest group to established party

The analysis of the evolution of the Irish Greens is divided into four periods demarcated by core events in their party history. While the party struggled with both sources of tension throughout its development, the first two periods centre more strongly around the challenge of building a functioning party organisation. The latter two periods, in contrast, centre around the challenge to professionalise and centralise the organisation without alienating core supporters. The first period starts with the party's foundation in 1981 in which the status of the party as 'electoral vehicle' is still highly contested. We move into a second period with the party's explicit decision to engage in electoral politics in 1988, when the victory of the pragmatists in the party settled the ongoing fight over the fundamental nature of the organisation, which helped to stabilise the party. The third period began in 2001 when the Greens formally nominated a party leader. At the 2002 elections, the Greens won six seats in the Dáil and began to perceive themselves as serious candidates for government, which triggered intense internal adaptation processes to become ready for such an event. The final period covers the party's experiences in government from 2007 to 2011.

## 1) The initial years 1981–87: organisation-building

The Ecology Party of Ireland was founded in 1981. At the party's inaugural meeting a steering committee of twelve was agreed upon by consensus and the party had a membership of about forty.[9] In 1984 the party formally registered candidates for the first time.[10] In 1985 it experienced its first electoral success when a Green candidate was elected to the Killarney Urban District Council.[11]

Green Party members were very individualistic and, as Dan Boyle recounts in this volume, the party's ambivalence to involvement in electoral politics was very pronounced, a basic conflict which could not be settled until 1988. Organisational capacities were weak and very few activists were willing to run for public office. To meet the requirements of formal party registration, the party adopted a more centralised decision-making structure that was not acceptable to more radical groups within the party such as the GANG. To resolve these tensions, a major reorganisation of the Green movement in 1983 and 1984 resulted in the formation of 'Comhaontas Glas/Green Alliance', an alliance of largely autonomous Green groups, each of which developed their own structures and policies.[12] This reform shifted the party back towards a more decentralised style of decision-making. This swing shows that, at that early stage, ideological preferences shaped the nature of the organisation more strongly than pragmatic considerations of organisational efficiency. At a time when the label 'party' still had negative connotations and was deliberately not included as a part of the Green Alliance's official name, the value of the organisation was defined by its correspondence to Green ideals about democratic decision making.

The capacity of the Greens to raise money was very limited, which is typical for new parties. The Greens do not receive union or business donations. Private funding tended to be small scale and flowed from collections or social events. Even these created internal difficulties: local groups refused to engage in fundraising methods if they consindered them as 'un-green', restricting the potential to generate party income even further.[13] The situation improved when the party started to win public office and gained access to public resources. Yet initially, the party was fully dependent on volunteers.

## 2) Becoming a (normal) party: the Greens turn to professional politics 1988-2000

*(a) Increasing intra-organisational efficiency*
After severe internal struggles within the party, another renaming, this time to Green Party/Comhaontas Glas, was decided in 1988. The rationale behind the name change was to avoid public confusion over the organisation's nature and indicated its final commitment to electoral politics. This move resolved considerable internal conflicts which circled around the question whether the organisation should be a decentralised campaigning movement or, alternatively, it should mainly focus – as a conventional party – on electoral activities. The main group mobilising against the latter was the GANG, supported by a sizable section of the Cork Green movement which in the end decided to leave the party in 1986.[14] The organisational costs had been high since the Greens needed any support they could get. Still, this step was crucial. It resolved a conflict between 'ideologues' (with strongly anarchist tendencies) such as GANG and the 'pragmatists' or 'realists' in favour of the latter, an outcome in line with developments in a range of other Green parties in Europe.[15]

At the same time, this decision does not imply that reforms to make the party ready for politics were easily accepted, which becomes visible in the debate around how intra-organisational decisions ought to be made. In essence, in the late 1980s it was still fundamentally contested whether the party could adopt any policy if there was not unanimous agreement amongst all members,[16] which meant that the party still struggled with the handling of consensus decision-making years after the anarchist groups had left. While consensus was the original procedure for internal decisions, it was manageable only as long as the deciding group remained small enough. Initially, given the size of the original steering committee of twelve members, this policy proved feasible. Applying the same decision-making rule in the National Council – comprising fifty members – proved comparatively difficult. A debate arose over how to interpret consensus and under which conditions individuals were entitled to block decisions (e.g. when core principles were violated). More particularly, in cases where there was wide majority support for a particular option and only a few rejections, was a majority decision potentially acceptable? In principle, a non-decision when lacking consensus can be regarded as a decision, and considerable parts of the party were reluctant to allow voting beyond the area of purely technical decisions, for example – choosing the venue for dinner.[17] Despite this reluctance, a report of the Constitution Group in 1990 indicated, 'Consensus isn't working at the moment. The spirit of our current constitution isn't being followed. Power is slipping back into the hands of those who set the agenda.'[18] In practice, consensus did not ensure an equal level of influence for each member but instead allowed skilled individuals a disproportionate say. To avoid regular blockades that were a consequence of strategic manoeuvring, a working compromise was to allow for voting in case of 'urgently needed decisions'. This solution, however, proved not satisfactory since it remained unclear which issue was urgent and which was not.[19] Another problem was which type of fallback option to choose and how to implement it practically.[20] In the end, the deviation from consensus was only formalised in the new constitution ratified in 1997. The reform process was slow and indicates that after the 1986 split disagreement about the basic nature of this new organisation was not resolved fully. Being asked to identify the most decisive organisational reform in the party history, a range of interviewees still active in the party today pointed to the new constitution and its introduction of majority voting, which enabled the party to make decisions more efficiently. Consensus remains the preferred method of making decisions, but in cases of failure the 'preferendum' (that is, the Borda Count) (in case of multiple alternatives) or majority voting are established alternatives.[21]

### (b) Responding to the pressure of public office

While the Greens had won seats in local councils since 1985 (and as a consequence gained some experience in public office), in 1989 they also entered the national parliament. The election of Roger Garland as TD strengthened the position of the pragmatists in the party who had pleaded for a serious engagement in professional politics. Its national return of 24,827 votes on a campaign budget of £5,000 was a pretty decent return; an investment of 20p per vote. In contrast, Fianna Fáil spent approximately £2.5 million and won 731,487 votes, a mean cost of £3.40 per vote.[22] In face of scarce resources, this surprising success was welcomed because Garland donated his salary to the party and, through him, the Greens had access to parliamentary resources, such as parliamentary assistants. Some of these resources proved particularly important since the party faced considerable trouble generating money internally. In 1990 the Co-ordination Committee of the party tried to introduce a group levy that took into consideration the number of members, but this was objected to by a number of groups that refused to pay. The same happened after a standard group levy (£12 per group) was put forward.[23] Local groups still forcefully oppose attempts to centralise party finance, which makes the running of the national party particularly dependent on resources provided by party office-holders and state funding.

While entering national parliament in 1989 was a considerable success, the capacity of Garland to engage in Dáil debates was limited, which proved frustrating for the Greens.[24] The grass roots were critical of his collaboration with other TDs, fearing their own influence on the TD to be diminished. Too small to have parliamentary group status, the Greens could not access a range of parliamentary privileges, which motivated their formation of a technical group with Democratic Left representatives and some independents in 1993, giving them access to private members' time, priority questions, representation on committees and full participation in whips' meetings.

Efforts to communicate more effectively with the media were not only difficult in practical terms but also a sensitive matter because they implied a personalisation of politics and an informal hierarchy between ordinary members and the party's public representatives. In theory, each policy area should be covered by one spokesperson but the party had trouble filling these positions. The required rotation of party offices intensified this problem, a problem with which several other Green parties in Europe struggled before. It usually led to the abolishment or at least the relaxation of this rule.[25] Active party spokespeople had little working group backup which meant they could use the freedom not to consult their policy group and push for particular viewpoints conflicting with Green egalitarian ideas. In a similar vein, the appointment of a chief spokesperson in 1991 was already a critical step. In his first press release, Trevor Sargent, who took over this position, twice called himself 'head of the party'. This caused uproar in the Greens, where the idea of a party leader (or some functional equivalent) was still strongly opposed. Sargent had to officially apologise to the party's national committee for his remarks.[26]

Having entered the national legislature, the party started to increasingly feel the conflict between Green politicians and the party organisation 'outside', which became more and more pronounced with the growth of the parliamentary party. On several occasions Garland's individual convictions clashed with party positions; one in particular resulted in his threat to leave the party, which would have weakened the party considerably given that the donation of his salary was an important source of party income. Other times he was asked by the media to comment on an issue on which the party had not yet an official policy position, which was resented by party members since the media interpreted his comment as the official Green position.[27] Finally, in 1994 Garland was close to being expelled from the party after he backed an independent Green candidate for the European elections instead of the official party candidate. Similar to the struggle over the abolishment of consensus decision-making, these incidents point to the particular difficulties of a party composed of very individualistic personalities to adapt to the requirements of public office. They further highlight the tensions Green TDs were subject to when pressed to take positions quickly. Getting permission from the party often required too much time, a dilemma also faced by Green ministers.

Despite the rather critical position of the media, and the loss of Garland's seat, the Greens maintained its solitary representation at the 1992 Dáil election through the victory of Trevor Sargent in Dublin North. Sargent proved to be a decisive figure in the Green's process towards further professionalisation as well as centralisation. Immediately after his election in 1992 it became clear that he was – to a stronger extent than Garland - driven by the goal to get re-elected. Sargent held a constituency clinic and made sure that the needs of his constituents were met. A support team began to develop around him, and his Fingal Green Group became the most effective political machine in the party.[28] This development reflects a movement towards those organisational patterns common in the major Irish political parties, where structures evolve around individual incumbents and are directed towards maintaining their personal support rather than ensuring citizen participation. The party in public office constitutes these parties' locus of power – a structure conflicting with Green egalitarian ideals that oppose a dominance of professional politicians over activists in intra-party decision-making.[29]

The increasing weight of the parliamentary party changed the balance of power within the organisation. Its strengthening moved the party closer to organisational patterns in established parties, where core decisions such as policy formulation are dominated centrally. The availability of more financial means meant that the party could hire professional staff, which led to the creation of a research office. Taking the drafting of party policy as an example, in the initial years policy initiatives were drafted in policy committees by dedicated members. Later on also the research office had the capacity to launch initiatives, a body run by professionals who can invest more time in initiatives than ordinary members. In a similar vein, the access of each TD to parliamentary assistants and the growth of the parliamentary party over time meant that more and more policy initiatives originated in the Dáil. Both these types of initiatives tend to pass more easily through the National Council than those coming from the party base.

Eventually Sargent, in his inaugural speech in the Dáil in 1992, publicly announced the Greens' governmental ambitions. He indicated that 'the Green Party is determined to be constructive and responsive … in the formation of Government',[30] a position that was not shared by everyone in the party and still is not today. Garland, for instance, considers formal cabinet seats as a risk since small coalition partners are easily dominated by their bigger partners and can suffer strongly from electoral punishment,[31] a scepticism which was not unfounded considering the fate of other minor parties joining government coalitions earlier. Nonetheless, the desire to enter national government becomes important once a party wants to influence actual policy. Leaving independents aside, who have been regularly able to extract concessions from minority governments, the usual parliamentary channels available to opposition parties (e.g. through standing committees) are particularly weak compared to other parliamentary systems.[32] Confronted with this dilemma, Sargent pushed for the Green Party's transformation from an opposition party to a coalition partner, a process which would take more than one decade to be realised.

### 3) Getting ready for government 2001–2006

The turn towards electoral politics had already led to a more pronounced intra-organisational hierarchy. This tendency was reinforced by the party's growing parliamentary representation. One expression of this was the selection of a formal leader (as well as a deputy leader and a secretary general) in 2001. A proposal to select a leader had been made for years but regularly rejected. More ideologically-driven members regarded it as a move towards centralisation, restricting the influence of ordinary members opposed to an institutionalised party leadership able to dominate the organisation. However, in the end, the pragmatists won out by arguing for the need to have a face for the party, a leader to represent the party in public. As a small party, the Greens always had a difficult time attracting media attention and getting their message out to the voters. The long-lasting refusal to put forward a personality standing for the party as a whole with whom voters could identify and the media could direct their attention towards, made this even more difficult than for conventional small parties. The leader's allowance, a source of income which the Greens could not access as long they refused a formal party leadership, provided another incentive to moderate their anti-hierarchical credentials. Despite all these advantages of having a leader, it was in 2001 only, at a special convention in Kilkenny, that the party selected its first formal leader: Trevor Sargent. Thinking back to the outrage in the party when Sargent, ten years earlier, after having taken over the role of a Chief Spokesperson, dared to call himself in a press release the 'head of the party', the relevance of this reform cannot be underestimated. Similar to the reform of internal decision making in the 1990s, the amount of time to get this proposal through again reflects the on-going strength of the ideologues in the party.

In the long run, however, the balance shifted more and more towards the parliamentary party. The creation of a formalised leadership stabilised its power base which was closely tied to the – however small – party in public office. Before the 2002 election a policy was adopted to target the strongest constituencies, indicating the parties' increasing professionalisation, a strategy that paid off. Following the election of six Greens in 2002, the party could rely on extra resources such as a parliamentary group secretary, the leader's allowance, as well as voluntary contributions of parts of TDs' salaries to the party organisation, compensating for its rejection of corporate donations and its rather modest contribution of membership fees to its income.

The electoral success strengthened the confidence of the party, which was increasingly recognised as a serious political player. Back in 1989, the party's success in entering the Dáil was considered an accident and took the party itself by surprise. After the 2002 success reform processes were particularly intense, initiating the streamlining of decision-making processes to allow for faster responses of party elites if necessary. Furthermore, a separate communications officer was appointed, and the party started to organise its annual conference as a major event. The party's growing parliamentary strength and its increasingly professionalised parliamentarians facilitated the party's transformation into a serious candidate for government, both in size and personnel capacities.

## 4) First time in government and its consequences 2007–2011

### (a) The spoils of government

On 13 June 2007 Green delegates voted 441 to 67 at a specially convened party conference in favour of entering government with Fianna Fáil and the Progressive Democrats. A day later the six Green TDs voted for the re-election of Bertie Ahern as Taoiseach. The Greens received two senior ministries: John Gormley became Minister for the Environment, Heritage and Local Government and Eamon Ryan became Minister for Communications, Energy and Natural Resources, both core areas for Green members. In addition, the party received one junior ministry and two Seanad seats.

The party was well prepared for coalition negotiations. Already in 2006, as part of their pre-election preparations, the Greens formed a committee of John Gormley, Dan Boyle and the party's general secretary Dónall Geoghegan who formulated strategies for talks to enter government. This committee also led the later negotiations.[33] In strategic terms, however, the Greens were neither indispensible for Fianna Fáil nor did they play the pivotal role of a 'kingmaker' able to threaten its larger negotiation partner with the option of joining a rival coalition. This reduced their bargaining power. The party was forced to make a range of painful compromises to secure an agreement in terms of policy, such as the use of Shannon Airport by American troops as well as the construction of a new motorway near the 'Hill of Tara', an area central to the cultural heritage of the country, which made the deal unpopular with a range of active members. Nor was Fianna Fáil the most preferred coalition partner, in ideological terms. The Green Party deliberately had not entered a pre-election pact and had strategically refrained from specifying preconditions for government participation during the 2007 elections. Nonetheless, Green candidates had intimated earlier on that their preferred government partners were Labour and Fine Gael, while the Fianna Fáil government was heavily criticised by the Green Party. Joining government with Fianna Fáil was even harder to digest for some than government participation *per se*. Trevor Sargent, who had refused the possibility that his party would join a Fianna

Fáil-led government, stepped down as the party leader after the deal was made and served as Minister of State in the Department of Agriculture between 2007 and 2010.

Nonetheless, the confirmation by the rank and file (despite short notice more than 500 of 1,000 members attended) was broad. One main argument which convinced sceptical members, as the party's press officer Damian Connon put it, was the policy progress that would not happen without their involvement in government – even though it went at the cost of policy purity. Others left as a response to the party's participation in government and supported new formations that competed at the 2011 election; one example being the left-wing party Fís Nua.

It has been widely recognised in the literature that government participation needs to be assessed in terms of its costs and benefits.[34] In terms of the benefits, it is important to note that in Ireland policy making is monopolised by the government. Opposition parties have little influence on policy through parliamentary committees (until they achieved parliamentary group status in 1993, the Greens had no right to be appointed to committees). Since most legislative proposals are drafted in the ministries and initiated by the government, taking over government posts improves considerably the position of a policy-oriented party. Furthermore, in terms of material resources, ministers have considerable access and discretion to make appointments to committees and boards, an opportunity which has been used extensively by Fianna Fáil and Fine Gael as a pay-off for party support.[35]

*(b) The price of governing*
Even leaving the unfortunate timing (with the financial crisis just around the corner) of the Greens' decision to enter government aside, the costs of governing could be expected to be particularly pronounced. After all, the party was without previous governing experience, formed a coalition with a bigger, highly experienced partner with very different ideological orientations and is characterised by a strong participatory tradition and decentralised modes of decision making.[36]

Beginning with the implications of the latter, existing tensions between parliamentary party and external party organisation are likely to intensify further when members of the parliamentary party enter government. Furthermore, those TDs outside government are affected by the pressure to support government bills. Inevitably, the leeway for individualistic TDs to pursue their own viewpoints will be more limited in government than in opposition. As the majority of bills are drafted in ministries, policy initiative inevitably shifts towards the party in government. This, in turn, creates a divide between those parliamentarians taking over government posts (i.e. become ministers) and those who do not.

Some of the consequences of government entry were evident in interviews with party staff and representatives early after the party had entered government. When asked whether the party profited in terms of resources linked to government participation, interviewees pointed out that, in fact, the party as an organisation had 'lost' active and prominent members who were – after entering the coalition – preoccupied with government responsibilities and had little time left for party work. Another problem was one of reduced access of the organisation to their ministers, who tried to get things done within the coalition, were advised by civil servants rather than party representatives, and spoke to the public through their own governmental press officers. Similarly, a tight flow of information between the parliamentary party and the grass-roots organisation was difficult to maintain.

Neither Green followers inside nor outside public office found that adequate mechanisms were in place to ensure sufficient linkages between office-holders and the membership organisation. On the ground, the demand was to ensure sufficient grass-roots control over what their party in government was doing. Office-holders and more pragmatic activists, however, pointed to the 'realities of governing' as a small partner in a coalition, which conflicts with tight and cumbersome intra-organisational control mechanisms that undermine the party's capacity to respond quickly and make the necessary compromises. Furthermore, given much more intense media attention, information needed to be handled with care which complicated an open communication of elites with the broader membership as envisaged by some activists.

The adaptation of organisational structures tends to be a slow process, which often lags considerably behind the initial conflict that creates the need for reform in the first place. Defections, in contrast, are a more immediate sign of intra-organisational distress. In 2009 Chris O'Leary (a member of Cork City Council) and the Dublin city councillor Bronwyn Maher resigned, indicating dissatisfaction with the party leadership holding national office and its handling of internal criticism. Their resignation fuelled a debate within the national party executive after Patricia McKenna, one of the members of the executive, publicly complained about the lack of response on behalf of the leadership to the resignations and criticised the party's 'stay-in-government-at-all-costs' agenda. McKenna consequently ran as an independent at the European Parliament elections in June of that year.

One reason brought forward by the councillors was the party's lack of policy achievements in government, which brings us to the dominance of the bigger partner and its very different preferences in many policy areas from the Green agenda, which threatened to erode the party's distinctive policy profile and identity. These expressions of dissatisfaction appeared not long after the party had entered government, reflecting critics' earlier warnings against Green government participation. The resignation of Déirdre de Búrca, a Green Senator, in early 2010 was another major blow that left the party 'shell-shocked'.[37] Not only did the party lose a high-profile member of its parliamentary party, who had served the party on the local and later national level for more than ten years, De Búrca's letter of resignation publically articulated fundamental criticisms of the Green Party's operation in government. In her view, the Greens had, 'become no more than an extension of the Fianna Fáil party'. She accused the party in government of a lack of assertiveness and of failing to protect the party's values and integrity. Remaining in office had become 'an end in itself', which combined with the Greens' lack of experience, was exploited by Fianna Fáil by bypassing the smaller partner in major decisions, and undermining its attempts to realize its own policy initiatives.[38]

No matter what was the main trigger for de Búrca's resignation,[39] her criticisms reflect what research on small (more particularly new) parties in government has identified as the major challenges with which minor, often inexperienced, coalition partners tend to struggle. They tend to have a hard time pushing through their preferences in cases of conflict with their stronger coalition partners. On top of that, if policies supported by all coalition partners are realised, it is equally difficult for small parties to claim the credit for those. This means even if 'their' policies are realised, they nonetheless risk being considered as superfluous.[40] Not only might this alienate supporters, it might make it difficult for voters to see the small partner's distinct contribution, generate disappointment and provoke an electoral backlash. The notion of cabinet responsibility putting pressure on government members to present a unified front in face of unpopular decisions (think, for instance, of budget cuts) makes it impossible for individual parties to criticise cabinet decisions in public.

Looking back at the party's record during its time in government, a range of policy innovations were achieved, such as the introduction of a carbon tax or the 2010 Planning Act. Party elites are right to stress that these achievements were only possible because the party joined government (a point echoed by Dan Boyle in this volume). The problem was less an issue of the party's 'objective' achievements in its core areas of interest that might have been satisfying for a small coalition partner during normal times, but rather its incapacity to distance itself from its dominant coalition partner and, with it, a range of unpopular policies. This would have been essential to reduce the electoral damage the party leadership must have expected, especially later in the term.

The fact that disappointed people leave a party while in government is not a Green peculiarity, but reflects the challenges that minor parties in Ireland more generally face. Both the Progressive Democrats and Labour have regularly suffered from resignations after going into government. Further, the timing of the Green councillors' resignations, close to the local elections, suggests that motives other than points of principle might have been at stake. The party's problems to effectively maintain its profile and to highlight its achievements became visible early on. The decision of the Green Party to publicly call for a review of its 'Programme for Government' with Fianna Fáil indicated the elite's awareness of this problem. It signalled a desire to put as much distance as possible between itself and its coalition partner in advance of the European elections in 2009, which was interpreted as an attempt to put a deeply unpopular Fianna Fáil party at arm's length for the rest of the election campaign.[41] In spite of this, at the European and local elections in June 2009 the Green Party turned out to be the biggest loser with no European seats and the loss of all bar three of its council seats.[42] This first shock, however, proved only a prelude to the electoral disaster of 2011. Whether the damage could have been reduced by leaving the coalition slightly earlier remains questionable.[43] What seems to be the more general issue that transcends the exceptional circumstance of the economic crisis is the high risk the Green Party took by joining a big coalition partner with such a different ideological profile.

## Conclusions: the Irish Greens and why they might come back

Despite the transformation the Greens have undergone over thirty years, the party is still less centralised and more member-oriented than the longer-lived Irish parties. At the same time, as Green parties in other countries, the party is not only programmatically more moderate than it was in its initial period, its organisation is more centralised with decision making more driven by the party in parliament and shaped by the resources linked to public office. The party runs more professional campaigns than in earlier years and is more reliant on professional staff. The move from protest to mainstream party was not an easy one. It had to overcome severe internal conflicts over the nature of organisation which led to a split in the 1980s. While pragmatists succeeded in the long run, some resistance against the 'normalisation' of the party is still present.

Until very recently, the parallels with the long-term experiences of other Green parties in Europe were striking.[44] Most notably, since its foundation in 1981, professionalisation and centralisation have been reinforcing each other. The increasing role of professional staff was tied to resources accessed through office-holders, be it the donations from TD salaries, public funding, which allowed the hiring of professional personnel, or be it the support of parliamentary assistants in the formulation of party policy. The main weight of party activities shifted away from active volunteers to professionals, from the extra-parliamentary party to the party in public office. Once government ambitions were pursued more openly by organisational elites, various reforms (such as the introduction of a formal leadership in 2001 or the streamlining of decision-making processes before the 2007 elections) centralised the organisation. To some extents, this development seems to be a natural consequence of growing electoral success which made particular types of resources available, inevitably shifting the balance of power in the party organisation towards those who control these resources, the office-holders who naturally care about staying in office more than the ordinary members.

Since the 2011 elections, the party is forced to again rely exclusively on its extra-parliamentary arm, with the party in public office on the national level – that had increasingly become a central locus of the organisation – being wiped out, which initiates a fundamentally new phase in the evolution of the Irish Green Party. In some respects the party might return to its roots. Over twenty years ago, David Farrell described the Green Party in Ireland as a 'party without support base':[45] a party with an active organisation, committed volunteers running the national headquarters and a steady output of policy documents which, however, lacks a ready electorate. He argued that organisational reasons for this deficit were first, the lack of a party leader which prevents voters from identifying with one aspect of party image and hinders media focus and second, the emphasis on consensual decision making which does not augur well for a smooth-running campaign machine. Both have been reformed, despite considerable internal resistance. As far as joining a national government is a valid indication of Green success, these difficult steps paid off – as they did for other Green parties in Europe, which moved from protest party status to government party much earlier.

However, for the Irish Greens, they paid off only in the very short run. In the medium and long term, the price the Irish Green Party paid for government participation was exceptionally high compared to other Greens' experiences in government, which at times were turbulent but rarely similarly disastrous.[46] While the party was to some extent unlucky to govern during the Irish economic crisis, the types of problems the party faced were by no means unusual compared to experiences of other minor parties that joined coalition governments, be it in Ireland or elsewhere. To enter government with Fianna Fáil, a party with very different economic orientations, which the Green Party had heavily criticised most of its history, might have been more damaging for the credibility of the Greens than joining government as such.

The crucial question to be addressed by future research is whether the Greens can recover outside parliament and win back sufficient support to re-enter as did the Belgian Greens or the Swedish Greens before them.[47] Despite the disastrous 2011 results, it seems unlikely that the Greens will vanish from Irish political life completely (see also Boyle in this volume). Thanks to considerable efforts to build up an organisational support base at the local level in some strongholds, the Greens have shown considerable ability to outlive periods of low levels of electoral success and scarce resources earlier in their history. While the strong bottom-up structures might have complicated the life of Green Party elites in parliament and government, their organisational backup might help them now to deal with the heavy costs of governing they had to pay in 2011, suffering from a massive withdrawal of electoral support. These elections cost them most of their resources, not only in terms of parliamentary posts but also in terms of state funding, which had paid for their offices and staff. However, unlike the Progressive Democrats which dissolved in 2009, Green activists are intrinsically motivated rather than career-oriented. Consequently, electoral success is no necessary condition for the Green Party's persistence as an organisation, which could constitute the starting point for a national comeback.

# 7

# The Party That Ran Out of Lives:
# The Progressive Democrats

*Séin Ó Muineacháin*

## Introduction

On 10 November 2008, a special conference of the Progressive Democrats (PDs) voted to wind itself up.[1] There was something significant in the fact that one of the documents submitted to the conference was a letter from the party founder, Des O'Malley, calling on delegates to face electoral realism and to bring the party to an end. It was made all the more significant by the fact that it was a speech by O'Malley, then a former Fianna Fáil minister, in 1985 that put in train a series of events that brought the party into existence (see chapter 4). As opposed to a letter calling for common sense, this speech stood apart as a unique piece of oratory and went some way towards defining the new party.

In many ways, the Progressive Democrats saw themselves as a typical liberal party in the European sense, economically pro-market, fiscally conservative and socially open. They affiliated themselves with the European Liberal Democrat and Reform Party and were members of Liberal International. What made the emergence of the PDs significant was the fact that Irish politics heretofore had not featured the existence of a European-style liberal party. Almost as interesting is the fact that the party, or at least one with a similar ideology, did not persist.

The aim of this chapter is to show that as a party, the PDs were no different from many other minor parties that had existed in Ireland before them. From their foundation, the PDs were in terminal decline, like many other minor parties, and escaped demise by reinventing their distinctiveness as a political force. Though they certainly exerted a substantive influence on policy during their time in power, their participation in government may have hampered their development as a party to the extent to which they could put down strong organisational roots. Over time, other parties started to borrow the PDs' 'clothes' and it became difficult to identify their particular distinctiveness, and while the party may not have necessarily 'broken the mould' as Clark, in chapter 14, claims, they may well have catalysed the direction of policy while they existed.

The structure of this chapter is as follows. The first section gives an account of the formation of the party and how they fared electorally and in government. We then pay particular attention to the profile of the PD voter and the appeal that the party had to particular social groups. We discuss how this changed over time. The third section analyses the policy platform of the Progressive Democrats, how it changed over time and how it influenced the policy of other parties. Finally, we look at the demise of the PDs and why they were not replaced by another successor party and look at their experience in the context of the broader study of minor political parties.

## The Progressive Democrats (1985-2009)

The foundation of the PDs in December 1985 was the culmination of a series of events that had resulted in O'Malley's expulsion from Fianna Fáil for 'conduct unbecoming' (he abstained on a vote where Fianna Fáil opposed a bill that would have liberalised the sale of contraceptives in Ireland). Approaching their first election in 1987 with five TDs, the PDs were scoring extremely well in opinion polls and were firmly placed as the third most popular party. Given that this campaign came in the aftermath of the collapse of the Fine Gael–Labour coalition over measures of fiscal austerity, it is no surprise that that the economy was foremost in the minds of voters. The PDs advocated a raft of economic and political reforms, including the reduction of taxation rates and the cutting of state expenditure.[2]

Surveys found that PD supporters were predominantly middle-class and lived in urban areas.[3] They were more than twice as likely to have voted for Fine Gael as Fianna Fáil in the past.[4] The issues that they considered most important were unemployment, the need to cut taxes and reduce government spending, followed by the need to crack down on crime. During their first election campaign, the PDs capitalised on the high regard in which Des O'Malley was held by ensuring that he featured prominently on election materials. Indeed, the party's first slogan was 'Dessie can do it'.

The PDs managed to overtake the Labour Party and won fourteen seats with almost 12 per cent of the vote. The Fianna Fáil minority government that was formed after the election implemented a substantive amount of the PDs' economic policy, especially in terms of cutting government spending and reforming tax policy.[5] While this could be deemed a partial success for the PDs, it eroded their distinct appeal, particularly in terms of fiscal policy. Girvin claims that another concern for the PDs was the apparent evaporation of their previous support base.[6] This was a function of the fact that their previous support was quite volatile, and was a 'protest' vote of sorts against the two main parties.

The PD manifesto of 1989 offered little that was radically different.[7] Having rejected the overtures of Fine Gael two years previously, the PDs now presented an 'Agreed Agenda for Action' to the electorate with a view to forming a coalition government if both parties were successful. Des O'Malley pointed out that both were 'like-minded parties and there is broad compatibility between our policy priorities'.[8] Even the titles of the manifestos were almost identical: Fine Gael's platform was named *Putting the Country First* and the PD document was named *Putting the People First*.

At the 1989 election the PDs lost over half of the votes received in 1987 and eight of their seats. Somewhat in forewarning, Gallagher argued that the only way for the PDs to overcome near-certain electoral oblivion was to focus on broadening the appeal of the party from personal votes of TDs to a more durable party vote.[9] The post-election outcome proved slightly better, however, as Haughey's desperation to remain in power led him to look to the PDs to form an unprecedented Fianna Fáil-led coalition. Two PD TDs were appointed to the government (Des O'Malley and Bobby Molloy), and Mary Harney was appointed a minister of state.

This period in government was a tense one,[10] and one of the tactics employed by the PDs to maintain their distinct identity was to use Michael McDowell, one of the 1987 parliamentary party who had lost his seat in the election, as a conscience of sorts for the party. The tipping point was the new Fianna Fáil leader Taoiseach Albert Reynolds' refusal to apologise for describing the evidence of O'Malley to the Beef Tribunal as 'reckless, irresponsible and dishonest'.[11]

In the ensuing election campaign of 1992, the PDs argued that much of what had been achieved was due to their participation and that Reynolds had caused an unnecessary general election by his unreasonable behaviour. This resonated with voters.[12] During the campaign, the PDs shifted focus from fiscal policy towards employment policy – the 1987 fiscal crisis had now become an employment crisis.[13] While the PDs did not enter an alliance with other parties in this campaign, they did not rule out the rainbow coalition of Labour, Fine Gael and the PDs proposed by the Fine Gael leader, John Bruton. The PDs gained four seats, bringing them up to ten, but as Gallagher argued, 'for the PDs, electoral success and power have been inversely related' and they went into opposition.[14]

The years in opposition proved tumultuous for the party, as first its leader and founder resigned; later its general secretary left the party to run as an independent at the 1994 European Parliament elections against O'Malley himself; and then one of its TDs defected to Fianna Fáil. There was also talk of a possible merger between Fine Gael and the PDs in 1993 until it was ruled out by O'Malley.[15]

The party recovered from this turmoil, began working with Fianna Fáil in opposition, and presented an alternative coalition to the country in 1997. The PDs once again had an opportunity to present themselves as a distinct force of the right in Irish politics, given that Fine Gael had attached themselves to two parties of the left.[16] At the beginning of 1997, opinion polls indicated positive support trends for the party but an election campaign that involved controversies over the PDs' perceived desire to introduce 25,000 redundancies in the public service as well as a proposal over single mothers put paid to any sort of bumper yield of seats.[17] Winning just four seats, it formed a minority government with Fianna Fáil. Once again, the PDs had been decimated at the polls, but still managed to enter government. This administration ran much smoother than its 1989-92 predecessors, and the Fianna Fáil leader Bertie Ahern maintained a positive relationship with Mary Harney. It was also aided by the fact that a number of Fianna Fáil ministers shared a similar philosophy with the PDs, such as Minister for Finance, Charlie McCreevy; much of what was implemented could be identified as PD party policy.

Conscious of the fact that failure to distinguish themselves from their coalition partners and other parties in the past usually resulted in poor results at the polls, for the 2002 election, the PDs made the decision to launch attacks on their Fianna Fáil allies, and questioned the desirability of a single-party majority government, which was considered a real possibility. The PDs doubled their representation and, significantly, entered government with Fianna Fáil again. On this occasion, as O'Malley claims, the PDs had not hugely increased their share of the vote, but had been much more prudent in their candidate selection.[18]

The dynamic of this government was changed when Charlie McCreevy was appointed as European Commissioner, following a poor local election for Fianna Fáil in 2004. This deprived the PDs of one of their closest philosophical allies in government. Despite the fact that they got a new leader in Michael McDowell in 2006, the party did not seem to be gaining traction among the public. What further compounded its lack of distinctiveness was the indecisive manner in which McDowell handled allegations of financial impropriety by Ahern in 2006 and 2007. This contrasted significantly with the manner in which Des O'Malley had acted as an 'ethical watchdog' in the 1989-1992 coalition.

The 2007 election proved to be the party's last. It lost six of its eight seats, including that of party leader Michael McDowell. Like 1989 and 1997, when it had suffered electoral losses, the party entered into coalition with Fianna Fáil and the Green Party. Mary Harney was appointed to the government again and a new leader was elected, Senator Ciarán Cannon. The party failed to consolidate itself in the opinion polls and by the end of 2008 came to the decision that its time had come. The remaining four members of the parliamentary party went their separate ways: the party leader Ciarán Cannon was recruited by Fine Gael, while the remaining three sat as independent members of the Oireachtas, and Mary Harney was kept on as a member of the government.

Murphy claims that in the aftermath of the emergence of the PDs, other political parties in Ireland emulated their characteristics and copied their policies, which meant that political debate in electoral competition was distilled down to a discussion of what party was better suited to manage the economy.[19] The distinctiveness of the PDs over time was eroded. On every occasion, bar one, where it was anticipated that the PDs would face electoral oblivion, they reinvented their distinctiveness and subsequently emerged considerably more successful than was expected. In 1987, their low tax and small government policies set them apart from other parties. In 1992, on the foot of leaving government with Fianna Fáil, they made much of the fact that they were well placed to secure high ethical standards in politics and that they struck a chord with the public on the urgency for policies to create and sustain employment. In 2002, they emulated their approach of 1992 and painted themselves as a 'watchdog' for Fianna Fáil in government, best summed up in the slogan, 'One-party government: no thanks!'

Conversely, in elections where the PDs did relatively poorly, this distinctiveness was not so evident. In 1989, Fine Gael and the PDs were broadly supportive of the fiscal path pursued by the Fianna Fáil minority government. In 2007, the PDs had been in government for ten years and there was little to set them apart from their coalition partners, or other political parties. The interesting case is the 1997 election campaign, where arguments that 'Fine Gael tying itself to its left-wing partners' meant that pre-election opinion polls suggested the electorate would welcome for a distinct agenda.[20] However, a disastrous election campaign put paid to any prospective gains, and indeed caused a haemorrhaging of seats. This election showed the volatility of the support base of the PDs. This volatility was a good thing when the PDs offered something distinctive, but could work against them if they did not. In 2007 the fact that the PDs had been in government continuously for ten years did not set them apart from other parties, most of all their coalition partners in Fianna Fáil.

Table 1 presents the PDs' results from general elections. There was a sharp decline in support after the 1987 election and the party never managed to acquire double-digit support after that, suggesting that the party was in terminal decline since its establishment. However, sensible candidate selection masked this, suggesting that while the party met with some success at times in maintaining a distinctive characteristic, it never really succeeded in making its niche area secure from encroachment by other parties. This meant that the party never extended beyond a collection of good candidates rather than one with an organisational base throughout the country, something that a former general secretary John Higgins claimed cost the PDs in the long run.[21]

This terminal decline was evident in the share of the vote won in European and local elections. In the two European elections contested, 1989 and 1994, the party did reasonably well but this was because of the candidates that it had nominated. Over the three local elections contested, the number of local authorities on which the PDs were represented declined over time, suggesting that the geographic concentrations that defined their support in general elections

*Table 1: PD election results 1987-2007*

| Year | Election (type) | First preference vote | % vote | Seats won | No. of candidates |
|------|-----------------|----------------------|--------|-----------|-------------------|
| 1987 | (General) | 210,583 | 11.8 | 14 | 51 |
| 1989 | (General) | 91,013 | 5.5 | 6 | 35 |
| 1989 | (European) | 194,059 | 11.9 | 1 | 4 |
| 1991 | (Local) | 70,415 | 5 | 28 | 78 |
| 1992 | (General) | 80,787 | 4.7 | 10 | 20 |
| 1994 | (European) | 73,696 | 6.5 | 0 | 4 |
| 1997 | (General) | 83,765 | 4.7 | 4 | 26 |
| 1999 | (Local) | 41,362 | 2.9 | 25 | 62 |
| 2002 | (General) | 73,628 | 3.8 | 8 | 20 |
| 2004 | (Local) | 69,650 | 3.9 | 19 | 104 |
| 2007 | (General) | 56,396 | 2.7 | 2 | 30 |

Sources: ElectionsIreland.org

Note: There were PD councillors on 14 of the 34 local authorities after the 1991 and 1999 local elections, and on 11 local authorities after the 2004 elections.

reflected local level. Collins claims that this feature illustrates the 'paradox of the PDs', in that the party managed to achieve a loyal vote in areas like Limerick and Galway where the original Fianna Fáil defectors were represented, but that ultimately a natural PD vote was never actually developed.[22]

To look at the PDs' vote from a comparative perspective, we take their average share of the vote during the 1980s (3.5 per cent), 1990s (4.7 per cent) and 2000s (3.4 per cent) and compare this with the Western European average share of the vote for liberal parties – 11.1 per cent in the 1980s, 11.3 per cent in the 1990s and 10.5 per cent in the 2000s.[23] The striking pattern here is that the proportion of the vote won by Irish liberal parties (i.e. the PDs) is much lower than the average share won by their European neighbours. This is not unusual when comparing minor parties in Ireland with their Western European neighbours. As Clark shows in chapter 14, minor parties in Ireland win a smaller share of the vote than their Western European counterparts. The electoral fate of the PDs does not challenge this.

From an organisational perspective, they never developed a strong organisation around the country. Looking at the membership numbers over time, the trend here mirrors the trend of the electoral support won by the party – a breakthrough in the 1980s, followed by a rapid decline soon after, and then a period of stabilisation towards the mid-1990s. One reason for the rapid decline after 1985 is that the initial membership list was a mailing list, and that once this was filtered to identify active members, reported membership numbers plummeted. However, the party never actually succeeded in putting together a strong organisational base across the country or a slate of party candidates that could consolidate themselves over time in a local area from election to election.

*Figure 1: PD membership figures (1986-2008)*

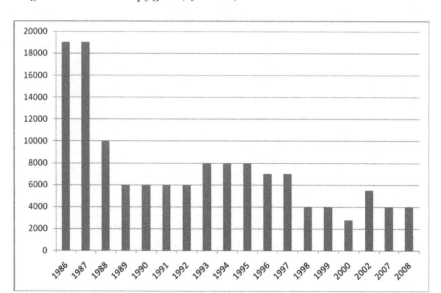

Source: *Irish Political Studies Data – Yearbooks*.
Information was not available for 2001, 2003, 2004, 2005 and 2006.

This weakness was particularly evident in terms of the local roots of the PDs. Collins describes it best when he argues that the party could 'only win votes with very strong candidates'.[24] Mair's argument that politics in Ireland takes place in two spheres which rarely intersect is of particular interest here.[25] Parties must participate in both spheres in order to be successful, i.e. tend to local concerns in the first sphere while engaging in political competition at the national level in the second sphere. As Collins argues, the PDs managed a very distinctive national image, though they did not maintain a strong vote that was independent of the candidates.[26] They needed strong personalities to win seats, and there are many anecdotes of individuals with a high profile being headhunted by the party leadership as potential candidates. A consequence of this was that local organisations were usually no more than an individual candidate's electoral machine. This is borne out if we examine the records of those candidates that were elected to the Dáil for the PDs between 1987 and 2007. Of the twenty elected, just six had never contested any election (local, Dáil and European) before, and five failed to hold the seat at the subsequent election). Two of these six were related to former Fianna Fáil TDs and one had been the president of the Irish Farmers' Association.

A further consequence of this lack of organisation and reliance on a number of strong candidates was a familiar one in the context of minor parties. While quite a number of minor parties, in Ireland and internationally, are personality-driven parties whose prospects for success are inextricably linked to the preferences (and fortunes) of the leader, parties such as the PDs (as well as Clann na Talmhan and Clann na Poblachta) did exist beyond the constituencies of their leaders.[27] However, where a party is a collection of strong candidates, this can lead to a situation where they may have an exceptionally powerful role in the direction of a party. For example, the decision in 2002 to enter government after a successful election was a consequence of the office-seeking motivations of those strong candidates, and the lack of ability of a grassroots organisation to prevent this.

## Profile of the Progressive Democrats' support base

We saw above that the PDs' share of the vote was in terminal decline since its foundation. What is of interest to us in a comparative context is the profile of this voter base. Weeks states that the PDs had a distinct younger middle-class support base.[28] Below, we discuss how the characteristics of their voter base changed over time. Figure 2 shows the annual polling mean of estimated support for the Progressive Democrats. While we report the PDs' electoral results in Table 1, the use of opinion polls provide us with a fuller picture of the size of the PD support base over time.

Like a lot of minor parties, the profile of the PDs' electoral lifespan is unimodal – the high point of their electoral support comes directly after their foundation. They were politically active for just over twenty-two years (six general elections), which is similar to the life-span of other minor parties in Ireland. The downward slope of their electoral support suggests that they were on a trajectory of decline, in that they suddenly appeared and then gradually disappeared over time.

On the basis of socio-economic background, the social group which was more likely to support the PDs was that of those voters who were members of the middle class, or in market research terms, the ABC1 group. However, it is worth noting that the PDs polled quite well across all social groups immediately after their formation. Over time, their appeal among the working class waned significantly as it did among farmers, and middle-class voters were the most consistent group in their support. As Mair suggests, this data gives some support to the claim that the PDs illustrated new social bases of political support in Ireland of the 1980s – voters who were better off were more likely to support a party that followed policies associated with the right, and conversely voters with a working-class background were less likely to support the PDs' policy positions at the ballot box.[29]

*Figure 2: PD opinion poll support (per cent), 1986-2008*

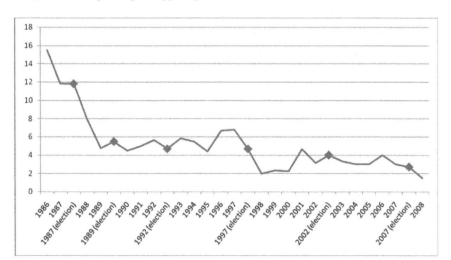

Note: Each year represents the average polling score of the PDs. The diamonds indicate the share of the first preference vote won at the general election in that year.

As with the socio-economic groups, when the PDs came onto the political scene, they polled well among all age groups, apart from the oldest voters. Additionally, the liberal attitude of the PDs towards social issues made it attractive as a party for younger voters and those under sixty-five would not have had the same level of party attachment as those older than them. Generally, the PDs seemed to fare best among voters between twenty-five and forty-nine, but this became less pronounced as time went on, which would suggest that they lost the 'radical' element that set them apart at their formation, especially when appealing to the younger voter. In fact, their lack of appeal to the younger voter contrasts with the ability of other minor parties active at the time to appeal to those groups, such as the Green Party and Sinn Féin, something that is discussed by Marsh *et al.*[30] In terms of gender, there was little discernible difference in levels of support. For a brief period in the late 1990s, women were more likely to support the PDs than men and this could be explained by the election of Mary Harney as Ireland's first female party leader, though that difference did not persist for the entirety of her leadership.

There are distinct patterns in the regional characteristics of the PD support base. Similar to the other categories discussed above, both urban and rural voters supported the PDs at the time of their establishment. As the PDs' share of the vote declined, however, it lost disproportionately more support from rural voters than urban ones. In terms of the provincial breakdown, opinion polls show that in the years immediately following the PDs' foundation, voters in Munster were more likely to be supporters of the PDs. This is due to the personal popularity of

Des O'Malley in his Limerick base, and the fact that other founding members of the PDs represented constituencies in Cork, Waterford and Limerick. This shifted when O'Malley resigned as leader and Dublin then became the most electorally fertile region for the party. After this point, regional support in other parts of the country began to converge.

What the above discussion tells us is that the PDs started off appealing to most categories of voters, and some more than others. As time went on, this universal appeal was eroded and the PDs came to rely on certain categories of voter – usually middle class, young to middle-aged, living in urban areas. If we wanted to paint a picture of a common PD voter it would be one that lived in an urban area (probably Dublin, or anywhere in Munster before 1994), was generally between twenty-five and forty-nine, and a member of the ABC1 social group. Given the discussion that preceded this analysis about the emphasis that the PDs placed on championing policies that appealed to segments of the electorate, the results presented in Figure 2 suggest that they met with some success in so doing. However, their reliance on this particular part of the electorate was akin to putting all the electoral eggs in one vulnerable basket. Once the larger parties succeeded in adopting and campaigning on PD policies, and as the PDs appeared to lose relevance, their appeal to these particular groups became less apparent and ultimately contributed to their electoral demise.

## Progressive Democrats' policy

At the beginning of this chapter, we claimed that the Progressive Democrats saw themselves as a liberal party in the European sense. In order to verify whether or not this is true, it is useful to place the PDs ideologically, drawing on the classification offered by Mair.[31] Mair distinguished nine party families, including a liberal category. However, Coakley, in chapter 3, offers six categories of ideological classification, none of which include a liberal category, but he does include right-wing parties. Coakley argues that while the PDs were not a party of the new right, as understood in the continental European sense, they certainly did feature characteristics that would be attributed to right-wing parties. Manifesto analyses by Laver[32] and Benoit and Laver[33] corroborate this, finding that the Progressive Democrats were towards the right of the ideological spectrum, especially on matters of economic policy.

Using data from the Comparative Manifesto Project,[34] we attempt to shine a light on whether or not the PDs had much in common with a typical liberal party. We analyse the emphasis that the PD manifesto placed on certain policy areas, and compare this with the most emphasised policy areas of an average liberal party from the CMP dataset. There are some slight similarities in that there are four categories that feature in the top ten categories of both parties, such as 'welfare state expansion', 'governmental and administrative efficiency', 'technology and infrastructure' and 'positive sentiments towards equality'.

However, in general, the PDs placed a very clear emphasis on the need for law and order – the third most emphasised priority, something that is not a common feature of an average liberal manifesto. On the other hand, according to this data, the average liberal manifesto has a very clear focus on issues pertaining to political freedom and citizen engagement, as well as the need to pay attention to the most marginalised in society, neither of which feature prominently in the PDs' manifestos. There are only two categories in the top ten categories of the average liberal manifesto pertaining to economics – support for a free market economy, and expansion of the national infrastructure. The PDs' manifestos were primarily concerned with economic matters, such as the opening up of markets, the need to reform taxation, a commitment to economic orthodoxy (i.e. fiscal rectitude) and the need to invest in infrastructure. They did not contain the liberal emphasis on individual rights and freedoms. This calls into question the PDs' self-classification as a liberal party and lends more credence to Coakley's argument that the PDs are better classified as a right-wing party.

Tracking the change in the emphasis placed on certain policy areas over time is a useful exercise in that it gives us a picture of the different priorities of the PDs at each particular election. Economic matters featured prominently in all PD general election manifestos, but differed on the priority given to specific issues. For example, the 1987 manifesto emphasised tax reform and fiscal rectitude, while employment and care for the unemployed were considered priorities in 1989. Again, economic goals were important in 1992, as was an emphasis on governmental efficiency. The attention given to law and order became more pronounced in manifestos from 1989 on, suggesting that the party was embracing characteristics more associated with the right, as opposed to the freedoms and rights associated with liberalism. The PDs constantly focused on the need for civil-service reform and the need to make government administration cheaper. Equality featured quite extensively, as did the need to expand education.

The final perspective from which we can examine PD policy positions is whether or not they caused the other main parties to adjust their own manifesto priorities. It is often argued that the PDs lost their distinctive appeal because the more traditional parties mirrored their policies. In order to assess whether this is truly the case, we took the top ten policy areas emphasised across the PDs' manifestos and compared the pre-1987 average proportion of each category with the post-1987 proportion across the manifestos of Fianna Fáil, Fine Gael and Labour.

Across all three parties, extra emphasis is placed on law and order after the emergence of the PDs. Extra attention is given to the need to open up markets, regulate in favour of consumers and invest in infrastructure across all three, markedly so in the case of Fianna Fáil. Both Labour and Fianna Fáil gave more attention to the need to pursue economic orthodoxy after the PDs entered the political fray. Generally, Fianna Fáil gave more emphasis to nine of the top ten PD policy areas after 1987. This bears out the 'smothering' hypothesis discussed by O'Malley – Fianna Fáil sought to erode the distinctiveness of the PDs by emphasising PD policy as their own.[35] In relation to Fine Gael, there is little drastic change, which probably bears out the similarities between the two parties and may explain why Fine Gael was damaged electorally by the existence of the PDs. Even the Labour Party's policy platform was affected, especially on economic matters. Indeed, the first party to announce a commitment to cut the basic rate of taxation in 2007 was the Labour Party – real evidence of the fact that other parties had sought to move into the space traditionally occupied by the PDs.

There is an interesting point to make here about the adoption of minor parties' policies by larger parties from the above analysis. We have shown that the emergence of the PDs had consequences for the policies emphasised by the main parties. Around the time of the foundation of the PDs, the Green Party had also started to gain traction. This combined with a noticeable positive change in the emphasis given to environmental protection on across all three parties. This is to be expected, given the mirroring that happens between larger parties and smaller parties. Interestingly, however, we notice that the PDs started to place more emphasis on the environment and anti-growth politics over time. This suggests that large parties are not the only ones who can attempt to emulate the policies of minor parties. The evidence from PD manifestos shows that they were more than capable of adopting green policies, especially after the Green Party became electorally relevant. Another example of this, while not necessarily supported by the manifesto analysis, was the PDs' attempt to challenge Sinn Féin as the self-appointed guardians of the nationalist tradition. This became clear on Michael McDowell's accession to leadership, and he made much of his pedigree as a grandson of Eoin MacNeill, one of the founding members of the Irish Volunteer Force. While such movement is difficult to track, it does illustrate the point that parties will copy or mirror the policies of others which has consequences for the distinctiveness of individual parties.

## The demise of the Progressive Democrats

An obvious starting point from which to address the PDs' demise is to examine the political destinations of those candidates who contested elections for the party. We examine the two groups of candidates that contested the last local and general election before the PDs were wound up. There were 104 such candidates in the 2004 local elections, of whom seventy-six did not contest another electoral contest, either locally or nationally. Of the remaining twenty-eight candidates, over half of them (fifteen) contested subsequent elections as independents, of whom eleven were elected. Five joined Fianna Fáil, of which three were successful in subsequent elections. Seven joined Fine Gael, all of whom were successful in subsequent elections. One candidate fought under the Labour banner and was unsuccessful. None joined Sinn Féin or the Green Party.

Thirty candidates ran for the PDs in their last general election in 2007. Of this group, four were elected to the Dáil and Seanad, of whom one defected to Fine Gael, while the remaining three remained on as independents. Of the thirty candidates, eighteen did not pursue their political career any further after 2007. From the remaining twelve, six became independent, three joined Fianna Fáil, two joined Fine Gael and one joined the Labour Party.

There are a number of things clear from the breakdown presented above. Firstly, in both groups the majority of candidates did not contest any further elections. This suggests two things – they did not feel that there was another party that represented their views, or alternatively, they were not strong local candidates who considered that their electoral prospects would not be improved by joining another party. Secondly, of those who did decide to pursue a political career, there was no clearly preferred party for people who had run for the PDs in the past. That being said, it is noticeable that Sinn Féin, the Green Party, and to a lesser extent, the Labour Party were not attractive homes for former PDs. This is unsurprising given the centre-right ethos of the party. The majority of continuing former PDs opted to compete under an independent label. This lends weight to the point made a number of times in this chapter – that the PDs lacked a strong national organisation throughout the country, but rather selected strong local notables as candidates who then built up a personal organisation around them. Of those who drifted to other parties, Fianna Fáil and Fine Gael were the preferred choices, given that both parties were successful in adopting the PDs' policies over time, and that both offered strong electoral brands for prospective members.

The destination of those voters who voted for the PDs is also of interest. Marsh and Cunningham show that almost 45 per cent of PD voters from 2007 voted for Fine Gael in the 2011 general election.[36] The next most popular option for them in 2011 was the 'Independents/Others' category – a quarter of former PD voters supported such candidates. Unsurprisingly, left-wing parties such as the Greens and Sinn Féin proved to be unpopular to this group – only 3 per cent of the 2007 PD voters supported such candidates in each case, and 11 per cent chose to vote Labour. Fianna Fáil was able to attract only 14 per cent of this group, despite being the PDs' coalition partner for so long.

There are three things clear from these results. The centre-right ethos of PD voters is clear, given the unpopularity of the left-wing options to them. Secondly, Fine Gael's appeal to former PD voters is also clear. This is not unexpected given the fact that the PDs had always been a threat to the Fine Gael vote because of the similarities between the two.[37] Ultimately, the demise of the PDs saw Fine Gael win the lion's share of the old PD vote. Thirdly, similar to the study of the candidates above, a significant cohort of PD voters opted for independent candidates or other smaller parties. Two things can be implied from this: (1) strong local candidates previously with the PDs retained support after the party's demise, and (2) there was a significant segment of the PD voter base that was unhappy with the choices available to them and opted for non-establishment alternatives, showing that the larger parties did not entirely succeed in catering to the preferences of former PD voters.

In understanding the demise of the PDs, it is useful to look at them in a comparative context in terms of Irish politics and international experience. In line with Coakley's analysis in chapter 3, the PDs are classified as a breakaway party as well as being a challenger party (a party that competes with established parties on the basis of the capacity to deliver, as opposed to just policy difference). This classification has consequences for understanding their demise, but also for understanding their emergence. The story around the emergence of the PDs is a familiar one in the case of most minor parties in Ireland. The electoral system, as Weeks points out,[38] assisted in facilitating the emergence of the PDs. Also, their success in the 1980s can be attributed in some part to a public frustration with larger parties, something cited by Coakley in his chapter when he is discussing the emergence of parties in Ireland, and something that is used to explain the emergence of minor parties internationally. Interestingly, looking at where former PD voters went after 2007, we observe that a quarter of them chose not to vote for established parties, suggesting a lasting distrust of or disillusionment with larger parties.

The second area of interest, comparatively speaking, is the life-span of the PDs. As highlighted in Table 1 and in Figure 2, the PDs' share of the vote has been in terminal decline since their foundation. The PDs' life cycle is similar to that of Clann na Talmhan, Clann na Poblachta and the Farmers' Party, in that it followed a pattern of steady decline following initial electoral success. Pedersen's framework for discussing the life cycle of minor parties is insightful in relation to the PDs.[39] The PDs crossed the first three thresholds of proclamation, authorisation and representation easily in its first few years. The fact that Fine Gael identified them as a potential coalition partner in 1989 (and their subsequent entry into government) indicated their passing of Pedersen's fourth threshold – relevance. However, as O'Malley argues in chapter 5, relevance need not be equated with entering government, but rather an interaction of entering government and being able to stay distinct while in government. Once the PDs fell below this threshold of relevance, most clearly between 2004 and 2007 (because they brought nothing distinctive to government), their next step was to fall below the threshold of representation which can be described as the beginning of their end. Similarly, Weeks, in chapter 1, claims that the reasons for the emergence of minor parties can also explain their decline. There is some truth in this when discussing the PDs – they set themselves up as being outside of the political establishment, but may have undermined this claim on their entry into government in 2002 and 2007. As opposed to the breakaway party of 1985, they became integrated into the political establishment.

Throughout their existence, the PDs could be regarded as a 'challenger' party, which came about because of internal leadership challenges in Fianna Fáil. This has consequences for understanding their demise. Ultimately, they did not have the organisational strength of larger parties (explained somewhat by their frequency in government) and the distinctiveness of their particular policy agenda was eroded over time by their more established competitors.

Coakley, in his chapter, argues that Pedersen's definition of 'relevance' is subjective, that is, it is more than just entry into government. This is especially true in the case of the Progressive Democrats. Throughout their existence, the PDs hovered around the threshold of relevance, and constantly sought to make sure that they passed it either through strategic candidate selection, or distinctive campaigning or policy positions. Every time that the PDs came close to supposed oblivion, they found a reason upon which they could reinvent themselves and illustrate their distinctive characteristic, whether that was in fiscal policy in 1987, in employment and ethics in 1992, or as a watchdog for Fianna Fáil in 2002. Their record suggests that there was only so much reinventing that would work. Added to this was the fact that after ten years in government, by 2007 the PDs had become part of the 'establishment', no longer seen as 'radical' but certainly thought of as 'redundant', given the vigour with which other parties had succeeded in emulating their agenda by the time of their demise.

As a very final point, it is worthwhile to consider why no successor party emerged to replace the PDs, given the parallels which can be drawn between the economic stagnation that faced Ireland in the 1980s and the economic crisis that has existed in Ireland since 2008 (see chapter 1). As Weeks discusses, prior to the 2011 election there was speculation that a number of high-profile figures would band together to form a grouping similar in nature to the PDs, though it never made it off the ground.[40] Why did a 'new PDs' not form? The economic policy for which the PDs stood in the 1980s – the reduction of government expenditure, the privatisation of state assets and the opening up of sheltered parts of the economy to competition formed a substantive section of the programme of reform that was outlined in the IMF (International Monetary Fund)–ECB (European Central Bank)–EC (European Commission) agreement. Given that a 'forced consensus' existed in the form of this agreement, there was little appetite among the electorate for a party that supported a large amount of the IMF-ECB-EC deal that manifested itself in the form of severe austerity. It is interesting to observe the success of parties of the left in 2011, which compares and contrasts with the breakthrough of the PDs in 1987. While no new party emerged, the United Left Alliance was brought together to contest the election, winning 2.7 per cent of the vote and five seats in the Dáil. Sinn Féin also dramatically increased its Dáil representation to fourteen seats and managed to secure almost 10 per cent of the vote. While economic policy (and to some extent social policy) was challenged by the emergence of the PDs in the 1980s, the breakthrough of the

ULA and Sinn Féin in 2011 would seem to indicate that there were significant challenges to the policy consensus (as brought about by the IMF–ECB–EC agreement) from outside the main establishment parties. The comparison is not entirely clear-cut, but it can provide some useful preliminary observations as to why a new (right-wing) party has not emerged.

## Conclusion

It is difficult to do justice to the story of the rise and fall of the Progressive Democrats in one chapter. Following elections where the party had fared poorly commentators often stated that the PDs were irretrievable, only for the party to bounce back in the following election. However, the PDs eventually ran out of lives. They were more successful than other Irish minor parties, being in government for the majority of their existence. This success masked the fact that the traditional parties became adept at embracing the economic philosophy espoused by the PDs and that the PDs themselves were organisationally quite weak. While it is true that the PDs exercised massive influence in the governments in which they participated, this was also as much a result of the fact that their partners (Fianna Fáil) had seen the appeal of that agenda and adopted it as their own. However, the fact that other parties did try to 'steal the PDs' clothing' is testament to the fact that the emergence of the PDs did bring about a change in policy. They may not have broken the mould, but for a short time at least, they certainly changed its colour.

# 8

# Seeking the Fianna Fáil Vote: Why do Interest Groups Run for Office in Ireland?

*Gary Murphy*

## Introduction[1]

Since independence, political parties have been central to the stability of Irish democracy. Schattschneider's decades-old controversial view that democracy is unthinkable save in terms of parties seemed particularly relevant to Ireland.[2] The dominance of political parties is unquestioned at government level.[3] Yet a major part of the public astonishment over the result of the 2011 general election was due to the fact that the collapse of the Fianna Fáil vote, a loss of fifty-eight seats and 25 per cent of the vote since 2007, although heralded by the opinion polls, still came as a significant surprise to much of the population, including many within Fianna Fáil itself. That Fianna Fáil, the most successful party of modern European democracies, the natural party of Irish government, the party that had dominated the state since it first took office in 1932, could be reduced to 17 per cent of the first-preference vote and twenty seats out of 166, seemed to show that in Ireland the survival of no political party could be taken for granted. Irish political parties including minor parties who had played active parts in government had come and gone before; Clann na Talmhan, Clann na Poblachta, Democratic Left and the Progressive Democrats were all part of inter-party or coalition governments with party members serving in senior ministries. All eventually disappeared.

This chapter will explore the reasons interest groups run candidates for national office. It assesses why interest groups in Ireland have not been particularly successful in attracting the votes of the people at general elections. Finally, it offers some thoughts on why, with the collapse of the Fianna Fáil vote in 2011, a single-issue interest group did not emerge to offer an alternative to what seemed to be the failed policies of the political party elites. While independents did remarkably well, a puzzle remains as to why no new party emerged to offer themselves as an alternative to the existing party status quo (on this theme, see chapter 1). Although not strictly minor parties *per se*, interest groups are very much relevant as they often exhibit the features of a micro-party, and in many cases tend to be the precursor to the emergence of political parties. In 2011 the political conditions leading up to the general election seemed somewhat conducive to the possibility of such a minor party emerging. This did not happen.

## The demise of Fianna Fáil

A classically populist party since its foundation in 1926, Fianna Fáil could prob-ably best be described as a catch-all party, as it drew support from all sections of the population.[4] Small and large farmers alike, businessmen, the skilled artisan middle class, the manual working class, labourers, and the unemployed, all saw Fianna Fáil as a party that could represent them and their ambitions. That it con-sistently took over 40 per cent of the vote at general election time was testament to this remarkable chameleon-like ability to attract support from all groups and social classes. By the 2011 general election Fianna Fáil had been in power for sixty of its eighty-four-year existence.[5] In many ways it mirrored the state it theoreti-cally served. In 1981 Tom Garvin said of Fianna Fáil that its penetration 'into the bureaucracy appears to be very great, and is due mainly to the fact that the party has had a near monopoly on public office for almost fifty years and has, by its own success, generated social categories created in its own image'.[6] This articulate explanation seemed to hold up to, and immediately beyond, the general election of 2007. All then went spectacularly south with the infamous bank guarantee scheme of 29 September 2008.

In the May 2007 election Fianna Fáil received 42 per cent of the vote. A series of polls up to the beginning of September 2008 showed them consistently within the 40-per-cent bracket and comfortably Ireland's most popular party. However, once the guarantee was enacted and the consequences of that decision began to become apparent, support for Fianna Fáil plummeted to a degree never witnessed before. The first TNS MRBI poll after the guarantee had Fianna Fáil at 27 per cent, a gargantuan drop in Irish terms of 15 per cent from which it would never recover, while the first Red C poll taken in late October 2008 had them at 26 per cent.[7] Once it became clear throughout 2009 that the bailout of the banks and the establishment of the National Assets Management Agency (NAMA) were not the panacea for the Irish economy as they had been portrayed by Fianna Fáil as being, then it simply became a matter of how low Fianna Fáil would go.[8] The social categories it had created in its image right across the Irish state had deserted it once its reputation for economic competency was lost.

One of the traditional benefits of interest-group activity for democratic societies is that it strengthens representation by articulating interests and advancing views that are, for the most part, ignored by political parties. In Ireland, however, such interests were usually catered for by Fianna Fáil and, for the most part, were not ignored. That is why Fianna Fáil governed so successfully in Ireland for so long and that is also why the result of the Irish general election of 2011 is so fascinating. Interest-group activity also theoretically provides a means of influencing governments between elections as interest groups are largely focused on, 'influencing policy outcomes, trying to force issues onto, or up the political agenda, and framing the underlying dimensions that define policy issues'.[9] This is also the case in Ireland, but again in Ireland Fianna Fáil usually proactively reacted to policy issues from interest group actors to sustain its hold on the electorate.[10]

Interest group activity in Ireland spans numerous strands and tends to be associated in the public mind on one level through the process of social partnership, where sectional groups such as trade unions, employers, and farmers interests have had central roles since 1987, driven on politically by Fianna Fáil, and on another level through various cause-centred groups who have attempted to influence policy outcomes in a specific area. One of the fundamental precepts of interest group study is that such groups do not seek public office. As Allern and Bale point out, both political parties and interest groups, 'aggregate individual interests and preferences into collective demands and seek to influence the form and content of public policy'.[11] Thus a satisfactory definition of an interest group will stipulate two criteria: that the organisation has some autonomy from government and that it tries to influence policy outcomes.[12] Beyers, Eising and Maloney refer to the concept of informality as a key factor in defining an actor as an interest group noting that such informality relates to the fact, 'that interest groups do not normally seek public office or compete in elections, but pursue their goals through frequent informal interactions with politicians and bureaucrats'.[13] Political parties, however, attempt to influence public policy and stand for office.[14] The essence of a political party as Katz points out, lies in its intention and willingness to 'rule and to take responsibility for ruling'.[15] In Ireland, Fianna Fáil in essence pulled off the neat trick of being Ireland's dominant political party who clearly wanted to rule and take responsibility for ruling while at the same time governing through seeking to accommodate the sectional interests of society.

With political competition in Ireland becoming both more congested and competitive in recent years, some interest groups have attempted to move beyond the informality stage by putting forward members of their groups for election at both national and local level. This has met with varying degrees of success and gives rise to conceptual difficulties as to whether those who seek public office can be categorised as interest groups at all. In that context this chapter asks why interest groups put forward candidates for public office. One way of looking at this question is to suggest that such groups were, in essence, trying to replace Fianna Fáil in that their own particular interest did not fit into the image of the Irish state created by Fianna Fáil. Such groups thus ran for election as they saw the Dáil as the place where Fianna Fáil had made modern Ireland in its own image. This was the nirvana for interest groups to get their message across:

a message they saw Fianna Fáil, and indeed by extension any opposing coalition government alternative, as ignoring.

## Seeking office: the political party interest group dichotomy

Interest groups have long been divided into those who advocate on behalf of sections of the population (trade unions, employers' groups and farmers), and those who advocate for particular causes. Different interest groups will have different spans of longevity depending on whether they are sectional interests who exist perpetually to defend their members' interests within the farming community, the labour movement, and business organisations, or those groups who exist for a particular cause and tend to dissipate when that cause is completed. Interest groups can also have articulation at a local and national level depending again on the type of group. Where interest groups certainly do differ from political parties is that when they put forward candidates for election in Ireland they are not interested in capturing the main organs of power and in ruling *per se*, but rather are more interested in supporting political parties and by extension governments that can provide largesse for the group's members and their goals. That essentially is where the difference lies between interest groups and political parties no matter even if interest groups put forward members for election to public office. The Standards in Public Office Commission (SIPOC) for instance offers a clear distinction in relation to political parties and lobby groups and the electoral acts do impose certain obligations on what SIPOC calls Lobby/Campaign groups. These relate to groups which: receive donations for a campaign that is conducted to promote or procure a particular outcome in relation to a policy or policies or functions of the government or any public authority or to influence the outcome of a referendum or election, or intend to incur expenditure to promote or oppose a candidate or a political party at a Dáil, European Parliament or presidential election, or to otherwise influence the outcome of the election. (Standards in Public Office Commission)

While interest group activity in Ireland is best categorised between sectional groups and cause-centred groups, we can place those interest groups who are involved in explicit political action in four separate categories:

- Those that (permanently) lobby outside the political system and do not put themselves forward for election
- Those that lobby within the system such as the social partnership sectional groups
- Those that run candidates for elected office at both local and national level;
- Those that campaign in specific referendums

There can be some carryover between the latter two categories as some groups both run candidates at elections and also campaign at referendums. Nevertheless there are groups which come into existence just to campaign at referendums, the emergence of Cóir during the Lisbon Treaty referendums is a good example, and thus we are justified in including four categories.

*Table 1: Examples of groups involved in explicit political action*

| Lobby groups within the political system | Groups which run for office | Groups which campaign at referendums |
|---|---|---|
| Trade Unions (ICTU) | National H-Block Committee (1981) Independent Health Alliance (2002) | Pro-Life Amendment Campaign (1983) Anti-Amendment Campaign (1983) Mother and Child Campaign (2002) |
| Farmer's Organisations (IFA) | People Before Profit (2007, 2009) United Left Alliance (2011) | Divorce Action Group (1986, 1995) No-Divorce Campaign (1986, 1995) |
| Business Organisations (IBEC) Libertas (2008, 2009) | | Cóir (2008, 2009) Ireland for Europe (2009) We Belong (2009) |

While the latter two categories cause specific problems for students of interest-group politics, sectional groups have also strayed into the electoral scene on occasions. The question of interest group definition is important here as some of the main sectional interest groups (labour, farmers, business) have had links to various political parties going back many years. The trade union movement for instance has long been a breeding ground for politicians on the left. A number of former Democratic Left TDs, including subsequent Labour Party leaders such as Pat Rabbitte and Eamon Gilmore were full-time trade union officials before becoming members of Dáil Eireann while the Labour Party itself has a long history of union officials running under its banner at election time. Of even more importance is the fact that there are twelve trade unions officially affiliated to the Labour Party. These include SIPTU and the Amalgamated Transport and General Workers' Union, which between them account for about 44 per cent of union membership in the Republic. The modern association between the Labour Party and the organised trade union movement goes back to the early 1960s when a number of trade unions, including the Irish Transport and General Workers' Union, re-affiliated to the party. Originally, the Labour Party was conceived by the Irish Trades Union Congress in 1912 to act as the political voice of organised labour and came into being in 1922 as a party committed to defending workers' rights.[16] Over the years, the trade union movement has also played an important financial role within the Labour Party through affiliation fees. For its part, the Irish Farmers' Association, while it has had links with both Fianna Fáil and Fine Gael has also spawned the political careers of people as diverse as Tom Parlon of the now defunct Progressive Democrats and Rickard Deasy of the Labour Party. Nevertheless sectional groups do not as a rule engage in electoral politics.

As Varley discusses in chapter 9, the farming community dallied occasionally with electoral politics but never made any long-term breakthrough in the electoral game, ultimately coming to the conclusion that as they could not win in this game they were better off influencing the result from the sidelines. In this they have proved remarkably successful, gaining official government recognition in the early 1960s in relation to input into the formal agricultural policy of the state and being central players in the social partnership process from 1987.[17] There were a variety of business parties in the early years of the Irish state but these quickly disappeared and were subsumed into Cumann na nGaedheal in particular.[18] A key point to make here is that parties which defend or promote specific sectional interests such as the farming and business communities are not necessarily interest groups *per se* but stand for election on a platform which tends to be limited towards specific sections of the population

Other interest groups, however, have not been shy to either put members up for election to public office or attempt to sway referendum results. Moving beyond the major sectional interests, the relationship between interest groups and the political process is becoming more important in an age where the decline of party membership in European democracies has resulted in parties in contemporary Europe losing their capacity to engage citizens.[19] Interest groups have moved into this gap. Concomitant to the decline of party membership has been a significant rise in both interest group numbers and numbers in interest groups across Europe.[20] In an Irish context, despite the fact that party loyalism persists, with those who 'feel close' to a particular party hovering at about 25 per cent since the 1980s,[21] this is not reflected in party membership. With the collapse of the Fianna Fáil vote in 2011, this figure must now be seen as outdated. Marsh suggested that about 80,000 people, under 3 per cent of the population, were members of political parties.[22] Mair and van Biezen gave a slightly higher figure of 86,000 or 3.14 per cent at the end of the 1990s.[23] A decade later, however, they were estimating that it was at 2 per cent.[24] Weeks, using figures supplied by individual party headquarters, reckoned party membership in Ireland stood at 118,500.[25] The figure of 65,000 for Fianna Fáil seems excessively high and apparently includes lapsed members who the party would like to entice back into the fold. In fact, one of Fianna Fáil's own internal party reports from 2004 estimated that the true figure was only about a quarter of this.[26] For comparative purposes membership of the Irish Farmers' Association stands at about 85,000.[27]

More instructively is that in a WorldValues Survey conducted at the beginning of the 1990s, the percentage of the population in Ireland belonging to a voluntary organisation was 49 per cent.[28] The most recent data for Irish membership of voluntary organisations shows that over 47 per cent of people are active on a weekly basis in meeting with other members of their organisation, and 58 per cent meet fellow members at least twice a month.[29] A recent government report suggested that in 2006 almost two thirds of people aged sixteen and over participated in at least one group activity while participation in political groups was as low as one per cent across all age groups.[30]

## Seeking office: the independent politician – interest group dichotomy

Once Fianna Fáil accepted the politics of coalition by going into government with the Progressive Democrats in 1989, and copper fastened it in 1992 by coalescing with the Labour Party, Irish party competition became more volatile and unstable. Since then the unpredictable nature of the Irish party system has opened up scenarios whereby interest groups have viewed elections to the Dáil as an attractive avenue to achieve their goals. Such groups in effect turned away from Fianna Fáil and the party system to get things done and decided that becoming part of the system was the way to policy success. Mair and Weeks note that one future scenario, 'might envisage many voters turning away from party politics as such, and relying more heavily on competing personal appeals of the party leaders or even the local candidates, which could lead to even greater successes for independent, single-issue candidates'.[31] The rise of independents as a major factor in Irish electoral politics has ensured that candidates representing various organisations such as hospital action groups and other similar causes have had a significantly increased profile. Weeks notes that independents, along with the Labour Party, are the only grouping to have had continuous representation in the Dáil and regularly occupy between one in fifteen and one in twenty seats.[32]

Bolleyer and Weeks, in a survey of why Irish independents ran for office, noted that significantly more independents than party candidates rated being asked to run by a group or organisation campaigning for specific issues as an important incentive in their decision to run.[33] Independent candidates thus, somewhat surprisingly, seem more motivated by substantial policy objectives when compared to party candidates. Yet 89 per cent of independents cited representing their area as an important factor in their decision to run for public office, with over 70 per cent ranking this as the most important reason. While independents can be motivated by both policy and local issues, a convergence of the two often leads to independents seeking the vehicle of a group when putting themselves forward for election. This can also act in the other direction where groups may also seek high profile independents to attach themselves to. The puzzle for students of interest group politics remains why some such groups, in effect, betray a seemingly key *raison d'être* of their existence by putting themselves forward for election. Seeking public office in effect means groups attempt to articulate their interests from within the charmed circle of power that is the Dáil as distinct from trying to influence governments from outside the electoral process as should be the theoretical norm in interest group politics.

One of the major strands of interest group study is corporatism. While corporatism has a number of varying definitions, the corporatist model, in the main, suggests that interest groups are closely associated with the formal political process and play a critical role in both the formulation and the implementation of major political decisions. Pope Pius XI's papal encyclical Quadragesimo Anno of 1931, with its call for a reconstruction of the social order, served as the intellectual stimulus for Irish corporatists.[34] Ireland in the 1930s and 1940s flirted with elements of corporatist thought, which condemned both material capitalism as well as the traditional bogeyman, material communism. This form of corporatism, with its demands for a national vocational council, which would either advise or supersede parliament, did not have much to recommend it to the main political parties, particularly Fianna Fáil, as it would have curbed their growing power in the nascent Irish state. The National Guard founded in 1932 was the first incarnation of this new type of politics with the party showing certain elements of a type of fascism in terms of programme, organisation and public profile. After supporting Cumann na nGaedheal in the 1933 election it later merged with the larger party and the National Centre Party to form Fine Gael with Eoin O'Duffy as its first leader. O'Duffy later left Fine Gael to form his own party the National Corporate Party which collapsed almost immediately under the weight of vanity of its leader.[35]

A decade after the National Guard vanished from the scene, a new flowering of corporatist thought emerged with the formation of Ailtirí na hAiséirigh which dedicated itself to establishing a truly Gaelic, Christian Ireland under the direction of an all-powerful leader who would be advised by a Council of a Hundred in which there would be no political parties.[36] One commentator has argued that Ailtirí na hAiséirigh was a, 'response to a desire for action and committed leadership within a section of the republican population disillusioned with the stagnation of post independence Ireland and … was very much a party of its time'.[37] However, in a democracy that had quickly stabilised itself after the bloodshed of the civil war, Ailtirí na hAiséirigh was really nothing more than a corporatist fantasy party; in reality a fascist project of Gearóid O'Cuinneagáin, supported financially by Ernest Blythe, which quickly went under and faded away after the 1948 general election. A corporatist revival of sorts re-emerged in 1954 as National Action and later as the Christian Democratic Party in 1961 but this was in reality nothing more than a personal vehicle for the political ambitions of the equally amorphous Sean Loftus, who in later guises would appear on ballot papers in different elections as Sean D. Christian Democratic and Sean Dublin

Bay-Rockall on which he was elected as an independent in 1981. Another short-lived political party which was in reality a personal political project was the Monetary Reform Association of the 1940s led by Oliver J. Flanagan. This, like many other like-minded crypto right wing parties, was subsumed into Fine Gael when Flanagan, joined them in 1952. One final personal political project worth mentioning here is Aontacht Éireann. Founded in September 1971 by Fianna Fáil activists who broke with the party following the so-called 'Arms Crisis' of 1970, it was in essence a vanity project of Kevin Boland who resigned from the government at that time in sympathy with sacked ministers, Neil Blaney and Charles Haughey and was later expelled from Fianna Fáil. Advocating, rather bizarrely considering the nature and strength of the Irish army, an overtly aggressive policy towards Northern Ireland, Aontacht Éireann performed spectacularly badly in the 1973 general election and did not put itself forward as a party for election again, although Boland did unsuccessfully fight a by-election in 1976, gaining a paltry 4.75 per cent of the vote.

In contrast to the crypto-corporatist groups described above, there have also been a number of groups who we may describe as harbingers of pluralism. The pluralist model of interest group behaviour maintains that individual interest groups apply pressure on political elites in a competitive manner and attributes power in policy making to individual groups operating in particular areas at particular times. In that context there have been a number of minor sectional interest groups which formed as political parties, ran for office, tended to be unsuccessful and then disappeared again. Amongst these were the Ratepayers' Association, the Town Tenants' Association, the Irish Housewives' Association, and a Blind Men's Party, while a National Army Spouses' Association fielded three candidates under the Army Wives' banner in 1989.[38]

More recently, the People before Profit Alliance first ran candidates on a broadly socialist agenda in the 2007 general election and won five seats in Dublin in the 2009 local elections. The People before Profit Alliance is slightly different from the other groups listed above in that their agenda is certainly wider but we can still accurately describe them as evidence of a type of pluralism in action as they are clearly targeting a certain section of the population to apply pressure on political elites in an attempt to get their policies enacted. In any event, they made a significant breakthrough when, as part of the United Left Alliance, two of their candidates, Richard Boyd Barrett and Joan Collins, were elected in the 2011 general election.

Categorising interest groups into sectional and cause-centred groups allows us to reassess the role of independents in Irish politics. The reality is that many of the independents who have ran for, and been elected to, Dáil Eireann are representatives of interest groups which advocate a particular cause. Cause-centred groups can be divided into two categories: those who are *ad hoc* groups formed to press for a single measure and who then disband once the measure has been enacted or fades from the political scene, and organisations with a more permanent mission.[39]

These groups have used a variety of methods to raise public consciousness in their attempts to influence public policy. While their tactics initially took the form of simple lobbying of both local and national politicians, groups who form for a single measure are now much more likely to actually put up members for election. Why is this so? Cause-centred candidates tend to be at their most influential, and thus effective for their own groups, when they have minority governments looking for their vote. The main reason for running candidates in elections is the hope of having a disproportionate influence on government should their candidate get elected and be in a position to influence votes within the Dáil. For example, the Roscommon hospital candidate Tom Foxe was elected in Longford–Roscommon in 1989 with a massive 22 per cent of the first preference vote, and used his pivotal position in the Dáil to secure guarantees concerning the status of Roscommon hospital in exchange for his support in a crucial vote in 1990 when a motion of no confidence in the Minister for Health was defeated only when he switched his vote.[40] Foxe, a member of the Roscommon Hospital Action Committee, in effect a single issue interest group, stood and was elected solely on a platform of opposition to health cuts, then being implemented by the minority Fianna Fáil government. While he retained his seat at the 1992 election, his vote fell by 10 per cent and he eventually lost his seat at the 1997 election.

The Roscommon Hospital Action Committee, however, did not simply go away with Foxe's Dáil defeat and has run candidates at both local and national level ever since. It re-emerged, much to the Fianna Fáil-led government's annoyance, during the 2008 Lisbon Treaty campaign. This group was one of many lobby groups, who, opposed to the downgrading of various hospitals around the state, actively campaigned against the Lisbon Treaty, although they accepted that there was no link between the treaty and the hospital issue. In an era, however, where lobby groups are happy to use any means to highlight their own issue this group maintained that this was the only way to get the government's attention. In any event, the Lisbon Treaty was decisively rejected in the constituency of Roscommon–South Leitrim with 54 per cent of people voting no. As the treaty was rejected throughout rural Ireland, it is difficult to estimate how much influence groups like the Roscommon Hospital Action Committee actually had. For instance, the two most rigorous examinations of the treaty result to date do not mention local factors at all in their analysis of the result.[41] But it is reasonable to assume, given the high profile nature of this group over many years, that its opposition to the Lisbon Treaty must have had some impact on voter intentions in the referendum in that particular area.

## Interest groups and referendums

One of the categories in which we placed interest groups who are involved in explicit political action related to those that campaign in specific referendums. Thus the question arises why interest groups involve themselves in referendums. One of the main reasons why cause-centred groups sprung to prominence in Ireland in the early 1980s was due to the referendums that took place on the question of abortion and divorce between 1983 and 1995. These in turn can be placed side by side with the emergence of a number of women's interest groups who became important lobbying agencies for changes in family law and the status of women during the 1970s from issues such as the wider availability of contraception to family home protection.[42]

One of the main women's interest groups AIM (Action, Information, Motivation) had lobbied governments throughout the 1970s, without success, for the repeal of the constitutional ban on divorce. On the other side of the moral fence were a number of groups who wished to impose a distinctly catholic view of morality on the Irish state who would become the acknowledged leaders in the field of pressure group politics. Indeed the Society for the Protection of the Unborn Child sprung up completely unannounced in 1981 and within two years had, along with other like-minded groups, under the umbrella of the Pro-Life Amendment Campaign (PLAC), successfully persuaded the government of the day to call a referendum with the purpose of introducing an amendment which would, in effect, guarantee the rights of the unborn child and constitutionally outlaw abortion.[43] Thus it was interest groups who effectively manoeuvred the government into calling a referendum in which they would play the key role. The Fine Gael–Labour government of the day was completely ill-equipped to deal with such a highly organised pressure group and the result was a decade of social division, whose effects still linger as evidenced by the refusal of abortion to disappear as a political issue. For instance, during the Lisbon Treaty referendum campaign in 2008, the interest group Cóir, which was a vigorous opponent of the treaty from an ultra conservative stance, argued that its acceptance through the adoption of the Charter of Fundamental Rights would change Irish law in the areas of abortion and euthanasia.[44]

How did it come about that referendums would become the vehicle through which moral interest groups would attempt to influence public policy in this area? Previous Irish referendums had seen some interest group involvement but none on the scale of the 1980s. The original 1937 referendum on the constitution spearheaded by Fianna Fáil saw a number of women's groups complain that the constitution discriminated against women and denounced the omission of any statement regarding women's rights as sinister and regressive.[45] The 1972 referendum on EEC membership saw sectional groups actively campaign; farmers were enthusiastic supporters of a yes vote, while the trade union movement advocated a no vote, but given the final outcome, it is likely that significant numbers of trade unionists actually voted yes.

The 1980s, however, saw interest group activity in referendums go to a whole new level. The principal reason for this was that, while earlier referendums were very much driven by political parties, the impetus for the original abortion referendum in 1983 came from a specific interested lobby group: PLAC. Gaining access to both Fianna Fáil and Fine Gael senior politicians, PLAC was the driving force behind persuading both major parties that the legal ban on abortion could be overturned in the courts and that a constitutional ban on abortion was imperative. This, in reality, was a very unlikely scenario and was in many respects a very simplistic argument, but one that was very persuasive to politicians and to the electorate as a whole. Eventually the wording that Fianna Fáil had put forward, which was acceptable to PLAC, was adopted against the advice of the government's attorney-general, Peter Sutherland.

Paradoxically, when those groups who campaign on a conservative view of morality enter the mainstream political arena seeking electoral support in national elections, they garner a risible amount of support. After the 1995 divorce referendum was barely carried by only 9,000 votes, both the then No-Divorce Campaign vice-chairman, and Christian Solidarity Party chairman Dr Gerard Casey, and Richard Greene of another anti-divorce group Muintir na hÉireann stated that they would be looking at the next general election for the 50 per cent of voters, as they saw it, whose views were now no longer represented in the Dáil. Yet in the 1997 election held just over eighteen months later, Greene lost his deposit in Dublin South, polling just over 1,400 first preferences, while Casey, running in the generally liberal Dún Laoghaire constituency, also lost his deposit, receiving exactly 2,000 first preferences. Two years later, in the 1999 European elections, Casey again lost his deposit running on a generally conservative Catholic agenda in Dublin, receiving 3.3 per cent of the first preference vote. What this clearly shows is that individuals who play major roles in mobilising large sections of the population to vote a certain way in morality-based referendums struggle at national election time when the issue base is obviously much wider. It may also show that both Fianna Fáil and Fine Gael overestimated the ability of pro-life groups to hurt them electorally in the early to mid-1980s. However, with the contest between the two major parties as close as it had ever been since both had been founded over a half century previously, it is not perhaps surprising that both parties made every effort possible to placate the pro-life group. Ignoring this group was a risk neither political party was willing to take.

Two further abortion referendums took place in 1992 and 2002 due to the Supreme Court's decision in the X case of 1992 when it found that the threat of suicide provided grounds for abortion within the meaning of the eighth amendment to the constitution. Fundamentally, this was an interpretation which had intrinsically the opposite effect to that anticipated by those who had supported the 1983 amendment. Notwithstanding the Supreme Court's judgement in 1992 and subsequent referendums, the reality remains that abortion is not available on demand in Ireland and the Irish Medical Organisation does not allow its members to perform them. In that context the *raison d'être* of all interest groups, that of achieving public policy, would seem to have been achieved by pro-life lobbying groups in that abortion remains constitutionally illegal except in extremely rare circumstances and it is most unlikely that any there will be any change to the *status quo* in the foreseeable future.

Many of the same individuals who were involved in the abortion referendums on different sides also showed up in differently named groups, particularly on the no side, during the two divorce referendums of 1986 and 1995. Moreover, it was the constant campaigning of such interest groups as AIM, the Divorce Action Group and the Irish Council for Civil Liberties in lobbying for divorce from 1981 onwards which was a critical factor in persuading the Fine Gael–Labour government of 1982-1987 to eventually seek a change in the constitution to allow for divorce in 1986, and laid the foundation for the second referendum in 1995 after the original referendum was defeated. In the words of journalist, Carol Coulter, who followed the campaign closely, 'without the efforts of members of voluntary organisations with direct experience of marriage breakdown who ... felt it was necessary to campaign for divorce independently of the government, the amendment would have been lost'.[46]

The other main area of referendum politics where interest group politics have been important has been on the European issue. A new dynamic emerged in interest group politics during the 2008 Lisbon Treaty referendum, when a previously unheard of organisation called Libertas became a key driver in the no campaign. Depicting itself as a movement dedicated to campaigning for greater democratic accountability and transparency in the institutions of the EU, although it would be more accurate to describe it as a group set up to defeat the Lisbon Treaty, Libertas under its leader, businessman Declan Ganley, brought a completely new dynamic to opposing EU referendums in Ireland. Up to the Lisbon Treaty such opposition mostly came from groups on the left of the political spectrum, but for Lisbon, Libertas, arriving onto the political scene early in 2008, actively campaigned on the idea that the treaty was bad for Irish business. The Lisbon Treaty campaign became a melting pot of sorts for lobby groups from across the political divide with those on the no side ranging from Cóir, an offshoot of Youth Defence, and other anti-abortion elements, to Libertas on the right of the political spectrum and from the Peace and Neutrality Alliance, to People Before Profit on the left. After the referendum was successfully defeated, Libertas announced that it was considering running candidates in the 2009 elections to the European parliament and reckoned it could win up to seventy seats.[47] In that it was true to its word as it reconstituted itself in December 2008 as a party, rather than simply a movement, or more strictly speaking an interest group, declaring its intention to run candidates in all the states of the European Union. Libertas eventually contested elections in fourteen European states, running over 600 candidates but performed spectacularly badly, winning only one seat in France. Ganley came close to winning a seat in the Ireland North West constituency, but on coming up short he subsequently declared that he was retiring from politics. He returned, however, to the Irish political scene just three months later to campaign, unsuccessfully this time, against the second Lisbon Treaty referendum.

Prior to the European Parliament elections one commentator argued that with the disbandment of the Progressive Democrats there was room for a niche party promoting value for public money and acting as an advocate for private enterprise.[48] Yet the residual strength of both Fianna Fáil, Fine Gael and indeed the Labour Party, combined with the history of parties such as Clann na Talmhan, Clann na Poblachta, Democratic Left, and the Progressive Democrats would suggest that any gains to be made by such a party would dissipate sooner rather later, but dissipate they will. The Irish electorate, while occasionally happy to vote promiscuously, no more so than 2011 in their crushing rejection of Fianna Fáil, seems always to ultimate reject the newcomer, forcing them to either disband or join with one of the larger parties. As Weeks indicates in chapter 1, in the hectic political atmosphere prior to the general election of 2011, while there was much talk of new political parties and movements, none materialised. In that context there is no evidence at all in Ireland that any interest group can emerge as a major political force which can, to use Katz's phrase, rule and take responsibility for ruling.[49]

## The 2011 general election

Ireland's earthquake election of 2011 saw national priorities come to the fore with a plurality of voters viewing national issues as the most important criterion in deciding how they would vote.[50] Yet if the demise of Fianna Fáil proved to be the main story of the election, the rise in the independent vote was no less noteworthy. The reduction in the independent vote in the 2007 general election might well have suggested that this route to influencing public policy might be less fruitful than in the past.[51] Notwithstanding the reduction of independents from thirteen to five in that election however, Fianna Fáil, or more specifically its leader, Bertie Ahern, during the negotiations to form a government, agreed deals with three of them which mainly concerned the provision of resources to local amenities in those TDs' constituencies.[52] The 2011 general election, however, saw the independent vote reach an eighty-year high with fourteen independents elected. Another five members of the United Left Alliance, featuring two Socialist Party candidates, two People before Profit Candidates, and one other independent, were also elected. The combined vote of over 12 per cent was the highest since June 1927.[53] This dramatic increase came of course in the middle of the meltdown of the Fianna Fáil vote but it would seem to give sustenance to the

Mair and Weeks view of voters relying more heavily, to a certain extent at least, on competing personal appeals.[54] This would seem to be particularly the case in times of economic uncertainty. How else is it possible to explain the victory of Mick Wallace in Wexford who decided to run at the proverbial last minute in Wexford and was subsequently elected on the first count topping the poll and exceeding the quota? The same goes for Stephen Donnelly who also decided to run late in the day and won the last seat in Wicklow despite having begun his campaign with no public profile to speak of, unlike Wallace, but who used the national media to great effect in his campaign.

Political parties in Ireland now compete on an increasingly narrow issue base. The ingrained nature of social partnership has removed much of the economic debate from the political sphere and what is left is reduced to who can best manage the economy. This reductionism in economic policy making has dwindled even further as the parameters of independent government action are constrained by the paymasters of the EU/ECB/IMF.

When Fianna Fáil clearly failed to manage the economy the voters took a swift and brutal revenge on them in the February 2011 general election. Independents from across the political spectrum did well but no interest groups emerged to fill the vacuum. A number of new groups did put themselves forward but sank without trace as none of them could organise a national campaign with candidates in every constituency.[55] Fís Nua, an offshoot of disaffected Green Party members, and New Vision, a hotch potch of independents led by Eamonn Blaney, a son of the former Fianna Fáil minister and later independent Fianna Fáil MEP Neil Blaney, put forward a small number of candidates under their respective banners to no effect with the electorate. Luke Ming Flanagan, successfully elected in Roscommon–South Leitrim aligned himself with New Vision but had a long history as an independent activist. There was some excitement, in media circles at least, when a group known as Democracy Now emerged on the scene (see also chapter 1) and floated the idea in private and eventually public of running as a specific group but in the end they did not put themselves before the electorate.[56] As Seán Donnelly, the veteran astute electoral commentator, pointed out on RTÉ's radio election programme in the immediate aftermath of the 2011 election, the Irish people are very protective of their vote; the idea that they would simply hand it away to any of these groups when there was established political alternatives was something they were not willing to countenance.[57] While these established political parties may not be able to respond to the demands of their voters or meet their interests as Mair points out,[58] and this particularly remains the case in relation to the politics of austerity as demanded by the EU/ECB/IMF troika, nevertheless, the potential for any new party emerging onto the political scene remains most unlikely.

Running a national election campaign involves significant organisational and financial commitments. In Ireland after the Fianna Fáil-led government accepted the access to the EU/ECB/IMF loan facility, a number of groups articulated opposition to the so called bailout and threatened to run on the general notion of restructuring bank debt and ending Irish cronyism.[59] All these groups, however, substantially underestimated the hurdles to be overcome in facing the electorate in a general election. In essence, candidates from those groups like Fís Nua and New Vision which did run under putative party banners in reality ran independent campaigns. And while a record number of independents were successful, they came from across the political spectrum with candidates such as Shane Ross and Stephen Donnelly on one side and those such as Mick Wallace, Luke Flanagan on the other. A final category of independents included those who had previously represented other political parties, most notably Fianna Fáil. The independent vote can thus perhaps best be interpreted as an anti-Fianna Fáil vote but it is clearly a vote that went in different directions.

## Conclusion

One of the significant puzzles yet to be satisfactorily answered in interest group politics has been why some groups in effect betray a seemingly key *raison d'être* of their existence by putting themselves forward for election and thus trying to influence policy from within parliament. By remaining as an interest group and not fighting elections, groups should theoretically be able to influence policy outcomes and force issues onto the political agenda by frequent informal interactions with politicians and bureaucrats. Some interest groups have, of course, been quite happy to operate in this way by lobbying intensively behind the political scene for their particular cause. The divisive abortion referendum of 1983 is a good example of how interest groups use the threat of the ballot box to pursue their ends. The threat of PLAC throwing its weight behind either Fianna Fáil or Fine Gael, as distinct from forming a party themselves, in the atmospheric hothouse that was Irish politics in the early 1980s, was enough to persuade both parties that they had to sign up to a referendum. Those groups which have thrown themselves into the political sphere have tended to come unstuck in a quick and brutal fashion as an electorate which can be mobilised to act in a significant way on certain issues at referendums has shown no appetite to vote in a similar way at national level.

Political parties freed from strong ideological class-based identities have demonstrated, 'the flexibility to adjust readily to changing circumstances without risking loss of support'.[60] Herein lies the difficulty for interest groups who stand for electoral office. The catch all nature of Irish politics makes it extremely difficult for new groups or parties seeking electoral support. Once such a grouping begins to show signs of gaining support around an issue, larger parties will simply shift their policies to accommodate them. Simply put this is what happened to the Progressive Democrats as once both Fianna Fáil in particular, and Fine Gael to a lesser extent, followed their low taxation mantra, they found themselves out in the political cold.

Moral issues and attitudes towards Europe have been consigned to referendums. Then why do interest groups still put forward candidates rather than simply trying to influence the political process through normal channels? Why do they seek to go beyond the informality stage of representation through the articulation of interests and pursuit of their goals through interactions with politicians and civil servants? Why do they in effect try to replace Fianna Fáil? The answer may lie in the fact that cause-centred groups in particular simply do not feel that they are able to influence the political process from outside. Sectional groups with the access they enjoy to the levers of power, even in an era where social partnership has ended, feel no such need to contest elections. For cause centred groups, however, Dáil Éireann is a sort of manna from heaven, and election to it a sign of their maturity as an important and influential group with a serious cause. In an increasingly congested political market, and now one where the very future of Fianna Fáil itself is at risk, interest groups consider that putting themselves forward to an electorate, potentially disaffected on any number of issues, is a better way to influence policy than accessing and influencing political parties from outside the charmed circle of potential power that is having a seat in Dáil Éireann.

# 9

# Irish Farmers' Parties, Nationalism and Class Politics in the Twentieth Century

*Tony Varley*

Since southern Ireland was substantially an agrarian society for much of the twentieth century (and became even more so with partition), historians and political scientists have often seen the absence of a major farmers' party as something of a puzzle. Of course some farmers' parties did emerge, but these remained minor in stature and decline and death was to be the ultimate fate of the three main farmers' parties that appeared in the inter-war period. Why these parties – the Farmers' Party, the National Centre Party and Clann na Talmhan (Family of the Land) – should suffer such a fate is the question posed in this chapter.

In the academic literature on Irish parties, four main explanations have been offered, either singly or in combination, to account for the absence of a major farmers' party and for the weakness and eventual dissolution of the three main farmers' parties that did materialise. For contextual reasons associated with nationalism and modernity, two of these explanations suggest that there was no real need for a major farmers' party to begin with. The two other explanations point to the inability of the three main farmers' parties that did emerge to transcend the internal class divisions that prevented farmers becoming a coherent and well-organised political class, and to counter various other inadequacies that left them organisationally and tactically disadvantaged *vis-à-vis* their nationalist political rivals.

The plausibility of these four explanations will provide a convenient means of framing our discussion here. To proceed we will, after briefly sketching our four explanations, profile our three farmers' parties by considering their origins, early aims and analysis as well as their organisation and tactics. With these profiles in hand, we will then turn to the question of appraising the adequacy of our four explanations. It is argued that the difficulties generated by class and political divisions were mutually reinforcing, and that these difficulties impacted on both organisational and tactical prospects and were in turn aggravated by organisational and tactical shortcomings.

## Four explanations

Why were the conditions not right for the emergence of a major farmers' party in post-independence Ireland? One view points to the wider context and contends that no such party was needed because by 1900 farmers could depend on nationalists, and (after 1921) on a nationalist-controlled state, to represent, safeguard and advance their interests.[1]

A second contextual explanation focuses on the wider society and suggests that rural Ireland, compared to the peasant societies of eastern Europe, was relatively modern (in the sense of integrated into the market economy) by 1900 and therefore didn't require a large peasant party. 'Post-Famine Ireland', in Lee's words, 'had a land question. It had no peasant question'. What crucially discouraged any yawning economic, political or cultural divide opening up between the countryside and the city was a well-established 'market-oriented agriculture'.[2]

A third attempt at explaining Ireland's lack of a major agrarian party combines contextual and internal factors by pointing to the potential for class divisions (primarily based on farm size) among farmers to undermine their capacity to become a major well-organised political party. This view echoes the general claim that as large and small farmers have different economic interests, they cannot realistically hope to form a single, coherent and autonomous political class, one capable of becoming a major force in a competitive party system.[3]

While many commentators would accept that Irish farmers were divided internally along class lines, there is no complete agreement as to which class was dominant. Once the power of the Irish landlords 'as a class had been broken' by the mid-1880s, Emmet Larkin sees it as 'inevitable' that much of their economic power should pass to the larger tenant farmers in a 'social revolution', and that 'the new nation-state … would be run in the interests of the larger farmers as a, class'.[4] As landowners these larger or 'strong' farmers would remain, 'the dominant social, economic and political class in Ireland almost to the present day'.[5] Fergus Campbell's contrasting interpretation sees Ireland's agrarian and nationalist revolutions combining to, '… create a class of sturdy smallholders who would dominate Irish society for most of the twentieth century'.[6]

Did intra-farmer class divisions result in serious conflict? Conflicts centred mainly on land redistribution had surfaced in the western Land League[7] and later on in the United Irish League.[8] To the extent that these conflicts never disappeared, subsequently,[9] attempts at using farmers' parties to instil a sense of class unity among farmers would always face an uphill battle.

A fourth explanation suggests that once farmers' parties appeared they were apt to be weakened by being organisationally limited and amateurish as well as tactically naïve and inept. Thus the Farmers' Party, according to Mitchell, was but, 'a loosely bound group with little party discipline'.[10] Similarly, Manning points to how it was 'never really a coherent political party with a national organisation. Its candidates were selected by the individual farmers' unions and its TDs tended to act more as independents than as members of a political party'.[11] In Gallagher's judgement, 'its leaders were not adroit politically and lacked the ability (and perhaps the will) which enabled Labour to preserve an independent existence'.[12]

Comparable characterisations have been offered of the National Centre Party and Clann na Talmhan. The former Manning describes as 'essentially a two-man band with little real development potential'.[13] Garvin sees Clann na Talmhan as, 'an almost anti-political party'.[14] 'It had', in Manning's appraisal, 'energy and anger, but little judgement, and lacked a leader of stature'.[15] In the hands of, 'political innocents abroad', Murphy judges the party's Dáil performance as 'never impressive'.[16] Uninterested in rising above its 'sectional aims' or in becoming a genuinely countrywide political force, Clann na Talmhan was content to pursue a narrow agenda and to remain within its western and southern heartlands.[17]

## Profiling our three cases

### Origins

How well do these four explanations fit the experience of our three cases? To begin with, how do the three parties compare in the circumstances of their appearance? Although each one was born out of crisis conditions, the nature of these conditions differed in important respects, as did the responses they evoked. Conceived as the political wing of the Irish Farmers' Union (IFU), the architects of the Farmers' Party never saw it as having an entirely independent existence. They were impelled to mobilise in 1922 by a combination of economic and political crisis conditions. By 1921 Irish farmers were feeling the effects of the post-war price slump, and with the country emerging from the Anglo-Irish War and descending into civil war in 1922, public disorder and economic dislocation looked set to continue. Adding substantially to the strong farmers' security fears during the revolutionary years was the rise of a frequently militant rural labour movement.[18]

The crisis conditions that helped call forth the National Centre Party in 1932-3 were similarly complex. By late 1932 the IFU and the Farmers' Party were defunct, Cumann na nGaedheal had been voted out of office and the tariff dispute known as the economic war (1932-8) was combining with the effects of the Great Depression to cut farming incomes sharply. The National Centre Party's beginnings can be traced to the 1932 general election victories of county-based farmers' and ratepayers' associations in Roscommon and Cavan.[19] By October 1932 a National Farmers' and Ratepayers' League (NFRL) had come into being. Despite making 'rapid headway', de Valera's snap election of January 1933 forced the NFRL, 'into political action before it was ready'.[20] Only after the Dáil was dissolved on 2 January 1933 did the National Centre Party, under the leadership of Frank MacDermot and James Dillon, begin to appear alongside the NFRL.

When what emerged as Clann na Talmhan in 1939 began first to stir in County Galway in 1938, the political crisis conditions that had provoked the appearance of the Farmers' Party and the National Centre Party, with civil and class wars real or imagined possibilities, were substantially absent. There were nonetheless considerable economic grievances among the farmers. Two events in 1938, disruptive bad weather and the decision in October to establish a new commission to inquire into the condition of Irish agriculture, combined to convert western discontent into collective action.

Further encouraging the western mobilisation was the knowledge that farmers in the eastern counties – especially those active in the Irish Farmers' Federation (IFF) founded in 1936-7 and registered as a trade union in 1937 – had recently re-organised in defence of their interests. A central IFF aim was to bring together elements associated with the now extinct NFRL/National Centre Party (and that had grown disenchanted with Fine Gael) and the United Farmers' Protection Association (UFPA), an originally pro-protection and pro-Fianna Fáil group founded in 1930. Partly influenced by an apparently effective English National Farmers' Union (NFU), the IFF leadership saw a wholly union-based approach as vital to its chance of creating corporatist-style relations between organised farmers and the state.[21]

### Early aims and analyses

Two themes pervaded the aims and analysis of the IFU activists who formed the Farmers' Party in 1922. Ample evidence for the view that the state was partly the author of the farmers' economic difficulties was found in the wartime state's perceived excessive regulation of agriculture. State interference, in the form of compulsory tillage in 1917, had also helped stimulate a new and menacing rural labour movement.[22] A second theme ran in a different direction and involved IFU activists looking to the state to buffer Irish farmers against further economic and political disturbance.

It proved impossible for the leadership of the new Farmers' Party to ignore the security threats posed by anti-Treaty militant nationalists and by militant labour. By contesting the 1922 general election, and so enduring 'intimidation of various kinds',[23] the IFU had publicly recognised the new state's legitimacy and displayed its readiness to participate in its representative assemblies. Of course the decision to enter the new parliament also reflected a conviction that nationalists in power could not be fully trusted to safeguard and advance the farming interest. 'There was no one', as the IFU president (R.A. Butler) put it in 1923, 'better fitted to look after the farmers' interests than a man put forward and elected by the farmers themselves'.[24]

What were the early aims of the NFRL/National Centre Party? Many strong farmers had reason to fear that Fianna Fáil in particular was intent on turning back the economic clock. Radical land redistribution, and a self-sufficiency policy of downgrading the cattle economy (the mainstay of export agriculture) in favour of tariff-protected tillage agriculture, were capable of tipping the balance in favour of peasant farming. Such fears partly inspired the National Centre Party's desire to preserve 'individual liberty and individual ownership'.[25]

By far the NFRL/National Centre Party's most pressing concern in the 1933 general election was to see economic war hostilities cease.[26] And to avoid anything like future economic wars, the NFRL/National Centre Party pressed for, 'more influence for the agricultural community over government policy'.[27]

Only gradually, and not without contention, did Clann na Talmhan acquire a firm identity. At first, the form the new mobilisation should assume, its platform and its spatial reach were all matters of debate. Some, mindful of the fate of the Farmers' Party and the National Centre Party (and with them the IFU and the NFRL), conceived of the new mobilisation more as a league or as a union of the western smallholder than as a national farmers' party that would contest elections. This position had its proponents, but it would not ultimately prevail.

By 1941 Clann na Talmhan had evolved into a party, albeit a professedly 'non-political' (or 'vocational') one that claimed a membership of 40,000 (half of which was in Galway).[28] The party's early programme shared with the IFU/Farmers' Party an aversion to excessive state regulation and tariff-protected manufacturing, a desire to defend farmers against the depredations of processors and commercial middlemen, and proposed a raft of public spending cuts to protect the farmer ratepayer from perceived runaway local authority and central government spending.

*Tactics and organisation*

Whether to organise as a party was an early tactical choice for each of our three cases. Prior to the Farmers' Party's formation, the IFU had been making substantial (if sometimes fleeting) organisational advances. When it formally registered in 1920 as a trade union,[29] it had attracted 60,000 members and established a presence in twenty-five counties.[30] And by 1921 it ,'had become a fairly powerful lobby in Irish politics'.[31]

As part of a tactical approach that sought 'to avoid involvement in "politics" and to apply pressure to all political factions, whatever their colour', the IFU had consciously stood aloof from the 1918 general election and the 1920 local elections.[32] What changed this stance, in Fitzpatrick's view, was the Anglo-Irish Treaty of December 1921.[33] Yet even before the treaty, and inspired by feelings of powerlessness in response to a state perceived to be too eager to regulate and too sympathetic to organised labour, the idea was gaining currency within IFU circles that 'candidates from the farming class' were required.[34]

As with the IFU/Farmers' Party, the NFRL had both predated the National Centre Party and provided the basis of its local organisation.[35] The demoralisation that followed the disappearance of the IFU/Farmers' Party encouraged a belief that farmers would need the support of business ratepayers if they were to overcome their representational weakness.[36] By December 1932, the NFRL was claiming to have six Oireachtas members,[37] though soon afterwards MacDermot admitted that the organisation, 'while strong in a few counties is in a rudimentary stage in most parts of the country'.[38] From the beginning the desire was, 'to form a Balance of Power Party'.[39]

The IFU and Clann na Talmhan leaderships may have agonised initially about the wisdom of forming a farmers' party, but once the nettle was grasped the idea was to build a party that would traverse the country and appeal to a wide spectrum of farmers and rural voters. This is not to say that all links to unions or leagues were to be severed. The central IFU leadership's early expectation was that the Farmers' Party would generally act as the IFU's agents where agriculture and related matters were concerned. Behind the National Centre Party, and supplying the organisation for its 1933 election campaign, stood the NFRL. A more tenuous link with trade unionism was to be found in Clann na Talmhan.

After a failed commodity strike in 1939 exposed the limitations of any exclusive reliance on trade unionism, some leading IFF activists (including the independent farmer TD, Patrick Cogan) launched the National Agricultural Party in 1942. This new party, 'would not be a rival to the IFF', in Cogan's view, but would be, 'another type of organisation to meet and beat the politicians on their own ground'.[40] As the 1943 general election approached and the need for farmer unity strengthened, the National Agricultural Party leadership made sufficient concessions (especially on the derating of agricultural land) to permit a merger between the westerners and the easterners under the title of 'Clann na Talmhan – the National Agricultural Party'.

How well our three farmers' parties became established depended critically on the ability of the union, league or federation to organise and on their own ability to win and hold parliamentary seats. The Farmers' Party fielded sixty-four candidates in twenty-six constituencies in 1923 and won fifteen seats.[41] Although a promising result (Labour won fourteen seats), the uneven spatial spread of its victories – no Dáil seats were won in Connacht for instance – had to be a worry for an organisation aspiring to be a genuinely national political force.[42] Nor was the Farmers' Party able to build on its 1923 result. In the June and September elections of 1927 nine Dáil seats were lost.[43] What remained of the Farmers' Party (some standing as independents) contested seven constituencies and returned with three seats (all in Munster) in 1932.[44]

The National Centre Party had barely appeared when it had to face the general election of January 1933. The eleven seats it won, mainly in Leinster and Munster constituencies where the Farmers' Party had succeeded in the past, has prompted the suggestion that the, 'new party is probably best seen as simply a revival of the old Farmers' Party ...'.[45]

In the 1943 election Clann na Talmhan won an impressive ten seats (five in Connacht), though five other farmer TDs opted to remain as independents rather than join the party. Even before Fine Gael's revival in the 1950s, Clann na Talmhan's electoral decline was well under way, with the party's national vote being, 'halved in 1948 and halved again in 1951'.[46]

Did levels of electoral support have a bearing on parliamentary tactics? While some optimistic farmer activists had hoped for a landslide that would sweep farmers into power, the more realistic thought in terms of the farmers securing sufficient representation to hold the parliamentary balance of power and so be able to influence government composition and policy. After the September election of 1927 the support of the Farmers' Party proved crucial to Cumann na nGaedheal's ability to form a government.[47] Clann na Talmhan also held the balance of power after the 1943 election. Seemingly influenced by a desire to preserve stable government in wartime, its national executive decided on a Dáil strategy of not opposing Fianna Fáil in forming a government.[48]

## Assessing our four explanations

*Competing with Nationalists*
With our three cases profiled, we are now ready to assess the four reasons offered to explain the fate of the Irish agrarian parties. The first of these, in light of the way nationalists were already representing farming interests adequately, questions the very need for an Irish farmers' party. From what we have seen, such a view clashes with the early subjective perception of the leaderships of our three farmers' parties that the manner nationalist politicians were representing farmers' interests was seriously deficient.

But how well were the farmers' parties able to compete with nationalists? Compared to the twenty-five years or so that Clann na Talmhan existed, the Farmers' Party stayed the course for about a decade. Not for even a year did the NFRL/National Centre Party survive as an independent party. What is also true of course is that both the Farmers' Party and the IFU were clearly disintegrating by 1927, and that Clann na Talmhan was visibly failing by the late 1940s. With the exception of the Farmers' Party in 1923 when it more than doubled its Dáil representation, both the Farmers' Party and Clann na Talmhan lost seats at every successive election. At their best elections where seats were concerned (1923, 1933 and 1943 respectively) our three farmers' parties averaged twelve seats and 10 per cent of the vote.

Why then were farmers' parties unable to compete better with nationalists? Clearly, the latter were hugely advantaged by the virtual monopoly they had achieved in representing farming interests in parliament prior to independence.

Although the volatility of the 1920s gave class parties possibilities to exploit, the three farmers' parties faced a situation where the rival nationalist parties were each claiming to be the real voice of Irish agriculture, had their own agricultural policies and owed their position largely to 'agricultural support'.[49] An occupational analysis reveals how 25 per cent of Cumann na nGaedheal/Fine Gael TDs up to 1948 and 31 per cent of Fianna Fáil TDs were farmers.[50]

In such a context, and to counter the view that they were merely class or sectional parties, the farmers' parties were at pains to show that they were just as national-minded (if not more so) than their nationalist rivals. As early as 1922 the IFU's national executive advised its county associations that 'any candidates selected be "men with a national record"'.[51] Frank MacDermot and James Dillon, the leaders of the National Centre Party, were first and foremost nationalist figures within the Irish Parliamentary Party tradition.[52] National unity and the ending of partition took pride of place in the manifestos of the National Centre Party and Clann na Talmhan.[53]

What critically went against the farmers in competing with nationalists was the manner the treaty split interacted with economic class divisions to weaken the ability of farmers' parties to constitute farmers as a single, unified political class. The tendencies for larger farmers to be pro-treaty, and for smaller ones to be anti-Treaty, were not long in revealing themselves,[54] and to a degree the policy stances of the main pro- and anti-Treaty parties came at once to reflect and strengthen such tendencies.[55]

What further told against the farmers was their closeness to (evident in the pattern of lower preference vote transfers),[56] and ultimate absorption by, the main pro-Treaty party. Absorption came piecemeal and gradually for the Farmers' Party, all at once for the National Centre Party (in 1933) and over a protracted period for Clann na Talmhan. But why did our three cases all gravitate to the pro-Treaty side? Cumann na nGaedheal possessed features that endeared it to many Farmers' Party' activists and supporters.[57] Besides accepting the treaty and upholding it against its enemies, it had asserted the primacy of the cattle economy and free trade and seen off the challenge of militant rural labour. The Economic War and its humiliations weighed heavily on the leaders of the NFRL/National Centre Party and those of the early Clann na Talmhan and IFF, thus strengthening the trend for farmer party activists to see the pro-Treatyites as natural allies and Fianna Fáil as an ever more dangerous threat.

There is therefore considerable irony in the way that both the National Centre Party's and Clann na Talmhan's electoral gains tended to be made mainly at Cumann na nGaedheal's and Fine Gael's expense. What later transpired – instantly in 1933 and more gradually for Clann na Talmhan – was that Fine Gael would retrieve the seats it had lost to the farmers.[58]

## Modernity and agrarian politics

Lee sees Irish agriculture's commercial character as indicative of its modernity and as what ultimately denied Ireland the possibility of having a major farmers' party.[59] As much as our three cases were modern in the sense of being pro-commercial agriculture, they also displayed some of those 'streaks of peasantism' that Lee detects 'in all major parties'.[60] Certainly land redistribution was of some importance to them. And a stridently anti-urban populist rhetoric that could sound distinctly ambivalent about parliamentary democracy infused Donnellan's early speeches.[61]

As the different farmers' parties fell apart, a viewpoint that links agricultural modernity with organisational forms as well as with commercialisation vigorously re-asserted itself. Here the contention was that organising exclusively along interest-group lines offered a more modern and effective mode of mobilising Irish farmers than forming small and inevitably ill-fated farmers' parties.

## Class conflict

A leading goal in all three farmers' parties was to mobilise farmers in a manner that would transcend internal economic, political and cultural differences and so constitute them as a single, coherent and powerful political class. Projecting all farmers as a single embattled class was important to this ambitious project, as was the desire to suppress or de-emphasise potentially divisive issues. Thus IFU activists, to minimise the risk of incapacitating divisions, desired to promote issues on which farmers could agree and to avoid issues that were likely to prove divisive.[62] Likewise, the Farmers' Party had, 'tried to play down class differences in the farming community' in 1923.[63] Within the IFU, however, conflict between different farming classes became a debilitating source of factionalism. We thus find the first leader of the Farmers' Party, Denis Gorey, who identified very much with the unpurchased tenants, being contemptuous in public of such leading IFU figures as Col. George O'Callaghan-Westropp and Sir John Keane, whom he took to be members of an 'old gang' of Irish landlords and ex-landlords.[64]

Historically, redistributive land reform was an issue capable of exposing diverging class interests and bringing large and small farmers into serious conflict. Alongside the suppression of radical versions of redistributive land reform, we find some acceptance in our three cases that large and small farmers had to be prepared to accommodate each other's diverging interests to some degree.[65] At least in principle large farmers would have to yield something on land redistribution, while small farmers would have to acknowledge 'fixity of tenure' as a strong farmer core value. Of course their political enemies rejected any suggestion that the farmers' parties could reflect and build class solidarity among farmers. The IFU's early critics had dismissed it as a landlord and strong farmer-controlled organisation that had little to offer the smallholder.[66] As the 1920s progressed the Farmers' Party drew the hostility of Fianna Fáil activists who similarly saw both the IFU and the

Farmers' Party as essentially the pro-rancher allies of Cumann na nGaedheal. In its turn the NFRL was castigated for its association with landlordism and for being 'a league of graziers',[67] a charge MacDermot vigorously denied.[68]

A decade later the same charge that small and large farmers had incompatible economic interests, and therefore could never form a coherent political class, was levelled at Clann na Talmhan.[69] In the party's 1943 election manifesto we find an attempt to balance a commitment to land division and to preserving the principle of fixity of tenure.[70] The following year saw the tensions associated with accommodating the divergent economic interests of big and small farmers contributing to the change of party leader. Late in 1946 Patrick Cogan chose to resign from the Clann na Talmhan parliamentary party in protest at the part two of his parliamentary party colleagues (both advocates of accelerated land redistribution) had played in an agitation over the sale of a Mayo farm that, early in 1947, saw them serving a month in Sligo jail.[71]

Of course divisions other than class differences (mainly reflecting farm size) could also prove to be divisive. Three of Clann na Talmhan's southern TDs revolted and quit over dissatisfaction with various items of government policy (such as the government's treatment of milk producers) during the life span of the 1948-51 inter-party government.[72] These departures also illustrate how some of the Clann na Talmhan deputies tended, as with their earlier Farmers' Party counterparts,[73] to ultimately see themselves as independents accountable to their local executives in the first instance.[74]

*Organisation and tactics*

Not surprisingly, the decision to enter competitive politics greatly influenced aims, organisational forms and tactics in our three cases. When the IFU launched the Farmers' Party in 1922 the preference was for the union and the party to work in tandem. By 1927 the two pillar assumptions of the dual approach: that the Farmers' Party would generally act as the central IFU's parliamentary agent and that the party and union would complement one another, had been substantially eroded. Only after the Farmers' Party had already agreed to enter what was effectively a coalition government in late 1927 did the IFU's national executive give its approval.[75]

Earlier in 1927 the IFU had vetoed a Farmers' Party proposal to merge with Cumann na nGaedheal,[76] but this act prompted the party leader to defect to Cumann na nGaedheal. Another leader, Michael Heffernan, after serving as a parliamentary secretary during Cumann na nGaedheal's last term of office, followed suit in 1932. Nor were our two other agrarian parties free of leadership-related difficulties. MacDermot and Dillon helped found the United Ireland Party (or Fine Gael) in 1933. Many Clann na Talmhan activists (especially in Galway) came to view Joseph Blowick as a less dynamic party leader than Donnellan.

The uneven spread of Farmers' Party seats encouraged the local level to eclipse the national level, as did the practice (equally evident in the NFRL/National

Centre Party and Clann na Talmhan) of leaving each county to build its own organisation, select candidates and contest elections.[77] Clann na Talmhan's organisation quickly came to revolve around fighting elections. And only in those constituencies where TDs were elected did its organisation endure. What organisation survived tended in addition to become the local constituency machines of the sitting TDs and councillors, ever more dependent on clientelism to retain their seats.[78]

Further contributing to the dominance of the local over the national level was the way nobody among the top leadership, with the partial exception of Dillon and MacDermot (neither of whom were farmers) and Donnellan (a renowned Gaelic footballer), was a prominent national figure comparable to the likes of Cosgrave or de Valera.

Only when its vote was in steep decline, observes Sinnott,[79] did Clann na Talmhan have 'most impact, participating in both inter-party governments in 1948-51 and 1954-7'. The same might equally be said of the Farmers' Party in the aftermath of the September election of 1927. Far from it bringing a reversal of electoral decline, however, participation in government hastened the Farmers' Party's partial absorption by Cumann na nGaedheal and Clann na Talmhan's substantial absorption by Fine Gael.

## One explanation or many?

How adequate then are our four explanations? Each one is revealing up to a point, but their explanatory power greatly expands when they are combined. Here I would stress how decisive to party survival chances in the inter-war years and beyond was the manner divisions based on class (centred on farm size and exemplified by the small v. large farmer distinction) and nationalism (pro- and anti-Treaty) overlapped and accentuated each other. Transcending these intertwined class and political divisions presented our three cases with challenges that ultimately proved to be beyond them.

Rather than transcending class divisions among farmers, the way our farmers' parties came to be identified with either larger farmers (the Farmers' Party and National Centre Party) or smaller and mainly western farmers (Clann na Talmhan) at once reflected and helped reproduce internal class differentiation in Irish agriculture. Similarly, rather than transcending the basic political opposition in post-independence Ireland, the way our farmers' parties tended to be pro-Treaty in practice at once reflected and added to the underlying strength of the party system's fundamental polarisation. As time passed, and with their autonomy compromised and their efficacy ever more questionable, it became progressively harder to argue that it took a farmers' party farmer to represent a farmer.

The difficulties thrown up by the way nationalism- and class-based divisions interacted also had an important bearing on organisational and tactical prospects. As much as the electoral vulnerability of Cumann na nGaedheal and Fine Gael presented the NFRL/National Centre Party and the early Clann na Talmhan with opportunities, attempts at building organisation were always dogged (substantially for class- and nationalism-related reasons) by an inability to be competitive with the mainstream nationalist parties on a national basis. Broadly the same reasons contributed to the IFU's organisational and tactical difficulties in striking a dynamic balance between the union and the party.

What is also true of course is that organisational and tactical difficulties not only existed in their own right but were sufficiently serious to add significantly to the problems created by class and political differences. Power in all three of our farmers' parties tended to concentrate at the local as against the central or national level. Combining the union, league or federation with the party was always to prove difficult. Indeed, forming its own party, something the NFU had consciously shunned, was to be a divisive and enervating move within the IFU. It became harder to expect Farmers' Party deputies to follow the IFU Congress's direction in agricultural and related policy matters if the central IFU itself was frequently in disarray as the 1920s wore on. For its part the IFF was irreparably damaged by its decision to back the 1939 failed farm strike.

### Explicating the Irish experience comparatively

So far our discussion has confined itself to Ireland, but can light be shed on the fate of the Irish farmers' parties by comparing them with the Scandinavian farmers' parties that have survived to the present day? Why the Scandinavian parties have survived can be heavily attributed to the way they benefited from participation in coalition governments.[80] The Scandinavian agrarian parties also succeeded in creating more effective working relationships with farmers' unions.[81] Something else present in Scandinavia but absent in Ireland was the presence of vibrant youth and women's sections.[82] Adeptness at re-inventing themselves, especially by evolving (in the 1950s and 1960s) into centre parties capable of appealing to more broadly rural and even urban constituencies, became vital to the longer term survival chances of the Scandinavian parties, even if this was to dilute their identities as class parties somewhat.[83]

Conditions were very different, and significantly more adverse, in inter-war Ireland. Here the civil war split that left nationalists deeply and bitterly divided, late industrialisation, a lingering red scare that turned first the rural proletariat and then the early Fianna Fáil into the strong farmers' political and class enemies, the trauma of the economic war, and Fianna Fáil's virtual stranglehold on political power after 1932 conspired to rule out the sort of red-green class compromises and governing coalitions that proved so beneficial for the Scandinavian agrarian parties. Besides Fianna Fáil's preference for single-party government, the party's early leadership projected a distinctive vision of Irish agriculture that regarded farmers' parties as natural allies of the pro-Treatyites and therefore as political and even class enemies.[84]

Under such circumstances, the Irish farmers' parties failed to grow in ways that allowed for identity development and the widening of their appeal to new constituencies. Compared to the Farmers' Party's 'stodgy conservatism',[85] the Swedish Agrarian Party for instance, partly as a consequence of a struggle that saw the party's conservative leadership replaced by moderates,[86] came to project itself as a force for social progress.[87]

It is true that Clann na Talmhan's commitment to improving the lot of agricultural labourers and small farmers did commend it to some on the Irish Left, notably to Roddy Connolly and to R.M. Burke. At different times Connolly even saw possibilities for an alliance between the Labour Party and Clann na Talmhan as part of a wider progressive alternative to Fianna Fáil, though in the end nothing came of these possibilities.[88]

## Conclusion

There is a clear sense that the patterns we find in attempts at representing Irish farming interests autonomously came full circle in the twentieth century: starting out with an exclusively union-based interest group approach, then adopting a dual approach based on the ideal of having the union, league or federation work in tandem with a farmers' party, before reverting once again to an exclusively interest group approach. As early as the mid- to late 1930s the learning process at work here is detectable in the IFF's insistence – mindful of the fate of the IFU/Farmers' Party and the NFRL/Centre Party – on remaining strictly non-political.

For the upcoming generation of farming activists that put its energies into building Macra na Feirme (Young Farmers' Clubs) in the 1940s and the Irish Creamery Milk Suppliers' Association and National Farmers' Association shortly thereafter, the lessons of history were even clearer: party politics was a game which organised farmers could never play with any real hope of winning at the national level. These activists could see more clearly how the conditions conducive to the appearance of farmers' parties in Ireland – civil war and the political, economic and social turmoil of the inter-war years – were much the same conditions that helped ensure, as many of the fears of the inter-war period faded yet 'civil war politics' endured, that those farmers' parties that did appear would always be small, weak and transient.

Even so, the idea of forming new farmers' parties in Ireland did not entirely die in the 1940s. It was strongly rumoured, in the agriculturally troubled early 1980s, that T.J. Maher, a former Irish Farmers' Association (IFA) president and then a sitting independent MEP, was about to launch a new farmers' party.[89] While these rumours came to nothing, Maher exemplifies the tendency for farmers in the recent period to steer clear of forming farmers' parties while intermittently seeking representation for agricultural interests in parliamentary politics. Reflecting the centrality of Brussels to present-day Irish agriculture, two former IFA presidents (Paddy Lane and Alan Gillis who stood for Fianna Fáil and

Fine Gael respectively) would – substantially by appealing to the farming vote – follow in Maher's footsteps in winning seats in the European Parliament.

Two general questions raised in the study of the minor Irish parties are highly pertinent to us. Can small parties, the first of these asks, make the transition from minor to major standing? And, secondly, why do Irish minor parties expire? We have suggested that for the three farmers' parties to become major parties in the inter-war years and beyond, or even to survive as minor parties, they would have had to establish the primacy of a particular class politics in a party system heavily dominated by divided nationalism and in an agrarian society heavily divided along class lines. The three farmers' parties might have improved their chances of making the transition from minor to major party standing, and of surviving for longer as minor parties, had they been more coherently organised and tactically more savvy, but the wider adverse nationalism- and class-related circumstances they battled against constituted formidable, and ultimately insurmountable, hurdles.

If new minor parties are to appear at some future date in Ireland, they are highly unlikely to be farmers' parties. The emergence of strong 'non-political' lobbies to represent agricultural interests in the post-war decades,[90] along with urbanisation and a rapidly shrinking farming population have progressively diminished the chances of new farmers' parties appearing. Of course, long before such developments farmers had already learned the lesson from bitter experience that farmers' parties – largely in view of their inability to transcend the related class and political divisions that prevented farmers becoming a powerfully organised autonomous political force – were a relatively ineffective means of representing and defending farming interests. For the rising generation of wartime and post-war farmer activists, it therefore was not a question of reconfiguring the party approach to representing farming interests, but of striking out in an entirely different (and more NFU-style modern) direction that would look to constituting farmers as a powerfully organised economic as against political class.

# 10

# To the Left of Labour: The Workers' Party and Democratic Left, 1982-97

*Kevin Rafter*

## Introduction

Over the last ninety years new parties have repeatedly attempted to break into the national political arena in Ireland to challenge the longtime dominance of Fianna Fáil, Fine Gael and Labour. The new entrants have periodically challenged the established order in terms of shaping policy agendas, winning seats and participating in multi-party governmental arrangements. A limited number of small parties have achieved these three outcomes: impact on policy, Dáil representation and governmental involvement, including Clann na Poblachta, Clann na Talmhan, the Progressive Democrats, Democratic Left and the Green Party. Others, including the Workers' Party, while not experiencing a period in power, have both impacted policy formation and enjoyed national electoral success. All these new entrants, however, share one common trait, namely, a poor record in sustaining their challenge to the big three parties. It has been pointed out that smaller parties can, 'add a richness and depth that has an impact on democracy and representation'.[1] In an Irish context, however, despite this democratic value, these parties have failed to sustain a lasting political and electoral presence.

Ireland's so-called 'two and a half party system' was defined, until the general election in 2011, by Fianna Fáil, Fine Gael and Labour repeatedly filling the same pecking order in terms of votes and seats. The 2011 outcome while dramatic, but not unexpected given the country's economic decline, did not, however, bring about a new party political order. Instead the results delivered a re-ordering of the established rankings of the three main parties. This situation is in sharp contrast to a previous period of national turmoil when Ireland won its independence from Britain in 1921. Such were the dramatic changes that, as Chubb observed, 'the party system that emerged in the 1920s bore little resemblance to the system before independence'.[2] The moderate nationalist Irish Parliamentary

Party disappeared, the Labour Party, formed in 1912, continued, while Sinn Féin divided into what was the first in a series of splits that would become a recurring feature associated with the party. Sinn Féin, which was established in 1905, is the starting point, albeit a distant one, for tracing the origins of many of the political parties that emerged post-independence including the two parties of interest in this chapter: the Workers' Party and Democratic Left.

Both parties enjoyed some success, the Workers' Party in electoral terms in the 1980s and Democratic Left in government participation in the 1990s. The Workers' Party emerged out of the contemporary republican movement and the post-1969 conflict in Northern Ireland. Divisions over ideology and criminality in the Workers' Party led to the formation of Democratic Left in 1992. Throughout the 1980s and the 1990s these two parties sought to challenge Labour's position as the dominant left voice in Irish politics. Ultimately, however, neither of these 'breakthrough' parties sustained a presence on the Irish political landscape. This chapter examines the development of these two parties in relation to Labour, first in terms of electoral competition and second in terms of creating distinct ideological space from the larger party. Their respective failure to achieve their stated objective of replacing Labour as the dominant presence on the left of Irish politics is discussed in the context of a failure to create discernible ideological differences.

## Electoral competition

The failure of the left to develop a significant political presence in Ireland in a manner similar to other western European countries has been the subject of considerable discussion. Mair focused on a number of historic factors in attempting to account for this marginalisation.[3] First, the absence of a substantial and politically self-conscious working class which denied the left a natural constituency. Second, the strength of a clientelist culture that stresses individual political relations over collective action. Third, the catch-all appeal of Fianna Fáil which allowed the party to promote welfarist policies. Fourth, the salience of nationalist issues in the early years of Irish politics meant that there was simply little scope for a party which devoted itself almost exclusively to working-class socialist concerns. Allied to this was the decision of the Labour Party to stand aside from the 1918 Westminster general election when many voters casting their ballot for the first time were influenced by the nationalist political agenda.[4]

These factors combined to lessen the electoral success of the left – as evident in Table 1 for the 1973 to 1997 elections. This constituency has primarily been represented by the Labour Party. There have been periodic electoral successes, for example, Labour achieved a record national vote in 1969 and historic seat gains in 1992 and, more recently, in 2011. But there have also been periods of despondence, particularly in the 1980s when the political landscape became more crowded and complex with the emergence of several smaller parties including the Workers' Party. The latter party emerged out of a split in the hardline Irish republican tradition in 1969-70 with internal differences over electoral participation and the use of violence. Those who favoured violence, the Provisional wing of the republican movement, went on to wage a thirty-year campaign against British rule in Northern Ireland. The alternative group, styled the Official wing, had a preference for political activism. Its leadership argued against the use of violence but there was ambiguity about the continued existence of the Official IRA with sufficient evidence to support the argument that the organisation 'remained active throughout the 1980s'.[5]

Official Sinn Féin, as the organisation's political wing was known, renamed in 1977 as Sinn Féin the Workers' Party and in 1982 became the Workers' Party as it attempted to move from a past association with republican paramilitarism to stress a new attachment to left-wing political activism. This evolution of the Workers' Party was assisted by its positioning as a radical alternative to Labour's more moderate policy stance. The party matches Coakley's categorisation as a 'breakaway party' – one that origniated in a split within an existing party, but one which was defined by a left-wing ideological dimension that challenged the mainstream party of the left through adoption of 'radical positions of principle'.[6] In the latter respect, in the 1982 to 1987 period, the Workers' Party had free reign to articulate a left alternative while Labour struggled in bleak economic times as part of a coalition government with Fine Gael. The party pushed for higher taxation and greater state involvement in the running of the economy and in ownership of strategic assets. During this time the party was able to function as an alternative voting outlet for disgruntled Labour supporters. The Workers' Party won more first-preference votes than the Labour Party at the 1985 local elections, a performance the party built on as it took full advantage of Labour's negative appeal arising from its involvement in government with Fine Gael. Relations were poor; as Labour leader Dick Spring recalled, the two parties were essentially fighting for the same territory.[7]

The Dublin-based leadership of the Workers' Party effectively rewrote the party's mission statement to such an extent that Rooney, writing in 1984, pointed to a potential difficulty for the Workers' Party as a self-styled 'revolutionary party' with, 'the increasingly social democratic nature of its politics, and the fact that these tend to be confined to an internal debate within rather than against capitalism'.[8] The type of ideological transition in European left-wing politics discussed below was underway. The Workers' Party promoted a policy agenda with heavy state involvement in all facets of socio-economic life including nationalisation of the banking sector and the creation of a national health service. In the economically depressed 1980s this alternative to the agenda of the main parties won a significant audience. As mentioned previously, the unpopularity of the Fine Gael-Labour coalition also assisted Workers' Party growth.

The statist-type underpinning of domestic policies was coupled with a foreign policy that backed the communist leadership in the USSR. From the mid-1970s

*Table 1: Parties of the left, electoral support 1972-97 (% vote)*

| Year | Election | Workers' Party | Democratic Left | Labour |
|------|----------|----------------|-----------------|--------|
| 1973 | Dáil | 1.1 | – | 13.7 |
| 1977 | Dáil | 1.7 | – | 11.6 |
| 1979 | European Parliament | 3.3 | – | 14.5 |
| 1981 | Dáil | 1.7 | – | 9.9 |
| 1982 (Feb) | Dáil | 2.2 | – | 9.1 |
| 1982 (Nov) | Dáil | 3.3 | – | 9.4 |
| 1984 | European Parliament | 4.3 | – | 8.4 |
| 1985 | Local | 3.0 | – | 7.7 |
| 1987 | Dáil | 3.8 | – | 6.5 |
| 1989 | Dáil | 5.0 | – | 9.5 |
| 1989 | European Parliament | 7.6 | – | 9.5 |
| 1991 | Local | 3.6 | – | 10.5 |
| 1992 | Dáil | 0.7 | 2.8 | 19.5 |
| 1994 | European Parliament | 1.9 | 3.5 | 11.0 |
| 1997 | Dáil | 0.4 | 2.5 | 10.4 |

Sources: Donnelly, Seán (ed.) *Poll Position: An Analysis of the 1991 Local Elections* (Dublin; Sean Donnelly, 1992); Sinnott, R. *Irish Voters Decide: Voting Behaviour in Elections and Referendums Since 1918* (Manchester; Manchester University Press, 1995); www.election-sireland.org

there was vocal support for Soviet foreign policy even in the face of the Soviet military interventions in Afghanistan and Poland. There were some internal doubts about this strategy but ideological purity and membership discipline necessitated that the debate was shut down. The fall of the Berlin Wall in 1989 came as a relief to many on the reformist wing of the party as it provided a strong justification to quicken the pace of ideological reform. During this period of transformation the party also fundamentally altered its approach to Northern Ireland, where hostility to traditional republicanism was considerable.

The Workers' Party was organised on an all-Ireland basis. In Northern Ireland it contested elections to the Sunningdale Assembly in 1973 but on an abstentionist platform. This policy remained in place until internment ended and the emergency powers were dropped. The party's ten candidates in 1973 polled poorly, receiving less than 2 per cent of the first-preference vote across Northern Ireland. In local district elections, in May 1977, six official Sinn Féin candidates were elected with the party taking 2.6 per cent of the overall vote. But three of those seats were lost in 1981 as the party's support slipped back to 1.8 per cent. There was a slight recovery four years later but throughout this period, as their colleagues south of the border were making decent electoral gains, the party in Northern Ireland failed to make an electoral breakthrough of any note.

The first evidence of electoral progress for the Workers' Party in the south came in June 1981 with the election of its first TD to Dáil Éireann (Joe Sherlock in Cork East). Eight months later, following the February 1982 general election, support from three Workers' Party TDs – and independent TD Tony Gregory – facilitated the election of a minority Fianna Fáil government. The arrangement was short-lived as Workers' Party support (and Gregory's) was withdrawn in November 1982 amid proposals for austere fiscal policies. This support for Charles Haughey's government caused little political or electoral damage. Indeed, Dunphy and Hopkins write that the Workers' Party, 'was almost alone amongst West European communist and workers' parties in having experienced steady, if modest, electoral growth throughout the 1980s'.[9] From its initial breakthrough with Sherlock the party went on to make strong electoral gains, increasing its Dáil representation to a high of nine seats in 1989. The party had a strong Dublin base, illustrated by its 1985 local election results and its candidate Prionsias de Rossa winning a European Parliament seat in the Dublin constituency in 1989 when he topped the poll with over 70,000 first preference votes.

Throughout this period the position of the Labour Party was a very different story. Labour's share of the first preference vote had declined at each general election since 1969. There is some limited evidence that the competition between the two parties contributed to an increase in overall left support, but this strengthened support base was restricted as the smaller party was primarily taking votes from its larger rival. Labour rejected overtures for a transfer pact at the 1987 general election, which Girvin concluded 'reflected the threat Labour felt'.[10] Nevertheless, even before the emergence of Democratic Left in 1992 there had been a, 'slow but steady rise in the rate of transfers between the two left parties during the 1980s, though this still falls short of the degree of solidarity between Fine Gael and the PDs, and indeed between Labour and Fine Gael before 1987'.[11] The Workers' Party was the party on the move while Labour was in trouble. The former organisation won seats in 1987 in Dublin Central and Dún Laoghaire – both from Labour – and in Dublin South West from Fianna Fáil. After the 1987 contest there were six Workers' Party deputies in the Dublin region, twice that of Labour. Gallagher, however, highlighted a salient weakness in the Workers' Party position – an inability to match Labour's claim to be a national party because it had only one seat outside of Dublin.[12]

There were very mixed views in the Labour Party about its smaller rival, fuelled by both the origins of the Workers' Party and the legacy of the official republican movement. There was also the natural antipathy between two parties seeking to draw support from a similar support base. There was strong competition in terms of Dáil seats with continued movement prevailing over the entire 1981 to 1997 period between the two groupings. Relations were poor between individual party members in a variety of constituencies. Workers' Party (later Democratic

Left) TD Eric Byrne recalled, 'We were always looking at the Labour Party as the natural enemy'.[13] One senior Labour official remarked upon, 'a history of intense rivalry verging almost on hatred on the ground'.[14] Yet, coupled with the negative Labour responses there was also private, and often begrudging, respect for the work ethic and strong Oireachtas performances of the Workers' Party/Democratic Left TDs. Finlay describes the differing Labour Party views about their rivals as, 'ranging from envy for their discipline and coherence to outright hatred, arising from individual incidents in the past'.[15]

Having enjoyed electoral success throughout the 1980s, the onward march of the Workers' Party was halted by disappointing results in the 1991 local elections. The Labour Party had regrouped in opposition, and was therefore better able to compete with its smaller rival, while the Workers' Party was left hugely embarrassed by a renewed media focus on the criminal activities of those associated with its organisation in Northern Ireland. The internal debate about its ideological positioning in light of developments in Central and Eastern Europe was also coming to a head. In the aftermath of the 1991 local elections the general assessment within Labour was that the Workers' Party, 'had run out of steam'.[16] Labour, now in opposition, regrouped and was repositioned to account for the threat of its rival. Labour strategists believed there was even a possibility that some Workers' Party TDs could be persuaded to join them. It was against this backdrop that relations between the Labour Party and the newly formed Democratic Left must be seen. Moreover, the issue of the new party's individual identity was closely linked with Labour. In early April 1992 Pat Rabbitte addressed these inter-party relations, 'There is a good deal of convergence … and I certainly would look forward to maximum co-operation between our parties, but I think that there is a space in our society, to the left of the Labour Party and it is important that that space is filled.'[17]

The question of a merger with Labour was informally on the agenda at the time of the split in the Workers' Party in early 1992. There was, however, little support among the De Rossa (their party leader) group for joining Labour – on an individual basis or *en masse* at that time. The larger party was seen as 'very staid and not open to change' and of its members it was said that they would 'sell their souls'.[18] Pat Rabbitte was the only senior party figure to give serious consideration to the Labour option in 1992, and only loyalty to his colleagues prevented his departure. Even at that stage fundamental policy differences between the two parties were hard to identify. Many accepted that the differences were driven more by personality and individual political ambition than political ideology. 'Very often relations were defined by what relations were like in the constituencies,' Eamon Gilmore admitted.[19] For Gilmore, the ultimately unsuccessful talks about government formation with Labour in late 1992 helped to overcome many personal difficulties at leadership level in the two parties, 'The discussions between Labour and Democratic Left in that post-1992 election period, that's what really brought about the subsequent merger. We had the same objectives.'[20]

During the 1980s the Workers' Party put Labour under considerable electoral pressure, as their fortunes at the polls went in opposite directions. But the split in 1992 meant the Workers' Party never got to continue its challenge and to see if its objectives could be realised. The post-1987 period undoubtedly presented a greater challenge, as Labour had returned to the opposition benches in 1987. While regrouping for the larger party was difficult – evident by the 1989 general and European election results – it was better positioned to more vigorously battle its smaller rival. In any event the 1992 split sundered the Workers' Party; the party never again won a Dáil seat, and stripped of its leading public representatives it became a marginal actor in political life. But neither was Democratic Left able to build on the Workers' Party previous strong electoral showings. The performance of Democratic Left in the period between 1992 and 1997 can best be described as poor, with a singular failure to make a substantial electoral breakthrough most particularly in the general elections in 1992 and in 1997. Democratic Left never achieved an 'electoral spectacular' such as when De Rossa was elected to the European Parliament in 1989. The new party failed to seriously expand and develop beyond the number of constituencies where the Workers' Party had previously enjoyed success. Democratic Left's vote was very much confined to constituencies where the Workers' Party had established an electoral presence. Indeed, the election of Liz McManus in Wicklow was the only constituency where Democratic Left won a Dáil seat beyond those where the Workers' Party had successfully returned a candidate. There was also a failure to attract new names to stand for the party. The personnel pool from which Democratic Left selected candidates was very much the one formerly associated with the Workers' Party.

## Ideological convergence

Few political parties positioned under the broad left umbrella remained unchanged by the events of 1989 in central and eastern Europe and the advance of economic globalisation. In Ireland, the ideological conflict, coupled with other internal issues, split the Workers' Party and led to the formation of Democratic Left. The pressures had been building over several years. Prior to 1989, throughout western Europe, socialist and social democratic parties had been engaged in internal debate and searching analysis. Over a protracted period of time those to the left of mainstream left parties in countries like Britain, Austria and Sweden, and including the Workers' Party in Ireland, were increasingly confronted with the reality that their positons, policies and outlooks were indistinguishable from the social democracy of their so-called more moderate left rivals. As Dunphy observed about the more radical left in Spain, Denmark, Greece and in Ireland (the Workers' Party), these parties were, 'all relatively small organisations forced to define themselves in opposition to social democratic parties which seem to be post-socialist, never mind post-Marxist'.[21]

The advance of economic globalisation reduced the individual influence of national governments. In this environment the power of the Keynesian economic tools traditionally favoured by the left significantly weakened. This transformation was underway at a time when the left was challenged to comprehend and deal with the consequences of the collapse of the Soviet model. In this new world many parties on the left struggled to forge a new political identity and distinctive economic policy agenda. For many, socialism's theory and past practice has been hard to discern in the policies of left-wing governments in countries like Britain, France and Spain in the 1990s and the early years of the twenty-first century. Reviewing these developments, Gottfried argued that the, 'policy differences between the right and the left have narrowed down to mere detail. The right accepts and even expands the welfare state, while the left has scuttled plans for government control of industries. Talk about a 'third way' between capitalism and socialism has replaced the radical left's appeal to class conflict.'[22] It was a scenario familiar to those in the Workers' Party who departed to form Democratic Left in 1992.

The Workers' Party was never formally styled as a communist party, and there remains, among its former leading political figures, differing views as to its ideological classification. Eamon Gilmore was emphatic that, 'the Workers' Party was never a communist party. It had within it people who were Marxists, people who were social democrats, people who were Left Labourites, if I can put it that way, you know, people who were socialists in a wide sense of the word.'[23] This broad definition is in sharp contrast to the view offered by Proinsias De Rossa, 'My clear understanding about the party was that it had evolved into what might nowadays be termed a communist party. It was much more like the communist party in Italy.'[24] Despite these alternative opinions, the Workers' Party did in fact share many of the characteristics of the communinst identity in western Europe. Bull isolated three factors binding west European communist parties together including a privileged link with Moscow; a commitment to building a society different from the capitalist one; and an internal organisation underpinned by democratic centralim.[25] It can be reasonably concluded that the Workers' Party met the Bull criteria as it had links to the Soviet Union, a commitment to a post-capitalist future and an adherence to democratic centralism as a mode of organisation.

The Workers' Party has been categorised as one of the reformist Eurocommunist parties which emerged in the 1970s.[26] Certainly taking the definition of Eurocommunism as parties commited to revolutionary goals, adhering to democratic socialism and defined by considerable membership uniformity, then the Workers' Party in the late 1970s and throughout 1980s, in effect, ticked the correct boxes. But, just like the communist model in the Soviet controlled areas, Eurocommunism was inadequate as an ideological position. It was, as Kindersley noted, 'a good sales pitch'.[27] But it was also an inadequate sales pitch as it failed to offer a new voice and saw the left on a trajectory towards convergence with the social democractic tradition.

The internal Workers' Party debate was undoubtedly given added impetus by developments in the Soviet Union where Mikhail Gorbachev was opening up the possibility of an alternative definition of socialist democracy. The first sign of new thinking came at the Workers' Party annual conference following De Rossa's election as party president in 1989. Television producer Eoghan Harris was a key player in the background at this stage. Harris, who heavily influenced De Rossa's approach, had, 'acute sensitivity to those epochal changes that radically transform the basic contours and language of politics …'.[28] Heavily influenced by the Gorbachev revolution as well as the new approaches adopted by the Italian Communists among others, Harris argued for a reassessment of the socialist model. The move surprised many in the Workers' Party. According to long-time member and De Rossa adviser, Tony Heffernan, the Harris-inspired speech at the 1989 Ard Fheis, 'shocked lots of people in the party [as] it raised questions about a whole series of assumptions that people had'.[29]

Harris's intervention hastened an internal debate among his colleagues but the collapse of the communist-controlled regimes in Central and Eastern Europe forced the Workers' Party to speed up the reconsideration of its ideological identity and organisational model. 'At stake were not merely organisational choices but also the party's political and ideological direction', Dunphy and Hopkins noted.[30] There was some unease that senior members were clinging to the increasingly discredited ideology as represented by the Soviet-controlled states, as Eric Byrne outlined, 'At annual conferences we would be most embarrassed when we'd see invitations … bringing in people from North Korea and other weird communist countries …'.[31] Another party veteran, Tomás MacGiolla, did not see the wider debate about the Left in Europe, and in eastern Europe in particular, as impacting on the Workers' Party. 'I was a total anti-communist and there were no Stalinists in the party. So it was never an issue [within the Workers' Party]'.[32] But a more nuanced debate than MacGiolla acknowledged was well underway in party ranks. Others recognised the wider debate. Proinsias De Rossa recalled, 'I remember making a speech where I pointed out that the fall of the Berlin Wall and what was happening in Russia was going to have far-reaching effects on the Left and on the Right, and that people didn't know quite yet what the outcome would be.'[33] The debate may have consumed much greater energy within the party than it did with the wider electorate, and even a large section of the voters who supported the Workers' Party, but the debate was energy-sapping and the uncertainty drained morale.

There were other pressure points in the Workers' Party in the 1980s unique to the party's Irish experience and removed from the wider debate about European left-wing politics. The party was dogged by questions about the continued existence of the illegal Official Irish Republican Army (OIRA), an overlap in membership between the two organisations and the possibility that monies obtained by illegal means were funding legitimate political activities. While the ideological debate had been developing throughout the 1980s, the question of members with links to criminal activities had been a recurring theme since the 1970s and eventually pushed the divisions to a stage where even reconstitution of the party was not going to overcome the deep internal tensions. For many of those who ultimately exited the Workers' Party criminality was the main motivation for the split. The Official IRA had called a ceasefire in May 1972 – and very much disappeared from the public sphere by 1975 – but questions about the organisation's continued existence lingered. The official line from all leading Workers' Party figures for well over a decade had been that the party was not associated with the OIRA nor was it funded from criminal activity. But the negative publicity arising from media speculation about the OIRA was a source of considerable frustration within the De Rossa wing of the party. As one senior party member observed: 'We tolerated too many excuses within the North, special circumstances and conditions in which they lived … We didn't want any taint of illegality.'[34]

The ideological debate had been developing over several years. The issue of members with criminal associations now augmented these internal differences. Reconstruction although attempted was an unlikely solution and, even if successful, was probably not going to be a permanent one. In the latter half of 1991, talk within the De Rossa group turned to the possibility of forming a new political party. Such a move would immediately remove the burden of the history and ideology dogging the Workers' Party. Before this next step was taken, a decision was reached to make one final effort to reach an accommodation within the Workers' Party. Ultimately, however, an attempt to reconstitute the existing party at a special conference in February 1992 was unsuccessful. The outcome only increased the likelihood of the formation of a new party. 'Most of us then decided there was nothing more we could do and we left,' De Rossa admitted.[35]

At the time Democratic Left was formed, there was a belief in left circles across Europe that a new form of left poltics would emerge, a politics more radical than social democracy. Various labels were applied to this new thinking including 'third way' and 'new revisionism'. It was, Sassoon concluded, driven by, 'the idea that capitalism would not be destroyed by a self-generated crisis, or by a revolution, or by the steady expansion of public property'.[36] This 'New Revisionist' theme was addressed at the founding conference of Democratic Left in 1992. Senior member Des Geraghty was one of those who attempted to place the formation of the new party in the post-1989 political context in Europe, 'We have rejected any utopian or elitist politics which seek to act on behalf of people but fails to involve the people in setting their political agenda for change.'[37]

Various contributors at the foundation conference pointed towards the 'third way' debate. But this third way politics and new revisionism was somewhat ill-defined. Politicians like Proinsias De Rossa in Ireland were in the difficult role of trying to explain how their new positioning was different from the outlook held by their social democratic opponents. Those who departed the Irish Workers' Party in early 1992 were not yet prepared to make the leap into a new social democratic future. They were intent on finding, and maybe even creating, a new type of politics. Although his contribution came at the end of the conference proceedings, De Rossa posed some pertinent questions, 'some people ask – do we need a new party? And what is this new party? How does it differ?' The party leader could not avoid the subject as elsewhere the issue of difference between the new undertaking and the Labour Party was being discussed. One media commentator, Dick Walsh, who had close links with the Workers' Party noted, 'On most fronts, Labour and Democratic Left will find themselves in broad agreement, although they still differ on the North and ... may employ different tactics.'[38]

De Rossa was hoping to lead a new political party, which would be an active democratic socialist party with a strong presence in parliament. There is little doubt but that De Rossa's speech at the Democratic Left founding conference – and indeed the various documents approved by delegates – fitted with the Sassoon neo-revisionism thesis. But the founding vision was never defined in a way that explained the party's distinctiveness, nor was it made clear what policy instruments were to be used to implement the same vision. Democratic Left's search for ideological relevance became a recurring theme in the party's short life. In early 1992 the party and its leading members embarked upon a political journey in search of a middle ground, or third way between a discredited communist/ socialist/republican past, and an unsatisfactory social democratic compromise. But left politics – and in particular the type of ideology framed as more radical than social democratic thinking – struggled to find a coherent programme. Like its counterparts in Italy and France, Democratic Left was confronted with the rejection of a Marxist past and its replacement with a variation of social democracy. David Arter has written how post-1989 politics led to, 'the neo-liberalisation of social democracy, and the associated phenomenon of the social democratisation of the radical Left'.[39] Democratic Left's weakness was tied to its rejection of social democracy as a political and ideological programme. The party wanted a more radical prescription but struggled to create a new coherent ideological blueprint, especially in the economic arena.

Despite the best efforts of those involved, and the work of a number of internal task forces established to address the issue, no clear understanding emerged as to what exactly was understood by 'Democratic Left'. In his report to the 1993 annual conference, the party's general secretary acknowledged the challenge. 'One of the unsatisfactory aspects for members must be the continuing low poll ratings for Democratic Left. There is no simple explanation for this situation, although it is obvious that the party has still to develop a clear identity in the public mind.'[40]

The identity issue was not one that was easily resolved. It emerged once more in July 1994 in a short internal document, Youth Report, prepared for an Executive meeting. 'There is a crisis of identity and purpose in Democratic Left. This has resulted, externally, in continually low voter identification and recognition for the party as a unit, its politics and its policies; internally, with the membership's morale and motivation.'[41] The prescription offered was a variation on a theme repeated time and time again in internal party documents, 'The very immediate task and objective of this party is to clearly establish and define itself as a democratic socialist party on the radical left of the Irish political spectrum. This must be done on an unambiguous and unapologetic way.'[42] Included among the practical solutions put forward to enhance the party's identity was the need for a campaigning section, a party newsletter, promotion of internal debate and a change in the language and symbols of the party.

The identity problem was widely acknowledged by leading Democratic Left figures. Senior advisor Tony Heffernan said more should have been made of differences with the Labour Party, 'We described ourselves as a democratic socialist party. I suppose we should have tried to explain the difference between that and social democracy which wasn't all that easy and which wasn't something that the voters were terribly interested in. We should have explained ourselves more in terms of criticising the positions that the Labour Party had taken and criticising the previous record of the Labour Party.'[43] But for others the 'Labour question' was one that did not have an easy answer. 'That bedeviled every left wing party that has emerged because there has always been the Labour Party, and in the mind of the people – "why are you different?" – that certainly was an issue for Democratic Left,' the party's former general secretary, John Gallagher, concluded.[44]

The lack of a clearly defined identity stifled the party's growth. This situation was even more difficult during the life of the 1994-7 rainbow government when the points of differentiation with Labour became even more blurred, especially for the electorate.[45] The identity issue was again the focus of discussions at meetings of the post-general election task force that convened in the summer of 1997. 'The precise position and purpose of a socialist party like Democratic Left needs to be re-stated', the report concluded, adding the recommendation that a new strategic approach involved other like-minded parties to create a Left-led government.[46] In a significant recommendation, and a significant acknowledgement of the troubles facing the party at the time, the task force members said they, 'would favour a change in the party name but believes that this is not politically practical. However, it recommends that the party should style itself Democratic Left – the Socialist Party on literature and elsewhere as appropriate.'[47] The party's National Executive did not accept the name change idea although its members agreed to commission a report, 'on projection of our name and policy and the production of a new logo.'[48] In the end, this failure to carve out a clear difference of identity in the public mind from the Labour Party meant Democratic Left did not achieve its aim of becoming a strong left alternative in Irish politics.

## Conclusion

The split in the Workers' Party and formation of Democratic Left came at a time when the wider European Left in all its various hues was engaged in a debate about the forging of a new radical identity in response to the challenges arising from the collapse of communism and the rise of the New Right's free market dogma. There was a failure to find a consistent and coherent voice. The Workers' Party backed away from change after the split in 1992, moving into a political *cul de sac* that brought only political irrelevance. But its successor party Democratic Left, like many other Left groups in Europe, never decided what it wanted to become, never offering a coherent explanation of how it would use a given set of policy instruments to deliver its stated goals.

The unravelling of the Workers' Party, and the short, but eventful life of Democratic Left, was shaped by the debate in European Left politics. The blurring of ideological identity had an impact on both parties. As the rules of the game changed in the late 1980s and throughout the 1990s, neither the Workers' Party nor Democratic Left found themselves able to articulate a distinct message for Irish voters. The exit from the Workers' Party was also prompted by a specific local issue: criminality, and there is little doubt that those embarassing revelations created a climate in which, having failed to reconstitute the party, the formation of a new political grouping was inevitable. But even if the reconsitution had been accepted, it is likely that a stronger Workers' Party would also have been confronted by the same issues which challenged Democratic Left. In such a scenario it might have been possible to move beyond the criminality allegations but a reformed Workers' Party would also have had to explain what were the substantive policy differences with the Labour Party.

Neither did the experience in government assist Democratic Left in this regard. While the small Irish parties that have experienced government come from different ideological perspectives they all share in common initial electoral success followed by steady decline. On first analysis it would seem that participation in government shortened their respective life cycles. Involvement in a coalition government with one or more of the three big parties – Fianna Fáil, Fine Gael or the Labour Party – may possibly have blurred the lines of difference with their rivals. This collection of small parties were each, to use O'Malley's phrase, 'smothered' by their larger governmental partner.[49]

In the aftermath of the 1997 general election, serious questions were being asked within Democratic Left about the party's future, not to mention its future direction. Some members believed they had a role to play as a critical niche political party offering an alternative on the left to the more moderate Labour Party. This argument was rejected by several senior party figures who were no longer able to distinguish real differences between themselves and their counterparts in the Labour Party. These two schools of thought were, however, united in appreciating the task involved in rejuvenating the party after the disappointing election results in 1997 which had seen Democratic Left exit government and return to the opposition benches in Leinster House. Certainly, by the end of 1997, there was a realisation among many leading party figures that the process of rebuilding was going to be very difficult. Des Geraghty was not alone in addressing the scale of the work and effort being shouldered by a small group of individuals and the resulting pressure this generated. 'I think we were faced by just too many elections, too quickly, and then there was the strain in a very small party, intellectually, physically and mentally ...'.[50] Eamon Gilmore also referred to the energy required to maintain the party when, for many senior members and the vast majority of the electorate, the party was no different from the Labour Party, 'we certainly saw no future in effectively two Labour parties with little or no difference.'[51]

Ahead of Democratic Left's founding conference, Proinsias De Rossa received a letter of best wishes from Dick Spring, the leader of the Labour Party, in which he wrote of, 'continuing the co-operation that we have enjoyed in the Dáil on a wide range of issues' and establishing, 'a strong and coherent left-wing voice'.[52] The hostility between the two parties reduced significantly during the 1994-7 Rainbow coalition. Many involved mention increased trust and the development of friendships between individuals who previously would have had no opportunity to associate with each other. The period in government also only served to highlight the perception issue, that is, how the voters saw the two parties. This identity conundrum was set alongside continuing organisational problems and mounting financial difficulties. The party's future was leading in one direction, according to John Gallagher, 'The Labour Party had moved on. In 1992 there would have been a more confrontational view of the Labour Party. But by 1997 a lot of old battles were over and [many] constituency battles had also sorted themselves out.'[53]

The Democratic Left experience, and that of the Workers' Party, show, however, that the challenges and threats to small parties are more fundamental than the dangers of cosying-up with their larger rivals in government. When faced with a multitude of challenges such as membership, organisation, leadership and, more recently, money, new parties in Ireland struggle to sustain their political involvement. They also fail to deal with the larger parties adapting their programmes and positions to preserve their predominance. In seeking to identify why small parties have been unable to achive longevity in an Irish context no one answer is sufficient. Democratic Left was essentially a challenger party but one without significant ideological difference from its larger rival. It was in competition with Labour based on its capacity to deliver, and what Coakley defined as a self-proclaimed superior competence and integrity in formulating and implementing policy.[54] But challenger parties, partly due to their relative smaller size as new entrants, remain open to renewed vigorous competition from their long established and better resourced larger rivals. In the latter respect, the durability of the main parties has been impressive, even when faced with a decline in their first preference vote, Fianna Fáil, Fine Gael and the Labour Party have adapted to changes and challenges so that they continue to win more or less the same percentage of Dáil seats.[55]

As Weeks indicates in Chapter 1 on new parties, the emergence of new small parties is often a reflection of a failure by the established parties to respond to new political agendas; the new entrants are in tune with voter concerns. They also act as a means of registering protest or discontent with the political system, and represent certain principles. In this way, small parties tend to be agenda-setters. But their agendas may be limited and once the large parties adjust their stance voters tend to gravitate away from the small parties. In this way, the electorate's support for small parties may be highly promiscuous beyond a limited core vote. The Workers' Party experience in the 1980s is an example of this fact as Labour's support declined in government but the party subsequently countered the threat of the new entrant.

Fianna Fáil and Fine Gael – and to a lesser degree the Labour Party – as catch-all parties with a flexibility to reach accommodation with societal changes rely upon broad coalitions of support. In general, catch-all parties dilute their ideological individuality in order to maximise their appeal to centre-oriented middle class voters. They compete for votes not on significant policy difference but rather on competency and personality with competency equating with economic management and personality defined by the likeability of a party leader. A narrowing of party difference has been evident in the main areas of political debate in Irish society over the last three decades – Northern Ireland, the economy and the liberal/moral agenda. This uniquely Irish convergence played out as the global political scene was transformed in a post-Berlin Wall environment with a merging of economic ideology and a blurring in the differences in political orientation between most mainstream parties which had their origins in twentieth century left and right politics.

Those involved in founding Democratic Left in early 1992 were aware of the poor record new entrants had in challenging the traditional dominance of Fianna Fáil, Fine Gael and the Labour Party in Irish electoral and governmental history. 'It is extremely difficult to build a new party in Ireland from the ground up,' Pat Rabbitte acknowledged.[56] The challenge for Rabbitte and his colleagues was made even harder still by the uncertainty over their political identity in the context of left politics in the 1990s, the rate of change in Ireland in the same decade as many of their core issues were resolved, and the specific organisational and financial demands placed upon small political parties. It is the combination of these factors, varying in importance between different parties, which has caused the death of a multitude of small Irish parties despite the enthuasitic ambitions of their founding members.

# 11

# Major Breakthrough or 'Temporary Little Arrangement'? The Labour Party's 2011 Electoral Success in Historical Perspective

*Shaun McDaid and Kacper Rekawek*

## Introduction

The place of the Labour Party within the Irish party system has been historically difficult to classify. Whether the party can be defined as a major or minor one is also problematic. Prior to the 2011 election, the Irish party system was characterised as a 'two and a half party system' with centre-right Fianna Fáil and Fine Gael as first and second parties and Labour usually a distant third.[1,2] Labour was classified by one of its former parliamentarians as an entity which goes through, 'cycle[s] of decline and recovery, always on a small electoral base', but which always fails to make a quantum political leap.[3] However, in 2011, Labour effectively ceased to function as the 'half' in the Irish party system, relegating Fianna Fáil into third place. After an impressive electoral performance, Labour received its highest number of first preference votes (FPVs) (431,786 or 19.4 per cent of the total vote) and saw the highest number of its candidates (thirty-seven) elected to the Dáil in its history.[4] What is the significance of this result for the Irish party system?

The primary political cleavage in Ireland has been the legacy of the Civil War (1922-23). Both Fianna Fáil and Fine Gael, traditionally the two largest parties, owe their origins to opposing factions of the Irish revolutionary movement which fought for independence from Britain between 1919 and 1921. While the legacy of civil war has affected other European party systems, such as Greece, post-Franco Spain[5] and Finland,[6] its effects in Ireland have resulted in the retardation of a left–right alignment in the party system. However, the two largest parties are now the centre-right Fine Gael and centre-left Labour. The latter, for many years, strove to terminate the aforementioned 'Civil War' political cleavage. However, it is by no means certain that Labour has been enduringly successful in its quest to re-align the Irish party system, despite its tremendous electoral successes in 2011. Indeed, the party achieved a similarly impressive result in the 1992 general election, despite remaining the third largest party, when it won more than 333,000 first preference votes (19.3 per cent of the total vote) and saw thirty-three of its candidates elected to the Dáil.[7]

The so-called 'Spring tide', named after the party's telegenic and impressive leader, Dick Spring, propelled the party to unprecedented levels of popularity and transformed it into an effective political kingmaker in Ireland. Between 1992 and 1994, it coalesced with Fianna Fáil, and between 1994 and 1997 it was an integral part of the 'rainbow coalition' with Fine Gael and the Democratic Left (DL).[8] In a 2010 article, we argued that the 'Spring tide' was in fact a blip in the party's electoral history due to a number of exceptional factors.[9] This was evidenced by Labour's failure to sustain the 1992 gains in subsequent general elections, and its return to its average share of the party system. Given the current economic realities in Ireland, Labour is faced with a daunting challenge, and its members could be forgiven for bitterly remembering their party's history, especially the build-up to the 1992 electoral success, and the subsequent return to the 'half' in the Irish party system in the late 1990s and beyond. Thus interesting parallels can be drawn between Labour's 'Spring tide' and the recent 'Gilmore gale', which can help us assess the extent to which Labour's second party status is truly an enduring major breakthrough or merely a Reynoldsian 'temporary little arrangement'.[10]

## Methodology

This chapter compares Labour's performances during the 1987-92 and 2007-2011 periods, and examines the reasons why the party achieved its lowest percentage share of the vote in over fifty years in 1987, and the processes by which it recovered in 1992. It will also assess the reasons behind the party's reversal of fortunes from 2007 to 2011. Between 1987 and 1992, Labour managed to almost triple its total number of voters. This led to a more than threefold increase of its percentage of the vote and expanded its Dáil team by 175 per cent (twelve TDs in 1987 compared to thirty-three in 1992). During the next fifteen years, however, the party's vote share slumped to 10.3 per cent and its parliamentary presence comprised a respectable, but relatively insignificant, twenty TDs. Nonetheless, a mere four years later the party staged a remarkable comeback and won twice as many votes as in 2007, almost doubling its Dáil team.

Through the means of a thematic analysis, we study the evolutionary and transformative factors which led to Labour's reversal of fortunes in 1992, and compare the extent to which these factors were also important between 2007 and 2011. No observer will be able to account for all the factors and account for all the variables behind a political success or failure. Sometimes, these are by-products of seminal extraordinary events outside the influence of political leaders, (and beyond the control of researchers seeking to establish independent variables). Extraordinary factors were co-responsible for Labour's slide into minor party status in 1987, when it was blamed by the electorate for the state of the economy, despite there being little it could have done to improve the situation. Five years later, however, fortune was on Labour's side, as it was the beneficiary of the electorate's anger at the performance of the Fianna Fáil-led government. This was to be repeated nineteen years later, as Labour, under Eamon Gilmore, could confidently portray itself as economically and politically detached from the succession of Fianna Fáil-led governments that presided over the slide from Celtic Tiger to IMF rescue. Nevertheless, it would be naive to suggest that extraordinary factors alone, such as the current Irish financial crisis, explain the change in Labour's fortunes during both these periods. Such an analysis would fail to appreciate the far-reaching structural changes within the party, its effective leadership, nullification of its internal squabbles and successful competition with other left wing forces in the 1987-92 and 2007-11 periods respectively.

The key factors we investigate during both periods are: internal divisions within the party, party leadership, organisational structure, and rivalry with the non-Labour left. Our analysis of the two periods is based on privileged access to Labour Party documents, election materials, contemporary newspaper articles, transcripts of Dáil debates, electoral data and retrospective interviews with senior Labour members, including the most influential figures from 1987-92 and 2007-11. The information from these sources is triangulated with secondary sources already in the public domain and extant secondary literature which addresses different aspects or periods of Labour's history.[11]

## Labour: a 'proximal mainstream' party

Before analysing the implications of Labour's recent gains, it is worth reflecting on the party's electoral performances in historical perspective. An examination of the data illustrates that Labour cannot simply be classified as either a 'major' or 'minor' party. In general elections between 1923 and 2007, it polled an average of 11 per cent of the total vote, with a mean of sixteen candidates elected per Dáil. The large gains of 2011 failed to radically alter this statistical image of the party. Its average vote (between 1923 and 2011) increases by one quarter of a per cent and the average number of TDs continues to hover around sixteen, still less than 10 per cent of the Dáil which has 166 members. If we agree with Mair's suggestion that a major party is one that normally polls at least 15 per cent in general elections,[12] then Labour would not qualify as such, having only received the necessary mandate on five occasions throughout its history (see Table 1). However, if Labour is not a major party, then neither is it a minor one. Many scholars have recognised the problematic nature of deciding what constitutes a minor party.[13] If the criterion of a minor party is that it has less than one quarter of the midpoint number of seats of the two largest parties, then Labour has fallen into the minor category only in the periods 1981-2 and from 1982-7, despite being a coalition partner in government on both occasions. Given Labour's position as an occasional party of government, size is not the only factor which needs to be considered when addressing this question.[14]

A party's small size will not necessarily restrict it from playing an 'active and significant role' in the party system.[15] Returning to Sartori, perhaps 'relevance' is helpful in defining major or minor party status. 'Relevance' is not judged by electoral strength alone, but also the potential of any party to affect the balance of power, or 'coalition potential'. An irrelevant minor party would be one never needed or put to use in a coalition government. A relevant minor party would be one which had been in coalition, at least once. If this is the case, then Labour has certainly been a 'relevant' party, whether numerically major or minor. It has also achieved Pedersen's four 'thresholds' in relation to party relevance.[16,17] Labour might also be classified as a 'hinge' party.[18] Such parties, in theory, operate near the centre of the left–right axis, and are free to support parties of both the left and right. Traditionally, the two major parties in Ireland have both been centre-right in orientation; however, Labour has, at various times, switched its support between Fine Gael and Fianna Fáil to form coalition governments, whilst successfully avoiding the tag of a 'detached' party, displaced from the left-right axis and relying on electoral support from particular societal groups.[19]

During the 1923-2011 period, Labour increased its FPV at Dáil elections on sixteen out of twenty-eight occasions, and its proportion of votes on thirteen occasions. Concurrently, its number of seats increased fifteen times (1969 was the one occasion when an increasing vote return did not deliver an increased number of seats). Therefore, in 55 per cent of general elections, the party saw its fortunes rise in one way or the other, with a decrease in the remaining 45 per cent. Labour found it extremely difficult to maintain long periods of electoral growth, thus not qualifying as a 'major' party. However, it also defended itself relatively well against terminal electoral decline, carving a distinctive niche for itself in the party system and successfully avoided becoming a 'minor' party.

Effectively, Labour has, for most of its history, functioned as the third largest party in Ireland, and participated in coalition governments led by both Fianna Fáil and Fine Gael. It was only beaten into fourth place, an obvious sign of demotion in the 'two and a half' Irish party system, on three occasions in its history (in 1933 by National Centre Party, 1944 by Clann na Talmhan and in 1987 by the Progressive Democrats). Thus we argued that Labour, for most of its history, might best be classified as a 'mainstream', rather than 'minor' party.[20] 'Mainstream' in the Irish context is the 'half' in the 'two and a half party system', or the third largest party. Mainstream parties are potential parties of government, not ideologically constrained from taking part in coalitions, as is often the case for far-right or far-left parties. For example, the French and Italian Communist parties, which won between a third and a quarter of electoral support at various

*Table 1: Labour's results in general elections 1923-2011[22]*

| Year | First preference votes for Labour* | Percentage of the vote for Labour | Seats won by Labour** |
|---|---|---|---|
| 1923 | 111,939 (1,053,955) | 10.62 | 14 (153) |
| 1927 June | 143,849 (1,146,460) ▲ *** | 12.55 ▲ | 22 (153) ▲ |
| 127 Sept | 106,184 (1,170,869 | 9.07 | 13 (153) |
| 1932 | 98,286 (1,274,026) | 7.71 | 7 (153) |
| 1933 | 79,221 (1,386,558) | 5.71 | 8 (153) ▲ |
| 1937 | 135,758 (1,324,449) ▲ | 10.25 ▲ | 13 (153) ▲ |
| 1938 | 128,945 (1,286,259) | 10.02 | 9 (138) |
| 1943 | 208,812 (1,331,079) ▲ | 15.68 ▲ | 17 (138) ▲ |
| 1944 | 106,767 (1,217,349)**** | 8.77 | 8 (138) |
| 1948 | 115,073 (1,318,650)**** ▲ | 8.72 | 14 (147) |
| 1951 | 149,293 (1,304,542) ▲ | 11.4 ▲ | 16 (147) ▲ |
| 1954 | 153,919 (1,309,976) | 11.7 ▲ | 18 (147) ▲ |
| 1957 | 111,747 (1,227,019) | 9.1 | 11 (147) |
| 1961 | 136,111 (1,168,404) ▲ | 11.6 ▲ | 15 (144) ▲ |
| 1965 | 192,740 (1,253,122) ▲ | 15.4 ▲ | 21 (144) ▲ |
| 1969 | 224,498 (1,318,953) ▲ | 17.0 ▲ | 18 (144) |
| 1973 | 185,117 (1,350,537) | 13.7 | 19 (144) ▲ |
| 1977 | 186,410 (1,603,027) ▲ | 11.6 | 16 (148) |
| 1981 | 169,990 (1,718,211) | 9.9 | 15 (166) |
| 1982 Feb | 152,053 (1,665,353) | 9.1 | 15 (166) |
| 1982 Nov | 158,115 (1,701,093) ▲ | 9.3 ▲ | 16 (166) |
| 1987 | 114,551 (1,777,165) | 6.4 | 12 (166) |
| 1989 | 156,989 (1,656,813) ▲ | 9.5 ▲ | 15 (166) |
| 1992 | 333,013 (1,724,853) ▲ | 19.3 ▲ | 33 (166) |
| 1997 | 186,045 (1,788,997) | 10.4 | 17 (166) |
| 2002 | 199,059 (1,860,333) | 10.7 ▲ | 20 (166) |
| 2007 | 209,185 (2,025,903) ▲ | 10.3 | 20 (166) |
| 2011 | 431,796 (2,243,146) ▲ | 19.4 ▲ | 37 (166) ▲ |

\* In brackets – total number of votes cast.

\*\* In brackets – total number of seats.

\*\*\* ▲ equals rise in either first preference votes, percentage of the votes or number of seats for Labour in contrast to the preceding election.

\*\*\*\* Result for the Official Labour does not include National Labour Party.

stages of their existence, had a coalition potential of virtually zero due to their ideological heritage.[21] A mainstream party thus has the potential influence of a major party and often more influence than a mass party of the far-right or far-left, without necessarily breaking Mair's 15 per cent threshold and without becoming, in the Irish context, the second or first party.

A 'proximal mainstream' party has precisely the same characteristics in terms of potential to participate in coalition government, but would usually poll slightly less than a mainstream party. To differentiate a 'proximal mainstream' party from a relevant minor party, the 'proximal mainstream' party would be expected to consistently poll an average of above 10 per cent in national elections – Labour's average is 11.25 per cent. Sartori's relevant minor parties need only have participated in coalition once to guarantee their relevance, whereas an average vote of above 10 per cent, regular coalition participation, and occasional gains to major party status suggest that Labour is more than just a relevant minor party but less than a fully fledged 'mainstream party'.

Given that Labour maintained an average of 11 per cent of votes and circa 10 per cent of Dáil seats throughout its history, it is clear that the 1987-92 period represents the most turbulent shifts between lows and highs in Labour's history. In fact, during this period, the party went from minor, its second worst result, to major, its second best in twenty-eight elections, before returning to 'proximal mainstream' status in the post-1992 period. As mentioned, the 2011 gains have not significantly affected the party's overall average share of the party system. Thus it cannot be taken for granted that the party has yet broken through to major or fully-fledged mainstream rank. Indeed, Labour's post-1992 experience suggests that it may yet return to its usual, proximal mainstream status at the next election. Interesting parallels can thus be made between the 1987-92 and 2007-11 periods, and perhaps serve as a warning to a party determined to cement its major and mainstream status, thus avoiding a Reynoldsian 'temporary little arrangement' with regard to its electoral standing and strength.[22]

## Internal divisions within the party

Between 2007 and 2011, the Labour leadership did not have to deal with significant internal divisions. Although, following the party's decision to coalesce with Fine Gael in March 2011, there is evidence of some dissent from some of the party's more left-wing members. Westmeath junior minister Willie Penrose resigned from government over the decision to close Columb Army barracks in his Westmeath constituency.[23] Dublin TDs Tommy Broughan and Patrick Nulty lost the party whip, for voting against the government: Broughan on a procedural motion to discuss the extension of the bank guarantee scheme, Nulty on the austerity measures demanded by Ireland's EU-IMF creditors.[24] While Penrose's decision was perhaps, 'based on a number of factors, not all of which were ideological',[25] Broughan and Nulty were regarded as being on the 'hard left' of the party.[26] Their actions were not entirely surprising, since both had 'already voted against the [coalition's] programme for government'.[27]

Nevertheless, there is no faction of TDs representing the hard left within the Parliamentary Labour Party (PLP) at present. Indeed there is, 'no formal group of any kind' within the PLP.[28] The PLP is regarded as, 'more homogenous than it ever was in terms of the ideological spectrum of its members'. PLP divisions were 'much greater' during the 1970s and '80s, particularly between those 'from "provincial" Ireland ... who weren't always personally conservative, but ... knew they couldn't go too far ahead of their own constituency' and the more socialist inclined urban TDs.[29]

Despite media reports in late 2011 playing up divisions within the party,[30] former Labour general secretary Ray Kavanagh argues that both Broughan and Nulty want to, 'make the party more left-wing', but whilst remaining within the 'umbrella' of Labour.[31] This is confirmed by Nulty himself, who plans, 'to be very much involved in Labour politics, even though at the moment [is] outside the PLP.' Indeed, one of the quirks of the Irish party system itself may partially explain why Labour may appear more divided than it actually is. In Ireland, there is a 'very rigid whip system'.[32] Backbenchers who vote against the government are sidelined immediately which can stifle internal policy debates within the party. This is much less frequent in Westminster where there is a tradition of, 'backbenchers from both Labour and the Tories voting with their consciences on issues of importance to them'.[33] Such MPs do not usually lose the party whip.[34] There is also a 'strong tradition of that in the US Senate. The Irish tradition ... doesn't foster democratic debate and discussion.'[35]

By contrast, Labour was crippled by divisions between 1987 and 1992. Its participation in coalition with Fine Gael between 1982 and 1987 left it open to criticism from Labour Left, the political tendency within Labour opposed to coalition.[36] Labour Left was emboldened by Labour's poor electoral performance and the perceived weakness and unpopularity of Dick Spring. Labour Left sought an amalgamation with the hard-left Workers Party (WP)[37] and wanted to abolish the central role of the PLP in selecting the party leader to undermine Spring, who was supported by most Labour TDs.[38] This disunity threatened Labour's ability to confront the 'three strong parties of the right [Fianna Fáil, Fine Gael and the PDs]'.[39]

The threat from Labour Left diminished after 1987 but did not entirely abate. This was only partially achieved in the aftermath of the 1989 party conference in Tralee when prominent Labour Left TD Emmet Stagg of Kildare was marginally defeated in the contest for party chairmanship. Nonetheless, Labour continued to court Stagg and other leading Labour Left members such as Michael D. Higgins, now the Irish President, who had the support of their local party branches. Disciplinary action or expulsions would have meant losing Dáil votes and seats, at a time when Labour had to regain its 'mainstream' status and face a left-wing challenge from the WP.[40] According to Stagg, Labour Left actually had a revitalising effect on the party's, 'lazy, long established leadership' which was forced to, 'start working and talking, communicating like any political party'. This allegedly helped reshape the internal dynamics of Labour and restore its competitiveness.[41]

Labour Left was not the only divisive element within Labour. The presence of the 'mad extremists' in the Militant Tendency, an entryist, Trotskyite group, was tackled in 1988-89 with the expulsion of Militant branches.[42] This was an attempt to 'box [the Militants] off' to increase the party's acceptability to the electorate.[43] Moreover, the Militants were also attacked by Labour Left, incorrectly perceived by some as the former's allies. Both groups might have disliked Spring's leadership but were 'plotting from different directions'.[44] In fact, Labour Left helped the Spring leadership purge the Militants from the party. Both effectively conceded defeat at the aforementioned Tralee conference, and henceforth supported the leadership.[45] During both the 1987 to 1992 and 2007 to 2011 periods, the role of the party leader has been an important factor in Labour's improved electoral performances.

## Leadership of the party

In 2007 Labour polled, for the third consecutive election, less than 11 per cent of the popular vote. Party leader Pat Rabbitte resigned and was replaced by yet another former WP/DL member, Eamon Gilmore, the only contender for the job. Gilmore, with eighteen years of parliamentary experience and over three decades of political involvement, plus a three year stint as Junior Minister for the Marine,[46] has consistently remained a 'mystery' – low key, private, and serious but immensely popular with the electorate, who considered him as better leadership material than Fine Gael's Enda Kenny.[47]

Gilmore successfully utilized his political and managerial experience to 'change' the way his party organised, presented and ran itself during what was dubbed 'Project of Renewal',[48] in line with the recommendations of the 21st Century Commission.[49] The new leader was thus transformed into a centralising, 'Managing Director type figure',[50] leading a seemingly open, vibrant and campaigning party which consciously disassociated itself from the limitations of Rabbitte-era electoral pacts with Fine Gael, and after more than a decade in opposition unashamedly sought power. He also became renowned for his 'excellent media performances' and policies which 'resonated with the people'.[51] His accusation that the Fianna Fáil–Green government was guilty of 'economic treason' for pumping taxpayers' money into the insolvent Anglo-Irish Bank struck a chord with the electorate.[52]

Such an approach, combined with Gilmore's national standing, allowed the party to record considerable gains in the 2009 local elections, and consequently to reach unprecedented support levels in opinion polls. Indeed, in June 2010, an *Irish Times* poll suggested Labour was the most popular party in the state for the first time in its history, the so-called 'Gilmore gale' which brought back memories of the 1992 'Spring tide'.[53]

Twenty years before Gilmore's accession, *The Phoenix* magazine referred to then Labour leader as 'Groucho' Spring, a reference to his gruff manner and apparent haplessness.[54] The disastrous 1987 result, combined with his uninspiring 1987-89 parliamentary performance led many party members to question his ability to establish himself as a decisive leader: 'Did he have the balls to lead the party? ... It was touch and go ...'.[55] Unexpectedly, Spring managed to focus Labour's attention on electoral success and oversaw a reorganisation of party structures, resulting in a centralisation of control over the different constituencies,[56] establishment of a communications committee,[57] and standardisation of election literature for the whole country, in line with the recommendations of its Commission on Electoral Strategy (CES).[58] This had previously been resisted by rural TDs who, 'didn't like that stuff from Dublin'. Afterwards, 'the party was speaking with one voice ... and it was Dick Spring ['s].'[59] The Labour leader also met the challenge of holding the government to account in the Dáil, through forensic attacks on successive Fianna Fáil leaders.[60]

This strengthened the public perception of Spring and Labour as proponents of accountability in government. As a result, Spring, 'grew in stature, people began to see – "hey, this guy can do it"',[61] and came to be regarded as *de facto* leader of the opposition. Additionally, Spring benefited from his association with Mary Robinson, whose candidacy for the Irish presidential election helped revive Labour's fortunes. Although technically an independent, Robinson's nomination papers were signed by Labour parliamentarians, and Labour led her campaign. Most Labour sources agree that the decision to propose a candidate in the presidential election was a masterstroke on Spring's part.[62] Such an approach allowed the party to register important gains in the 1991 local elections and paved the way for the 1992 electoral success.

## Electoral strategy and organisation

Labour's organisation changed significantly between 2007 and 2011. A comprehensive review of its organisation and strategy was undertaken by the 21st Century Commission, under the direction of Greg Sparks, a former advisor to Dick Spring.[63] This 'completely revised' the party's internal decision making structures. In particular, 'the move to a directly elected leader strengthened the relationship between the party leader and the party members'. This resulted in a more rationalised system than the previous 'Trade Union set-up', and lessened tensions between party members and the National Executive.[64] There is much more 'central control' by party Head Office than in 2007, and the organisation is, 'much more professional; the key goal is winning elections', with the focus on 'the nuts and bolts of clinical campaigning'.[65] In addition, the party has two professional, full-time organisers in Dublin alone, (where it is the largest party), in the guise of Councillors Dermot Lacey and Brian McDowell.[66]

Candidate selection during the 2011 election was also much more centralised than before. There was a 'completely different process' compared to 2007, with prospective candidates being interviewed by personnel from Head Office. Existing TDs, however, were exempt from this process.[67] Head Office was thus in a position to hand-pick its preferred candidates throughout the country. This generally caused few difficulties, although in a number of instances local branches resisted this change, such as in Sligo, where a number of ex-Labour candidates stood against the official candidate and split the party vote.[68]

Despite the increased centralisation of the party's organisation, further work may be required to ensure the policies of Head Office are followed fully. The concept of, 'paper branches and paper members is still very much a part of the [party's organisational] culture' and is something which, 'hasn't really been eliminated'.[69] Equally, the increase in central control has not met with complete approval from all party members due to the lessened, 'grass-roots autonomy and participation' in the decision making process.[70] However, the more professional organisation, and the party's decision to field its highest number of candidates since 1969, certainly contributed to the increased share of the vote in 2011. The contrasts between the 2011 election, Labour's best performance, and the 1987 election, its second worst, could not be starker.

On the eve of the 1987 election, party elites argued that Labour resembled a '"rainbow" coalition of minority groups and interests which may be impossible to reconcile'.[71] The party's organisation was described by the then leader, Dick Spring, as 'the world's worst'.[72] This was unsurprising, given that Labour lacked a centralised administration.[73] Electorally, it functioned like, 'a federation of 15, 16 independent republics [which] varied from place to place [and] was a very light ... in terms of number of people in it'.[74] Far-reaching organisational changes, like taking decision making powers away from the annual conference and the disbandment of the Administrative Council (AC), were suggested to rectify this.

There was a loose structure of party fiefdoms centred on rural TDs, often beyond the control of the Dublin Head Office. Thus Labour was prone to factionalism and infighting, which surfaced publicly at the party's annual conference.[75] Conferences were dominated by tedious policy debates,[76] with the party leader or the general secretary often forced to personally lobby delegates to assure crucial motions were passed.[77] The leadership also had to thwart attempts by Labour Left and the Militant tendency in their bid to 'dump Dick Spring'.[78]

This structural disorganisation was corrected during the 1987-9 period when the party got 'its house in order'.[79] The Militants were expelled, and controversial left-wing TD Emmet Stagg was successfully marginalised.[80] This helped the party, 'clean [up its] act internally'.[81] Thus, by 1989 'the shock of the near obliteration'[82] of the 1987 election subsided and the Spring leadership was firmly 'in control' of the party.[83] Under Spring, party structures and operational activities were centralised, which strengthened and renewed the party's image. Labour enjoyed a steady rise in the opinion polls from 1988 onwards,[84] and successfully utilised Spring's popularity to convince the electorate that it was a coherent political unit.[85]

Furthermore, Labour's 'morale [was] boosted' by Mary Robinson's presidential election victory in 1990 and the 1991 local election results. The party began preparing for the next general election almost two years in advance, targeting thirteen constituencies where it might potentially gain a seat.[86] The leadership 'hand picked' or 'hand beheaded' many candidates[87] and decided it, 'wouldn't disrupt the organisation by trying to parachute another layer of candidates on the eve of elections'.[88] Dealing effectively with its leftist rivals also ensured that Labour improved its chances of electoral success.

### Rivalry on the Irish left

In 2007 the Green Party and Sinn Féin constituted Labour's primary left-wing competitors. In 2011, almost all the left-wing parties recorded some kind of increase, including Sinn Féin's seemingly unthinkable election of fourteen seats in the new Dáil.[89] Moreover, the newly formed United Left Alliance (ULA), (consisting of People Before Profit Alliance, Socialist Party, and Workers and Unemployed Action Group) won five seats.[90] The Greens were the only party not to benefit, and were electorally annihilated, the result of participation in coalition with Fianna Fáil.

All the left-wing parties that made electoral gains benefited from being in opposition during the most unprecedented economic crisis in the history of the state. In theory, their left-wing ideologies enabled them to offer more comforting alternatives to the electorate bracing itself for the prolonged period of austerity. The radical left could also attempt to present itself as an alternative to the three main parties which were allegedly responsible for Ireland's sordid state of affairs. This strategy definitely helped the 'disparate' alliance of Joe Higgins's Socialist Party, (SP), effectively a 'one man band', and the SP's ULA partners make electoral gains.[91]

Sinn Féin, despite suffering from 'stagnation', electoral disappointments and a resignation of prominent councillors in the 2008-9 period,[92] made calls for Labour to explore with it, 'and others the potential for co-operation in the future'.[93] At the same time, Sinn Féin learnt the lessons of 2009 local elections and its activists began to operate and, 'represent "good areas"' which enlarged its potential pool of voters. The republican party therefore managed to appear more 'acceptable' and 'palatable'[94] without addressing its ideological dilemma of how to mix Irish republicanism and socialism while competing for electoral endorsement in the Republic of Ireland.[95] In short, Sinn Féin, 'established itself as a long-term force in Irish politics', which might benefit from an intake of former Fianna Fáil voters in rural areas where Labour is often sparsely represented.[96] Indeed, despite the discrediting of Fianna Fáil, Labour failed to make major gains in Connacht and Ulster. Nevertheless, at national level, the improved performance of the left aided Labour most of all, catapulting it to second place in the party system.

Two decades earlier, the left-wing threat to Labour was much more menacing, as non-Labour left parties and candidates almost equalled Labour's share of the vote.[97] However, by 1992 this threat was minimised by Labour's merger with two leftist micro-parties the Democratic Socialist Party (DSP) and the Independent Socialist Party (ISP). These mergers resulted in gains for Labour in the constituencies where these parties operated.[98]

Labour was also inadvertently helped by a split in the ranks of its main leftist rival, the WP. The latter emerged in 1982 as the political wing of the Official republican movement after a long period of transformation. Labour's coalescing with Fine Gael between 1982 and 1987, combined with devoted membership of the WP, electorally 'fishing in the same pond [as Labour]',[99] ensured that the WP made serious electoral advances and threatened to become the major force on the Irish left, particularly in Dublin.[100] This forced Labour to embark on a policy of confrontation with the WP, to regain the influence and seats lost to the latter.[101] Elements within both parties, however, still made, 'ritual declarations about the desirability of unity on the Left' but remained in a state of both covert and overt political conflict.[102]

The fact that Labour managed to reduce the electoral threat of the WP by the early 1990s was the result of a combination of factors, including Labour's organisational renewal, the unpopularity of other main parties associated either with scandals (Fianna Fáil) or muted political opposition (Fine Gael), and Dick Spring's reasserted leadership of the party. However, more important was the internal divide and consequent split within the WP, between members favouring a more social democratic approach and those controlling the administrative apparatus of the party, who favoured communism and allegedly retained links with the theoretically moribund Official Irish Republican Army (OIRA).[103] Thus, Labour was, for the majority of those with left-of-centre politics, the only acceptable party with a credible political programme.

## Conclusion – The perpetuation of Labour's cycle?

For most of its history, Labour has occupied a unique place in the Irish party system, a space somewhere between major and minor party status. Between both 1987-92 and 2007-11, Labour witnessed a significant revival of its electoral fortunes. Whilst both key elections, 1992 and 2011, occurred during periods which witnessed extraordinary political circumstances, a number of important organisational and structural factors contributed to the party's advances in both contests, specifically, party leadership, organisation and electoral strategy, the internal unity of the party, and the challenge of the non-Labour left.

In both these core periods, Labour has had a popular and credible leader, in the guise of Gilmore and Spring. Both men were also helped by the lacklustre performance of their rivals: in Gilmore's case, Enda Kenny's lack of charisma has certainly benefitted the Labour leader, while Spring was aided by the decision of the then Fine Gael leader, Alan Dukes, who pursued the so-called 'Tallaght strategy', supporting the Fianna Fáil-led government's programme of austerity measures in the 1980s and early 1990s.[104]

Spring and Gilmore were both keen to ensure that the party they led focused on electoralism. They professionalised their organisations, and exercised greater control over candidate selection and campaign literature, although in Gilmore's case, this was already under way before he became leader.[105] Both Spring and Gilmore also pursued an independent campaign strategy, which did not limit Labour's options for future coalition partners. By contrast, under Pat Rabbitte, Labour signed the Mullingar Accord in 2004, effectively a pre-election pact with Fine Gael. However, Gilmore was forced to rule out a deal with Fianna Fáil when, 'their absolute unpopularity became known'.[106]

Whether or not Gilmore's decision to coalesce with Fine Gael will be less damaging than Spring's decision to govern with Fianna Fáil, however, remains to be seen. Indeed, previous results suggest that Labour tends to fare badly regardless of which party it governs with.[107] As O'Malley has noted, junior parties in government are vulnerable to being 'smothered' by the larger coalition partner.[108] Also, whilst Spring took time to build up a profile as leader, the electorate eventually warmed to him, following a number of impressive performances in the Dáil. By contrast, there are already signs that Gilmore will be unable to sustain his initially high approval ratings, which have recently plummeted by 11 per cent to just 35 per cent. Gerry Adams, leader of Labour's main rival, Sinn Féin, is now the most popular Irish political leader.[109] Like Gilmore, however, Adams may find that personal popularity does not necessarily mean that voters are willing to vote for the party of which he is leader. Indeed, Labour's 'Gilmore for Taoiseach' campaign never gained much momentum, with Gilmore himself conceding that Fine Gael would lead the government a few days before the election took place.[110]

This republican–left threat is a common theme for Labour during both the 1987 to 1992 and 2007 to 2011 periods. In 1987, the non-Labour left polled almost as many votes as Labour. By 1992, this trend was reversed, with Labour making the primary gains on the Irish left. However, in 2011, all the left-wing parties did well, a process aided both by the micro-parties contesting under the banner of the ULA, and the 'protest, anti-establishment vote' due to anti-government feeling.[111] Whereas in 1992, the republican–left threat to Labour diminished due to the split in the WP, the threat posed by Sinn Féin is markedly different. If Sinn Féin can resist the ideological ruptures which doomed the WP, then it could feasibly threaten Labour's electoral position. In March 2011, many Irish voters did not consider Sinn Féin an 'acceptable' party of government,[112] but further tough budgets, populist policies, and consistently strong Dáil performances from Sinn Féin's younger members such as Pearse Doherty and Mary Lou MacDonald, both untainted by previous involvement in government, might increase Sinn Féin's acceptability.

Whatever challenges Labour faces, it appears to be a more united party internally than it has ever been. The pragmatism and skill of Dick Spring and his supporters in expelling the Militants and marginalising Labour Left between 1987 and 1992, and ensuring the party rallied around its leader certainly improved its electoral prospects in 1992. The party was transformed from a disparate coalition of quasi-independent TDs into a professional, organised and more ruthless political organisation. Historically, better organisation always appears to help Labour's electoral performances. This was certainly true during the 1960s, a decade when the party grew consistently,[113] and evidence from the 1987-92 and 2007-11 periods confirms this trend.

Internal unity has also helped Labour in its quest for electoral advancement. Nowadays, despite some opposition to the programme for government from some high profile members such as Joanna Tuffy, Patrick Nulty and Tommy Broughan, there is no organised group of left-wing TDs within the party, as there was during the 1987-92 period and earlier, which augurs well for its future internal coherence. Equally, even these more left-wing voices appear to want to move Labour's policies further to the left from within the party, rather than break away from it. Whether or not Gilmore, whose ideological heritage is democratic centralism, will continue to allow those who do not subscribe to government policy to remain within Labour is yet to be seen.

Despite Labour's position as the second largest party, there remain a number of significant challenges. Labour is the weakest ever second largest parliamentary party in terms of FPVs. The second party has always polled more than 20 per cent (with the sole exception of Fine Gael in 1948 which polled 19.8 per cent).[114] Also, as a party of government, it will undoubtedly face criticism for implementing the austerity measures which the country's external creditors demand. Labour received similar treatment in 1987 from an electorate which was 'up in arms', at the introduction of water charges while in government with Fine Gael.[115]

But does Labour's new-found status as the second largest party truly represent a re-alignment of the traditional, Civil War, party system in Ireland? It is difficult to make political predictions of this sort. In 2008, none of our interviewees believed that this was an imminent possibility: 'It's an ongoing civil war ... Will there be a realignment of politics in the Republic of Ireland? No'.[116] Three years on, and despite Labour's position as the second party, there is little certainty about a potential left-right realignment of the party system.

Many believe it is simply too early to say whether or not we are witnessing a lasting change in the party system. Assessing just how damaged Fianna Fáil is by the economic crisis is difficult at this remove.[117] Equally, Labour could face a similar electoral backlash to that received by the left-wing parties in Greece and Spain, due to its role in implementing cuts and tax rises. Those on the left of the party opposed coalition on the grounds that coalescing with Fine Gael merely 'reinforces the previous pattern' and potentially hinders the sought-after left–

right realignment.[118] Others, however, are more sanguine, believing that Fianna Fáil's lack of talent, and the contempt in which it is currently held, means that, 'Fine Gael and Labour will be the two major parties going forward, certainly for the next five to ten years, until things have improved.'[119]

Opinion polls from late 2011 onwards, however, suggest difficult times ahead for Labour. While support for the centre-right Fine Gael has fallen, it remains the largest party, with 30 per cent support ratings. In the same poll, Sinn Féin was the second most popular party (21 per cent support), just one point ahead of Fianna Fáil, which appears to be staging somewhat of an early recovery. By contrast, Labour was only the fourth most popular party, with 11 per cent support, precisely the same figure as its average share of the vote throughout its electoral history since 1923.[120] However, in the most recent poll, it has recovered somewhat with 16 per cent, but still lagging behind Fianna Fáil as third largest party.[121] In the last three polls, Labour has been only the third or fourth most popular party among those surveyed.[122] Thus the unprecedented gains of 2011 may yet prove to be a 'temporary little arrangement' for Labour. Indeed, it may yet require a number of 'tides' or 'gales' to cast off its 'proximal mainstream' status, and establish itself as a major player in the Irish party system.

### Acknowledgements

The authors sincerely thank those who helped with both our 2010 article and the current chapter: Paul Dillon, Keith Martin, Brendan Halligan, Ita McAuliffe, Aoife Carroll, Ian O'Mara, all our interviewees and their support staff.

# 12

# The Slow Growth of Sinn Féin: From Minor Player to Centre Stage?

*Dawn Walsh and Eoin O'Malley*

## Introduction

In the elections of 2011 Sinn Féin made something of a breakthrough. It received almost 10 per cent of the national vote in the Dáil election, a three-point increase on its 2007 result. Later in the year its candidate for the presidential election, Martin McGuinness, polled almost 14 per cent. The party's return in Dáil seats, though less than its vote would have commanded in a purely proportional system, was a significant improvement on its disappointing result in 2007. Its return of fourteen seats compared favourably to Fianna Fáil's total of twenty seats. The latter party's decision not to contest the presidential election, while probably wise in hindsight, caused some to wonder if the party was leaving itself open to further encroachment of its position by Sinn Féin.

Throughout this book, we see examples of small parties who blaze brightly for a short period, only to die out. O'Malley suggests that this might be because of the impact of government on small parties. The experience of Sinn Féin south of the border seems to support this point. It is one of the extant few parties to have maintained a Dáil representation and not gone into government. The party has made steady progress and in 2011 was larger than any of the minor parties since the initial breakthrough of the PDs in 1987. Sinn Féin is approaching the size of the Labour Party in the 1997, 2002 and 2007 elections. In short, it seems to be moving from minor to mainstream party.

In this chapter we ask if Sinn Féin can truly break the mould of Irish politics by moving to overtake Fianna Fáil or Labour to become such a mainstream party, or if it is likely to play at best a supporting role, which may have some relevance because of its coalition or blackmail potential. We can attempt to answer this question, which essentially looks to the future by examining the nature of Sinn Féin as it stands. We have some expectations of mainstream and minor parties in Ireland, which may differ from mainstream and minor parties in other countries. Mainstream parties tend to be heterogeneous in their support base, so the three established parties in Ireland tend to have broadly stable support across class, gender and age. Their support also tends to be reasonably evenly divided throughout the country, rather than focused in a small number of strongholds, often associated with individual politicians. Because minor parties are usually dependent on a small number of notable political figures, the political organisation is often personalised and less rule-based than in major parties. Minor parties tend to be ideologically on the fringes, whereas mainstream parties tend to be more centrist, or more difficult to pin down in policy terms. By looking at how Sinn Féin performs in these areas, we can make a better informed judgement as to whether Sinn Féin is likely to move centre stage.

There is a paucity of literature on Sinn Féin as a 'normal' political party. Most works deal with the more violent wing of the organisation, the IRA, and its involvement in the move away from conflict. However, a number of works consider the party in normalised politics. Murray and Tonge look at Sinn Féin policies beyond just the constitutional issues, although the main focus of the book is to tell the story of its movement to party politics.[1] Maillot devotes a good deal of space to studying 'New Sinn Féin' and finds that it is a leftist party with a strong equality agenda.[2] Another study of Sinn Féin as a normal political party found no evidence that it is anything other than a radical left-wing party. Policies which are associated with the right such as Sinn Féin's use of public–private partnerships to fund education in Northern Ireland, in contravention of its stated policy, are examples of the party's 'pragmatism'.[3]

This chapter builds on this nascent work. We are interested primarily in the party as an electoral organisation in the Republic of Ireland, although we also make references to its operation in Northern Ireland. We first explore the roots and history of the party, its growth strategies, policies, support bases and organisation in order to decide how best Sinn Féin's role in the Irish political party system can be understood. We conclude that its policies are broadly left of centre and its nationalism has undergone a transformation in line with the transformation of the situation in Northern Ireland. There is a strong potential for growth as Sinn Féin builds a grassroots-based campaigning organisation that targets the socially marginalised and young people. It may also benefit from being seen as the main opposition party (as Fianna Fáil struggles to criticise the Fine Gael–Labour coalition's policies due to its central role in the economic crisis). However, Sinn Féin also faces challenges as it seeks to move the leadership of the party from the charismatic old guard to a new younger grouping and to maintain consistency north and south of the border in radically different contexts in order to fulfil its own claim to be an all-Ireland party.

## Roots of the party

While Sinn Féin (variously translated as 'Ourselves', inelegantly as 'We Ourselves' or incorrectly as 'Ourselves Alone') was founded in 1905 by the non-violent nationalist, Arthur Griffith, it has split so many times that practically all political parties in Ireland (and none) can claim to be descended from this original party. Sinn Féin was a small, insignificant party in Ireland until, following the 1916 Easter Rising, it reconstituted as a broad nationalist party, having become the focus for the electoral efforts of the unsuccessful military revolt. The British wrongly assumed Sinn Féin had been behind the uprising. Before that it was a nationalist party looking for a joint-sovereignty arrangement to achieve similar terms to Hungary in the Austro-Hungarian Empire. In the December 1918 general election it received 47 per cent of the vote on the whole island, and had all the seats been contested would probably have received two-thirds of the vote (Sinn Féin won twenty-five seats without a contest).[4] Though some of this support can be put down to Sinn Féin's anti-conscription policy, the party's success is a measure of the extent to which Irish political consciousness had changed in the previous years. It won 73 out of the 105 Irish seats and proclaimed the First Dáil (Assembly). The party's fate in the 1920s has been well-documented, with little need to repeat this in much detail. The split in 1921 (over the Anglo-Irish Treaty) and in 1926 (over abstention from the Dáil) reduced Sinn Féin to a largely irrelevant rump party ignored by its military wing and master, the IRA. Further splits on the issue of abstention led to the creation of Clann na Poblachta and Republican Congress. Renewed IRA military campaigns in the 1950s and 1960s, and the assumption of radical socialist policies reduced Sinn Féin's relevance even more.

In the late 1960s the IRA seized the opportunities provided by Unionist over-reaction to civil rights demands and assumed responsibility for 'defending' Catholic areas. The Sinn Féin/IRA leadership in Dublin, which had become increasingly leftist and engaged in politics, was seen as militarily inactive and a split ensued. One of the Provisional's leaders, Joe Cahill 'had a feeling that ultra-left politics were taking over. As far as I was concerned, the main purpose of the IRA and Sinn Féin was to break the connection with England and get the Brits from Ireland.'[5]

For the existing leadership of Sinn Féin, Cahill and people like him, 'were simply right-wingers living in a fantasy world and clinging to a romantic past'.[6] The Provisional IRA was founded in Belfast in 1970 with its political wing Provisional Sinn Féin. This is what is commonly referred to by the name Sinn Féin. Official Sinn Féin, as the original party became known, went on to split again; the splinter group going on (eventually) to merge with the Irish Labour Party.

The leadership of Provisional Sinn Féin (hereafter Sinn Féin) was northern-based and closely connected with the armed campaign of the Provisional IRA. Anti-communism was high on the agenda for the new organisation. *Republican News*, the Belfast organisation's mouthpiece complained that, 'into executive posts both in the IRA and Sinn Féin, the Red agents infiltrated … young men and women were brainwashed with the teachings and propaganda of the … Red infiltrators.'[7] The same paper later claimed, 'our allegiance is to God and Ireland'.[8] For one IRA member, an early leader of the Provisionals, Billy McKee, was 'an arch-Catholic bigot'.[9] However, this conservatism was not uniform in the Provisional movement and the ever-present tensions between conservatives and socialists re-emerged. As time went on, a debate on Sinn Féin's politics took place and a left-wing agenda became current, but in the late 1970s Gerry Adams rejected the idea that Sinn Féin was or should be an extreme-left organisation, declaring, 'There is no Marxist influence within Sinn Féin. I know of no one in Sinn Féin who is a Marxist or would be influenced by Marxism.'[10] By the mid-1980s Adams claimed that socialism, never a popular ideology in Ireland, was not on the agenda.[11] From the early 1980s an electoral strategy was pursued and Sinn Féin moved to moderate its public statements to make them more acceptable to the broader nationalist community in Northern Ireland. But Sinn Féin was still largely seen as beyond the pale in the south, never receiving over two per cent support. In the aftermath of the 1989 election, Gallagher commented that Sinn Féin's, 'performance suggests it has little future in the south'.[12] He remarked that its 'long road' to success looked more like a *cul de sac*.

Continued negotiations with the British and Irish governments led to an IRA ceasefire in 1994 and eventually to the Belfast Agreement, a consociational peace agreement institutionalising the ethno-national divisions in Northern Ireland, in 1998. This 'peace' was broadly welcomed, with Sinn Féin dramatically increasing its support in Northern Ireland as it became seen as the party best able to ensure the implementation of the Belfast Agreement for nationalists. In the south the party's increased acceptability enabled it to increase its support base. However its campaigns in the south (understandably) had less to do with the 'peace process' agenda, but emphasised and campaigned on issues such as housing shortages, bin charges and anti-social behaviour, the concerns of its voters in deprived urban areas.

## Sinn Féin's growth strategy

These campaigns are fundamental to the party's growth strategy. By operating in areas of deprivation Sinn Féin is able to persuade traditional non-voters that the party can address the issues which concern them. There have been many commentators who have argued that Sinn Féin's growth may come from winning the votes of traditional Fianna Fáil voters who are angry or disappointed by the party's recent performance. However, Sinn Féin members and representatives are more focused on the traditional non-voting groups.[13] Winning the votes of these groups has greater potential to build a loyal Sinn Féin vote. If the party targeted the dissatisfied voters of another party there is a risk that such voters would only temporarily vote Sinn Féin and would revert to voting for their former party once their anger dissipated.

These campaigns give the party a can-do image and help it to differentiate itself as an activist or campaigning organisation as opposed to just a political party concerned with gaining and maintaining power for its own sake.[14] They also allow the organisation to maintain a larger active membership than other small parties. These campaigns provide a focus for the membership in the respective areas, particularly during quiet times in the electoral cycle. However, the party also recognises that different strategies are appropriate for different constituencies, and that these campaigning activities that are effective in socially-deprived areas will not be successful in more middle-class areas where the profile of candidates or representatives may be more important.[15] This is a lesson the party has learned from its experience in Northern Ireland, despite the very different contexts, where it has success outside the working-class areas it seems confined to in the south.

Another area of potential growth which the party focuses on is winning votes from young voters. This is seen as a strong area of possible expansion. There is a view within the party that these voters represent fertile ground for the Sinn Féin message for two reasons. Firstly, young people are seen as less attached to a party than those who have a life-long history of voting for a particular party. The current economic difficulties which the country faces are also viewed as presenting the party with an opportunity to persuade young voters not to follow generational voting patterns which are so deterministic within the Irish context. Secondly, younger people have less direct experience of the party's involvement in violent nationalism. This lack of direct experience means that Sinn Féin may not be as toxic to these voters as it was to their parents or grandparents.

This growth strategy that involves targeting traditional non-voters and young voters leads to slower growth than would be achieved by an electoral swing. There are only a certain number of young people becoming part of the electorate in each election and votes from traditional non-voters are won by labour-intensive campaigning on social issues. However, this slow and steady growth is seen as a positive form of growth by the party. While there has been excitement regarding potential electoral swings and a sudden breakthrough in the lead up to certain elections the dangers of such rapid growth is apparent. Such swings can easily be reversed and if they result in a single term in government any gains made can quickly be undone as the Green Party has recently learned.[16] Slow and steady growth in Northern Ireland has proven to be a successful strategy for the party and this experience informs growth plans in the south. Data from exit polls indicates that this is a successful strategy in so far as support for the party is significantly higher among young people and the working-class. This point is returned to in our discussion of support bases below and Table 1 illustrates data from exit polls which supports this point.

## What kind of party?

The strategy of slow growth indicates that the party has no expectation to become mainstream in the short term. Minor parties seem to be qualitatively different to mainstream parties in a number of ways. In this section we investigate to what extent Sinn Féin appears like a minor or mainstream party.

## Ideology

Sinn Féin is unusual in that it contests elections in two jurisdictions. It is systemically in very different positions in the two places. In Northern Ireland it is one of the largest parties, and the largest party within its ethno-national block. In the south, it has been a minor party with just a handful of seats. In Northern Ireland, the unusual governmental structure means that it has consistently been represented in the devolved government there – though there is no opposition. In the south, the party has not just consistently been in opposition, it has been assumed 'uncoalitionable' in a *conventio ad excludendum* among the other political parties that they would not enter government with Sinn Féin. This is not unlike the similar convention in Italy that any coalition was preferable to one that included the Communist Party, though some have alleged that Enda Kenny suggested approaching Sinn Féin in 2007 in a bid to form a government.[17] It is not clear whether its systemically different positions in the two jurisdictions mean that the party has presented itself in different ways to voters in the two places. In the south, it presents itself as a radical left-wing, even anti-system party. In Northern Ireland, even though it actually is anti-system, its support among middle-class Catholics might mean that it tends to offer a more mainstream position.

In one area, it is qualitatively different from other parties in the south. It alone has a radically nationalist policy towards Northern Ireland and the British position there. Yet it has positions which are not at all nationalist, or exclusive in tone, in areas such as immigration. O'Malley argued that Sinn Féin's position in the south was akin to those of what are commonly termed radical right-wing parties, but which might more accurately be termed populist nationalist parties.[18] However, unlike other populist nationalist parties, Sinn Féin is among the most openly pro-immigrant parties in Ireland. Ireland had seen a rapid rise in the immigrant population: from negligible levels to ten per cent of the population in as many years. While a Labour Party leader has expressed concerns about immigrants driving down wages and job security in 'a race to the bottom',[19] Sinn Féin has consistently called for greater supports to immigrants and in its 2002 manifesto called for, 'the right to work or study for asylum seekers while their claims are being processed'.[20] It explicitly states that immigrants should not be blamed for housing shortages or hospital waiting lists. Sinn Féin is vocal in its support for a pluralist society and its opposition to sectarianism.

Though the attitude to modern immigrants is welcoming, the attitude to those who settled in Ireland centuries ago is hostile. The party leader, Gerry

Adams, has written many books in which he sets out his political beliefs. These tend not to show a desire for a pluralist society. His justification for his campaign is that Ireland has a right to self-determination which the British prevent the Irish exercising. By contrast unionists cannot claim this right, 'They are a national minority; a significant minority but a minority nonetheless. To bestow the power of veto over national independence and sovereignty on a national minority is in direct contravention of the principle of self-determination.'[21]

As Whyte points out, Adams assumed what is to be proved. There seems no recognition that Ulster Protestants may themselves form a separate nation with its own identity and rights. Murray and Tonge report that, in 1987, early drafts of the document Scenario for Peace contained a suggestion that Unionists unable to accept a united Ireland could be repatriated (presumably to somewhere they are not from).[22] Even post-Belfast Agreement Adams displays basic majoritarian instincts by suggesting that unity can come about when there is a 50 per cent plus one majority in favour of unity.[23] Nor does the attitude to recent immigrants sit easily with the activities of Sinn Féin/IRA during the Troubles, many of which were blatantly sectarian such as the murder of Protestants in Tullyvallen Orange Hall, La Mon, or the Enniskillen Remembrance Day bomb in 1987. While it may support the plight of modern-day immigrants, the descendants of those who travelled to Ireland 400 years ago appear less welcome.

Sinn Féin is similar to populist nationalist parties in other ways. It has consistently opposed EU treaties and regards the single currency as a diminution of Irish sovereignty. Though it has tempered its language against globalisation, its economic policies emphasise support for small indigenous business. Sinn Féin argues that it would develop,[24] 'World-class infrastructure to attract Foreign Direct Investment *and* support indigenous enterprise for longer-term employment creation. This sustainable long-term employment would broaden and secure the tax base.' (Emphasis added.)[25]

Its main policy proposals focus on support for small business and local brands, though it calls for maintenance of the low rate of corporation tax. In education it calls for greater investment and for Irish culture and language teaching to be improved. Unusually for an avowed left-wing party, the document focuses heavily on crime. It calls for community policies, victims' rights and measures to tackle drug pushing and anti-social behaviour. The focus is on populist local action and a distrust of the state. Sinn Féin also gives some attention to human rights. This may be interpreted as being a post-material concern, consistent with its radically liberal-left self-description, but others have shown that the appeal to human rights in Northern Ireland is less a reflection of post-materialist values and more a reflection of politics in that place.[26]

For a socially radical party, Sinn Féin's social policies are at times surprisingly conservative or non-committal. For instance Sinn Féin joined the DUP to support a motion in the Northern Ireland Assembly (20 June 2000) against extending the 1967 UK Abortion Act to Northern Ireland. Ambivalence on the abortion issue may only reflect social realities in Ireland which makes all Irish politicians uneasy. Adams, despite describing himself as a devout Catholic, also said he would not oppose gay marriages. However, he was willing to allow Sinn Féin to participate in a New York St Patrick's Day parade from which gays were banned. Mixed with this are calls which are quite typical of a radical left liberal party; the party was against the war in Iraq, calls for an end to the US blockade of Cuba, and for nuclear disarmament.

But an Irish election is a series of small local elections. It might be that the positions taken in manifestos (which are never read by voters anyway) may differ from the message being put to voters in deprived urban areas, or that different constituencies receive different messages. When one looks at Sinn Féin campaigns, it is making essentially populist appeals. Though it campaigns as an environmentally sensitive party it has opposed the efforts of councils to force householders to recycle by making them pay for refuse collection. It gives the incorrect impression that large businesses do not have to pay its waste disposal. One campaign is for a motorway to be built to the north-west of the country. A willingness to change ideology was noted by Moloney who is generally regarded as antagonistic to Sinn Féin, found that the:[27]

'move to the left' which Adams had launched to isolate the old guard in Sinn Féin, was eventually dropped as were other policies that characterized and even defined the Provisionals under his leadership in the 1970s and much of the 1980s.

Excepting the policy on Northern Ireland, Sinn Féin policy documents do not appear radical; rather (like other Irish parties) they are often statements of desired outcomes rather than actual policies to achieve those outcomes. Where policies are proposed these too are platitudinous. For instance, an aspiration of the party's 2002 election manifesto was,[28] 'Sinn Féin supports the development of a comprehensive all-Ireland strategy to eradicate poverty and deprivation in Ireland. This must be properly resourced and carried out within a specified time frame.'

It might be hard to see a coherent political philosophy but arguably this is no different to other mainstream Irish parties. This would indicate that Sinn Féin, as Doyle implied, is pragmatic enough to make the shift in policy to the centre, if this is needed to move to the mainstream in politics in the Republic. A systematic study of Irish party manifestoes using computer-coded word-scoring found that, apart from its distinctive position on Northern Ireland, Sinn Féin appears, 'interested in moving into the territory of the mainstream Irish parties rather than marking out a distinctive position on the liberal left'.[29] Indeed, these authors point to the party's focus on urban crime, drug dealing, and the support for small and indigenous business, which would position the party closer to conservative parties than on the left. Overall, their study finds Sinn Féin to be an economically centrist party and socially the most conservative party after Fianna Fáil. More recently Suiter and Farrell found that in an analysis of party manifestos Sinn Féin maintained a distinctly left-wing stance compared to the other left-wing parties which had moved to the centre in 2011.[30]

Other measures of party policy exist. An expert survey conducted by Benoit and Laver, where academic experts are asked to place parties on a number of different dimensions, shows Sinn Féin to be clearly a party of the left on both sides of the border.[31] In a candidate survey conducted by Gilland-Lutz and Farrington,[32] party candidates to the 2003 Northern Ireland Assembly election were asked to place themselves on scales measuring policy positions on a number of dimensions. In these, Sinn Féin candidates placed themselves as the most liberal on moral issues, most environmentally friendly, most tolerant of minorities, and among the most left-wing of the four mainstream parties in a generic left–right scale. On the EU it was at the mid-point, much more Eurosceptic than the SDLP, and more pro-European than the unionist parties. It should be noted that this was based on a very small number of candidates, just thirteen from Sinn Féin.

## Support bases

A party's voters can tell us a good deal about a party. If its voters are systematically more left-wing than other voters we might expect that the party itself is left-wing. If its voters are working class, or predominantly urban, older or male, this might indicate something about the party. Garry, in a study of voters in Northern Ireland, finds that Sinn Féin voters are no more left-wing than those from the SDLP, usually regarded as a centrist party.[33] Nor did its voters differ from those of Unionist parties on the subjective left-right scale. Sinn Féin voters were no different to the SDLP voters on social issues, where the two nationalist parties were more liberal than the unionist parties. Overall there is mixed evidence on the placement of Sinn Féin as a party. This ambiguity and the apparent willingness of the party to adapt its policies to the needs of the electoral campaign indicate that it is more like a pragmatic, mainstream party than an ideologically committed fringe party. This would tally with our view of Sinn Féin as a mainstream party in Northern Ireland.

A few years ago, a respected Irish political commentator proposed that there are two types of Sinn Féin voter in the Republic: traditional anti-British nationalists, mainly in rural areas; and people living in deprived urban working class areas disenchanted with the 'Celtic Tiger' economy and the established parties.[34] Where the former may be conservative and Catholic the latter has the potential to be more radical. Sinn Féin's support in the Republic is strongest in rural border counties and in working-class areas of Dublin.

One of the unusual features of Irish political parties is the heterogeneous basis of their support.[35] Tables 1 and 2 show some demographic characteristics of Sinn

Féin voters in the last four elections. Overall we see an increase in support for Sinn Féin. Within that, the figures are very much in line with what we might call fringe parties, of either the left or right. Sinn Féin's voters are (statistically and substantively) significantly more likely to be working class. There is an obvious and strong relationship with age. Support among the young is much higher than among over pensioners. Should Sinn Féin voters be similar to radical nationalist party voters we would expect to see a gender gap. This also exists.

*Table 1: Sinn Féin voters 1997-2007*

|               | 1997 | 2002 | 2007 |
|---------------|------|------|------|
| Total         | 3.3  | 7.1  | 7.3  |
|               |      |      |      |
| Middle class  | 1.4  | 4.5  | 4.6  |
| Working class | 5.0  | 10.3 | 10.8 |
| Farmers       | 1.0  | 2.4  | 3.5  |
|               |      |      |      |
| 18–24         | 5.4  | 14.5 | 10.7 |
| 25–34         | 4.4  | 8.7  | 9.9  |
| 35–49         | 3.1  | 6.7  | 7.9  |
| 50–64         | 1.8  | 4.6  | 5.6  |
| 65+           | 1.8  | 3.6  | 1.5  |
|               |      |      |      |
| Male          | 4.4  | 8.4  | 8.4  |
| Female        | 2.0  | 5.8  | 6.1  |

Sources: own analysis of RTÉ/ Lansdowne exit polls 1997, 2002 and 2007.

These tables show that Sinn Féin lacks the even distribution across social class that the three mainstream Irish parties possess. There is remarkably little difference in class support for the Labour Party or Fianna Fáil and the differences across class in support for Fine Gael, though they exist, are not substantial if we consider the magnitude of the party's support. For Sinn Féin we still see different support levels across class, age and sex. However, these are perhaps less pronounced than in earlier elections, which might indicate that Sinn Féin is not just increasing, but also broadening, its support base. Particularly encouraging for Sinn Féin might be that its younger voters seem to remain with the party as they get older. It would seem that the slow growth strategy might be working. In 2012 the party's support as measured by various opinion polls indicated that Sinn Féin was increasing its support. A Millward Brown/ *Sunday Times* Poll in mid-February showed the party at 25 per cent and clearly the second biggest party. Although there continues to be age and class difference in the party's support, this poll also shows that Fine

Gael too has quite a big age and class difference in its support bases. While it should be noted that this is just one poll, and the numbers are very small for such an analysis, might we be seeing a move to politics with social bases?

*Table 2: Breakdown of party support in 2011*

|  | **Fine Gael** | **Labour** | **Fianna Fáil** | **Sinn Féin** |
|---|---|---|---|---|
| Total | 36.1 | 19.4 | 17.4 | 9.9 |
|  |  |  |  |  |
| AB | 41 | 22 | 14 | 6 |
| C1 | 36 | 23 | 14 | 9 |
| C2 | 30 | 23 | 15 | 14 |
| DE | 30 | 21 | 16 | 17 |
| Farmers | 53 | 5 | 23 | 7 |
|  |  |  |  |  |
| 18–24 | 31 | 24 | 12 | 14 |
| 25–34 | 30 | 26 | 12 | 13 |
| 35–49 | 35 | 24 | 12 | 11 |
| 50–64 | 35 | 22 | 16 | 10 |
| 65+ | 39 | 18 | 25 | 5 |
|  |  |  |  |  |
| Male | 36 | 20 | 15 | 12 |
| Female | 35 | 23 | 15 | 9 |

Sources: Marsh and Cunningham 'A Positive Choice, or Anyone but Fianna Fáil?' and Appendices in in Michael Gallagher and Michael Marsh (eds) *How Ireland Voted 2011: The Full Story of Ireland's Earthquake Election* (London; Palgrave, 2011)

Less encouraging for Sinn Féin is that the party still does not get a seat bonus. This is because, unlike mainstream parties, there is still quite a deal of antagonism towards the party. In 2011 when asked whether they were likely to vote for Sinn Féin on a 1 to 10 scale, where 1 was completely unlikely, 52 per cent of voters score 1 for Sinn Féin – more even than for Fianna Fáil which was especially unpopular in that election.[36] The same was true of the party's presidential election candidate in 2011.[37] Sinn Féin polarises voters, as we might expect for a minor, ideologically-driven party, perhaps comparable to the experience of the PDs after 1989.

Another feature of the 2011 election is that Sinn Féin did not take support from Fianna Fáil defectors, attracting just 9 per cent of these voters. This has two possible implications for Sinn Féin. First, it challenges the idea that the party will naturally inherit the constitutional republican mantle of Fianna Fáil should the latter fail to recover to its past glories. On the other hand, it also demonstrates that

Sinn Féin's growth strategy is working, and that it did not just 'borrow' votes from Fianna Fáil in 2011, which might, in changed circumstances, return to that party.

The geographic spread of a party's support indicates something about its nature. Mainstream parties tend to attract support reasonably evenly across constituencies, whereas minor parties, because they are more dependent on party strongholds and personalities, have a much greater variation in support. For instance, North Kerry might be a stronghold for Sinn Féin because of Martin Ferris, but in the neighbouring constituencies of Kerry South, Limerick and Clare it is not strong enough to run a candidate. To measure this spread in support we use the coefficient of variation (CV). This takes the average of each constituency's percentage support for a party and divides it by the standard deviation, a measure of the spread of each party's results. The coefficient of variation is an adjusted measure of spread that takes into account the magnitude of the mean and so makes it comparable across parties. The coefficient is scale-free but in this case has a theoretical minimum of zero. Zero indicates that the party's support is distributed perfectly evenly throughout a country. In Ireland we might think of this as a measure of how mainstream is a party's support base.

For Fine Gael in 2011 its CV is 0.24, Labour's is 0.45 and Fianna Fáil's 0.28. The Sinn Féin coefficient of variation is greater at 0.70, though not as large as that for the ULA (1.76) or the Green Party (0.95). The Sinn Féin figure is comparable to the PDs' coefficient of variation in 1987. About the most evenly distributed support of a political party in Ireland in recent years was in 1997 when Fianna Fáil's coefficient of variation was 0.17. Thought the trend for Sinn Féin is to becoming a more nationally-based party – the equivalent figure for 1997 was 1.9 – Sinn Féin is therefore less nationally-based than the three established parties in Ireland. It indicates that Sinn Féin does well in specific areas, but does not have a significant base throughout the country, even in its best election yet. This patchy support is something of which the party is aware and is reported to be targeting.[38]

A more intensive study of Sinn Féin's voters in 2011 than Table 2 demonstrates that the party's voters are closer to the mainstream of Irish society than the party's policies might lead us to expect. Using data from the Irish National Election Study in 2011 we can estimate the position of Sinn Féin's voters, and compare these to the voting electorate as a whole. On left–right self-placement, Sinn Féin's voters in the 2011 general election place themselves at 4.6 on a 0 to 10 scale where 10 means most right. This compares to an average position of 6.0 for the general population, 5.4 for the Labour Party and 4.6 for Socialist Party voters. The attitude to immigrants of Sinn Féin's voters is marginally less welcoming than the mainstream parties. On Europe it is no more hostile than any of the parties, in fact only the Socialist Party's voters appear to stand out. On social issues – the position of women in the home, abortion and belief in God – Sinn Féin voters are significantly more conservative than the general population. Sinn Féin voters do not appear to be typical of supporters of a radical left party, and, in fact, are quite similar in many respects to Fianna Fáil's voters.

## Organisation

Organisationally Sinn Féin portrays itself as a grassroots campaigning party. Members are quick to point out that the parliamentary party has no special role within the organisation in relation to issues such as candidate selection or policy development. They argue that the party is not hierarchical and point to the fact that all those employed full-time by the party earned the average industrial wage in order to signal that elected representatives do not become disconnected.[39] However, certain high-profile representatives undoubtedly exercise a large amount of control. One can see in the decision to field a candidate in the presidential election in 2011 that the leadership can effectively make a decision which will then be ratified by the party's organisational structures.

Numerous books make the point that Sinn Féin and the IRA are essentially two branches of the same organisation.[40] It is also obvious that within the IRA factional disputes are sometimes ended using violence. One work in particular alleges that Gerry Adams has been the effective leader of both branches since before he became the titular leader of Sinn Féin in 1983. The insinuation is that Adams' critics have been effectively silenced. Moloney in particular suggests that the organisation is tightly controlled by the leader and a cabal around him.[41] Adams' tenure as leader (especially when compared with his predecessors) would certainly indicate that Sinn Féin is a leader-driven party and less democratic than it likes to portray itself.

One Sinn Féin TD has said about Adams that he, 'has the charisma of a pop star'.[42] Adams dominates the press coverage of the party. He is regarded as its main electoral asset and within the Provisional organisation he 'commands almost unswerving support and inspires deep loyalty … He is the strong leader. He has the quality of decisiveness.'[43] For others he is the, 'undisputed leader of Sinn Féin'.[44] In policy terms, the move towards political strategy was Adams' own strategy which he pursued successfully if slowly. That the Sinn Féin leader can direct the IRA is demonstrated by the IRA's willingness to turn off its violent campaign for electoral purposes. If military hard-men controlled the IRA, this would not happen.

This strong leadership undoubtedly had the benefit of maintaining coherence within the party and allowing it to move away from violence towards constitutional politics. However, organising a party around a strong individual also brings with it challenges. Firstly, when Adams retires from his central role, a massive power vacuum may be left within the party and the attention his profile brings to the organisation electorally will be lost. There are clearly attempts being made to build up high profiles for representatives such as Pearse Doherty and Mary Lou McDonald to enable them to become similar electoral assets. However, the absence of a clear front-runner to take over from Adams may result in a divisive leadership battle. Furthermore, Adams has been able to unite the party North and South; whether there exists a successor who could maintain this unity is an important question for the party's future as a cross-border entity.

This position as a cross-border party has been an asset to the party in a number of ways. Given that the election cycles in the two jurisdictions are not in sync, the party can call on its northern members to assist south of the border during campaigns. As one Northern representative put it, 'we come south en masse'.[45] Furthermore, the party can learn from its experiences in the North. Party members highlight how being in coalition in Northern Ireland has taught the party how to coalesce with those it is diametrically opposed to and how to negotiate for the implementation of its policies. The party in Northern Ireland is further into a journey that it hopes to make in the South.[46]

Despite the lessons the party can learn from its experiences in the North, its position as a cross-border entity also challenges its organisational coherence. Sinn Féin's experiences north and south of the border are so divergent and the contexts so different that maintaining unity is a massive challenge. The different contexts in relation to policy making on issues such as health and education pose problems for the party but it tries to overcome these by using the different tools to achieve the same aims. While this can lead to coherence in manifestos alone, it does not overcome the challenges posed by the party's different levels of organisation north and south of the border. In Northern Ireland, the party is the main party of nationalists from all socio-economic groups and is in a powerful position on councils and in the Assembly. In the Republic its leadership on councils is limited to the border region and it is in a weaker position in parliament. These differences lead to different focuses and in light of this a strong frame work needs to be in place to ensure unity.

Nevertheless compared to other small parties in Ireland, Sinn Féin is remarkably well-organised and active. It is not a cadre party in the way the PDs might have been. Its membership in the south of 6,748 represents an increase by a third in the year up to March 2012.[47] The party is driving to have a cumann (branch) in every local electoral area in Ireland. There seems to be an active membership visible at elections, and Ard Fheiseanna (party conferences) are organised democratically (on paper at least) and do not always produce decisions that the leadership suggest, although the leadership has been able to reverse decisions subsequently. The membership is also active in community issues, and this is possibly one reason for its success in the south. The issues on which Sinn Féin campaigns tend to be populist in nature, and are not always consistent with the image it portrays of itself as a radical left party. Anti-drugs campaigns have been high on Sinn Féin's list of activities, and given the types of communities Sinn Féin aims to represent, this is unsurprising. After Fianna Fáil it was in the past probably the best funded party, receiving donations from American supporters and there is evidence to suggest from illegal activities.[48] The party also funds itself though a 'levy' on its representatives, whereby they reportedly take the 'average industrial wage' and return the balance to the party, which it uses to hire more support staff. The support staff work for the party as a whole, rather than for individuals as is the case in other parties. TDs we spoke to from other parties 'envy' the support and briefing notes that Sinn Féin TDs and senators have.

Furthermore, as the party has increased its representation in the Dáil cooperation has become easier. Previously TDs were forced to take on a large number of portfolios. This made it more difficult for them to have the necessary in-depth knowledge of lower profile areas needed to effectively work with their counterpart in the Assembly. It is now much easier for TDs to be on top of their brief and thus to work with the party's minister or spokesperson on the issue in the North. Maintaining links between the parliamentary and local parts of the organisations is important to the party and it holds weekly meetings by TDs and Assembly members with the local councillors and organisers on the ground. This allows for the communication of issues and priorities in both directions. The party's organisational structure and framework of meetings also brings together members from north and south of the border and this may help to avoid the aforementioned possible divisions based on the different contexts in which the party operates.

## Future directions

In the immediate future Sinn Féin has an opportunity to position itself as the effective opposition in the Dáil. While Fianna Fáil has more TDs the former governing party may find it difficult to criticise the policies of the Labour–Fine Gael coalition because of its role in the economic crisis and its strategy in the election 2011 of supporting the strictures of the EU–IMF agreement. Sinn Féin benefits from having more active members than other small parties and uses these effectively to campaign on social issues. The party aims to maximise potential growth by first setting up working groups in areas and nurturing them into full scale branches.[49] It can also distinguish itself from the other parties in the Dáil by being the main party on the side of certain debates, such as the referendum on the Fiscal Compact. The decision of Fianna Fáil to take an unambiguously pro-European line on the Stability Treaty gave Sinn Féin the opportunity to distinguish itself from the other parties.

However, the party faces a number of challenges. Its position in power in Northern Ireland may offer important lessons but it also allows electoral opponents in the south to draw attention to policy inconsistencies and may damage the party's self-promoted image as an anti-system party. Furthermore, its organisation around a strong and charismatic leader for a considerable period may result in leadership issues in the future. While there are clearly a number of high-profile representatives, there is no single clear successor to Adams who could command loyalty and maintain valuable unity. Sinn Féin's slow-growth strategy clearly worked in Northern Ireland, but it was different in that it could not be left behind because of its control of the IRA. It can hope, but maybe not necessarily expect, that the same strategy would succeed in the south. In the Republic the party is less relevant, and it would be unusual if it as a radically left-wing party managed to become as large as one of the mainstream parties. Another route to relevance might be to move to the centre and become 'coalitionable', but this is risky in that then it might alienate its current followers. That said, we can see that the party's voters are not distinct in terms of policy. The party may be at a crossroads as to whether to remain a fringe party or move to the mainstream of Irish politics.

Of course the party may feel it need not make this choice. The party may be consciously trying to move public opinion to its position. One senior party official told us that its strategy is to 'mainstream and popularise republican politics' and so the tactic of running Martin McGuinness in the Irish presidential election was a 'strategic initiative' in which the hope was to shift public opinion towards Sinn Féin's viewpoint. The 2011 election seemed a vindication of its 'slow growth' strategy. Sinn Féin succeeded in getting community activists elected in parts of the country where it had not traditionally received much support. In many ways the election suited Sinn Féin; as a party it could say it consistently opposed government policies and its anti-EU and austerity message resonated with many. The political environment might be perfect for an anti-system, anti-EU and anti-capitalist party, and Sinn Féin is uniquely placed to exploit this. We could also be witnessing a realignment of Irish politics where Sinn Féin could become a mainstream party while maintaining its left-wing, anti-system base. We might than ask, at whose expense?

# 13

# Voting in Dáil Éireann: The Changing Roles of Minor Parties and Independents, 1937-2011

*Martin Ejnar Hansen*

## Introduction

Being a successful politician rests on several factors. One of them is running in elections and getting elected. Another is how to act once elected. The knowledge of minor actors' (i.e. small parties and independents) impact in all aspects of Irish politics is slowly but steadily increasing.[1] Despite this, there are still a few white spots on the map, especially with regards to the parliamentary behaviour of minor parties and independents. Since the first coalition government of 1948-51, minor parties have been members of a number of administrations, including all bar one (the 1992-4 coalition with Labour) of the Fianna Fáil governments since 1989. At other times minor parties, together with a number of independents, have also had a significant influence on the survival of a government. Despite this, we are often left with little more than journalistic descriptions and anecdotal evidence concerning their influence and behaviour. This chapter contributes to this debate by exploring some empirical evidence concerning the parliamentary behaviour of independents and minor parties since 1937.

Specifically, the way minor parties and independents cast their vote in the Dáil is the source of data for the analysis. Using parliamentary voting behaviour was, for a number of years, near non-existent in the literature on European parliaments, including the Irish case. Recently, there has been an increase in the number of articles exploring this valuable data source, not least in the case of Ireland.[2] A number of these articles use methodologically advanced procedures to analyse the voting behaviour. However, there is a far simpler method, which is just as effective at analysing the behaviour of minor parties and independents both within these groups and also in comparison with the major parties

Answering the questions on how minor parties and independents act in terms of voting behaviour when elected to the Dáil makes it possible to draw an inference on how minor parties and independents perceive their role and whether this is different from what would be expected generally of a parliamentary actor. It also allows for information on the extent to which minor parties and independents are more or less supportive of one or the other of the major parties in Ireland. The extent to which independents act as 'genuine' independents – sometimes voting with government, sometimes voting with the opposition – can also be addressed. Thus, the chapter expands our knowledge of minor parties and independents both in general terms but also in the crucial moments of Irish politics when these groups have held the balance of power.

The findings fall into several categories. First, it is only very rarely that a party or independent is observed which sometimes vote with Fianna Fáil and sometimes with Fine Gael. The majority of minor parties and independents take a firm stand across the parliaments in which they sit. Secondly, participation in the divisions differs; some members have a high participatory rate, others are only infrequent guests in the voting lobbies of the Dáil. Generally, the findings corroborate recent works on Irish politics, both with regards to the dimensionality of party competition in the Dáil[3] and the Weeks typology of Irish independents.[4]

## Minor parties and independents at the parliamentary level

Placing political competition in Ireland in a comparative setting is difficult as it is often portrayed as being different from that of European countries.[5] Among the prevalent differences is that amongst the electorate there is no cleavage derived from the social structure of society.[6] When it comes to positioning the Irish parties in the party families of Europe it is also somewhat problematic. This is contentious though, as Laver[7] argues that Irish parties are in fact just variations of the classical European party families. Weeks argues that one reason for these problems might be that party competition among the Irish electorate is not left–right based as is normally found in most European countries.[8] However, as the focus of this chapter is not on the electoral arena, but on the parliamentary arena, it is worthwhile to examine the parliamentary party system of the Dáil more in detail.

## The parliamentary party system of the Dáil

As is detailed by others in this volume, up to 2011 Dáil Éireann was historically dominated by two large centrist/catch-all parties: Fine Gael, often described as a conservative/liberal party, and Fianna Fáil, portrayed as a party ranging from centre-left to right-wing.[9] Party competition in the Dáil does not take place on a left-right conflict dimension which is dominant in other countries, but a government-opposition divide, or as the two major parties have never been in government together; a pro/anti Fianna Fáil one.[10] This is corroborated by, among others, Mair[11] and Mitchell[12] who argue that the logic of 'Fianna Fáil versus the rest' has been strong in Irish politics for many years. Hansen demonstrates that the two main parties, Fianna Fáil and Fine Gael, are clear opposites in the Dáil when taking their voting behaviour into account.[13] Interestingly, they are more similar than different when it comes to the policy that they pursue.[14] This is somewhat of a paradox which suggests that to understand a party system it is necessary to have research not only on the electoral arena but also the parliamentary arena. The full picture cannot be drawn until both are known as there are major differences between the parties' behaviour in these two arenas.

This analysis covers nearly seventy-five years, and in those years a number of minor parties and independents have also been represented in the Dáil. In the analysis, all minor parties which have had candidates elected since 1937 are included. Pedersen put forward the idea that all minor parties eventually die. In the Irish case there is plenty of support for this idea.[15] Even the most successful minor party to date, the Progressive Democrats, has wound up. Being successful at one point, even with government participation, before succumbing to a slow death is also the story of the farmer-based Clann na Talmhan and the republican Clann na Poblachta, both of which had their place on stage in the 1940s and 1950s. As discussed by Boyle and Bolleyer (chapters 4 and 6), whether the Green Party will succumb to a similar fate remains to be seen. It should be noted that for a party to be recognized by the Dáil as a parliamentary party group a certain threshold of TDs is needed. This number has changed over the years making it more or less easy for minor parties to achieve speaking rights automatically. Hence, over the years a number of so-called technical groups have been formed with minor parties and independents in order to secure those much sought after rights. This is indeed also the case after the 2011 election when a very different batch of minor parties and independents joined forces in order to secure the right to automatic participation in the deliberations of the Dáil.

## What is a minor party and what is an independent?

Analysing how independents and minor parties act in the Dáil necessitates a theoretical basis and formulation of testable hypotheses in order to move beyond pure description. While describing the actions of minor parties and independents in each Dáil would be interesting, the goal of this chapter is to present a general judgement on minor parties and independents. In this part of the chapter the theoretical considerations of analysing minor parties and independents are discussed and on that basis the hypotheses are formulated.

A political party is an organisation which, whether loosely or strongly organised, presents candidates for public elections or intends to do so.[16] This is a very broad definition which is also too broad for the purpose of this analysis. Here the focus is not on the electoral fortunes of minor parties and independents but on their legislative performance. Hence, any definition of a party must take this into account. Instead, the definition of party used in this chapter is a number of people running more than one candidate, and getting at least one of them elected to the parliament under a party heading, who, when continuously re-elected, does so under the same party name. This definition means that a party can not function if its members do not continuously perform under the same party banner in the Dáil chamber. A whole other logic comes into play when a party gets elected. Behaving in parliament is different to behaving on the electoral arena. Any actor elected to a parliament has three options: supporting the government exclusively, supporting the opposition exclusively, or doing a bit of both. Party competition in the Dáil is shown not to exhibit the last option in any great way as it is dominated by two blocs; one for the government and one for the opposition.[17] An important factor for this is the absence of minority governments in the traditional sense, that is, governments negotiating support from vote to vote. Another factor any minor party must take into account is whether or not it wants to be considered a potential coalition partner, that is, whether the party can be trusted with the responsibility of governing. As this is not something which is expected to happen overnight, a party wishing to enter government may attempt to increase its credibility in preceding parliaments by courting possible coalition partners after an election. Once a minor party has chosen to support the government or the opposition it is also expected that the party will continue the support of the bloc even if it at a later point in time it enters government instead of opposition and vice versa.[18] Hence, we should first of all expect that:

> H (Hypothesis) 1: A minor party will, if not in government, act as a member of the opposition and vote against the government at every possible opportunity.

> H2: Parties who are entering government for the first time will have adapted their voting behaviour to fit their possible coalition partner in the preceding parliaments.

> H3: A minor party that has at one point in time been a member of a government will vote more in accordance with its former partners.

While political parties are well researched entities, the Irish case also has a high level of independents who have played important roles over the years. It is only in recent years that those independents have received scholarly attention.[19] In the overview of political parties in Ireland by Gallagher, he does not go into any detail on the various independents elected but states that a large number of candidates stood for election outside of parties and that in the early years of the state they were a significant force.[20] An independent is a member elected primarily on his or her own name or under a banner which can not be incorporated under the definition of party discussed above.[21] One such example is Monetary Reform, under whose banner Oliver J. Flanagan was elected in 1943 and re-elected in 1944, but which did not get any other candidates elected. Flanagan ran as an independent in the elections of 1948 and 1951 hence, Monetary Reform does not meet the criteria of continuous re-election and Flanagan is treated as an independent.

The most comprehensive definition of Irish independents is presented by Weeks,[22] who identifies six families of Irish independents. The six types are 1) Vestigal Independents, 2) Corporatist Independents, 3) Ideological Independents, 4) Community Independents, 5) Apostate Independents, and 6) Quasi-parties.[23] Vestigal independents refer to independents with a background in defunct parties, especially the Unionist Party and the Irish Parliamentary Party. Corporatist independents relates to independents with strong links to a certain profession or industry. Ideological independents are those for whom policy is the main goal. Most of the left-wing independents fall into this category. Community independents are those who primarily seek to enhance the standing of their community or local area and for whom the interest in national politics comes second, unless it can be used to enhance their primary goal. Apostate independents are related to vestigal independents with the key difference that for apostates their former party is still very much alive.[24] The sixth type of independents is quasi-parties where independents stand under a party banner. Weeks places the example of Monetary Reform used above in this category.[25]

Several hypotheses can be derived from this typology. Weeks relies primarily on data from campaigns and ideology, and includes all independent candidates, not just TDs.[26] Thus, rigorous testing is needed to determine the extent to which independents are placed in the same category when taking their parliamentary behaviour into account. The first of the hypotheses relating to independents is:

H4: Apostate independents will vote in accordance with the party from which they came if this party is still in the Dáil

Ideological independents are solely in the game for policy and thus will often, though not necessarily, have problems with the government, whichever party is in charge, as the government will rarely be able to accommodate ideologically distinct demands. Thus it is hypothesised that:

H5: Ideological independents will vote counter to the government no matter which party is in government and no matter if they are needed or not for the majority

Following an observation by Weeks concerning the reliance of governments on the support of independents to survive, it can be asked whether certain governments are more positively inclined towards the independents than others and whether it will lead to a general re-alignment of all independents' attitudes towards the governments in question.[27]

H6: In periods where independents are needed by the government the whole body of independents will vote more in accordance with the government than in periods where they are not needed

Data availability sets limits as to how it is possible to test these hypotheses. The low number of minor parties represented in the Dáil over the years covered in the analysis makes it near impossible to carry out advanced multivariate tests. This is in many ways also the case for the independents, which though much more numerous than the minor parties, still present challenges for even the most simple statistical tests as the number of observations in some categories is simply too low.

## Data and methodology

There are a multitude of options to analyse voting behaviour in parliaments, ranging from the very technical to very simple. One of the challenges when dealing with minor parties and independents is that they are not always present in parliament. In the British case it is argued that voting is not among the top strategies for gaining influence.[28] However, in the Irish case independents are more likely to be of key importance and to enhance their influence. Nevertheless, there is a large variation in the attendance of independent TDs. In one case a TD cast only one vote in his entire career as an independent.[29] In these cases, using highly technical methods for estimating the position of the independents would result in an estimate with an error term that the position recovered would be meaningless. Luckily, there are other options which are more appropriate for the data at hand. In the analysis a method is used to calculate the distance from each minor party and independent to Fianna Fáil and Fine Gael. The method is inspired by the Pedersen index of distances.[30] It is a crude measure expressing the distance from party A to a fixed point, for instance party B, or in this case one of the two major parties. Cowley and Stuart employed a similar measure in their analysis of the voting behaviour of independent MPs in the UK House of Commons.[31] Given the particularities of Irish party competition, in particular that Fianna Fáil and Fine Gael have never been in government together, a high agreement with one party will, *ceteris paribus*, entail a low agreement rate with the other party. Indeed, the correlation between the agreement rates of Fianna Fáil and Fine Gael is -0.89, virtually completely different. This supports the assumption that when looking at the vote of one of the two parties, it is for the most part possible to derive how the other party voted.

## Data

The analyses in this chapter is based on an updated version of the dataset used by Hansen which in this version consists of all 5,866 votes in the Dáil from 1937 to December 2011.[32] The vote of each party and each independent is recorded in the dataset. The assumption is that Irish parliamentary parties can be treated as unitary actors whether large or small in size. Voting against ones party will, *ceteris paribus*, lead to either the loss of the whip or loss of influence within the party. This also means that it is not the behaviour of individual TDs which has been coded but that of their party. Thus, it is not possible to address questions like the extent to which minor parties are more cohesive than larger parties or whether being an ideologically based party makes it easier to ensure cohesiveness than for the mass parties like Fianna Fáil or Fine Gael. The time periods used are those between elections. Determining whether a TD is an independent, as defined in the previous sections, or part of a party, is not as clear cut as it may appear. In the coding I have relied on three sources: Walker, who covers all elections in the Republic of Ireland until 1989;[33] the members' database of Dáil Éireann (available at oireachtas.ie), and the distinction presented in Weeks.[34, 35] In cases where a difference has been encountered between the two sources, I have also relied on Took and Donnelly's Elections Ireland website (electionsireland.org) and relevant literature. TDs that previously were independent and joined a party have been coded as independents for the entire period. The TDs who left their party between elections have not been treated as independents but as members of their original party. This, for example, means that the Progressive Democrats are not included before the 25th Dáil as this was the first time they presented themselves to the electorate, even though they came into existence during the 24th Dáil. A rule of thumb is not to include new parties or independents, or even the change in status of independents, before they have had a possibility to present themselves to the electorate.[36] An exception is where the TD in question either resigned his seat or passed away. In such cases the coding for the person was stopped and if the seat was won by an independent in the by-election a new coding was begun for that person.

## Analysis

In the analysis the main variables of interest are the agreement rates between all minor parties and independents and the two largest parties represented throughout the period covered in this chapter (Fianna Fáil and Fine Gael).[37] In a few instances this is substituted with the agreement towards the government of the day regardless of which party led the government. Instead of using the exact agreement rates it has for most of the analyses been chosen to recode the rates in three categories; one of low agreement, ranging from 0-39.99 per cent; middle agreement, ranging from 40-59.99 per cent; and high agreement, ranging from 60-100 per cent. These proportions of agreement relate to the outcome for each Dáil session.

## Minor parties

The first part of the analysis is focused on the three hypotheses dealing with minor parties. The first of these relates to how minor parties behave when they are not in government, which historically has been their dominant role. With each instance of minor party per Dáil session comprising our cases, Table 1 below indicates the agreement rates between the minor parties and the two main parties and the government of the day.

*Table 1: Agreement rates of minor party when not in government (per cent)*

| Agreement with | Fianna Fáil | Fine Gael | Government |
|---|---|---|---|
| Low | 69(32) | 25(12) | 77(37) |
| Middle | 10(5) | 8(4) | 8(4) |
| High | 21(10) | 67(32) | 15(7) |

Note: Percentages sum to 100 in columns. Number in parentheses are N for each cell. The unit of analysis is minor party not in government per Dáil.

The results tell us that when minor parties are not in government the vast majority is less in agreement with Fianna Fáil and more in agreement with Fine Gael. As Fianna Fáil is the party in Ireland which has spent the most time in government, it is not surprising that there is a large deal of correspondence between the agreement rates towards Fianna Fáil and that of the government of the day. Whether this is due to an active courtship by the main opposition party, which is usually Fine Gael, towards the smaller parties outside government or whether they are in fact against the policies of the government is not possible to say for certain. However, it should be noted that when Fine Gael has been in government it has in many cases been together with minor parties. This was the case in 1948 when National Labour, Clann na Talmhan and Clann na Poblachta joined the government, leaving no minor parties in opposition. The Fine Gael-led government from 1994 also included a minor party (Democratic Left). For Fianna Fáil on the other hand, it is only since 1989 that minor parties have been included in their governments, and to date only two minor parties: the Progressive Democrats and the Green Party. Overall, it is possible to confirm hypothesis 1 – minor parties do behave as an opposition and to a large extent vote against the government.

Once a party enters government there is no doubt that it enters what must be a cohesive body. The government in parliamentary systems votes as one unit. However, exploring the voting behaviour of the parties before they enter government and to what extent being in government matters for the voting behaviour in subsequent Dála could yield a new perspective on minor parties. Here it should be noted that we are limited in the possibilities of analyzing this question as minor parties do not necessarily have a long parliamentary life before entering government. Looking at the examples of Irish politics, it seems that until now a short parliamentary experience may be better than a long presence. The low number of minor parties actually participating in governments during the period covered in this analysis also severely limits the analytical sophistication. On the other hand, it is a luxury to be able to include all cases. The agreement scores for each party in the period before entering government can be found in Table 2 below. Before Clann na Talmhan entered government in 1948 with Fine Gael and Labour it was in high agreement with Fine Gael. Indeed, both Clann na Poblachta and National Labour, which also entered the 1948 government, exhibit the same patterns of high agreement with Fine Gael. However, when turning to the two modern examples of minor parties entering government, the results point in the other direction. In the preceding Dáil before entering coalition government with Fianna Fáil, both the Progressive Democrats and the Greens were significantly closer to Fine Gael than to Fianna Fáil. However, the agreement rates of the Progressive Democrats towards Fine Gael were significantly lower than the other cases listed, an early indicator that the party did not seek to become as strong a supporter of the leading opposition party as might have seemed at the time. The coalition pact which was in place between the two parties at the 1989 election did not manifest itself in the voting behaviour. The most recent example of a minor party entering government was that of the Greens, who formed a coalition government with Fianna Fáil and the Progressive Democrats after the 2007 election. If their voting behaviour in the preceding Dáil is to be believed then it was either a complete *volte-face* on their behalf or that in the preceding Dáil they took a clear oppositional role to the Fianna Fáil government. With only five examples of this behaviour and a count of three to two in favour of the hypothesised relationship it may well be best to be cautious and say that the hypothesis is for the moment confirmed but it may well change in the future if other minor parties end up in government.[38]

*Table 2: Voting Behaviour of minor parties before entering government*

| Agreement with | Fianna Fáil | Fine Gael |
| --- | --- | --- |
| Clann na Talmhan 1944-48 | 5.2 | 91.0 |
| Clann na Poblachta 1944-48 | 0 | 100 |
| National Labour 1944-48 | 22.6 | 73.3 |
| Progressive Democrats 1987-89 | 18.3 | 55.9 |
| Green Party 2002-07 | 0.8 | 89.3 |

Note: These figures denote the proportion of times each of the minor parties voted with either Fianna Fáil or Fine Gael in parliament.

With oft-changing governments as is the norm in multi-party systems life as a political party also encompasses periods outside of government office; indeed, these must be expected. Yet those periods are not a free for all where opposition parties can take positions randomly. A party that wishes to be considered a viable government option must keep being a credible coalition partner. One way of doing so is continually to vote in accordance with its former government partners. The agreement rates for the parties which served in government and went into opposition can be seen below in Table 3.

*Table 3: Voting behaviour of minor parties after entering government*

| Agreement with | Fianna Fáil | Fine Gael |
|---|---|---|
| Clann na Talmhan 1951-54 | 1.6 | 80.2 |
| Clann na Talmhan 1957-61 | 5.4 | 94.2 |
| Clann na Poblachta 1951-54 | 0.9 | 84.0 |
| Progressive Democrats 1992-97 | 51.9 | 46.3 |

These numbers show that both Clann na Talmhan and Clann na Poblachta did not change their voting behaviour much after being in government. They both had high agreement rates with the party which led the government in which they participated. Even though the numbers for the Progressive Democrats look a bit strange, they are very much what would be expected in the situation. For the first two years of the 1992-7 Dáil the previous partner of the Progressive Democrats, Fianna Fáil, formed a coalition with Labour. The Progressive Democrats voted with Fine Gael, and when that party joined Labour and Democratic Left in a coalition mid-term the Progressive Democrats voted with Fianna Fáil. The number of parties entering government and either not contesting elections after their tenure in government or failing to secure representation is as high as the those successfully contesting elections after government participation. Democratic Left merged with Labour; so did National Labour; the Progressive Democrats disbanded, while in government, in 2009; and the Green Party lost all their seats in the 2011 election. While the results presented in Table 3 point towards some form of 'socialization' of being in government, that a party does not leave their former partner behind is still problematic to convincingly confirm or reject the hypothesised relationship. Leaving the low number of cases aside, there is also an inherent problem of separating whether it is indeed government participation or a certain predisposition for each party to vote the way they do. Hence, a verdict of inconclusive must be given in this case but the evidence to hand does point in the direction of a confirmation.

## Independents

The second part of the analysis deals with independents. Treating independents as one group is perhaps problematic, which is also suggested by the Weeks typology.[39] However, when looking at the entire population of independents elected at elections since 1937, in total 130 observations, nearly 69 per cent, of these are in low agreement with the government of the day; only 6 per cent falls in the middle and 25 per cent are in high agreement. This does suggest that it more likely than not that being an independent will entail voting against the sitting government. Across time this is fairly stable relationship with the 1948-51 Fine Gael led government as the outlier where 83 per cent of the independents elected to the 13th Dáil were in high agreement with the government. Nevertheless, there are differences between the independents not least in their background in becoming independents.

What, for instance, happens when disgruntled party members leave one of the major parties either due to a scandal (e.g. Michael Lowry) or as a response to a lost nomination (e.g. Jackie Healy-Rae)? In the Weeks typology these are known as apostate independents. It should be noted that some apostate independents change over time, moving mostly to become community-based independents.[40] The agreement rates for such independents categorised as apostates are detailed in Table 4 below. It should be noted that due to the small number of apostates from a different background than Fianna Fáil and Fine Gael it has been chosen only to show the results for these two parties.

*Table 4: Agreement rates for apostate independents*

| Agreement with | Fianna Fáil | Fine Gael |
|---|---|---|
| Low | 4 | 1 |
| Middle | 2 | 0 |
| High | 7 | 6 |

Note: Apostate independents as defined by Weeks.[41] Numbers in cells are the actual counts of apostate independents per Dáil session.

Overall, the evidence presented in Table 4 is mixed in supporting the proposed hypothesis that apostate independents keep a high agreement rate with their party. This is indeed the case for the apostates with a background in Fine Gael. For the Fianna Fáil apostates it is mixed. In just over half of the cases there is high agreement with the former party, but four Fianna Fáil apostates have low agreement rates with their former party. This is an interesting finding and is contrary to what some commentators (and party politicians) claim that Fianna Fáil apostates are not real independents and tend to be Fianna Fáil in all bar name. Weeks argues that the relative success of Fianna Fáil apostates has increased markedly over the years.[42] However, he can not determine the extent to which this is due to better candidates or a disloyal electorate. The results presented here, and those of Hansen,[43] who also examines the more broad concept of 'gene-pool' independents, suggest that over time there might be two kinds of apostate Fianna Fáil

TDs: one group for whom it is electorally necessary and parliamentary useful to keep as close to Fianna Fáil as possible, and another group for whom it is electorally necessary and parliamentary irrelevant to keep a high agreement with Fianna Fáil. Whether this changes in the years to come after the electoral fortunes of the Fianna Fáil brand declined dramatically in the 2011 election remains to be seen. The mixed nature of this evidence means the hypothesis presented for this topic can not be fully confirmed.

Another category of independents in the Weeks typology is the ideological independents. They are characterised by running in elections in order to obtain or highlight specific policy goals.[44] Among the most well known in this category was the left-wing republican Tony Gregory, and in recent years candidates mobilised on the government's handling of the economic crisis; examples of the latter in 2011 were Stephen Donnelly and Shane Ross. In Table 5 below the agreement rates of the ideological independents are detailed.

*Table 5: Agreement rates for ideological independent*

| Agreement with | Fianna Fáil | Fine Gael | Government |
| --- | --- | --- | --- |
| Low | 60(21) | 40(14) | 186(30) |
| Middle | 17(6) | 11(4) | 11(4) |
| High | 23(8) | 49(17) | 3(1) |

Note: Percentages sum to 100 in columns. Number in parentheses are N for each cell. Unit of analysis is ideological independent per Dáil session.

Two distinct elements can be found in the results. First, the majority of ideological independent TDs are in very low agreement with Fianna Fáil. Second, the ideological independents are split in their agreement rates with Fine Gael. If we were to calculate the agreement rates with the government of the day, whether Fianna Fáil or Fine Gael, it is clear that there is something unique about ideological independents. By a large margin they are always in low agreement with the government. More than 80 per cent of the cases have ideological independents with an agreement rate that falls in the low category and only in one case in the high category. This suggests that if an independent is categorised as an ideological one, then it is quite likely that he will exhibit the same behaviour as his fellow ideologues. The proposed hypothesis is thus confirmed.

Over the years, a number of Irish governments had to rely on independents to control a majority in the Dáil. Of the governments that needed the votes of independents to survive, five of these resulted in some sort of agreement with the independents who Weeks describes as the 'true kingmakers' of independents.[45] Of perhaps the most infamous of these agreements was the Gregory deal which led to Charles Haughey being elected as Taoiseach in 1982, and Tony Gregory reading out in the Dáil what he was given in return for his support. Bertie Ahern's deal with three (later four) independents in the 1997-2002 government is also an example of the need of independents' support for the survival of the government. However, there are also an equally high number of cases where governments have had no need for the votes of independents. The question is whether there is a difference in the voting behaviour of independents generally when they are needed by the government and when they are not needed. In Table 6 below the agreement rates between independents and the government of the day can be found. The result confirms the hypothesis that the independents as a group have a higher agreement rate with the government of the day when they are needed than when they are not needed. Undoubtedly, a large part of this relationship is driven by those reaching an agreement with the government as they *de facto* move to support the government in most, if not all, votes.

*Table 6: Independents' agreement rates by position in Dáil*

|        | Not holding the balace of power | Holding the balance of power |
|--------|-------------------------------|------------------------------|
| Low    | 85.3 (64)                     | 45.5 (25)                    |
| Middle | 5.3 (4)                       | 7.3 (4)                      |
| High   | 9.3 (7)                       | 47.3 (26)                    |

Note: Columns sum to 100, numbers in parentheses are the number of actual observations. (Chi-square) $\chi^2 = 25.56$, $p < 0.000$. Fisher's exact test also confirms the significant difference. Unit of analysis is all independents per Dáil session, when they are needed by the government.

When looking at the overall results, it is important to keep in mind that the Irish electorate chooses minor parties and independent TDs for a reason. This is in all probability not because they want them to support the government, but to keep the government on its toes. A corollary to this is the campaign of the Progressive Democrats in the 2002 election. They argued that giving Fianna Fáil power on its own would be erroneous and the Progressive Democrats should be given a mandate to keep them in check. If it is accepted that independents get their votes primarily from being in opposition to, or at the very least critical of, the government, then it can be of no surprise that they actually vote accordingly in parliament. This is, in all probability, very much the case after the 2011 election when the Irish electorate in only fifteen constituencies elected no minor party or independent to represent them. In two constituencies both at least one minor party and one independent was elected, and in quite a few constituencies more

Figure 1: *Agreement rates with government*

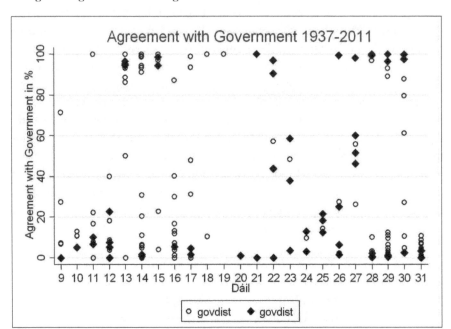

Note: Circles constitute independent TDs, diamonds minor parties. A score of 100 implies an actor voted on every occasion with the government; a score of 0 on no occasion.

than one minor party was returned or more than one independent. While it is not possible to produce a direct measure of the congruence between voter and representative, be it independent or minor party, it is still very likely that the chain of events is as perceived here. The electorate vote for independents or minor parties to ensure that a voice of opposition exists, a voice which hitherto only rarely has entered government. This provides the various independents and minor parties with a strong platform to argue and vote against the government. This does rest on the assumption that party competition in the Dáil occurs primarily on one dimension. Indeed, it is imperative for this understanding of the role of minor parties and independents in the Dáil that this does not change. Hansen has shown that this is indeed the case for the Dáil where party competition takes place on a government-opposition dimension.[46] This has been even more supported by the findings in this chapter that both minor parties and independents vote significantly more against the government when either they are not in government or when they are not needed by the government for its survival.

It should also be noted that the results presented in this chapter are consistent across time for both minor parties and independents. In Figure 1 above the representation of the agreement rates for minor parties and independents with the government of the day is highlighted. The results clearly suggest that voting against the government is not something new for either independents or minor parties. They tend to be either wholly pro-government (when in coalition or when an agreement of support has been formed) or anti-government, as indicated by the clustering around the axes of 0 and 100 per cent.

## Conclusion

The Irish earthquake election of 2011 resulted in a considerable change in minor party and independent representation in the Dáil. The Socialist Party returned and was joined on the left by the People before Profit Alliance. On the other hand, the 2011 election also saw two minor parties leave the Dáil; the Progressive Democrats had disbanded during the preceding Dáil and the Green Party was electorally wiped out. Various independents, from all sides of the political spectrum, had a field day (hence so many ran). The election also saw large gains for Sinn Féin and massive losses for Fianna Fáil. In particular, the fate of the latter is important for our understanding of minor parties and independents in the Dáil. In this chapter only the agreement rates in relation to Fianna Fáil and Fine Gael have been analysed. This choice has been made for analytic clarity. However, in the current Dáil, Fianna Fáil is neither a major party nor a minor party but in the middle category which for many years was where Labour was found. Whether Fianna Fáil will again become a major party or whether they will eventually become a minor party remains to be seen. For the sake of cross-temporal comparison Fianna Fáil has been treated as the major party it was from 1937 until the 2011 election. A second implication of the 2011 election is the somewhat fractious nature of the opposition. Now comprising Fianna Fáil, Sinn Féin and a technical group of the remaining parties and most of the independents, these groups have not previously been seen as natural cohabiters of the same political space. Indeed, both Sinn Féin and nearly the entire technical group spent much time and effort in the 2011 election campaign expressing their dissatisfaction with the Fianna Fáil-led government. However, they now share the burdens and prerogatives of opposition. Whether this can be built into a sharp and vigilant opposition that keeps the Fine Gael-Labour government in check remains to be seen.

When speaking of minor parties and independents, our knowledge primarily comes from their behaviour in the electoral arena, be it in the form of campaigns and issues or how they perform during the process of government formation; in the form of coalition participation for minor parties, and special deals in return for supporting the government for the independents. The latter seems to have been very fruitful for those independents negotiating such agreements. However, for minor parties, a spell in office can be a poisoned chalice; none have ever been successful in opposition when leaving government. Indeed, none have survived leaving government for more than two electoral periods after their last government participation. Thus the knowledge we have on how minor parties and independents behave when they are not in government is not complete. We lack knowledge of how a minor party behaves once out of office. Whether Fianna Fáil, in the years to come, can help provide this knowledge remains to be seen. This chapter has provided some evidence on a range of issues concerning the behaviour of minor parties and independents once elected.

However, there is still ample room for research in the parliamentary behaviour of minor parties and independents. An example of such a question for which currently the data is unavailable is whether there is a difference between minor parties and independents with regards to the issues they vote on. Another question is whether cyclical patterns exist in the voting behaviour of independents and minor parties within the duration of a Dáil. What happens to voting behaviour just before there is a split in a party or an independent joins a party? In summary, while our knowledge of minor parties and independents behaviour in parliament has increased, there are still many interesting questions to be explored.

If an overall conclusion should be given, it must first of all be that the most important factor in understanding the behaviour of minor parties and independents is whether they serve in government or not, or whether or not they are needed by the government. By and large that single factor helps us to understand and predict their behaviour. Secondly, while it is often useful to lump all independents together in one category, they are, in fact, quite different from each other, as shown with the examples of apostate and ideological independents. Minor parties and independents play an important role in Irish political life, both in the electoral arena and the parliamentary arena. The latter has been the focus of this chapter and it has been shown that in the Dáil minor parties and independents are important political actors in their own right.

# 14

# Radical, Redundant or Relevant? Minor Parties in Comparative and Systemic Perspective

*Alistair Clark*

## Introduction

Analysing Irish voting behaviour after the 2002 election, Laver observed that demographic trends in education, urbanisation and secularisation, among others, appeared to be moving in such a way as to potentially favour radical party options such as the Greens and Sinn Féin.[1] More recently, in 2011, the economic crisis appeared to create a further opportunity for minor parties. Yet, as Weeks notes earlier in chapter 1, these expectations were disappointed. While parties and independents polling less than 10 per cent of the vote certainly achieved a national vote share of around 27 per cent, picked up seventeen seats in the Dáil and now account for approximately 20 per cent of seats in the lower house, the proportion of seats held by Fianna Fáil, Fine Gael and Labour is at the same level as 2002. Müller-Rommel suggested more than two decades ago that while minor parties may have important political functions, 'they do not ... tend to "remould" the basic structure of the national party systems'.[2] In the aftermath of the electoral setbacks of 2009, the demise of the Progressive Democrats, a party sometimes presented as having 'broken the mould' of Irish politics,[3] and expectations of minor party success being disappointed somewhat in 2011, such a reminder seems particularly appropriate for analysts of the Irish party system.

Such fluctuations suggest the need for placing minor parties and independents in Ireland in a broader comparative and systemic context. This concluding chapter does so. Discussion proceeds in three sections. The first places Ireland in comparative perspective. As a number of chapters have suggested, Ireland's party system has not historically appeared particularly reliant on its minor parties. How then might Ireland be classified when compared with other European democracies and has this changed in recent years? The second section empirically assesses a number of claims that have been made about the contribution of minor parties to democratic politics. Does the emergence of such parties lead to a 'new' type of politics which mobilises hitherto disillusioned and disinterested voters? Does the arrival of minor party politics lead to an extension of issue space in electoral competition? The final section returns to the question of theorising about minor parties introduced earlier in this volume. In light of existing theories about minor parties, how do the preceding chapters contribute to knowledge and illuminate our ability to understand the role of minor parties in political systems?

## Minor parties in Ireland in comparative perspective

This volume has discussed various aspects of minor parties in Irish politics at some length. How does Ireland compare to other democracies however? Do minor parties play a greater or lesser role in political life in Ireland than they do in other established West European democracies?

*Table 1: Mean small party share of the vote in West European elections, 1970-2011[4]*

|  | Large party share | Small party share | 'Others' | Mean ENEP |
|---|---|---|---|---|
| Austria | 78.1 | 19.8 | 2.0 | 3.1 |
| Belgium | 20.3 | 59.1 | 25.8 | 8.3 |
| Denmark | 33.2 | 61.9 | 4.4 | 5.3 |
| Finland | 65.1 | 31.1 | 3.9 | 5.9 |
| France | 55.9 | 40.9 | 4.5 | 5.2 |
| Germany | 79.3 | 15.7 | 5.0 | 3.7 |
| Ireland | 72.9 | 18.4 | 8.8 | 3.4 |
| Italy | 46.3 | 28.0 | 25.8 | 5.3 |
| Netherlands | 67.3 | 16.2 | 16.4 | 5.3 |
| Norway | 58.7 | 40.6 | 3.1 | 4.7 |
| Sweden | 43.3 | 54.2 | 7.1 | 3.9 |
| Switzerland | 60.9 | 29.2 | 9.8 | 6.1 |
| UK | 81.7 | 13.6 | 4.7 | 3.2 |

Additional sources: Arter, David *Scandinavian Politics Today* (Manchester; Manchester University Press, 1999); Belgian Ministry of Internal Affairs (2008) Belgische verkiez-ingsuitslagen, available at: http://www.ibzdgip.fgov.be/result/nl/main.html, [31/10/08]; Coakley, John 'Appendix 2 Electoral Data', in John Coakley and Michael Gallagher (eds) *Politics in the Republic of Ireland*, 4th edition (London; Routledge/PSAI Press, 2005) pp. 465-72; Cole, A *French Politics and Society*, 2nd edition (London; Pearson Longman, 2005); Gallagher, Michael 'Election Indices', (2008), available at: www.tcd.ie/PoliticalScience/ staff/michael_gallagher/ElSystems/Docts/ElectionIndices.pdf, [22/10/08]; Ministro dell'Interno, 'Archivio Storico delle Elezioni', (2008), available at: http://elezionistorico. interno.it/index.php?tp=C, [31/10/2008]; Tetteh, E. 'Election Statistics: UK 1919-2007' (London; House of Commons Library Research Paper 08/12, 2008).

Table 1 presents the mean share of the vote for both large and minor parties in elections to the lower house of parliament across thirteen West European countries from 1970 to 2011. To aid comparison over time, Mair's analysis of minor parties in Western Europe provides a useful benchmark.[5] The calculations in Table 1 are therefore based on Mair's methodology, albeit with some modifications. While others in this volume have taken a more historical view, the base year for this discussion is taken as 1970. This is regularly seen as a useful point from which to track the onset of processes of dealignment and increased electoral fragmentation across advanced democracies.[6] Many breakthroughs for minor parties occurred from the 1970s onwards, whether the earlier 'earthquake' elections in Scandinavia in the 1970s, or the later rise of the far-right and Greens across Europe. Using 1970 as the base year allows for comparison of recent political dynamics to be more easily achieved. Large parties are those which achieve 15 per cent or more of the vote on average. Following Mair, minor parties are those that achieve less than 15 per cent but more than 1.5 per cent on average, and which have persisted for more than three elections. 'Others' are those receiving less than 1.5 per cent or which fail to persist for more than three elections. It is also useful to assess how many parties are 'relevant' to electoral competition in each country. This provides some assessment of the fragmentation or concentration of a party system. A widely used measure of party system fragmentation is the Effective Number of Parties (ENP), and this can be calculated in relation to parties in the electorate (ENEP) or in parliament (ENPP).[7] The final column therefore presents the mean effective number of electoral parties figure for each country as a further measure of electoral fragmentation; the higher the ENEP figure, the greater role small parties have in that country's electoral politics.

There is considerable variation in the share of the vote for each of the three categories of parties. By comparison with other West European countries, minor parties in Ireland appear to command a relatively small share of the vote in elections to the Dáil from 1973 onwards. The average minor party share between 1973 and 2011 is just 18.4 per cent and it ranges from 9.4 per cent in the second 1982 election, to a high of 31.1 per cent in 2011. This mean minor party share places Ireland fourth from bottom in a ranking of minor parties' share of the vote, with only Germany, the UK and the Netherlands having a lower proportion of the vote accounted for by minor parties. A further 8.8 per cent is accounted for by Irish parties and groupings classified as 'others' across this period. This appears to be a relatively high proportion in comparison and would rank Ireland fifth among these countries in terms of the share of the vote achieved by this group. Much of this vote share is accounted for by the appeal of personal voting for independents under Ireland's seemingly more open PR–STV electoral system and essentially 'localist' political culture.[8]

The impression of the Irish party system provided by Table 1 and highlighted in the preceding chapters confirms that Ireland has been dominated by the main three parties – Fianna Fáil, Fine Gael and Labour – at the expense of the minor parties.[9] Using Mair's classificatory schema, with its upper limit for minor parties means, however, that Labour is classified as a minor party.[10] While earlier discussion indicates such an assumption is somewhat debateable (see chapters 1, 3 and 11), to ensure consistency of comparison with Mair, Labour is treated as such for the remainder of this discussion. Far from 'breaking the mould', Irish minor parties from this perspective appear to have been very much in the shadow of their larger counterparts, Fianna Fáil and Fine Gael. Such an impression is underlined by the mean Irish ENEP figure of 3.4 between 1970 and 2011.This is the third lowest ENEP figure in table 1 with only Austria and the UK recording lower figures.

Using the figures reported in Table 1, it is possible to classify these party systems in relation to the success, or otherwise, of minor parties.This allows an extension of Mair's classification of West European party systems in relation to their minor parties between 1947 and 1987.Table 2 therefore presents a party -system classification based on a hierarchical cluster analysis of the vote share for both large parties and minor parties and 'others' combined in the thirteen democracies. Such a technique groups countries together according to their proximity on these two main variables.[11]

*Table 2: Party system classification, 1970-2011*

| **Large Party Systems** | **Small Party Systems** |
| --- | --- |
| Austria | Belgium |
| Germany | Denmark |
| Ireland | Sweden |
| UK | |

| **Weak Large Pary Systems** | **Fragmented Party Systems** |
| --- | --- |
| Finland | France |
| Netherlands | Norway |
| Switzerland | Italy |

Most countries were clustered together in both analyses, thereby allowing an over-all classification of party system types.The three small party systems are Belgium, Denmark and Sweden, each of which has over three-fifths of the mean post-1970 vote share falling to minor parties and 'others'. Equally unambiguous are the four large party systems – Austria, Germany, Ireland and the UK.These countries were also classified as large party systems by Mair,[12] and the large party mean share between 1970 and 2011 varies from around 73 per cent in Ireland to 81 per cent in the UK. Finland, the Netherlands and Switzerland are classified as weak large party systems. By comparison with large party systems, these have a higher share of the vote accounted for by minor party and 'other' options, but large parties still retain more than three-fifths of the average vote share in each country. The final category of fragmented party systems is somewhat more diverse and covers three countries where the minor party and 'others' vote share has averaged between 45 and 54 per cent, with France and Norway both recording between 43 and 45 per cent, while the respective Italian figure is approximately 54 per cent.

The key point to note from this categorisation is that Ireland's placement as a large party system is consistent across both the analysis reported here, Clark's earlier assessment before the 2011 elections,[13] and Mair's assessment from the post-war period to the late 1980s.[14] This suggests that minor parties have not 'broken the mould' of Irish electoral politics in either the post-war era, or the seemingly more volatile period from the 1970s onwards.

## The Systemic Contribution of Minor Parties to Irish Democracy

Given the comparative placement of Ireland as a large party system, it is worth changing the analytical focus and asking what impact minor parties have actually had upon the Irish party system. Implicit in theoretical discussions about minor parties is the idea that they contribute in a variety of ways to democratic politics. Herzog argues that minor parties help set the boundaries of political debate.[15] Others suggest that, against a backdrop of increasingly volatile electorates, their rise is a consequence of the declining ability of mainstream political parties to fulfil their traditional aggregation and representation functions having instead become part of a governing cartel increasingly separated from civil society.[16] As Copus *et al.* argue, minor parties, 'provide new channels of citizen engagement, political activism, participation and new avenues for political accountability'.[17] Coakley similarly argues in chapter 3 that, 'minor parties have played a distinctive role in Irish politics, one not dissimilar to their counterparts in Europe'. Given the backdrop to the 2011 election, these features are likely to have become, if anything, more important.[18]

The first idea to be examined is the extent to which there is a link between the decline of mainstream parties and a concomitant rise in the vote for minor party alternatives. Both Weeks and Coakley point to a 'third wave' of minor party success from the 1980s onwards.[19] Over the period, the two main parties have declined from a combined 81.3 per cent of first preferences in 1973, to 64 per cent in 2002 and 53.5 per cent in 2011. The corollary has been the sharp rise in the minor party and independent share of the vote which has increased from a combined 5 per cent in 1973, to 25 per cent in 2002, and over 46 per cent in 2011. Labour's share of the vote was relatively steady at just above or below 10 per cent from 1970, with the significant exceptions of the 1992 and 2011 elections when the party's share rose to just over 19 per cent. With the other minor parties, the sharp increase in 1987 can largely be accounted for by the 12 per cent achieved by the newly-formed Progressive Democrats, while the two most recent elections have seen increased levels of vote share for both Sinn Féin and the Greens with their combined 10 per cent in 2002 and almost 12 per cent in 2007. Their paths diverged in 2011, the Greens being punished for participation in the 2007-11 government and Sinn Féin benefiting from the collapse of the Fianna Fáil and Green vote to achieve 10 per cent. Much of the remaining increase in the vote for 'others' during this period, and particularly since the falling off of the PD vote from 1989, can be accounted for by the steady rise of the independent vote throughout the period, reaching almost 10 per cent in 2002 and over 12 per cent in 2011.[20] According to Mair and Weeks, the rise in such minor party support is 'symptomatic of voter dissatisfaction', not least with the traditional parties.[21]

Electorates have become increasingly volatile. Ireland has not been exempt from these dealigning dynamics. Marsh *et al.* point to declining party identification amongst Irish electors and indicate that short-term factors are increasingly important in explaining voting behaviour.[22] It should therefore be expected that the combined share of first preferences for minor parties and independents rises in more volatile elections. In short, the more volatile the election, the better minor parties and independents will do. This is easily tested. A widely used measure of volatility in comparative politics is the Pedersen index. This provides an estimate of net electoral volatility and is useful for assessing the gains and losses for all parties between two sets of elections. Table 3 sets out net volatility in Irish elections between 1973 and 2011 alongside the combined share of first preferences achieved by minor parties and independents in each respective election.[23] The index ranges from 2.9 in the first 1982 election, to 16.2 in the 1987 election, falling back to 6.5 in the 2002 and 2007 contests before rising sharply to 29.7 in 2011. Mean volatility between 1973 and 2011 is 9.1. The bivariate correlation coefficient between net volatility and the minor party and independent share of first preferences is 0.87 and this is statistically significant at the $p<.01$ level. Running this analysis with only the vote share for minor parties and not independents records a similar coefficient of 0.89, also significant at the 0.1 level.[24] In general terms, the higher the rate of electoral volatility, the better minor parties will do.

The consistency of this vote share suggests that some voters may have become used to giving their first preferences to minor parties and that a relatively loyal core of voters are now in the habit of doing so. For example, even if there had been some degree of turnover amongst Green voters, there is a consistency in the Green vote between 2002 and 2007,[25] while Marsh *et al.* point to Sinn Féin's strong party identity leading to high levels of attachment and stable voting among its voters.[26] While the sizeable decline of the Green Party vote in both the 2009 European and local elections and the 2011 general election might indicate that any such loyalties are somewhat fickle, that Sinn Féin's support in 2009, even if disappointing for the party, was essentially constant, before rising considerably in

*Table 3: Net electoral volatility and the minor party vote in Ireland*

| Election | Net volatility | 'Others' % 1<sup>st</sup> preferences (inc Ind) | Small party % 1<sup>st</sup> preferences only |
|---|---|---|---|
| 1973 | 3.5 | 5.0 | 2.0 |
| 1977 | 6.9 | 7.3 | 1.8 |
| 1981 | 7.1 | 8.4 | 2.2 |
| 1982-1 | 2.9 | 6.3 | 3.4 |
| 1982-2 | 3.2 | 6.3 | 3.8 |
| 1987 | 16.2 | 22.4 | 18.4 |
| 1989 | 7.0 | 17.1 | 13.2 |
| 1992 | 10.7 | 17.2 | 11.2 |
| 1997 | 8.9 | 22.4 | 15.5 |
| 2002 | 6.5 | 25.2 | 15.7 |
| 2007 | 6.5 | 21.0 | 15.2 |
| 2011 | 29.7 | 46.5 | 39.4 |
| Coefficient | | 0.87★★ | 0.89★★ |

Sources: Coakley, J. 'Appendix 2 Electoral Data', in J. Coakley and M. Gallagher (eds) *Politics in the Republic of Ireland*, 4th edition (London; Routledge/PSAI Press, 2005), p. 466; Gallagher, Michael 'The Earthquake that Never Happened: Analysis of the Results' in M. Gallagher and M. Marsh (eds) *How Ireland Voted 2007: The Full Story of Ireland's General Election* (Basingstoke; Palgrave Macmilan, 2008), p. 82; Weeks, Liam 'We Don't Like (To) Party: A Typology of Independents in Irish Political Life, 1922-2007', *Irish Political Studies*, 24(1), (2009), pp. 1-28; and Gallagher, Michael 'Ireland's Earthquake Election: Analysis of the Results' in Gallagher and Marsh (eds) *How Ireland Voted 2011: The Full Story of Ireland's Earthquake Election* (Basingstoke; Palgrave Macmillan, 2011), pp. 139-71

Note: ★★ significant at the p<.01 level

2011 instead suggests another explanation. This is that minor parties in Ireland are able to maintain voters' loyalties only while they are in opposition. In office, it becomes difficult to deliver on the often radical positions elaborated in election campaigns. As O'Malley notes, this is even harder in coalition when a minor party, such as the Greens from 2007, risks being 'smothered' by its larger partner in government. Under such conditions, any loyalties voters have towards minor parties are put under severe strain.[27]

Minor parties have also been argued to provide new channels for political participation for electors. The logic of this argument is that there is a relationship between the number of parties and the level of participation. If this were the case, the higher the number of parties contesting an election, the higher the levels of electoral participation ought to be. One way of assessing this is to use levels of turnout as a measurement of levels of participation. To take account of the relative size of parties, the Effective Number of Electoral Parties (ENEP), introduced above, can be deployed as a proxy variable for estimating the influence of parties beyond Fianna Fáil and Fine Gael. Therefore, the higher the ENEP ratio, the more influence smaller parties have. However, Ireland has been no exception to the international trend of declining election turnout during the period in question, even if this has risen by around 7 percentage points across the 2007 and 2011 elections.[28] This suggests that those who argue that minor parties lead to greater levels of participation are likely to be disappointed at the aggregate level. Consequently, the bivariate relationship between ENEP and turnout is a strongly negative coefficient of -0.78 which is statistically significant at the $p<.01$ level.[29] Alternatively, turnout might increase when there is a greater choice across the ideological spectrum of parties to choose from, regardless of their 'effective' size. The analysis was also therefore run using the raw number of parties contesting each election. The findings are similar and therefore confirm the negative relationship found between the effective number of electoral parties and turnout.[30] Greater numbers of minor parties contesting elections do not appear to, in and of themselves, lead to greater levels of turnout.

Nevertheless, it may still be the case that minor parties do mobilise parts of the electorate that hitherto have not been motivated to participate in politics. Some evidence appears to support such an argument. Kavanagh suggested that increased turnout in the 2004 local elections can partly be attributed to the success of Sinn Féin and other small left wing parties who played a significant role in politicising disaffected working class electorates over local policy issues.[31] Marsh *et al.* underline this argument at the national level by pointing out that Sinn Féin did better from increased turnout in 2002 than from vote switching.[32] Success in mobilising such electors continued in 2011; the Sinn Féin electorate in 2011 was drawn largely from C2DE social classes.[33]

Young people are notoriously difficult to engage in politics. Ireland is no exception. Age has clearly been a factor in explaining non-voting in Irish elections, with only just over half of eighteen to twenty-four year olds in the 2002 Irish National Election Study (INES) having voted.[34] Nevertheless, if the young are more radical, as one theory of age-related voting suggests, then it might be expected that minor parties appeal to the younger voter in Ireland. Both the Greens and Sinn Féin are pointed to in the 2002 study as having an electorate concentrated at the younger end of the age spectrum; the Greens had 8 per cent of the eighteen to twenty-four age group, while Sinn Féin had 9 per cent of eighteen to twenty-fours and 13 per cent of the twenty-five to thirty-four age group.[35] Similarly, the PD electorate was more likely to be at the younger end of the age scale, although much less distinct than that of Sinn Féin or the Greens.[36] In

2011, the Sinn Féin vote remained skewed towards younger age groups, achieving 14 per cent of the vote amongst eighteen to twenty-fours and 13 per cent of twenty-five to thirty-fours.[37] In some ways, the minor parties can therefore, albeit to different extents, be seen as broadening avenues for participation and mobilising voters who may otherwise have stayed at home.

*Table 4: Party membership estimates, 2002-2008*

| Party | 2002 | M/V 02 | 2008 | M/V 08 |
|---|---|---|---|---|
| Progressive Democrats | 5,500 | 7.5 | 4,000 | 7.1 |
| Labour | 3,700 | 1.8 | 7,500 | 3.6 |
| Sinn Féin | 2000 | 1.7 | 5,000 | 3.5 |
| Greens | 800 | 1.1 | 2,000 | 2.1 |
| **Total** | 12,000 | 2.6 | 18,500 | 3.7 |

Sources: Adapted from Marsh, Michael 'Parties and Society' in John Coakley and Michael Gallagher (eds), *Politics in the Republic of Ireland*, 4th edition (Abingdon; Routledge, 2005), pp. 169-70 and Weeks, Liam 'Parties and the Party System' in J. Coakley and M. Gallagher (eds) *Politics in the Republic of Ireland*, 5th edition (London; Routledge, 2009), p. 155

Research has shown that contact to mobilise young electors is crucial.[38] The organisational ability to undertake such activity is therefore as important in building and sustaining the vote of a minor party as their broad policy profile. To provide an estimate of organisation, Table 4 adapts figures on small-party membership reported in Marsh's and Weeks' discussion of party organisation in Ireland.[39] Membership figures should always be treated with some caution, since parties have incentives to overstate their membership and may not keep accurate records. These problems exist with all parties, but are particularly acute with minor parties. Nevertheless, they are often the only estimate available, and researchers have to make use of them while not being blind to their potential difficulties. Unfortunately, the most recent membership estimates predate the 2011 election, but can nevertheless serve as an indication of levels of mobilisation by minor parties.

The total estimated membership for the four minor parties in the 2002 election was around 12,000, and around 18,500 in 2008. To contextualise this, in 2008 Fine Gael had approximately 35,000 members. The M/V ratio reported in Table 4 estimates the proportion of members amongst a party's voters.[40] M/V provides an estimate for the party's penetration of its electorate; the higher the ratio, the closer the contacts between party and its electors are likely to be. In both years, the Progressive Democrats had the highest M/V ratio at around 7 per cent, while the Greens achieved the lowest M/V ratio of only around 1 per

cent in 2002, although this doubled to 2 per cent in 2008. Membership for the
minor parties clearly fluctuates both upwards and downwards. The Progressive
Democrats' membership was reported as having fallen to around 4,000 at the
time of the party's demise in 2008. Labour membership had increased to 7,500
in 2008. Similarly, both Sinn Féin and the Greens more than doubled their
membership between 2002 and 2008. Although a membership study is necessary
to assess motivations for joining, it is likely that without these parties contesting
elections, a considerable number of these members would not have joined a party
in the first place.[41] Minor parties do therefore provide an avenue to participation
for some electors. While membership numbers should not necessarily be equated
with levels of activity, these members, as underlined by Catherine Murphy earlier
in this volume, will also provide their parties with a wide range of benefits.[42]

A further claim made about minor parties is that they introduce a range of
distinct issues which distinguishes them from their larger competitors. Analysis
from recent contests suggests that, at least on some dimensions, minor parties
have presented alternative policy platforms to voters. In 1997, Laver notes that
the most significant issue distinguishing the Progressive Democrats was tax policy,
for the Greens environmental policy, and for Sinn Féin policy towards Northern
Ireland.[43] In left–right terms, minor parties clearly offered different profiles to
the centrist Fianna Fáil, Fine Gael, and Labour with the Progressive Democrats
clearly the most right-wing party and Democratic Left, the Greens and Sinn
Féin all firmly on the left. The Greens also promoted a 'new politics' agenda of
decentralisation, freedom of information and environmental matters. Benoit
and Laver found a similar situation in 2002, with a sharp move leftwards by the
Greens and moves towards the centre left by both Labour and Sinn Féin being
the main differences between the two elections.[44] They also note that the Greens
remained distinctive by promoting a liberal platform on social policy issues.
Marsh *et al.* also highlight a perception amongst voters that the Greens and Sinn
Féin were more Euro-sceptic than the mainstream parties, something that was
confirmed by Sinn Féin's prominent role in the 2008 and 2009 anti-Lisbon Treaty
referendum campaigns.[45] Analyses of party positioning in 2007 and 2011 similarly
place Sinn Féin furthest to the left, with the Greens and, in 2007, the Progressive
Democrats also having platforms that differentiated them from their mainstream
competitors.[46] It is important to note, however, that minor parties differentiate
themselves only in some policy areas. In others, they can be very much in the
mainstream; Benoit and Laver note that while Sinn Féin might be distinctive in
relation to Northern Ireland policy and on the left, on other issues the party is
located in mainstream policy space.[47, 48]

That most of Ireland's minor parties have been left-wing in orientation
poses an important question. Why has the left in general been weak in the Irish
party system and yet left-wing parties dominate minor party competition? One
explanation is that class-based cleavages have been much less important in the

development of the Irish party system than elsewhere, with Fianna Fáil and Fine Gael essentially being centrist parties. McDonnell develops this further and highlights the pro-growth nature of politics in Ireland, suggesting that 'class politics were accepted as being against the national interest'.[49] As party loyalties have broken down, Marsh *et al.* nevertheless provide some evidence to link the rise of left-wing minor parties with the class cleavage and left-wing views.[50] While Labour has had a declining hold on the working class vote from the 1970s onwards, over the last decade or so, this has coincided with Sinn Féin being able to attract a clear working-class electorate. At the same time, Green Party and Sinn Féin voters are clearly on the left of the political spectrum, in a way that most Irish voters have not been. Although what left and right have meant over time to Irish voters is unclear, minor parties have clearly tried to tap into such cleavages. Left-wing minor parties are therefore to some degree exploiting a demand among voters for such a policy platform which is not catered for by the two larger parties. However, the placement of most voters and parties in the 2002 INES suggest that such an appeal is likely to have limited traction, something that seemed to be borne out by minor parties' limited success in 2011.[51]

Ireland is, in another sense, a rare case in relation to minor parties. The main minor party representative of the right was the essentially centre-right free-market, and now disbanded, Progressive Democrats. In most advanced democracies however, parties of the radical right have had a significant presence.[52] In Ireland, this has not been the case. Garner explains this absence in terms of the politicisation of citizenship rules by the state and the ideological content of the mainstream parties in relation to citizenship.[53] In short, they have 'appropriated' an issue that has been exploited by radical right parties elsewhere. O'Malley suggests that the term 'radical right' is inappropriate in the Irish context and uses 'populist nationalist' attitudes to examine the potential for such a party amongst voters.[54, 55] His multivariate analysis shows that, while Ireland's attitudinal and social structure may be conducive to the rise of a radical right party, voters who may be attracted to such an option tend to vote for the left wing and pro-immigrant, Sinn Féin, attracted by the party's appeal to nationalism, nativism, authoritarianism and populism. McDonnell makes similar points, but also observes that for a minor party, Sinn Féin is well resourced.[56] This helps it to protect its position from any other minor party challengers who may want to exploit this electorate. McDonnell also points to the continuing importance of localised and personalised politics in Ireland.[57] This, he argues, limits the potential in Ireland for a populist, radical right party to emerge since these parties have tended to thrive in countries, such as Italy, France and the Netherlands, where the national appeal of the leader has been more important in explaining minor party success than virtually unknown candidates at local level. Consequently, there is currently no open opportunity structure for a populist or radical right party in the Irish political market.

Minor parties have had an increasingly important role in Irish government since Fianna Fáil's acceptance of the necessity of coalition in 1989, with the Progressive Democrats, Labour and the Greens all serving in government in recent years. To what extent can minor parties therefore be said to have been successful in implementing their policy commitments? Analysis of policy pledges enacted by the government between 2002 and 2007 suggests that they have been able to do so. Costello and Thomson indicate that of sixty-eight policy pledges in 2002, the Progressive Democrats had 47 per cent of those fulfilled while in government from 2002, while another 19 per cent were partially fulfilled.[58] While this might be expected since the Progressive Democrats were in government, Costello and Thomson also estimate the extent to which the policy pledges made by minor parties in opposition were also fulfilled. This can happen because either their policies are close to those of the governing parties, or because they have somehow been able to influence policy debate and consequently public policy. Between 2002 and 2007, Costello and Thomson find that a sizeable proportion of minor opposition party polices were fulfilled.[59] Of fifty-four Sinn Féin policies examined, 24 per cent were fulfilled and 19 per cent partially fulfilled, while for fifty-seven Green Party pledges, 18 per cent were fulfilled and 16 per cent partially fulfilled. This suggests that minor party relevance also needs to be thought of in pledge fulfilment terms, not just in relation to coalition potential or the introduction of new issues to campaigning.

## Minor party politics: the Irish contribution

Recent trends in political science have emphasized comparative research at the expense of detailed country studies. Nevertheless, inferences can be drawn from detailed single-country studies, and they are the basic building block of any robust comparative analysis. The argument thus far in this chapter has been that despite Ireland's classification as a 'large-party' country, minor parties and independents have nevertheless had an impact upon Irish political life. What contribution however does this volume make to understanding Irish party competition on the one hand, and comparative theories of minor parties more generally on the other?

Taking the question of Irish party competition first, a range of analyses help explain the rise and decline of minor parties in Ireland. A number of these are historical case studies. Such an approach can elaborate detailed political context which impacts upon minor party success or failure. Coakley provides a valuable up-to-date cataloguing of the minor parties that have contested elections to Dáil Éireann.[60] Varley provides a comprehensive discussion of why farmers' parties did not become a lasting feature of Irish party competition, indicating that they were unable to transcend the structures of class and party political competition they were faced with.[61] Murphy similarly catalogues and describes the overlap between pressure/interest groups contesting elections and whether or not they might be seen as minor parties.[62] McDaid and Rekawek's detailed discussion of the decline and rise of the Irish Labour Party highlights the impact that internal party politics, leadership and party competition had in explaining the fluctuations in the party's success.[63] Through studies of minor parties that have served in government in Ireland, O'Malley provides an account of their failure, or otherwise, to have an impact in office independent of their larger coalition partners.[64] While the Irish party system and its two main parties, Fianna Fáil and Fine Gael, are regularly presented as being sui generis, Bolleyer's study of the Irish Green Party reminds analysts that such an approach cannot necessarily be extrapolated to newer party options, demonstrating that the Irish Greens are following an organisational path well worn by other Green parties across Europe.[65] These analyses are complemented well by the accounts by minor party politicians contained in this volume.

Many of the issues raised contribute more broadly to the comparative study of minor parties and independents. The first contribution is classificatory and provides hypotheses for comparativists to test. Harmel and Roberston distinguish between 'contender' and 'promoter' parties.[66] 'Contender' parties have the perception that they can be eventually successful, while 'promoter' parties may think success unlikely but their major objective is to highlight attention to a particular cause or issue. Murphy, however, highlights the fact that there are two possible elements to this 'promoter' category.[67] The first is where a pressure or interest group decides to contest an election in order to attempt to achieve a policy goal. This might be termed, for want of a better term, a 'pressure party'. Such 'pressure party' policy goals are likely to be relatively short-lived single-issue objectives. A good example is the impact of Libertas in the 2008 Lisbon referendum campaign, success which after contesting the 2009 European elections, the organisation failed to follow up despite a relatively high-profile campaign. Consequently, as Murphy shows, such organisations are likely to rise and decline in a short timespan and are unlikely to outlive the three election limit often used to judge party system change.[68] By contrast, Coakley points to the Irish case to suggest that in the long run 'promoter' parties are more likely to persist over time than many other minor party options, not least since electoral reward is not necessarily their sole motivation.[69] Arguably, the idea of the 'pressure party' can therefore be placed somewhere between formal minor parties on the one hand and the various categories of independent falling closest to the quasi-party category identified by Weeks, while the longevity and success of such organisations remains to be tested comparatively by comparsion with 'promoter' parties.[70]

One of the major issues in minor party politics is that of which parties should be included in the analysis. This is not just a question of an upper limit, but also of setting a lower limit so that 'ephemeral' organisations and those who command miniscule levels of public support are excluded. Mair suggests an inevitably arbitrary cut-off point of 15 per cent of the vote.[71] While widely used, this is less than satisfactory because it sets quite a high maximum threshold. As noted above, using such a threshold means classifying a party such as the Irish Labour Party as minor. This is problematic because, as McDaid and Rekawek discuss and others have also argued, Labour, despite averaging around 11 per cent of the vote between 1973 and 2007 and breaking the 15 per cent threshold only once during that period, has actually been a key element in the Irish party system, having been crucial to both providing parliamentary opposition and having coalition potential.[72] Indeed, McDaid and Rekawek prefer the terms mainstream or proximal mainstream to explain the position of Labour and its fluctuating fortunes, and this underlines Smith's point that smallness is relative to specific individual party systems.[73]

O'Malley deals with these problems by proposing a new measurement for use in identifying minor parties when they participate in government, which also takes into account their size and position *vis-à-vis* their larger party opponents.[74] Minor parties in government are therefore those parties that are less than one quarter the percentage of seats of mid-point between the largest two parties. This method can of course also be used in relation to vote share. Between 1927 and 2007, O'Malley notes that the average cut-off for minor parties using such a method is 9.9 per cent. Such an approach means that parties such as Labour, with an average of 11 per cent, fall outside the minor party bracket. Taking an average of parties' results is important in order to avoid the fluctuations between different contests and to ensure consistency of classification.[75]

Central has been the idea that minor parties go through a lifespan of growth and decline.[76] In addition to identifying four thresholds of declaration, authorisation, representation and relevance, Pedersen goes on to outline a range of dimensions on which party lifespans can be measured: modality; dispersion, or the number of years the party has been operating; the flatness and the skewness of the party's lifespan curve.[77] While the process through which small parties choose to contest elections has been examined by a number of authors,[78] with the exception of Deschouwer's model of small parties in government,[79] the assumption is that minor parties will ultimately decline. Decline tends to be less well understood. Indeed, these thresholds fail to acknowledge the fact that the lifespan of minor parties can also be a dependent variable, dependent on the extent to which mainstream parties adapt organisationally and ideologically to see off the challenge small parties present. The Irish case presents new evidence, enlarging ideas regarding minor party decline. In particular, O'Malley tests the 'smothering' hypothesis to explain the decline and lack of effectiveness of minor parties in Irish government.[80] Ó Muineacháin's case study of the Progressive Democrats in chapter 7 illuminates why an apparently successful minor party might not only rise, but decline and chose to disband. Leaving aside the question of size, McDaid and Rekawek's studies of Labour also contribute to this debate, by challenging the unimodal assumption of rise and decline implicit in much of the minor party literature.[81] Instead, they highlight the internal and external factors that lead to minor party decline and rise again on more than one occasion. Similarly, Bolleyer highlights how minor parties can persist through organisational development even in a large party system in her discussion of the Greens.[82] While participation in government has clearly stalled the party's progress somewhat, the prevalence of environmental issues nevertheless suggests the party will persist, albeit with fluctuating results.

Finally, independent politics is a growing, if not yet well understood, field which is increasingly important in volatile times when the claim to not be aligned with a party is often appealing. Independents have variously been conceptualised as a symptom of party decline[83] and a way in which issues not effectively represented by parties can be voiced in a way that resonates with voters.[84] Irish research has been at the forefront of understanding both the rise of independent politics, and situating it as a normal element of political life. Weeks provides a comprehensive classification of independents in Ireland,[85] which contrasts with and develops further that utilised by Copus *et al.*'s discussion of the phenomenon in Britain.[86] Similarly, Bolleyer and Weeks utilise an incentives-based model to highlight that the decision to stand as an independent can be as rational as any made by a party organisation.[87] How independents behave in parliament when they are successful is also an open question. The few existing studies are hampered in their theory-building utility by either a small number of cases[88] or the uniqueness of the institutions.[89] Hansen deals with these difficulties in his use of cutting-edge techniques in the study of parliamentary voting by independent TDs in the Dáil between 1937 and 2011.[90] He tests hypotheses which find that independents, and minor parties, vote significantly more against the government in the Dáil when they are either in opposition or when they are not needed by the government for its survival. These hypotheses and findings are important and serve as the basis for which comparative analysis on the parliamentary behaviour of independents may be taken forward.

## Conclusion

With Ireland's consistent placement over time as a 'large party' country in both Mair's and this assessment of West European minor parties, it would be tempting to conclude that Irish minor parties and independents are of little relevance to the study of either Irish or comparative party competition.[91] Such a conclusion would be a mistake. As discussion at the systemic level has demonstrated, minor parties and independents have had a real impact on the Irish party system, offering, for instance, different policy options to voters, alternative avenues for participation, and also having an impact on government policy. While they may not be breaking the mould, nor are they merely fiddling at the edges of party competition. Indeed, while they may have fluctuating fortunes, minor parties and independents are nevertheless a permanent presence in Ireland as they are elsewhere. Important questions naturally remain for both Irish and comparative analysts. It is therefore to be hoped that this volume serves, not as the last word, but as the spur for further research into minor parties and independents in both Ireland and beyond.

# Bibliography

## Books

Abedi, Amir *Anti-political Establishment Parties: A Comparative Analysis* (London; Routledge, 2004)

Adams, Gerry *The New Ireland: A Vision for the Future* (Dingle; Brandon, 2006)

Adshead, Maura and Jonathon Tonge *Politics in Ireland: Convergence and Divergence in a Two-Polity Island* (Basingstoke; Palgrave Macmillan, 2009)

Ailtirí na hAiséirghe *Aiséirghe Says ... The New Order in the New Ireland* (Dublin; Ailtirí na hAiséirghe, 1943)

Aldrich, John H. *Why Parties?: The Origin and Transformation of Political Parties in America* (University of Chicago Press, 1995)

Arnold, Bruce and Jason O'Toole *The End of the Party: How Fianna Fáil Lost its Grip on Power* (Dublin; Gill & Macmillan, 2011)

Arter, David *Scandinavian Politics Today* (Manchester; Manchester University Press, 1999)

Barberis, Peter, John McHugh and Mike Tyldesley *Encyclopedia of British and Irish Political Organisations* (London; Pinter, 2000)

Bell, J. Bowyer *The Secret Army: A History of the IRA 1916-1979*, revised edition (Dublin; The Academy Press, 1979)

Benoit, Kenneth and Michael Laver *Party Policy in Modern Democracy* (London; Routledge, 2006)

Berry, R. *Independent: The Rise of the Non-Aligned Politician* (Exeter; Imprint Academic, 2008)

Bew, Paul *Ireland: The Politics of Enmity 1789-2006* (Oxford; Oxford University Press, 2007)

Bew, Paul, E. Hazelkorn and Henry Patterson *The Dynamics of Irish Politics* (London; Lawrence and Wishart, 1989)

Boyle, Dan *A Journey to Change: 25 Years of the Green Party in Irish Politics* (Dublin; Nonsuch, 2006)

Bradley, Dan *Farm Labourers: Irish Struggle 1900-1976* (Belfast; Athol Books, 1988)

Burchell, John *The Evolution of Green Politics: Development and Change within European Green Parties* (London; Earthscan Publications Ltd, 2002)

Campbell, Fergus *Land and Revolution: Nationalist Politics in the West of Ireland 1891-1921* (Oxford; Oxford University Press, 2005)

Carty, R.K. *Party and Parish Pump: Electoral Politics in Ireland* (Ontario; Wilfred Laurier Press, 1981)

Christian Solidarity Party *Policy Proposals* (Dublin; Christian Solidarity Party, 1997)

Chubb, Basil *The Government and Politics of Ireland* (London; Oxford University Press, 1974), reprinted 1992

Clann na Talmhan *The Book of Clann na Talmhan* (Drogheda; Drogheda Argus, 1944)

Coakley, John and Michael Gallagher *Politics in the Republic of Ireland*, 4th edition (London; PSAI Press/Routledge, 2005)

Coakley, John and Michael Gallagher *Politics in the Republic of Ireland*, 5th edition (London; Routledge, 2009)

Cole, Alistair *French Politics and Society*, 2nd edition (London; Pearson Longman, 2005)

Collins, Stephen *Breaking the Mould: How the PDs Changed Irish Politics* (Dublin; Gill & Macmillan, 2005)

Collins, Stephen *Spring and the Labour Story* (Dublin; O'Brien, 1993)

Collins, Stephen *The Power Game: Fianna Fáil since Lemass* (Dublin; O'Brien, 2000)

Communist Party of Ireland *The Communist Party of Ireland: An Outline History* (Dublin; Communist Party of Ireland, 1974)

Communist Party of Ireland *Ireland in Crisis: The Communist Answer* (Dublin; Communist Party of Ireland, 1975)

Coogan, Tim Pat *The IRA*, revised edition (London; Fontana, 1987)

Córas na Poblachta *Córas na Poblachta (The Republican Plan): Summary of Policy* (Dublin; Central Committee, Córas na Poblachta, 1940)

Craig, F.W.S. *Minor Parties in British Parliamentary Elections 1885-1979* (London; Macmillan, 1975)

Cronin, Mike *The Blueshirts and Irish Politics* (Dublin; Four Courts Press, 1997)

Daniels, C. *Prospects for a Greener Ireland: The Future of the Irish Green Party*, Paper submitted as Junior Independent Work (Department of Politics; Princeton University, 1990)

Deschouwer, Kris (ed.) *New Parties in Government* (London; Routledge, 2008)

Desmond, Barry *Finally and in Conclusion: A Political Memoir* (Dublin; New Island, 2000)

Donnelly, Seán (ed.) *Poll Position: An Analysis of the 1991 Local Elections* (Dublin; Sean Donnelly, 1992)

Donovan, Mark (ed.) *Changing Party Systems in Western Europe* (London; Pinter)

Douglas, R.M. *Architects of the Resurrection: Ailtirí na hAiséirighe and the Fascist 'New Order' in Ireland* (Manchester; Manchester University Press, 2009)

Dunphy, Richard *The Making of Fianna Fáil Power in Ireland 1923-1948* (Oxford; Oxford University Press, 1995)

Duverger, Maurice *Political Parties: Their Organisation and Activity in the Modern State*, 3rd edition (London; Methuen, 1969), first published 1954

Eley, Geoff *Forging Democracy – The History of the Left in Europe, 1850-2000* (Oxford; Oxford University Press, 2002)

English, Richard *Armed Struggle: The History of the IRA* (London; Macmillan, 2003)

English, Richard *Radicals and the Republic: Socialist Republicanism in the Irish Free State 1925-1937* (Oxford; Clarendon Press, 1994)

Finlay, Fergus *Snakes and Ladders* (Dublin; New Island Books, 1997)

Gallagher, Michael *Electoral Support for Irish Parties 1927-1973* (London; Sage, 1976)

Fitzpatrick, David *Politics and Irish Life 1913-21: Provincial Experience of War and Revolution* (Cork; Cork University Press, 1998)

Gallagher, Michael *Electoral Support for Irish Political Parties 1927-1973* (London; Sage Publications, 1976)

Gallagher, Michael *Irish Elections 1922-44: Results and Analysis* (Limerick; PSAI Press, 1993)

Gallagher, Michael *Irish Elections 1948-77: Results and Analysis* (London; Routledge and PSAI Press, 2009)

Gallagher, Michael *Political Parties in the Republic of Ireland* (Dublin; Gill & Macmillan, 1985)

Gallagher, Michael *The Irish Labour Party in Transition 1957-82* (Manchester; Manchester University Press, 1982)

Gallagher, Michael and Michael Marsh *Days of Blue Loyalty: The Politics and Membership of Fine Gael* (Dublin; PSAI Press, 2002)

Gallagher, Michael and Michael Marsh (eds) *How Ireland Voted 2011: The Full Story of Ireland's Earthquake Election* (London; Palgrave, 2011)

Gallagher, Michael, Michael Laver and Peter Mair, *Representative Government in Modern Europe* (New York; McGraw-Hill, 2011)

Gallagher, Michael and Richard Sinnott (eds) *How Ireland Voted 1989* (Galway; University College Galway, 1990)

Gallagher, Michael and Michael Laver (eds) *How Ireland Voted 1992* (Dublin; Folens and PSAI Press, 1993)

Galligan, Yvonne *Women and Politics in Contemporary Ireland: From the Margins to the Mainstream* (London; Pinter, 1998)

Garry, John, Niamh Hardiman, Diane Payne (eds) *Irish Social and Political Attitudes* (Liverpool; Liverpool University Press, 2006)

Garvin, Tom *The Evolution of Irish Nationalist Politics* (Dublin; Gill & Macmillan, 1981)

Gottfried, Paul *The Strange Death of Marxism: The European Left in the New Millennium* (Columbia; University of Missouri, 2005)

Greer, Alan *Rural Politics in Northern Ireland: Policy Networks and Agricultural Development Since Partition* (Aldershot; Avebury, 1996)

Hanley, Brian, and Scott Millar *The Lost Revolution: the Story of the Official IRA and the Workers' Party* (Dublin; Penguin Ireland, 2009)

Hesketh, Tom *The Second Partitioning of Ireland: The Abortion Referendum of 1983* (Dublin; Brandsma Books, 1990)

Hoppen, Theodore K. *Elections, Politics, and Society in Ireland 1832-1885* (Oxford; Oxford University Press, 1984)

Horgan, John *Labour: The Price of Power* (Dublin; Gill & Macmillan, 1986)

Horgan, John *Noël Browne: Passionate Outsider* (Dublin; Gill & Macmillan, 2000)

Hug, Simon *Altering Party Systems: Strategic Behavior and the Emergence of New Political Parties in Western Democracies* (Chicago; University of Michigan Press, 2001)

Jaensch, Dean and David Mathieson *A Plague on Both Your Houses: Minor Parties in Australia* (Sydney; Allen and Unwin, 1998)

Jordan, Grant and William A. Maloney *Democracy and Interest Groups* (Basingstoke; Palgrave, 2007)

Katz, Richard S. and Peter Mair (eds) *How Parties Organize: Change and Adaptation in Western Democracies* (Sage; London, 1994)

Kavanagh, Ray *Spring, Summer and Fall: The Rise and Fall of the Labour Party* (Dublin; Blackwater Press, 2001)

Keman, Hans and André Jrouwel *The Rise of a New Political Class?: Emerging New Parties and the Populist Challenge in Western Europe* (Vrije Universiteit Amsterdam, Department of Polictical Science, 2006)

Key, V.O. *Politics, Parties and Pressure Groups* (New York; Crowell, 1942)

Kitschelt, Herbert *The Logics of Party Formation: Ecological Politics in Belgium and West Germany* (Ithaca; Cornell University Press, 1989)

Kitschelt, Herbert, with Anthony J. McGann *The Radical Right in Western Europe: A Comparative Analysis* (Ann Arbor, MI; University of Michigan Press, 1995)

Laver, Michael and Norman Schofield *Multiparty Government: The Politics of Coalition in Europe* (Ann Arbor; University of Michigan Press, 1990)

Laver, Michael and Ken Shepsle *Making and Breaking Governments: Cabinets and Legislatures in Parliamentary Democracies* (Cambridge; Cambridge University Press, 1996)

Lijphart, Arend *Patterns of Democracy: Government Forms and Performance in Thirty-Six Countries* (New Haven; Yale University Press, 1999)

Lee, John J. *Ireland 1912-1985: Politics and Society* (Cambridge; Cambridge University Press, 1989)

Lysaght, D.R. O'Connor *The Irish Republic* (Cork; Mercier, 1970)

Mac an Bheatha, Proinnsias *Téid Focal le Gaoith [A Word Goes with the Wind]* (Baile Átha Cliath; Foilseacháin Náisiunta, 1967)

MacBride, Seán *That Day's Struggle: A Memoir 1904-1951* C. Lawlor (ed.) (Dublin; Currach Press, 2005)

MacCarron, Daniel *Letters about Ireland* (Dublin; DMC Universal, 1973)

MacDermott, Eithne *Clann na Pobachta* (Cork; Cork University Press, 1998)

MacGréil, Michael *Prejudice in Ireland Revisited* (Maynooth; Survey and Research Unit, St Patrick's College, 1996)

Maillot, Agnés *New Sinn Féin: Irish Republicanism in the Twenty-first Century* (London; Routledge, 2005)

Mair, Peter *The Changing Irish Party System: Organisation, Ideology and Electoral Competition* (London; Frances Pinter, 1987)

Manning, Maurice *Irish Political Parties: An Introduction* (Dublin; Gill & Macmillan, 1972)

Manning, Maurice *James Dillon: A Biography* (Dublin; Wolfhound Press, 1999)

Manning, Maurice *The Blueshirts* (Dublin; Gill & Macmillan, 1970)

Marsh, Michael, Richard Sinnott, John Garry and Fiachra Kennedy *The Irish Voter: The Nature of Electoral Competition in the Republic of Ireland* (Manchester; Manchester University Press, 2008)

McCracken, J.L. *Representative Government in Ireland: A Study of Dáil Éireann 1919-48* (London; Oxford University Press, 1958)

McCullagh, David *A Makeshift Majority: The First Inter-party Government, 1948-51* (Dublin; Institute of Public Administration, 1998)

McGarry, Fearghal *Eoin O'Duffy: A Self-Made Hero* (Oxford; Oxford University Press, 2005)

McGuire, Charlie *Roddy Connolly and the Struggle for Socialism in Ireland* (Cork; Cork University Press, 2008)

Meehan, Ciara *The Cosgrave Party: A History of Cumann na nGaedheal* (Dublin; Prism, 2010)

Micheletti, Michelle *The Swedish Farmers' Movement and Government Agricultural Policy* (New York; Praeger, 1990)

Milotte, Mike *Communism in Modern Ireland: The Pursuit of The Workers' Republic since 1916* (Dublin; Gill & Macmillan, 1984)

Minihan, Mary *A Deal with the Devil: The Green Party in Government* (Dublin; Maverick House, 2011)

Mitchell, Arthur *Labour in Irish Politics 1890-1930: The Irish Labour Movement in an Age of Revolution* (Dublin; Irish University Press, 1974)

Moss, Warner *Political Parties in the Irish Free State* (New York: Columbia University Press, 1933)

Moloney, Ed *A Secret History of the IRA* (London; Allen Lane, 2002)

Mudde, Cas *Populist Radical Right Parties in Europe* (Cambridge; Cambridge University Press, 2007)

Müller-Rommel, Ferdinand and Geoffrey Pridham (eds) *Small Parties in Western Europe: Comparative and National Perspectives* (London; Sage, 1991)

National Labour Party *Principles and Policy* (Dublin; National Labour Party, 1944)

Murphy, Gary *In Search of the Promised Land* (Cork; Mercier Press, 2009)

Murphy, John A. *Ireland in the Twentieth Century* (Dublin; Gill & Macmillan, 1975)

Murray, Gerald and Jonathan Tonge *Sinn Féin and the SDLP: From Alienation to Participation* (London; Hurst & Co., 2005)

Nohlen, Dieter C. and Philip Stöver (eds) *Elections in Europe: A Data Handbook* (Baden-Baden; Nomos, 2010)

Ó Brion, Eoin *Sinn Féin and the Politics of Left Republicanism* (London; Pluto Press, 2009)

O'Connor, Emmet *Reds and the Green: Ireland, Russia and the Communist International 1919-43* (Dublin; UCD Press, 2004)

O'Connor, Emmet *Syndicalism in Ireland* (Cork; Cork University Press, 1988)

O'Sullivan, Donal *The Irish Free State and its Senate: A Study in Contemporary Politics* (London; Faber & Faber, 1940)

Panebianco, Angelo *Political Parties: Organization and Power* (Cambridge; Cambridge University Press, 1988)

Patterson, Henry *The Politics of Illusion: A Political History of the IRA* (London; Penguin, 1997)

Penniman, Howard Rae and Brian Farrell *Ireland at the Polls 1981, 1982 and 1987* (Washington DC; Duke University Press, 1987)

Puirséil, Niamh *The Irish Labour Party, 1922-73* (Dublin; University College Dublin Press, 2007)

Quinn, Ruairi *Straight Left: A Journey in Politics* (London; Hodder Headline Ireland, 2005)

Rae, Douglas W. *The Political Consequence of Electoral Laws* (New Haven; Yale University Press, 1967)

Rafter, Kevin *Democratic Left the Life and Death of an Irish Political Party* (Dublin; Irish Academic Press, 2011)

Rafter, Kevin *Neil Blaney: A Soldier of Destiny* (Dublin; Blackwater Press, 1993)

Rafter, Kevin *The Clann: The Story of Clann na Poblachta* (Dublin; Mercier Press, 1996)

Rafter, Kevin *Sinn Féin 1905-2005; In the Shadow of Gunmen* (Dublin; Gill & Macmillan, 2005)

Regan, John M. *The Irish Counter-Revolution 1921-1936: Treatyite Politics and Settlement in Independent Ireland* (Dublin; Gill & Macmillan, 1999)

Reiser, Marion and Everhard Holtmann (eds) *Farewell to the Party Model? Independent Local Lists in Eastern and Western European Countries* (Wiesbaden; VS Verlag)

Rekawek, Kacper *Irish Republican Terrorism and Politics: A Comparative Study of the Official and the Provisional IRA* (Abingdon; Routledge, 2011)

Reynolds, Albert *Albert Reynolds: My Autobiography* (Dublin; Transworld Ireland, 2009)

Rokkan, Stein *Citizens, Elections, Parties: Approaches to the Comparative Study of the Processes of Political Development* (Oslo, Universitetsforlaget, 1970)

Ross, James F.S. *The Irish Election System: What it is and How it Works* (London; Pall Mall Press, 1959)

Rumpf, Erhard and A.C. Hepburn *Nationalism and Socialism in Twentieth-Century Ireland* (Liverpool; Liverpool University Press, 1977)

Sartori, Giovanni *Parties and Party Systems: A Framework for Analysis*, vol. 1 (Cambridge; Cambridge University Press, 1976)

Sassoon, Donald *One Hundred Years of Socialism: The West European Left in the Twentieth Century* (New York; New Press, 1996)

Scarrow, Susan E. *Parties and Their Members: Organizing for Victory in Britain and Germany* (Oxford; Oxford University Press, 1996)

Schattschneider, Elmer E., *Party Government* (Westport; Greenwood Press, 1942)

Sinn Féin *Éire Nua: The Social and Economic Programme of Sinn Féin* (Dublin; Sinn Féin, 1971)

Sinnott, Richard *Irish Voters Decide: Voting Behaviour in Elections and Referendums Since 1918* (Manchester; Manchester University Press, 1995)

Socialist Party of Ireland *Manifesto of the Socialist Party of Ireland with Declaration of Principles* (Dublin; Socialist Party of Ireland, 1949)

Taagepera, Rein and Matthew S. Shugart *Seats and Votes: The Effects and Determinants of Electoral Systems* (New Haven; Yale University Press, 1989)

Taylor, Peter *Provos: The IRA and Sinn Féin* (London; Bloomsbury, 1998)

Therborn, Goran *European Modernity and Beyond: The Trajectory of European Societies 1945-2000* (London; Sage, 1995)

Tweedy, Hilda *A Link in the Chain: The Story of the Irish Housewives Association, 1942-1992* (Dublin; Attic Press, 1992)

Urwin, Derek W. *From Ploughshare to Ballotbox: The Politics of Agrarian Defence in Europe* (Oslo; Universitetsforlaget, 1980)

Walker, Brian Mercer (ed.) *Parliamentary Election Results in Ireland: 1918-92: Irish Elections to*

*Parliaments and Parliamentary Assemblies at Westminster, Belfast, Dublin, Strasbourg* (Dublin; Royal Irish Academy, 1992)

Ward, Margaret *Unmanageable Revolutionaries: Women and Irish Nationalism* (Dingle: Brandon, 1983)

Weeks, Liam and Aodh Quinlivan *All Politics is Local: A Guide to Local Elections in Ireland* (Cork; Collins Press, 2009)

Whelan, Noel *Fianna Fáil: A Biography of the Party* (Dublin; Gill & Macmillan, 2011)

Whyte, John H. *Interpreting Northern Ireland* (Oxford; Clarendon Press, 1990)

Wilson, Graham K. *Interest Groups* (Oxford; Basil Blackwell, 1991)

## Articles and Book Chapters

Aars, J. and H.E. Ringkjob 'Party Politicisation Reversed? Non-Partisan Alternatives in Norwegian Local Politics', *Scandinavian Political Studies*, 28(2), (2005), pp. 161-81

Abramson, Paul R., John H. Aldrich, Phil Paolino and David W. Rohde 'Third-party and Independent Candidates in American Politics: Wallace, Anderson, and Perot', *Political Science Quarterly*, 110(3), (1995), pp. 349-67

Adams, Gerry 'A Sense of Hope and Purpose', (2009), available at: http://www.sinnfein.ie/contents/15516 (accessed 28 December 2011)

Adams, James, Michael Clark, Lawrence Ezrow and Garrett Glasgow 'Are Niche Parties Fundamentally Different From Mainstream Parties? The Causes and the Electoral Consequences of Western European Parties' Policy Shifts, 1976-1998', *American Journal of Political Science*, 50(3), (2006), pp. 513-29

Adshead, Maura 'Beyond Clientelism: Agricultural Networks in Ireland and the EU', *West European Politics*, 19(3), (1996), pp. 583-608

Allern, Elin H. and Tim Bale 'Political Parties and Interest Groups: Disentangling Complex Relationships', *Party Politics*, 18(1), (2012), pp. 7-25

Arter, David 'The Finnish Centre Party: A Case of Successful Transformation?' in David Arter (ed.) *From Farmyard to City Square? The Electoral Adaptation of the Nordic Agrarian Parties* (Aldershot: Ashgate, 2001), pp. 59-95

Arter, David 'Conclusion' in David Arter (ed.) *From Farmyard to City Square? The Electoral Adaptation of the Nordic Agrarian Parties* (Aldershot; Ashgate, 2001), pp. 162-83

Arter, David 'Scandinavia: What's Left Is the Social Democratic Consensus', *Parliamentary Affairs*, 36(1), (2003), pp. 75-99

Barnea, Shlomit and Gideon Rahat '"Out With the Old, in With the New": What Constitutes a New Party', *Party Politics*, 17(3), (2011), p. 303

Bartolini, Stefano 'The Membership of Mass Parties: The Social Democratic Experience, 1889-1978', in H. Daalder and Peter Mair (eds) *Western European Party Systems: Continuity and Change* (London; Sage, 1983), pp. 177-220

Bartolini, Stefano 'The Membership of Mass Parties: The Social Democratic Experience, 1889-1978', in H. Daalder and Peter Mair (eds) *Western European Party Systems: Continuity and Change* (London; Sage, 1983), pp. 177-220

Bélanger, Éric 'Antipartyism and Third-party Vote Choice: A Comparison of Canada, Britain, and Australia', *Comparative Political Studies*, 37(9), (2004), pp. 1054-78

Benoit, Kenneth and Michael Laver 'Estimating Irish Party Policy Positions Using Computer Wordscoring: The 2002 Election – A Research Note', *Irish Political Studies*, 18(1), (2003), pp. 97-107

Berrington, Hugh 'New Parties in Britain: Why Some Live and Most Die', *International Political Science Review*, 6(4), (1985), pp. 441-461.

Beyers, Jan, Rainer Eising and William Maloney 'Researching Interest Group Politics in Europe and Elsewhere: Much We Study, Little We Know?', *West European Politics*, 31(6), (2008), pp. 1, 103-28

Blais, André 'Third Parties in Canadian Provincial Politics', *Canadian Journal of Political Science*, 6(3), (1973), pp. 422-38

Bochel, Hugh and David Denver 'Minor Parties and Independents in Times of Change: Scottish Local Elections 1974 to 2007', *Local Government Studies*, 24(5), (2008), pp. 577-93

Boix, Charles 'The Emergence of Parties and Party Systems' in Charles Boix and Susan Stokes (eds) *Oxford Handbook of Comparative Politics* (Oxford; Oxford University Press, 2007), pp. 499-521

Bolleyer, Nicole 'Inside the Cartel Party: Party Organization in Government and Opposition', *Political Studies*, 57(3), (2009), pp. 559-79

Bolleyer, Nicole 'Small Parties – From Party Pledges to Government Policy', *West European Politics*, 30(1), (2007), pp. 121-47

Bolleyer, Nicole 'The Irish Green Party: From Protest to Mainstream Party?', *Irish Political Studies*, 25(4), (2010), pp. 603-23

Bolleyer, Nicole 'The Organisational Costs of Public Office', in Kris Deschouwer (ed.) *New Parties in Government* (London; Routledge, 2008), pp. 17-41

Bolleyer, Nicole and Liam Weeks 'The Puzzle of Non-Party Actors in Party Democracy: Independents in Ireland', *Comparative European Politics*, 7(3), (2009), pp. 299-324

Bull, Martin J. 'The West European Communist Movement in the Late Twentieth Century', *West European Politics*, 18(1), (1995), pp. 78-97

Carter, Elisabeth L. 'Proportional Representation and the Fortunes of Right-wing Extremist Parties', *West European Politics*, 25(3), (2002), pp. 125-46

Carty, R.K. 'Brokerage and Partisanship: Politicians, Parties and Elections in Ireland', *Canadian Journal of Political Science*, 14 (1), (1981), pp. 53-81

Central Statistics Office, 'Community Involvement and Social Networks 2006', July 2009, available at: http://www.cso.ie/releasespublications/documents/labour_market/2006/comsoc06.pdf

Christensen, Dag Arne 'The Norwegian Agrarian-Centre Party: Class, Rural or Catchall Party?' in David Arter (ed.) *From Farmyard to City Square? The Electoral Adaptation of the Nordic Agrarian Parties* (Aldershot; Ashgate, 2001), pp. 31-58

Chubb, Basil 'Ireland 1957' in D.E. Butler (eds) *Elections Abroad* (London; Macmillan, 1959)

Clark, Alistair 'Breaking the Mould or Fiddling at the Edges? Ireland's Minor Parties in Comparative and Systemic Perspective', *Irish Political Studies*, 25(4), (2010), pp. 661-80

Coakley, John 'Appendix 2 Electoral Data', in John Coakley and Michael Gallagher (eds) *Politics in the Republic of Ireland*, 4th edition (London; Routledge/PSAI Press, 2005) pp. 465-72

Coakley, John 'Centres, Peripheries, and Party Systems: Nested Secession Processes in Great Britain and Ireland', *Political Geography*, 27(7), (2008), pp. 740-60

Coakley, John 'Local Elections and National Politics', in Mary E. Daly (ed.) *Country and Town: One Hundred Year of Local Government in Ireland* (Dublin; Institute of Public Administration, 2001), pp. 77-87

Coakley, John 'Minor Parties in Irish Political Life, 1922-89', *Economic and Social Review*, 21(3), (1990), pp. 269-97

Coakley, John 'The Election and the Party System' in Michael Gallagher, Michael Marsh and Paul Mitchell (eds) *How Ireland Voted 2002* (Basingstoke; Palgrave, 2003), pp. 230-46

Coakley, John 'The Election that Made the First Dáil' in Brian Farrell (ed.) *The Creation of the Dáil* (Blackwater Press, 1994)

Coakley, John 'The Rise and Fall of Minor Parties in Ireland', *Irish Political Studies*, 25(4), (2010), pp. 503-58

Collins, Neil 'Still Recognisably Pluralist? State-Farmer Relations in Ireland' in R.J. Hill and Michael Marsh (eds) *Modern Irish Democracy: Essays in Honour of Basil Chubb* (Dublin; Irish Academic Press, 1993), pp. 104-22

Collins, Stephen 'Campaign Strategies', in Michael Gallagher, Michael Marsh and Paul
    Mitchell (eds) *How Ireland Voted 2002* (Basingstoke; Palgrave, 2003)

Copus, Colin, Alistair Clark, Herwig Reynaert and Kristof Steyvers (2009) 'Minor Party
    and Independent Politics Beyond the Mainstream: Fluctuating Fortunes but a Permanent
    Presence', *Parliamentary Affairs*, 62(1), 2009, pp. 4-18

Copus, Colin, Alistair Clark and K. Bottom 'Multi-Party Politics in England? Small Parties,
    Independents and Political Associations in English Local Politics', in Marion Reiser and
    Everhard Holtmann (eds) *Farewell to the Party Model? Independent Local Lists in Eastern and
    Western European Countries* (Wiesbaden; VS Verlag, 2008), pp. 253-76

Costello, Rory and Robert Thomson 'Election Pledges and Their Enactment in Coalition
    Governments: A Comparative Analysis of Ireland', *Journal of Elections, Public Opinion and
    Parties*, 18 (3), (2008), pp. 239-56

Costello, Rory and Robert Thomson 'The Fulfilment of Election Pledges' in Michale
    Gallagher and Michael Marsh (eds) *How Ireland Voted 2007: The Full Story of Ireland's
    General Election* (Basingstoke; Palgrave Macmillan, 2008), pp. 19-32

Courtney, Michael 'Appendix 2: Members of the 31st Dáil' in Michael Gallagher and
    Michael Marsh (eds) *How Ireland Voted 2011: The Full Story of Ireland's Earthquake Election*
    (Houndmills, Basingstoke; Palgrave Macmillan, 2011), pp. 304-9

Cowley, Philip and Mark Stuart 'There was a Doctor, a Journalist and Two Welshmen: the
    Voting Behaviour of Independent MPs in the United Kingdom House of Commons,
    1997-2007', *Parliamentary Affairs*, 62(1), (2009), pp. 19-31

Curry, Phillip and Michael O'Connell 'Post-materialist Values and Political Preferences:
    Some Unlikely Findings from Northern Ireland', *European Journal of Political Research*, 35,
    (2000), pp 19-30

Denemark, David and Shaun Bowler 'Minor Parties and Protest Votes in Australia and New
    Zealand: Locating Populist Politics', *Electoral Studies*, 21(1), (2002), pp. 47-67

Deschouwer, Kris 'Comparing Newly Governing Parties' in Kris Deschouwer (ed.) *New
    Parties in Government: In Power for the First Time* (London; Routledge, 2008), pp. 1-16

Dillon, Paul 'Explaining the Emergence, Political Impact and Decline of Labour Left,
    1983-1992' (MsocSc Thesis, University College Dublin, 2007)

Doyle, John 'Republican Policies in Practical Politics: Placing Contemporary Sinn Féin in a
    European Context', working papers in *British-Irish Studies*, 13, (2005)

Dunphy, Richard '"A Group of Individuals Trying To Do Their Best": The Dilemmas of
    Democratic Left", *Irish Political Studies*, 13(1), (1998) pp. 50-75

Dunphy, Richard 'From Eurocommunism to Eurosocialism: The Search for a Post-
    Communist European Left', *Occasional Papers*, 1(7) (Dundee; University of Dundee, 1993)

Dunphy, Richard and S. Hopkins 'The Organisational and Political Evolution of the
    Workers' Party of Ireland', *Journal of Communist Studies*, 8(3), (1992), pp.91-118

Eagles, Monroe, and Stephen Erfle 'Variations in Third/Minor Party Support in English
    Constituencies', *European Journal of Political Research*, 23(1), (1993), pp. 91-116

Farrell, David M. 'Campaign Strategies' in Michael Gallagher and Michael Laver (eds) *How
    Ireland Voted 1992* (Dublinl; Folens and PSAI Press, 1993), pp. 21-39

Farrell, David M. 'Ireland: The "Green Alliance"', in Ferdinand Müller Rommel (ed.) *New
    Politics in Western Europe: the Rise and Success of Green Parties and Alternative Lists* (Boulder;
    Westview, 1989)

Farrell, David M. 'Ireland: A Party System Transformed?', in D. Broughton and Mark
    Donovan (eds) Changing Party Systems in Western Europe (London, Pinter, 1999)

Farrell, David M. 'Campaign Strategies' in Michael Gallagher and Michael Laver (eds), *How
    Ireland Voted 1992* (Limerick; PSAI Press, 1993)

Farrell, David M. 'Ireland' in Katz, Richard S. and Peter Mair (eds) *Party Organisations: A
    Data Handbook* (London; Sage, 1992), pp. 398-458

Farrell, Sean, Ciara Meehan, Gary Murphy and Kevin Rafter 'Assessing the Irish General Election of 2011: A Roundtable', *New Hibernia Review*, 15(3), (2011), pp. 36-53

Finnegan, Richard B. 'The Blueshirts of Ireland During the 1930s: Fascism Inverted', *Eire-Ireland*, 24(2), (1989), pp. 79-99

Fisher, Stephen L. (1980) 'The "Decline of Parties" Thesis and the Role of Minor Parties' in Peter Merkl (ed.) *Western European Party Systems: Trends and Prospects* (New York; The Free Press, 1980), pp. 609-13

Gallagher, Michael 'Ireland's Earthquake Election: Analysis of the Results' in Gallagher and Marsh (eds) *How Ireland Voted 2011: The Full Story of Ireland's Earthquake Election* (Basingstoke; Palgrave Macmillan, 2011), pp. 139-71

Gallagher, Michael 'Parties and Referendums in Ireland 1937-2011', *Irish Political Studies*, 26(4), (2011), pp. 535-54

Gallagher, Michael 'Party Solidarity, Exclusivity and Inter-Party Relationships in Ireland, 1922-1977: The Evidence of Transfers', *Economic and Social Review*, 10(1), (1978), pp. 1-22

Gallagher, Michael 'The Earthquake that Never Happened: Analysis of the Results' in Michael Gallagher and Michael Marsh (eds) *How Ireland Voted 2007: The Full Story of Ireland's General Election* (Basingstoke; Palgrave Macmilan, 2008), pp.78-104

Gallagher, Michael 'The Election of the 27th Dáil' in Michael Gallagher and Michael Laver (eds) *How Ireland Voted 1992* (Limerick; PSAI Press, 1993)

Gallagher, Michael 'The Pact General Election of 1922', *Irish Historical Studies*, 21(4), (1979), pp. 404-21

Gallagher, Michael 'The Results Analysed' in Michael Marsh and Paul Mitchell (eds) *How Ireland Voted 1997* (Oxford; Westview Press, 1999), pp. 121-51

Gallagher, Michael, Michael Laver and Peter Mair *Representative Government in Modern Europe* (New York; McGraw-Hill, 2011)

Garner, Simon 'Ireland and Immigration: Explaining the Absence of the Far Right', *Patterns of Prejudice*, 41(2), (2007), pp. 109-30

Garry, John 'Consociationalism and its Critics: Evidence from the Historic Northern Ireland Assembly Election 2007', *Electoral Studies*, 28, (2009), pp. 458-66

Garry, John 'The Demise of the Fianna Fáil–Labour "Partnership" Government and the Rise of the "Rainbow" Coalition', *Irish Political Studies*, 10, (1995), pp. 192-9

Gerring, John 'Minor Parties in Plurality Electoral Systems', *Party Politics*, 11(1), (2005), pp. 79-107

Gilland, Lutz Karin and Christopher Farrington 'Alternative Ulster? Political Parties and the Non-constitutional Policy Space in Northern Ierland', *Political Studies*, 54, (2006), pp. 715-42

Gilland, Lutz Karin 'Irish Party Competition in the New Millennium: Change, or *Plus Ca Change?*', *Irish Political Studies*, 18(2), (2003), pp. 40-59

Girvin, Brian 'Political Competition, 1992-1997' in Michael Marsh and Paul Mitchell (eds) *How Ireland Voted 1997* (Oxford; Westview Press, 1999), pp. 3-29

Girvin, Brian 'Social Change and Moral Politics: The Irish Constitutional Referendum 1983', *Political Studies*, 34(1), (1986), pp.61-81

Girvin, Brian 'The Campaign' in Michael Laver, Peter Mair and Richard Sinnott (eds) *How Ireland Voted: The Irish General Election 1987* (Dublin; Poolbeg Press, 1987)

Girvin, Brian 'The Campaign' in Michael Gallagher and Richard Sinnott (eds) *How Ireland Voted 1989?* (Galway; PSAI Press, 1990)

Girvin, Brian 'The Road to the Election' in Michael Gallagher and Michael Laver (eds) *How Ireland Voted 1992* (Limerick; PSAI Press, 1993)

Gold, Howard J. 'Third Party Voting in Presidential Elections: A Study of Perot, Anderson, and Wallace', *Political Research Quarterly*, 48(4), (1995), pp. 751-73

Golder, Matt 'Explaining Variation in the Success of Extreme Right Parties in Western Europe', *Comparative Political Studies*, 36(4), (2003), pp. 432-66

Hansen, Martin E. 'Reconsidering the Party Distances and Dimensionality of the Danish Folketing' *Journal of Legislative Studies*, 14, (2008), pp. 264-278

Hansen, Martin E. 'The Positions of Irish Parliamentary Actors', *Irish Political Studies*, 24 (1), (2009), pp. 29-44.

Hansen, Martin E. 'The Parliamentary Behaviour of Minor Parties and Independents in Dáil Éireann', *Irish Political Studies*, 25(4), (2010), pp. 643-660

Harmel, Robert and John D. Robertson 'Formation and Success of New Parties', *International Political Science Review*, 6(4), (1985), pp. 501-23

Hazelkorn, Ellen 'Why is There No Socialism in Ireland? Theoretical Problems of Irish Marxism', *Science & Society*, 2, Summer (1989), pp. 136-64

Heinisch, Richard 'Success in Opposition–Fáilure in Government: Explaining the Performance of Right-Wing Populist Parties in Public Office', *West European Politics*, 26 (3), (2003), pp. 91-130

Herzog, Hanna 'Minor Parties: The Relevancy Perspective', *Comparative Politics*, 19(3), (1987), pp. 317-329

Hug, Simon 'The Emergence of New Political Parties from a Game Theoretic Perspective', *European Journal of Political Research*, 29(2), (1996), pp. 169-90

Hug, Simon 'Studying the Electoral Success of New Political Parties', *Party Politics*, 6(2), (2000), pp. 187-97

Hutcheson, Derek S. 'The Seismology of Psephology: "Earthquake Elections" from the Folketing to the Dáil', *Representation*, 47(4), (2011), pp. 473-90

Ignazi, Piero 'The Extreme Right in Europe: A Survey' in Peter H. Merkl and Leonard Weinberg (eds) *The Revival of Right-Wing Extremism in the Nineties* (London; Frank Cass, 1997), pp. 47-64

Ionescu, Ghina 'Eastern Europe' in Ghina Ionescu and E. Gellner (eds) *Populism: Its Meaning and National Characteristics* (London: Weidenfeld and Nicolson, 1969), pp. 97-121

Jordan, Donald 'Merchants, "Strong Farmers" and Fenians: The Post-Famine Political Élite and the Irish Land War' in C.H.E. Philpin (ed.) *Nationalism and Popular Protest in Ireland* (Cambridge; Cambridge University Press, 1987), pp. 320-48

Katz, Richard S. and Peter Mair 'Changing Models of Party Organization and Party Democracy: The Emergence of the Cartel Party', *Party Politics*, 1(1), (1995), pp. 5-28

Katz, Richard S. 'Party Government and its Alternatives' in Richard S. Katz (ed.) *Party Government: European and American Experiences* (Berlin and New York: Walter de Gruyter, 1987), pp. 1-26

Kavanagh, Adrian 'The 2004 Local Elections in the Republic of Ireland', *Irish Political Studies*, 19(2), (2004), pp. 64-84

Kavanagh, Ray 'Pride of our Past, Confidence in Our Future' in: *Labour Party, Killarney 1991* Labour Party Conference (Dublin; Labour Party, 1991)

Kindersley, Richard 'In Lieu of a Conclusion: Eurocommunism and 'the Crisis of Capitalism' in Richard Kindersley (ed.) *In Search of Eurocommunism* (London; Macmillan, 1981)

Laakso, Mogens and Rein Taagepera 'Effective Number of Parties: A Measure with Application to West Europe', *Comparative Political Studies*, 21(1), (1979), pp. 3-27

Labour *Labour's Policy Proposal, Election '89: Now More than Ever!* (Dublin; Labour Party, 1989)

Labour 'Never Again: Labour's Plan to Improve Standards in Business and Public Life', (2009), available at: http://www.labour.ie/download/pdf/never_again.pdf (accessed 2 January 2012)

Labour 'Report of the Commission on Electoral Strategy' (Dublin; Labour Party, 1986)

Labour 'Report of the 21st Century Commission', (2009), available at: http://www.labour.ie/download/pdf/21stcenturycommission.pdf (accessed 28 December 2011)

Labour 'Report to the National Conference 1989-1991' (Dublin; Labour Party, 1991)

Labour 'Report to the National Conference 1991-1993' (Dublin; Labour Party, 1993)

Larkin, Emmet 'Foreword' in William L. Feingold (ed.) *The Revolt of the Tenantry: The Transformation of Local Government in Ireland 1872-1886* (Boston; Northeastern University Press, 1984), pp. xi-xvii

Laver, Michael 'Analysing Structures of Party Preference in Electronic Voting Data', *Party Politics*, 10, (2004), pp. 521-541

Laver, Michael 'Are Irish Parties Peculiar?' in John T. Goldthorpe and Christopher T. Whelan (Eds) *The Development of Industrial Society in Ireland* (Oxford; Oxford University Press, 1992), pp. 359-82

Laver, Michael (1998) 'Party Policy in Ireland 1997: Results from an Expert Survey', *Irish Political Studies*, 13, (1998), pp. 159-71

Laver, Michael 'Voting Behaviour', in John Coakley and Michael Gallagher (eds) *Politics in the Republic of Ireland*, 4th edition(London; Routledge/PSAI Press, 2005), pp. 183-210

Laver, Michael and Kenneth A. Shepsle 'How Political Parties Emerged from the Primeval Slime: Party Cohesion, Party Discipline, and the Formation of Governments', in Shaun Bowler, David M. Farrell and Richard S. Katz (eds) *Party Discipline and Parliamentary Government* (Columbus; Ohio State University Press, 1999), pp. 23-48

Laver, Michael, Michael Marsh and Richard Sinnott 'Patterns of Party Support', in Michael Laver, Peter Mair and Richard Sinnott (eds) *How Ireland Voted: The Irish General Election 1987* (Dublin; Poolbeg, 1987), pp. 99-140

Lawson, Kay 'When Linkage Fails' in Kay Lawson and Peter H. Merkl (eds) *When Parties Fail: Emerging Alternative Organisations* (Princeton, N.J.; Princeton University Press, 1988), pp. 13-38

Leahy, Pat 'Campaign Strategies and Political Marketing' in Michael Gallagher and Michael Marsh (eds) *How Ireland Voted 2011: The Full Story of Ireland's Earthquake Election* (Basingstoke; Palgrave), pp. 68-88

Lipset, Seymour M. and Stein Rokkan 'Cleavage Structures, Party Systems and Voter Alignments: An Introduction' in *Party Systems and Voter Alignments: Cross-National Perspectives* (New York; The Free Press, 1967), pp. 1-64

Little, Conor 'The General Election of 2011 in the Republic of Ireland: All Changed Utterly?' *West European Politics*, 34(6), (2011), pp. 13

Lucardie, Peter 'Prophets, Purifiers and Prolocutors', *Party Policits*, 6(2), (2000), pp. 175-85

Lyne, Thomas 'The Progressive Democrats 1985-87', *Irish Political Studies*, 2, (1987), pp. 107-14

Mair, Peter 'Explaining the Absence of Class Politics in Ireland' in John T. Goldthorpe and Christopher T. Whelan (eds) *The Development of Industrial Society in Ireland* (Oxford; Oxford University Press, 1992), pp. 383-410

Mair, Peter 'Fianna Fáil, Labour and the Irish Party System' in Michael Gallagher and Michael Laver (eds) *How Ireland Voted 1992* (Limerick; PSAI Press, 1993)

Mair, Peter 'New Political Parties in Long-Established Party Systems: How Successful Are They?' in E. Beukel, K.K. Klausen and P.E. Mouritzen (eds) *Elites, Parties and Democracy: Festschrift for Professor Mogens N. Pedersen* (Odense; Odense University Press, 1999), pp. 207-24

Mair, Peter 'The Autonomy of the Political: The Development of the Irish Party System', *Comparative Politics*, 11(4), (1979), pp. 445-465

Mair, Peter 'The Election in Context' in *How Ireland Voted 2011: The Full Story of Ireland's Earthquake Election* (Basingstoke; Palgrave Macmillan, 2011), pp. 283-97

Mair, Peter 'The Electoral Universe of Small Parties in Post-war Western Europe' in Ferdinand Müller-Rommel and Geoffrey Pridham (eds) *Small Parties in Western Europe: Comparative and National Perspectives* (London; Sage, 1991)

Mair, Peter and Ingrid van Biezen 'Party Membership in Twenty European Democracies, 1980-2000', *Party Politics*, 7(1), (2001), pp. 5-21

Mair, Peter and Liam Weeks 'The Party System' in John Coakley and Michael Gallagher (eds) *Politics in the Republic of Ireland*, 4th edition (London; Routledge/PSAI Press, 2005), pp. 135-59

Manning, Maurice 'The Farmers' in John J. Lee (ed.) *Ireland 1945-70* (Dublin; Gill & Macmillan, 1979), pp. 48-60

Mansergh, Lucy and Robert Thomson 'Election Pledges, Party Competition and Policymaking', *Comparative Politics*, 39(3), (2007), pp. 311-29

Marsh, Michael 'Candidates or Parties? Objects of Electoral Choice in Ireland', *Party Politics*, 13(4), (2007), pp. 500-27

Marsh, Michael 'Parties and Society' in John Coakley and Michael Gallagher (eds), *Politics in the Republic of Ireland*, 4th edition (Abingdon; Routledge, 2005), pp. 160-82

Marsh, Michael and Kevin Cunningham 'A Positive Choice, or Anyone but Fianna Fáil?' in Michael Gallagher and Michael Marsh (eds) *How Ireland Voted 2011: The Full Story of Ireland's Earthquake Election* (London; Palgrave, 2011), pp. 172-204

McCluskey, F. 'Organisation as Ends: Comhaontas Glas Observed', unpublished MA Thesis, University College Dublin (1992)

McDaid, Shaun and Kacper Rekawek 'From Mainstream to Minor and Back – The Irish Labour Party, 1987-1992', *Irish Political Studies*, 25(4), (2010), pp. 625-42

McDonnell, Daniel 'The Republic of Ireland: The Dog That Hasn't Barked in the Night', in D. Albertazzi and Daniel McDonnell (eds) *Twenty-First Century Populism: The Spectre of Western Democracy* (Basingstoke; Palgrave, 2008), pp. 198-216

McGraw, Seán 'Managing Changes: Party Competition in the New Ireland', *Irish Political Studies*, 23(4), (2008), pp. 627-48

Millward Brown IMS, 'Post Lisbon Treaty Referendum Research Findings', September 2008, available at: www.dfa.ie

Mitchell, Paul 'Government Formation: A Tale of Two Coalitions' in Michael Marsh and Paul Mitchell (eds) *How Ireland Voted 1997* (Oxford; Westview Press, 1999), pp. 243-64

Mitchell, Paul 'Ireland: From Single-Party to Coalition Rule', in W. Müller and K. Strøm (eds) *Coalition Governments in Western Europe* (Oxford; Oxford University Press, 2000)

Morrissey, Hazel (1983) 'The First Communist Party of Ireland', *Irish Socialist Review*, (Summer, 1983), pp. 1-8

Mudde, Cas 'The Paradox of the Anti-Party Party', *Party Politics*, 2(2), (1996), pp. 265-76

Müller-Rommel, Ferdinand 'Small Parties in Comparative Perspective: The State of the Art', in Ferdinand Müller-Rommel and Geoffrey Pridham (eds) *Small Parties in Western Europe: Comparative and National Perspectives* (London; Sage, 1991), pp. 1-22

Müller-Rommel, Ferdinand 'The Lifespan and Political Performance of Green Parties in Western Europe' in Ferdinand Müller-Rommel and Thomas Poguntke (eds) *Green Parties in National Governments* (London; Cass, 2002), pp. 1-16

Murphy, Gary 'Influencing Political Decision Making: Interest Groups and Elections in Independent Ireland', *Irish Political Studies*, 25(4), (2010), pp. 563-80

Murphy, Gary 'Interest Groups in the Policy Making Process' in John Coakley and Michael Gallagher *Politics in the Republic of Ireland*, 4th edition (Abingdon; Routledge, 2005), pp. 352-83

Murphy, Gary 'Pluralism and the Politics of Morality' in Maura Adshead and Michelle Millar (eds) *Public Administration and Public Policy in Ireland: Theory and Methods* (London; Routledge, 2003), pp. 20-36

Murphy, Gary 'The 1997 Election', *Irish Political Studies*, 13(1), (1998), pp. 127-34

Murphy, Gary 'The Background to the Election' in Michael Gallagher and Michael Marsh (eds) *How Ireland Voted 2011: The Full Story of Ireland's Earthquake Election* (Basingstoke; Palgrave, 2011), pp. 1-28

Murphy, Gary 'The Irish Government, the National Farmers Association, and the European Economic Community, 1955-1964', *New Hibernia Review*, 6(4), (2002), pp.68-84

Murphy, Gary and John Hogan 'Fianna Fáil, the Trade Union Movement and the Politics of Macroeconomic Crises, 1970-82', *Irish Political Studies*, 23(4), (2008), pp. 577-98

Ní Lochlainn, Aoife 'Ailtirí na hAiseirge: A Party of its Time' in Dermot Keogh and Mervyn O'Driscoll (eds) *Ireland in World War Two: Neutrality and Survival* (Cork; Mercier Press, 2004), pp. 187-210

Ó Broin, Eoin 'Time for Sinn Féin to Work Out What it Stands for Now the Armed Struggle is over...', (2008), available at: http://sluggerotoole.com/2008/11/27/time-for-sinn-fein-to-work-out-what-it-stands-for-now-the-armed-struggle-is (accessed 28 December 2011)

Ó Culain, C. 'Sinn Féin – Moving to the Centre', (2011), available at: http://politico.ie/irish-politics/fair-comment/7626-sinn-fein-moving-to-the-centre.html (accessed 28 December 2011)

O'Halpin, E. 'Partnership Programme Managers in the Reynolds/Spring Coalition, 1993-4, an Assessment', *Irish Political Studies*, 12, (1997), pp. 78-91

O'Hare, Edward 'Getting to know Gilmore', (2011), available at: http://politico.ie/irish-politics/7462-getting-to-know-gilmore.html (accessed 28 December 2011)

O'Malley, Eoin 'Constructing and Maintaining Irish Governments' in K. Dowling and P. Dumont (eds) *The Selection of Ministers in Europe: Hiring and Firing* (London; Routledge, 2009)

O'Malley, Eoin 'Government Formation in 2007' in Michael Gallagher and Michael Marsh (eds) *How Ireland Voted 2007: The Story of Ireland's General Election* (Basingstoke; Palgrave, 2008), pp. 205-17

O'Malley, Eoin 'Ministerial Selection in Ireland: Limited Choice in a Political Village', *Irish Political Studies*, 21(3), (2006), pp. 319-336

O'Malley, Eoin 'Punch Bags for Heavyweights? Minor Parties in Irish Governments', *Irish Political Studies*, 25(4), 2010), pp. 539-62

O'Malley, Eoin 'The 2011 Irish Presidential Election: Culture, Valence, Loyalty or Punishment?', *Irish Political Studies*, 27(4), (2012)

O'Malley, Eoin 'Why is there no Radical Right Party in Ireland?', *West European Politics*, 31(5), (2008), pp. 960-77

O'Malley, Eoin and Matthew Kerby 'Chronicle of a Death Foretold? Understanding the Decline of Fine Gael', *Irish Political Studies*, 19, (2004), pp. 39-58

Pedersen, Mogens N. 'Consensus and Conflict in the Danish Folketing 1945-1965', *Scandinavian Political Studies*, 2, (1967), pp. 143-66

Pedersen, Mogens N. 'Towards a New Typology of Party Lifespans and Minor Parties', *Scandinavian Political Studies*, 5 (1), (1982), pp. 1-16

Pinard, Maurice 'One-party Dominance and Third Parties: The Pinard Theory Reconsidered', *Canadian Journal of Political Science*, 6(3), (1973), pp. 399-421

Poguntke, Thomas 'Green Parties in National Government: From Protest to Asquiescence?' in Ferdinand Müller-Rommel and Thomas Poguntke (eds) *Green Parties in National Governments* (London; Frank Cass, 2002), pp. 133-45

Pyne, Peter 'The Third Sinn Féin Party: 1923-1926. I. Narrative Account', *Economic and Social Review*, 1 (1), (1969), pp. 29-50

Quinlan, Stephen 'The 2009 European Parliament Election in Ireland', *Irish Political Studies*, 25(2), (2010), pp. 289-301

Quinlan, Stephen 'The Lisbon Treaty Referendum 2008', *Irish Political Studies*, 24(1), (2009), pp. 107-21

Quinlivan, Aodh and Liam Weeks 'The 2009 Local Elections in the Republic of Ireland', *Irish Political Studies*, 25(2), (2010), pp. 315-24.

Rafter, Kevin 'Leadership changes in Fine Gael and the Labour Party, 2002', *Irish Political Studies*, 18(1), (2003), pp. 108-19

Rafter, Kevin 'Wanted: A Champion of Public-sector Cuts', *The Sunday Times*, 19 April 2009

Red C. 'Vote Intention Opinion Poll', 12 Jan 2012, (2012), available at: http://redcresearch. ie/wp-content/uploads/2012/01/Paddy-Power-12th-Jan-Political-Poll-2012-Vote-Intention-Report2.pdf (accessed 29 January 2012)

Reich, Gary 'The Evolution of New Party Systems: Are Early Elections Exceptional?', *Electoral Studies*, 23 (2), (2004), pp. 235-50

Reidy, Theresa 'Candidate Selection' in Michael Gallagher and Michael Marsh (eds) *How Ireland Voted 2011: The Full Story of Ireland's Earthquake Election* (London; Palgrave, 2011), pp. 47-67

Rochon, Thomas R. 'Mobilizers and Challengers: Towards a Theory of New Party Success', *International Political Science Review*, 6(4), (1985), pp. 419-39

Rooney, Eddie 'From Republican Movement to Workers' Party: An Ideological Analysis' in Chris Curtin, Mary Kelly and Liam O'Dowd (eds) *Culture and Ideology in Ireland* (Galway; Galway University Press, 1984), pp. 79-98

Rose, Richard and Thomas Mackie 'Incumbency in Government: Asset or Liability?' in H. Daalder and Peter Mair (eds), *Western European Party Systems: Continuity and Change* (London; Sage, 1983), pp. 115-37

RTÉ News 'Sharp Decrease in Govt Support – Poll', (2011), available at: http://www.rte.ie/ news/2011/1217/politics.html, (accessed 18 December 2011)

Russell, Meg and Maria Sciara 'Independent Parliamentarians En Masse: The Changing Nature and Role of the 'Crossbenchers' in the House of Lords', *Parliamentary Affairs*, 62(1), (2009), pp. 32-52

Ryan, Raymond 'The National Farmers' and Ratepayers' League', *Studia Hibernica*, 34, (2007), pp. 173-192

Siaroff, Alan 'Two-and-a-half Party Systems and the Comparative Role of the "Half"', *Party Politics*, 9(3), (2003), pp. 267-90

Sinn Féin 'Sinn Féin General Election Manifesto 2002: Building an Ireland of Equals' from http://www.sinnfein.ie/pdf/GeneralElection02.pdf

Sinnott, Richard *et al.* 'Attitudes and Behaviour in the referendum on the Treaty of Lisbon', report prepared for the Department of Foreign Affairs, 2009, available at http://www.dfa. ie/uploads/documents/ucd percent20gearypercent20institutepercent20report.pdf

Sircar, Indraneel and Bjorn Høyland 'Get the Party Started: The Development of Political Party Legislative Dynamics in the Irish Free State Seanad' (1922-1936), *Party Politics*, 16, (2010), pp. 89-110

Smith, Gordon 'In Search of Small Parties: Problems of Definition, Classification and Significance' in F. Müller-Rommel and G. Pridham (eds) *Small Parties in Western Europe: Comparative and National Perspectives* (London; Sage, 1991), pp. 23-40

Smith, Gordon 'Small Parties: Problems of Definition Classification and Significance' in The Journal.ie. '"Gilmore for Taoiseach" Won't Become Reality, Hints Labour', (2011), available at: http://www.thejournal.ie/gilmore-for-taoiseach-wont-become-reality-hints-labour-2011-02/

Standards in Public Office, 'Lobby/Campaign Groups', available athttp://www.sipo.gov.ie/ en/QuickLinks/LobbyCampaignGroups

Sudulich, Maria L. and Matthew Wall 'Rewarding the Wealthy Versus Looking After The Poor: Affective Perception of Right and Left by Candidates in the 2007 Irish General Elections', *Irish Political Studies*, 25(1), (2010), pp. 95-106

Suiter, Jane and David M. Farrell 'The Parties' Manifestos' in Michael Gallagher and Michael Marsh (eds) *How Ireland Voted 2011: The Full Story of Ireland's Earthquake Election* (London; Palgrave, 2011), pp. 29-46

Tamas, Bernard 'The Self-Destructive Tendencies of Minor Parties: The Implosion of the Reform Party', paper presented at the annual meeting of the American Political Science Association, Boston Marriot, Massachusetts, 2002

Tavits, Margit 'Party System Change: Testing a Model of New Party Entry', *Party Politics*, 12(1), (2006), pp. 99-119

Tavits, Margit 'Party Systems in the Making: The Emergence and Success of New Parties in New Democracies', *British Journal of Political Science*, 38(1), (2008), p. 113-33

Tetteh, Edmund 'Election Statistics: UK 1919-2007' (London; House of Commons Library Research Paper 08/12, 2008)

Van der Brug, Wouter and Meindert Fennema 'What Causes People to Vote for a Radical-right Party? A Review of Recent Work', *International Journal of Public Opinion Research*, 19(4), (2007), pp. 474-87

Van der Brug, Wouter, Meindert Fennema and Jean Tillie 'Why Some Anti-immigrant Parties Fail and Others Succeed: A Two-step Model of Aggregate Electoral Support', *Comparative Political Studies*, 38(5), (2005), pp. 537-73

Varley, Tony 'Farmers Against Nationalists: The Rise and Fall of Clann na Talmhan in Galway' in Gerard Moran and Raymond Gillespie (eds) *Galway: History and Society* (Dublin; Geography Publications, 1996), pp. 589-622

Varley, Tony 'On the Road to Extinction: Agrarian Parties in Twentieth Century Ireland', *Irish Political Studies*, 25(4), (2010), pp. 581-602

Volkens, Andrea, Onawa Lacewell, Pola Lehmann, Sven Regel, Henrike Schultze and Annika Werner *The Manifesto Data Collection: Manifesto Project (MRG/CMP/MARPOR)* (Berlin; Wissenschaftszentrum Berlin für Sozialforschung (WZB), 2011)

Weeks, Liam 'Crashing the Party: Does STV Help Independents?', *Party Politics* (published online, 14 April 2012)

Weeks, Liam 'Independents in Government: A Sui Gereris Model' in Kris Deschouwer (ed.) *Newly Governing Parties: In Power for the First Time* (London; Routledge, 2008), pp. 136-56

Weeks, Liam 'Minor Parties: A Schema for Analysis', *Irish Political Studies*, 25 (4), (2010), pp. 481-501

Weeks, Liam 'Parties and the Party System' in John Coakley and Michael Gallagher (eds) *Politics in the Republic of Ireland*, 5th edition (London; Routledge, 2009) pp. 137-67

Weeks, Liam 'Rage Against the Machine: Who is the Independent Voter?', *Irish Political Studies*, 26(1), (2011), pp. 19-43

Weeks, Liam 'We Don't Like (To) Party: A Typology of Independents in Irish Political Life, 1922-2007', *Irish Political Studies*, 24(1), (2009), pp.1-28

White, Graham (1973) 'Third Parties in Canada Revisited: A Rejoinder and Elaboration of the Theory of One-party Dominance', *Canadian Journal of Political Science*, 6(3), (1973), pp. 439-60

Whiteman, David 'The Progress and Potential of the Green Party in Ireland', *Irish Political Studies*, 5, (1990), pp. 45-58

Whyte, John H. 'Ireland: Politics Without Social Bases', in Richard Rose (ed.) *Electoral Behaviour: A Comparative Handbook* (New York; Free Press, 1974), pp. 619-51

Widfeldt, Anders 'The Swedish Centre Party: The Poor Relation of the Family?' in David Arter (ed.) *From Farmyard to City Square? The Electoral Adaptation of the Nordic Agrarian Parties* (Aldershot; Ashgate, 2001), pp. 1-30

# Notes

## 1. *The Dog that Failed to Bark: Why Did No New Party Emerge in 2011*

1 It is described as such in the subtitle of the academic analysis of the 2011 election in Michael Gallagher and Michael Marsh (eds), *How Ireland Voted 2011: The Full Story of Ireland's Earthquake Election* (London; Palgrave, 2011)

2 Corcoran, Jody 'FF and FG Dissidents Planning New Party', *Sunday Independent* (20 June 2010)

3 Clifford, Michael and Shane Coleman 'The Truth about Fintan O'Toole's Aborted Dáil Bid', *Sunday Tribune*, (30 January 2011)

4 See for example a letter by Leo Armstrong, 'Call for a new party', *The Irish Times*, 13 July 2010

5 Reidy, Theresa 'Candidate Selection' in Michael Gallagher and Michael Marsh (eds) *How Ireland Voted 2011: The Full Story of Ireland's Earthquake Election* (London; Palgrave, 2011), pp. 47-67

6 Weeks, Liam 'Independents in Government: A Sui Generis Model' in Kris Deschouwer (ed.) *Newly Governing Parties: In Power for the First Time* (London; Routledge, 2008), pp. 136-56. Weeks, Liam 'We Don't Like (To) Party: A Typology of Independents in Irish Political Life, 1922-2007', *Irish Political Studies*, 24(1), (2009), pp.1-27. Weeks, Liam 'Rage Against the Machine: Who is the Independent Voter?', *Irish Political Studies*, 26(1), (2011), pp. 19-43

7 Mair, Peter 'The Electoral Universe of Small Parties' in Ferdinand Müller-Rommel and Geoffrey Pridham (eds) *Small Parties in Western Europe: Comparative and National Perspectives* (London; Sage, 1991), pp. 41-70

8 See Coakley, Murphy and Weeks in other chapters; see also Weeks 'We Don't Like (To) Party'

9 Weeks 'We Don't Like (To) Party'

10 Mair 'The Electoral Universe of Small Parties'

11 Weeks 'We Don't Like (To) Party; Weeks 'Rage Against the Machine; Weeks 'Independents in Government'

12 Bolleyer, Nicole and Liam Weeks 'The Puzzle of Non-Party Actors in Party Democracy: Independents in Ireland', *Comparative European Politics*, 7(3), (2009), pp. 299-324

13 Brennock, Mark 'McDowell's Radical Alternative: Is he the PDs' Messiah and if so will he have a Second Coming? *The Irish Times* (25 October 2000)

14 Barnea, Shlomit and Gideon Rahat '"Out With the Old, in With the New": What Constitutes a New Party', *Party Politics*, 17(3), (2011), pp. 303-320

15 Key, V.O. *Politics, Parties and Pressure Groups* (New York; Crowell, 1942)

16 Barnea and Rahat 'Out With the Old, in With the New', p. 304

17 Hug, Simon *Altering Party Systems: Strategic Behavior and the Emergence of New Political Parties in Western Democracies* (Chicago; University of Michigan Press, 2001)

18 Bochel, Hugh and David Denver 'Minor Parties and Independents in Times of Change: Scottish Local Elections 1974 to 2007', *Local Government Studies*, 24(5), (2008), pp. 577-93

19 Tavits, Margit 'Party System Change: Testing a Model of New Party Entry', *Party Politics*, 12(1), (2006), pp. 99-119

20 Gallagher, Michael, Michael Laver and Peter Mair, *Representative Government in Modern Europe* (New York; McGraw-Hill, 2011)

21 Barnea and Rahat 'Out With the Old, in With the New', pp. 308-9

22 Barnea and Rahat 'Out With the Old, in With the New' use a similar definition of newness, with the additional criteria that at least half of the new party's candidates are not from one former party

23 Hug *Altering Party Systems*, pp. 11-15

24 Keman, Hans and André Jrouwel *The Rise of a New Political Class?: Emerging New Parties and the Populist Challenge in Western Europe* (Vrije Universiteit Amsterdam, Department of Polictical Science, 2006)

25 Harmel, Robert and John D. Robertson 'Formation and Success of New Parties', *International Political Science Review*, 6(4), (1985), pp. 501-23

26 Lucardie, Paul 'Prophets, Purifiers and Prolocutors', *Party Politics*, 6(2), (2000), pp. 175-85. Hug, Simon 'The Emergence of New Political Parties from a Game Theoretic Perspective', *European Journal of Political Research*, 29(2), (1996), pp. 169-90. Hug, Simon 'Studying the Electoral Success of New Political Parties', *Party Politics*, 6(2), (2000), pp. 187-97. Boix, Charles 'The Emergence of Parties and Party Systems' in Charles Boix and Susan Stokes (eds) *Oxford Handbook of Comparative Politics* (Oxford; Oxford University Press, 2007), pp. 499-521. Tavits, Margit 'Party Systems in the Making: The Emergence and Success of New Parties in New Democracies', *British Journal of Political Science*, 38(1), (2008), p. 113.

27 Hug *Altering Party Systems*

28 Tavits 'Party System Change'

29 Harmel and Robertson 'Formation and Success of New Parties'

30 *ibid.*, p. 506

31 *ibid.*

32 *ibid.*

33 Keman and Jrouwel *The Rise of a New Political Class?*

34 See chapter 3

35 Aldrich, John H. *Why Parties?: The Origin and Transformation of Political Parties in America* (University of Chicago Press, 1995). Boix, Charles 'The Emergence of Parties and Party Systems' in Charles Boix and Susan Stokes (eds) *Oxford Handbook of Comparative Politics* (Oxford; Oxford University Press, 2007), pp. 499-521

36 Boix 'The Emergence of Parties and Party Systems', p. 501

37 Lucardie 'Prophets, Purifiers and Prolocutors'

38 Duverger, Maurice *Political Parties: Their Organisation and Activity in the Modern State* (London; Metheun, 1954), p. 205

39 Rae, Douglas W. *The Political Consequence of Electoral Laws* (New Haven; Yale University Press, 1967), p. 69

40 Lucardie 'Prophets, Purifiers and Prolocutors'

41 Laver, Michael and Kenneth A. Shepsle 'How Political Parties Emerged from the Primeval Slime: Party Cohesion, Party Discipline, and the Formation of Governments', in Shaun Bowler, David M. Farrell and Richard S. Katz (eds) *Party Discipline and Parliamentary Government* (Columbus; Ohio State University Press, 1999), pp. 23-48; Aldrich *Why Parties?*

42 Weeks, Liam 'Crashing the Party: Does STV Help Independents?', *Party Politics* (published online, 14 April 2012)

43 Abedi, Amir *Anti-political Establishment Parties: A Comparative Analysis* (London; Routledge, 2004)

44 Laakso, Mogens and Rein Taagepera 'Effective Number of Parties: A Measure with Application to West Europe', *Comparative Political Studies*, 21(1), (1979), pp. 3-27

45 Gallagher, Laver and Mair *Representative Government in Modern Europe*, Table 11.5

46 Extremely large parliaments, such as the Bundestag, the House of Commons and the French Chamber of Deputies are likely to act as outliers and distort our figures because of their electoral rules that limit the number of parties. In any case, the relationship between assembly size and party proliferation is weaker beyond a certain point, a pattern that affects our analysis.

47 Harmel and Robertson 'Formation and Success of New Parties'

48 Whyte, John H. 'Ireland: Politics Without Social Bases', in Richard Rose (ed.) *Electoral Behaviour: A Comparative Handbook* (New York; Free Press, 1974), pp. 619-51

49 Harmel and Robertson 'Formation and Success of New Parties', p. 509

50 Nohlen, Dieter C. and Philip Stöver (eds) *Elections in Europe: A Data Handbook* (Baden-Baden; Nomos, 2010)

51 Harmel and Robertson 'Formation and Success of New Parties'

52 Coakley, John 'Minor Parties in Irish Political Life, 1922-89', *Economic and Social Review*, 21(3), (1990), pp. 269-97

53 Garvin, Tom *The Evolution of Irish Nationalist Politics* (Dublin; Gill & Macmillan, 1981)

54 Mudde, Cas 'The Paradox of the Anti-Party Party', *Party Politics*, 2(2), (1996), pp. 265-76

55 O'Malley, Eoin 'Why is there no Radical Right Party in Ireland?', *West European Politics*, 31(5), (2008), pp. 960-77

56 Gallagher, Laver and Mair *Representative Government in Modern Europe*, Table 9.8

57 Corcoran 'FF and FG Dissidents Planning New Party'

58 McGee, Harry 'Technical Group Makes Voice Hard and Gives Bigger Parties Run For Their Money, *The Irish Times* (11 January 2012)

## 2. *From Cradle to Grave: The Impact and Evolution of Minor Parties*

1 Economist Seán Barrett on 'The PDs: From Boom to Bust', part II of a television documentary broadcast on RTÉ 1, 21 June 2010.

2 Bolleyer, Nicole and Liam Weeks 'The Puzzle of Non-Party Actors in Party Democracy: Independents in Ireland', *Comparative European Politics*, 7(3), (2009), pp. 299-324

3 Weeks, Liam 'We Don't Like (To) Party: A Typology of Independents in Irish Political Life, 1922-2007', *Irish Political Studies*, 24(1), (2009), p.5

4 Mair, Peter 'The Electoral Universe of Small Parties in Post-war Western Europe' in Ferdinand Müller-Rommel and Geoffrey Pridham (eds) *Small Parties in Western Europe: Comparative and National Perspectives* (London; Sage, 1991)

5 Pedersen, Mogens N. 'Towards a New Typology of Party Lifespans and Minor Parties', *Scandinavian Political Studies*, 5 (1), (1982), pp. 1-16

6 MacDermott, Eithne *Clann na Poblachta* (Cork; Cork University Press, 1998), p. 163

7 Gallagher, Michael *Political Parties in the Republic of Ireland* (Manchester; Manchester University Press, 1982), p. 113

8 Mair, Peter and Liam Weeks 'The Party System' in John Coakley and Michael Gallagher (eds) *Politics in the Republic of Ireland*, 4th edition (London; Routledge/PSAI Press, 2005), pp. 135-59

9 Weeks, Liam 'Parties and the Party System' in John Coakley and Michael Gallagher (eds) *Politics in the Republic of Ireland*, 5th edition (London; Routledge, 2009) pp. 137-67

10 The latter was revealed in part I of a television documentary, *The PDs: From Boom to Bust*, broadcast on RTÉ 1, 14 June 2010

11 Boix, Charles 'The Emergence of Parties and Party Systems' in Charles Boix and Susan Stokes (eds) *Oxford Handbook of Comparative Politics* (Oxford; Oxford University Press, 2007), p. 521

12 Berrington, Hugh 'New Parties in Britain: Why Some Live and Most Die', *International Political Science Review*, 6(4), (1985), p. 443

13 Tamas, Bernard 'The Self-Destructive Tendencies of Minor Parties: The Implosion of the Reform Party', paper presented at the annual meeting of the American Political Science Association, Boston Marriot, Massachusetts, 2002

14 Abedi, Amir *Anti-political Establishment Parties: A Comparative Analysis* (London; Routledge, 2004)

15 Tavits, Margit 'Party Systems in the Making: The Emergence and Success of New Parties in New Democracies', *British Journal of Political Science*, 38(1), (2008), p. 113-33

16 Abedi *Anti-political Establishment Parties*, p. 99

17 Minihan, Mary 'System Gives us Distracted TDs, says Dempsey', *The Irish Times* (22 January 2010)

18 *ibid.*

19 Bolleyer and Weeks 'The Puzzle of Non-Party Actors in Party Democracy'

20 Rae, Douglas W. *The Political Consequence of Electoral Laws* (New Haven; Yale University Press, 1967), pp. 138-40

21 Ross, James F.S. *The Irish Election System: What it is and How it Works* (London; Pall Mall Press, 1959), p. 64-6

22 Taagepera, Rein and Matthew S. Shugart *Seats and Votes: The Effects and Determinants of Electoral Systems* (New Haven; Yale University Press, 1989), p. 68

23 *ibid.*, p. xiii

24 *ibid.*, p. 114

25 Laver, Michael 'Analysing Structures of Party Preference in Electronic Voting Data' *Party Politics*, 10, (2004), pp. 521-541

26 McDaid, Shaun and Kacper Rekawek 'From Mainstream to Minor and Back – The Irish Labour Party, 1987-1992', *Irish Political Studies*, 25(4), (2010), pp. 625-42

27 Tamas 'The Self-Destructive Tendencies of Minor Parties'

28 *ibid.*, p. 9

29 Independent voters are analysed separately in Weeks 'We Don't Like (To) Party', but for reasons of continuity minor parties and independents are treated as a unitary category in this section.

30 Mair and Weeks 'The Party System', p. 153

31 Weeks, Liam 'Rage Against the Machine: Who is the Independent Voter?', *Irish Political Studies.* 26(1), (2011), pp. 19-43

32 Sinnott, Richard *Irish Voters Decide: Voting Behaviour in Elections and Referendums Since 1918* (Manchester; Manchester University Press, 1995); Gallagher, Michael *Electoral Support for Irish Political Parties 1927-1973* (London; Sage Publications, 1976)

33 Gallagher, Michael *Electoral Support for Irish Political Parties 1927-1973* (London; Sage Publications, 1976), pp. 47-54

34 *ibid.*, p. 49

35 *ibid.*, p. 56-61

36 Sinnott *Irish Voters Decide*

37 Marsh, Michael, Richard Sinnott, John Garry and Fiachra Kennedy *The Irish Voter: The Nature of Electoral Competition in the Republic of Ireland* (Manchester; Manchester University Press, 2008), pp. 173-9

38 *ibid.*, p 176

39 Marsh, Michael and Kevin Cunningham 'A Positive Choice, or Anyone but Fianna Fáil?' in Michael Gallagher and Michael Marsh (eds) *How Ireland Voted 2011: The Full Story of Ireland's Earthquake Election* (London; Palgrave, 2011), pp. 172-204

40 Tavits 'Party Systems in the Making'

41 MacGréil, Michael *Prejudice in Ireland Revisited* (Maynooth; Survey and Research Unit, St Patrick's College, 1996)

42 O'Malley, Eoin 'Why is there no Radical Right Party in Ireland?', *West European Politics*, 31(5), (2008), pp. 960-77

43 Marsh, Michael 'Candidates or Parties? Objects of Electoral Choice in Ireland', *Party Politics*, 13(4), (2007), pp. 500-27

44 Garvin, Tom *The Evolution of Irish Nationalist Politics* (Dublin; Gill & Macmillan, 1981), p. 182

45 Tavits 'Party Systems in the Making', p. 114

## 3. *The Rise and Fall of Minor Parties in Ireland, 1922-2011*

1 Gallagher, Michael 'Ireland's Earthquake Election: Analysis of the Results' in Michael Gallagher and Michael Marsh (eds) *How Ireland Voted 2011: The Full Story of Ireland's Earthquake Election* (Basingstoke; Palgrave Macmillan, 2011), p. 142

2 Mair, Peter 'The Election in Context' in *How Ireland Voted 2011: The Full Story of Ireland's Earthquake Election* (Basingstoke; Palgrave Macmillan, 2011), pp. 287; Hutcheson, Derek S. 'The Seismology of Psephology: "Earthquake Elections" from the Folketing to the Dáil', *Representation*, 47(4), (2011), pp. 473-90; Little, Conor 'The General Election of 2011 in the Republic of Ireland: All Changed Utterly?' *West European Politics*, 34(6), (2011), pp. 13

3 Clark, Alistair 'Breaking the Mould or Fiddling at the Edges? Ireland's Minor Parties in Comparative and Systemic Perspective', *Irish Political Studies*, 25(4), (2010), pp. 666-7

4 Fisher, Stephen L. 'The "Decline of Parties" Thesis and the Role of Minor Parties' in Peter Merkl (ed.) *Western European Party Systems: Trends and Prospects* (New York; The Free Press, 1980), pp. 609-10

5 Müller-Rommel, Ferdinand 'Small Parties in Comparative Perspective: The State of the Art', in Ferdinand Müller-Rommel and Geoffrey Pridham (eds) *Small Parties in Western Europe: Comparative and National Perspectives* (London; Sage, 1991), p. 1

6 Van der Brug, Wouter and Meindert Fennema 'What Causes People to Vote for a Radical-right Party? A Review of Recent Work', *International Journal of Public Opinion Research*, 19(4), (2007), pp. 474-87

7 Bélanger, Éric 'Antipartyism and Third-party Vote Choice: A Comparison of Canada, Britain, and Australia', *Comparative Political Studies*, 37(9), (2004), p. 1,055

8 Tamas, Bernard 'The Self-Destructive Tendencies of Minor Parties: The Implosion of the Reform Party', paper presented at the annual meeting of the American Political Science Association, Boston, Massachusetts, 2002

9 Gerring, John 'Minor Parties in Plurality Electoral Systems', *Party Politics*, 11(1), (2005), pp. 83

10 Coakley, John 'Minor Parties in Irish Political Life, 1922-89', *Economic and Social Review*, 21(3), (1990), p. 270

11 Copus, Colin, Alistair Clark, Herwig Reynaert and Kristof Steyvers (2009) 'Minor Party and Independent Politics Beyond the Mainstream: Fluctuating Fortunes but a Permanent Presence', *Parliamentary Affairs*, 62(1), 2009, p. 4

12 Bochel, Hugh and David Denver 'Minor Parties and Independents in Times of Change: Scottish Local Elections 1974 to 2007', *Local Government Studies*, 24(5), (2008), pp. 577-93

13 Abramson, Paul R., John H. Aldrich, Phil Paolino and David W. Rohde 'Third-party and Independent Candidates in American Politics: Wallace, Anderson, and Perot', *Political Science Quarterly*, 110(3), (1995), pp. 349-67; Gold, Howard J. 'Third Party Voting in Presidential Elections: A Study of Perot, Anderson, and Wallace', *Political Research Quarterly*, 48(4), (1995), pp. 751-73

14 Pinard, Maurice 'One-party Dominance and Third Parties: The Pinard Theory Reconsidered', *Canadian Journal of Political Science*, 6(3), (1973), p. 455

15 Blais, André 'Third Parties in Canadian Provincial Politics', *Canadian Journal of Political Science*, 6(3), (1973), p. 426

16 Bélanger 'Antipartyism and Third-party Vote Choice', p. 1,055

17 Hug, S. *Altering Party Systems: Strategic Behavior and the Emergence of New Political Parties in Western Democracies* (Chicago; University of Michigan Press, 2001), pp. 11-15

18 Adams, James, Michael Clark, Lawrence Ezrow and Garrett Glasgow 'Are Niche Parties Fundamentally Different From Mainstream Parties? The Causes and the Electoral Consequences of Western European Parties' Policy Shifts, 1976-1998', *American Journal of Political Science*, 50(3), (2006), p. 513. A yet more special subcategory is that of the 'extreme right' (Carter, Elisabeth L. 'Proportional Representation and the Fortunes of Right-wing Extremist Parties', *West European Politics*, 25(3), (2002), pp. 125-46; Golder, Matt 'Explaining Variation in the Success of Extreme Right Parties in Western Europe', *Comparative Political Studies*, 36(4), (2003), pp. 432-66), a category equated with 'radical-right' parties (Van der Brug and Fennema 'What Causes People to Vote for a Radical-right Party?') or with 'anti-immigrant parties' (Van der Brug, Wouter, Meindert Fennema and Jean Tillie 'Why Some Anti-immigrant Parties Fail and Others Succeed: A Two-step Model of Aggregate Electoral Support', *Comparative Political Studies*, 38(5), (2005), pp. 537-73)

19 Gerring 'Minor Parties in Plurality Electoral Systems', pp. 83 & 101

20 Bochel and Denver 'Minor Parties and Independents in Times of Change', pp. 580-1. Independents should not be regarded as an undifferentiated group whose members are equally remote from party organisation. One typology distinguished three categories: 'full' independents (devoid of organisation and of other links), 'conjoined' independents (who have links with other independent incumbents), and 'revealed party' independents (who describe themselves as independents but also point to sympathy with a particular party, such as 'Independent Labour'; Copus *et al.* 'Minor Party and Independent Politics Beyond the Mainstream', pp. 10-14). For a more elaborate classification of Irish independents which also identifies a 'quasi-party' category, see Weeks, Liam 'We Don't Like (To) Party: A Typology of Independents in Irish Political Life, 1922-2007', *Irish Political Studies*, 24(1), (2009), pp. 7-20.

21 McDaid, Shaun and Kacper Rekawek 'From Mainstream to Minor and Back – The Irish Labour Party, 1987-1992', *Irish Political Studies*, 25(4), (2010), pp. 625-42

22 Mair, Peter 'The Electoral Universe of Small Parties in Post-war Western Europe' in Ferdinand Müller-Rommel and Geoffrey Pridham (eds) *Small Parties in Western Europe: Comparative and National Perspectives* (London; Sage, 1991)

23 Chubb, Basil *The Government and Politics of Ireland* (London; Oxford University Press, 1974), p. 74

24 In the case of new parties registered for Dáil elections, the guidelines require (1) a certified record of the date and method of formation of the party, (2) the address of party headquarters, (3) a certified record showing at least 300 members of whom at least 50 per cent are registered electors, or certification that the party has at least one Dáil deputy, (4) evidence of organisation (including party constitution, date and venue of annual conference, membership of party executive, information on branches, and information on method of candidate selection), and (5) evidence regarding party finance, including names of trustees and bankers and method of raising funds (information supplied by the Registrar of Political Parties, June 2009). Similar provisions are made for parties registered to contest European elections, and slightly less demanding ones for parties contesting local elections, or elections in part of the state only. Unsuccessful applicants may refer the Registrar's ruling to an appeal board which is chaired by a judge of the High Court (nominated by the President of the High Court), with the chairs of the two houses of the Oireachtas as its other members.

25 Murphy, Gary (2010) 'Influencing Political Decision Making: Interest Groups and Elections in Independent Ireland', *Irish Political Studies*, 25(4), (2010), pp. 563-80

26 Pedersen, Mogens N. 'Towards a New Typology of Party Lifespans and Minor Parties', *Scandinavian Political Studies*, 5 (1), (1982), p. 5

27 Craig, F.W.S. *Minor Parties in British Parliamentary Elections 1885-1979* (London; Macmillan, 1975), p. vii

28 Hug *Altering Party Systems*, pp. 11-15

29 Tavits, Margit 'Party System Change: Testing a Model of New Party Entry', *Party Politics*, 12(1), (2006), p. 106

30 Bochel and Denver 'Minor Parties and Independents in Times of Change', pp. 580-1

31 Mair 'The Electoral Universe of Small Parties in Post-war Western Europe', p. 43-4

32 Pinard 'One-party Dominance and Third Parties', pp. 442-3

33 Harmel, Robert and John D. Robertson 'Formation and Success of New Parties', *International Political Science Review*, 6(4), (1985), pp. 517-18

34 Rochon, Thomas R. 'Mobilizers and Challengers: Towards a Theory of New Party Success', *International Political Science Review*, 6(4), (1985), pp. 421-3

35 This resembles a typology developed by Lucardie in 'Prophets, Purifiers and Prolocutors', *Party Politics*, 6(2), (2000), pp. 176-8, which distinguishes between four types of new parties: prolocutor parties, purifying (or challenging) parties, prophetic parties and personal vehicle (or idiosyncratic) parties.

36 Tavits 'Party System Change', p. 100

37 Adams *et al.* 'Are Niche Parties Fundamentally Different From Mainstream Parties', p. 513

38 Kitschelt, Herbert, with Anthony J. McGann *The Radical Right in Western Europe: A Comparative Analysis* (Ann Arbor, MI; University of Michigan Press, 1995), pp. 30-2

39 Ignazi, Piero 'The Extreme Right in Europe: A Survey' in Peter H. Merkl and Leonard Weinberg (eds) *The Revival of Right-Wing Extremism in the Nineties* (London; Frank Cass, 1997), pp. 52-3

40 Golder 'Explaining Variation in the Success of Extreme Right Parties in Western Europe', p. 446

41 Mudde, Cas *Populist Radical Right Parties in Europe* (Cambridge; Cambridge University Press, 2007), pp. 41-52

42 Mair 'The Electoral Universe of Small Parties in Post-war Western Europe', p. 48

43 Coakley, John 'Centres, Peripheries, and Party Systems: Nested Secession Processes in Great Britain and Ireland', *Political Geography*, 27(7), (2008), pp. 740-60; Lipset, Seymour M. and Stein Rokkan 'Cleavage Structures, Party Systems and Voter Alignments: An Introduction' in *Party Systems and Voter Alignments: Cross-National Perspectives* (New York; The Free Press, 1967), pp. 1-64; Rokkan, Stein *Citizens, Elections, Parties: Approaches to the Comparative Study of the Processes of Political Development* (Oslo, Universitetsforlaget, 1970)

44 See www.oireachtas.ie for the register of political parties in the Republic of Ireland, and www.electoralcommission.org.uk for Great Britain and Northern Ireland

45 Unlike other support groups for deputies who had parted company with their parties, such as that of Michael Lowry in Tipperary, the Independent Fianna Fáil organisation was more extensive and durable than would be needed simply to secure the re-election of its founder, Neil Blaney

46 Weeks, Liam 'Minor Parties: A Schema for Analysis', *Irish Political Studies*, 25(4), (2010), pp. 481-501

47 Communist Party of Ireland *Ireland in Crisis: The Communist Answer* (Dublin; Communist Party of Ireland, 1975), p. 38

48 Sinn Féin *Éire Nua: The Social and Economic Programme of Sinn Féin* (Dublin; Sinn Féin, 1971), p. 3

49 These may be extravagant, as in the case of the words attributed to Oliver J. Flanagan of Monetary Reform in 1943, 'Let the printing presses be put into action and let the pound notes, and fivers, aye, and tenners, too, be churned out. Put me into the Dáil and I'll guarantee that there will be rivers of money for all'; letter to the editor of *The Irish Times*, 18 April 1969, from Ms Helen Long, who claimed to have heard this in Portlaoise during the 1943 election campaign

50 O'Malley, Eoin 'Why is there no Radical Right Party in Ireland?', *West European Politics*, 31(5), (2008), pp. 960-77

51 The definitive study of populist radical right parties in Europe identified the Immigration Control Platform as the only Irish representative of this category, though that party had responded to an enquiry from the author of the study to the effect that 'since we are not a party and are strictly single issue I do not see how we can fall within your remit' (Mudde *Populist Radical Right Parties in Europe*, p. xi). Founded in January 1998, the Immigration Control Platform put forward candidates at the 2002 and 2007 general elections, and supported other candidates

52 Marsh, Michael, Richard Sinnott, John Garry and Fiachra Kennedy *The Irish Voter: The Nature of Electoral Competition in the Republic of Ireland* (Manchester; Manchester University Press, 2008), pp. 31-58

53 Laver, Michael 'Party Policy in Ireland 1997: Results from an Expert Survey', *Irish Political Studies*, 13, (1998), pp. 159-71

54 Pedersen 'Towards a New Typology of Party Lifespans and Minor Parties', pp 6-9

55 Sartori, Giovanni *Parties and Party Systems: A Framework for Analysis*, vol. 1 (Cambridge; Cambridge University Press, 1976), pp. 121-5

56 Deschouwer, Kris 'Comparing Newly Governing Parties' in Kris Deschouwer (ed.) *New Parties in Government: In Power for the First Time* (London; Routledge, 2008), p. 3

57 O'Malley, Eoin 'Punch Bags for Heavyweights? Minor Parties in Irish Governments', *Irish Political Studies*, 25(4), 2010), pp. 539-62

58 Adshead, Maura and Jonathon Tonge *Politics in Ireland: Convergence and Divergence in a Two-Polity Island* (Basingstoke; Palgrave Macmillan, 2009), pp. 100-1; Weeks, Liam 'Independents in Government: A Sui Gereris Model' in Kris Deschouwer (ed.) *Newly Governing Parties: In Power for the First Time* (London; Routledge, 2008), pp. 136-56; Weeks, Liam 'We Don't Like (To) Party: A Typology of Independents in Irish Political Life, 1922-2007', *Irish Political Studies*, 24(1), (2009), p.1-28

59 Tavits 'Party System Change'

60 Abramson, Paul R., John H. Aldrich, Phil Paolino and David W. Rohde 'Third-party and Independent Candidates in American Politics: Wallace, Anderson, and Perot', *Political Science Quarterly*, 110(3), (1995), p. 367

61 Golder 'Explaining Variation in the Success of Extreme Right Parties in Western Europe'

62 Carter 'Proportional Representation and the Fortunes of Right-wing Extremist Parties'

63 White, Graham 'Third Parties in Canada Revisited: A Rejoinder and Elaboration of the Theory of One-party Dominance', *Canadian Journal of Political Science*, 6(3), (1973), pp. 420; Gerring 'Minor Parties in Plurality Electoral Systems', p. 96

64 Eagles, Monroe, and Stephen Erfle 'Variations in Third/Minor Party Support in English Constituencies', *European Journal of Political Research*, 23(1), (1993), pp. 91-116

65 Gold, Howard J. 'Third Party Voting in Presidential Elections: A Study of Perot, Anderson, and Wallace', *Political Research Quarterly*, 48(4), (1995), pp. 751-73

66 Blais, André 'Third Parties in Canadian Provincial Politics', *Canadian Journal of Political Science*, 6(3), (1973), pp. 429-30

67 Bochel and Denver 'Minor Parties and Independents in Times of Change', p. 587

68 Denemark, David and Shaun Bowler 'Minor Parties and Protest Votes in Australia and New Zealand: Locating Populist Politics', *Electoral Studies*, 21(1), (2002), pp. 47

69 Pinard, Maurice 'One-party Dominance and Third Parties: The Pinard Theory Reconsidered', *Canadian Journal of Political Science*, 6(3), (1973), pp. 442-5

70 Bélanger 'Antipartyism and Third-party Vote Choice', pp. 1,071-2

71 Van der Brug, Wouter, Meindert Fennema and Jean Tillie 'Why Some Anti-immigrant Parties Fail and Others Succeed: A Two-step Model of Aggregate Electoral Support', *Comparative Political Studies*, 38(5), (2005), pp. 537-73

72 Coakley, John 'Local Elections and National Politics', in Mary E. Daly (ed.) *Country and Town: One Hundred Year of Local Government in Ireland* (Dublin; Institute of Public Administration, 2001), pp. 82-6; Weeks, L. and Aodh Quinlivan *All Politics is Local: A Guide to Local Elections in Ireland* (Cork; Collins Press, 2009), pp. 144-9

73 Marsh *et al. The Irish Voter*, pp. 63-4

74 Data is from the European Social Survey, third round, 2006, in respect of which the Irish fieldwork began in 2006 but was mainly conducted in 2007 (see www.europeansocialsurvey.org). The question was, 'Using this card, please tell me on a score of 0-10 how much you personally trust each of the institutions I read out. 0 means you do not trust an institution at all, and 10 means you have complete trust.'

75 Reich, Gary 'The Evolution of New Party Systems: Are Early Elections Exceptional?', *Electoral Studies*, 23 (2), (2004), pp. 235-50

76 Tavits, Margit 'Party Systems in the Making: The Emergence and Success of New Parties in New Democracies', *British Journal of Political Science*, 38(1), (2008), p. 133

77 Adams *et al.* 'Are Niche Parties Fundamentally Different From Mainstream Parties'

78 Pedersen 'Towards a New Typology of Party Lifespans and Minor Parties'

79 MacDermott, E. *Clann na Pobachta* (Cork; Cork University Press, 1998), pp. 163-5

80 Mair, Peter *The Changing Irish Party System: Organisation, Ideology and Electoral Competition* (London; Frances Pinter, 1987), pp. 217-21

81 Ailtirí na hAiséirhge *Aiséirghe Says ... The New Order in the New Ireland* (Dublin; Ailtirí na hAiséirghe, 1943); Mac an Bheatha, Proinnsias *Téid Focal le Gaoith [A Word Goes with the Wind]* (Baile Átha Cliath; Foilseacháin Náisiunta, 1967), pp. 119-23; Ní Lochlainn, Aoife 'Ailtirí na hAiseirge: A Party of its Time' in Dermot Keogh and Mervyn O'Driscoll (eds) *Ireland in World War Two: Neutrality and Survival* (Cork; Mercier Press, 2004), pp. 187-210; Douglas, R.M. *Architects of the Resurrection: Ailtirí na hAiséirighe and the Fascist 'New Order' in Ireland* (Manchester; Manchester University Press, 2009)

82 MacCarron, Daniel *Letters about Ireland* (Dublin; DMC Universal, 1973)

83 Christian Solidarity Party *Policy Proposals* (Dublin; Christian Solidarity Party, 1997)

84 Rafter, Kevin *The Clann: The Story of Clann na Poblachta* (Dublin; Mercier Press, 1996); MacDermott *Clann na Pobachta*; McCullagh, David *A Makeshift Majority: The First Inter-party Government, 1948-51* (Dublin; Institute of Public Administration, 1998)

85 Clann na Talmhan *The Book of Clann na Talmhan* (Drogheda; Drogheda Argus, 1944)

86 Varley, Tony 'Farmers Against Nationalists: The Rise and Fall of Clann na Talmhan in Galway' in Gerard Moran and Raymond Gillespie (eds) *Galway: History and Society* (Dublin; Geography Publications, 1996), pp. 589-622; Varley, Tony 'On the Road to Extinction: Agrarian Parties in Twentieth Century Ireland', *Irish Political Studies*, 25(4), (2010), pp. 581-602

87 Communist Party of Ireland *The Communist Party of Ireland: An Outline History* (Dublin; Communist Party of Ireland, 1974); Morrissey, Hazel 'The First Communist Party of Ireland', *Irish Socialist Review*, (Summer, 1983), pp.1-8; Milotte, Mike *Communism in Modern Ireland: The Pursuit of The Workers' Republic since 1916* (Dublin; Gill & Macmillan, 1984); O'Connor, Emmet *Reds and the Green: Ireland, Russia and the Communist International 1919-43* (Dublin; UCD Press, 2004)

88 Coogan, Tim Pat *The IRA*, revised edition (London; Fontana, 1987); Córas na Poblachta *Córas na Poblachta (The Republican Plan): Summary of Policy* (Dublin; Central Committee, Córas na Poblachta, 1940)

89 Mitchell, Arthur *Labour in Irish Politics 1890-1930: The Irish Labour Movement in an Age of Revolution* (Dublin; Irish University Press, 1974), p. 183-91

90 Varley 'On the Road to Extinction'

91 Boyle, Dan *A Journey to Change: 25 Years of the Green Party in Irish Politics* (Dublin; Nonsuch, 2006); Whiteman, David 'The Progress and Potential of the Green Party in Ireland', *Irish Political Studies*, 5, (1990), pp. 45-58

92 Bolleyer, Nicole 'The Irish Green Party: From Protest to Mainstream Party?', *Irish Political Studies*, 25(4), (2010), pp. 603-23

93 Rafter, Kevin *Neil Blaney: A Soldier of Destiny* (Dublin; Blackwater Press, 1993), pp. 88-111

94 Tweedy, Hilda *A Link in the Chain: The Story of the Irish Housewives Association, 1942-1992* (Dublin; Attic Press, 1992), pp. 61-2

95 Cronin, Mike *The Blueshirts and Irish Politics* (Dublin; Four Courts Press, 1997), pp. 17-27; Manning, Maurice *The Blueshirts* (Dublin; Gill & Macmillan, 1970); McGarry, Fearghal *Eoin O'Duffy: A Self-Made Hero* (Oxford; Oxford University Press, 2005)

96 Manning *The Blueshirts*, pp. 232-44; Finnegan, Richard B. 'The Blueshirts of Ireland During the 1930s: Fascism Inverted', *Eire-Ireland*, 24(2), (1989), pp. 79-99

97 National Labour Party *Principles and Policy* (Dublin; National Labour Party, 1944)

98 Gallagher, Michael *Political Parties in the Republic of Ireland* (Dublin; Gill & Macmillan, 1985), pp. 109-10; Lysaght, D.R. O'Connor *The Irish Republic* (Cork; Mercier, 1970), pp. 162-3; Puirséil, Niamh *The Irish Labour Party, 1922-73* (Dublin; University College Dublin Press, 2007)

99 Horgan, John *Noël Browne: Passionate Outsider* (Dublin; Gill & Macmillan, 2000), pp. 191-214

100 Lyne, Thomas 'The Progressive Democrats 1985-87', *Irish Political Studies*, 2, (1987), pp. 107-14; Collins, Stephen *Breaking the Mould: How the PDs Changed Irish Politics* (Dublin; Gill & Macmillan, 2005)

101 Laver, Michael, Michael Marsh and Richard Sinnott 'Patterns of Party Support', in Michael Laver, Peter Mair and Richard Sinnott (eds) *How Ireland Voted: The Irish General Election 1987* (Dublin; Poolbeg, 1987), p. 109

102 Collins *Breaking the Mould*

103 Pyne, Peter 'The Third Sinn Féin Party: 1923-1926. I. Narrative Account', *Economic and Social Review*, 1 (1), (1969), pp. 29-50

104 Bell, J. Bowyer *The Secret Army: A History of the IRA 1916-1979*, revised edition (Dublin; The Academy Press, 1979), pp. 247-8

105 Bell *The Secret Army*, pp. 77-8; Coogan *The IRA*, pp. 58-60, 77-92; English, Richard *Radicals and the Republic: Socialist Republicanism in the Irish Free State 1925-1937* (Oxford; Clarendon Press, 1994)

106 English, Richard *Armed Struggle: The History of the IRA* (London; Macmillan, 2003)

107 Horgan *Noël Browne*, pp. 265-77

108 Socialist Party of Ireland *Manifesto of the Socialist Party of Ireland with Declaration of Principles* (Dublin; Socialist Party of Ireland, 1949)

109 Rooney, Eddie 'From Republican Movement to Workers' Party: An Ideological Analysis' in Chris Curtin, Mary Kelly and Liam O'Dowd (eds) *Culture and Ideology in Ireland* (Galway; Galway University Press, 1984), pp. 79-98; Hanley, Brian, and Scott Millar *The Lost Revolution: the Story of the Official IRA and the Workers' Party* (Dublin; Penguin Ireland, 2009)

## 5. *Wipeout! Does Governing Kill Small Parties in Ireland?*

1 Dáil Debates, 30 November 2010 col. 461

2 Weeks, Liam 'Minor Parties: A Schema for Analysis', *Irish Political Studies*, 25 (4), (2010), pp. 481-501

3 Jaensch, Dean and David Mathieson *A Plague on Both Your Houses: Minor Parties in Australia* (Sydney; Allen and Unwin, 1998), p. 4

4 Bolleyer, Nicole 'The Organisational Costs of Public Office', in Kris Deschouwer (ed.) *New Parties in Government* (London; Routledge, 2008), pp. 17-41

5 O'Malley, Eoin 'Constructing and Maintaining Irish Governments' in K. Dowling and P. Dumont (eds) *The Selection of Ministers in Europe: Hiring and Firing* (London; Routledge, 2009), p. 184

6 O'Malley, Eoin 'Ministerial Selection in Ireland: Limited Choice in a Political Village', *Irish Political Studies*, 21(3), (2006), pp. 328-9

7 Finlay, Fergus *Snakes and Ladders* (Dublin; New Island Books, 1997), chapter 10

8 *The Irish Times* 25 February 2006

9 Mansergh, Lucy and Robert Thomson 'Election Pledges, Party Competition and Policymaking', *Comparative Politics*, 39(3), (2007), pp. 316-7

10 *ibid.*

11 Costello, Rory and Robert Thomson 'The Fulfilment of Election Pledges' in Michael Gallagher and Michael Marsh (eds) *How Ireland Voted 2007: The Full Story of Ireland's General Election* (Basingstoke; Palgrave Macmillan, 2008), p. 248

12 Mansergh and Thomson 'Election Pledges, Party Competition and Policymaking', p. 318

13 *The Irish Times* 27 July 1944

14 Chubb, Basil 'Ireland 1957' in D.E. Butler (eds) *Elections Abroad* (London; Macmillan, 1959), p. 190

15 McCullagh, David *A Makeshift Majority: The First Inter-party Government, 1948-51* (Dublin; Institute of Public Administration, 1998), p. 45

16 Dáil Debates 157, 6 June 1956

17 *The Irish Times* 31 May, 1956

18 Gallagher, Michael *Electoral Support for Irish Political Parties 1927-1973* (London; Sage Publications, 1976), p. 55

19 Manning, Maurice *Irish Political Parties: An Introduction* (Dublin; Gill & Macmillan, 1972), p. 100

20 Lee, John J. *Ireland 1912-1985: Politics and Society* (Cambridge; Cambridge University Press, 1989), 298

21 MacDermott, Eithne *Clann na Pobachta* (Cork; Cork University Press, 1998), p. 65

22 *ibid.*, p 79-80

23 MacBride, Seán *That Day's Struggle: A Memoir 1904-1951* C. Lawlor (ed.) (Dublin; Currach Press, 2005), p. 214

24 McCullagh *A Makeshift Majority*, p. 258

25 Lee *Ireland 1912-1985*, p. 318

26 *Irish Press*, 27 January 1969

27 MacBride *That Day's Struggle*, p. 151

28 Gallagher, Michael *Political Parties in the Republic of Ireland* (Dublin; Gill & Macmillan, 1985), p. 109

29 McCullagh *A Makeshift Majority*, p. 29

30 *The Irish Times*, 31 May 1956

31 Puirséil, Niamh *The Irish Labour Party, 1922-73* (Dublin; University College Dublin Press, 2007), p. 158

32 McCullagh *A Makeshift Majority*, p. 192-7

33 Puirséil *The Irish Labour Party*, chapter 5

34 Gallagher *Political Parties in the Republic of Ireland*, p. 86

35 Mair, Peter 'Explaining the Absence of Class Politics in Ireland' in John T. Goldthorpe and Christopher T. Whelan (eds) *The Development of Industrial Society in Ireland* (Oxford; Oxford University Press, 1992), p. 408

36 Farrell, Brian 'Government Formation and Ministerial Selection' in Howard Rae Penniman and Brian Farrell (eds) *Ireland at the Polls 1981, 1982 and 1897: A Study of Four General Elections* (Washington DC; American Enterprise Institute and Duke University Press, 1987)

37 Kavanagh, Ray *Spring, Summer and Fall: The Rise and Fall of the Labour Party* (Dublin; Blackwater Press, 2001), p. 7

38 Girvin, Brian 'The Campaign' in Michael Laver, Peter Mair and Richard Sinnott (eds) *How Ireland Voted: The Irish General Election 1987* (Dublin; Poolbeg Press, 1987), p. 2

39 McDaid, Shaun and Kacper Rekawek 'From Mainstream to Minor and Back - The Irish Labour Party, 1987-1992', *Irish Political Studies*, 25(4), (2010), pp. 625-42

40 Mair, Peter *The Changing Irish Party System: Organisation, Ideology and Electoral Competition* (London; Frances Pinter, 1987), p. 197-9

41 O'Halpin, E. 'Partnership Programme Managers in the Reynolds/Spring Coalition, 1993-4, an Assessment', *Irish Political Studies*, 12, (1997), pp. 78-91

42 *The Irish Times*/MRBI

43 *The Irish Times*, 13 May 1996

44 Garry, John 'The Demise of the Fianna Fáil–Labour "Partnership" Government and the Rise of the "Rainbow" Coalition', *Irish Political Studies*, 10, (1995), pp. 192-9

45 *The Irish Times*, 28 November 1994

46 *The Irish Times*, 22 May 1997

47 *The Irish Times*, 19 March 1997

48 *The Irish Times*, 25 February 1997

49 O'Malley 'Constructing and Maintaining Irish Governments', p. 209

50 *Hot Press*, 11 March 2009

51 *The Irish Times*, 23 January 2009

52 *The Irish Times*, 13 February 2010

53 *The Irish Times*, 22 March 2010

54 *The Irish Times*, 9 June 2010

## 6 *The Rise and Decline of the Green Party*

1 Poguntke, Thomas 'Green Parties in National Government: From Protest to Asquiescence?' in Ferdinand Müller-Rommel and Thomas Poguntke (eds) *Green Parties in National Governments* (London; Frank Cass, 2002), pp. 133-45; chapter 5

2 Among the few Green parties which lost parliamentary representation after having entered the national stage are the Swedish Greens which lost all seats right after their breakthrough election yet re-entered the next election. Similarly, Groen! Agalev in Belgium lost representation later in its history but similarly recovered at the follow-up elections. Only the latter lost representation after having been in government

3 Burchell, John *The Evolution of Green Politics: Development and Change within European Green Parties* (London; Earthscan Publications Ltd, 2002); Kitschelt, Herbert *The Logics of Party Formation: Ecological Politics in Belgium and West Germany* (Ithaca; Cornell University Press, 1989); Poguntke 'Green Parties in National Government'; for an overview see Bolleyer, Nicole 'The Organisational Costs of Public Office', in Kris Deschouwer (ed.) *New Parties in Government* (London; Routledge, 2008), pp. 17-41

4 Kitschelt *The Logics of Party Formation*

5 Whiteman, David 'The Progress and Potential of the Green Party in Ireland', *Irish Political Studies*, 5, (1990), p. 52

6 For an overview see Farrell, David 'Ireland' in Richard S. Katz and Peter Mair (eds) *Party Organisations: A Data Handbook* (London; Sage, 1992), pp. 398-458

7 Katz, Richard S. and Peter Mair (eds) *How Parties Organize: Change and Adaptation in Western Democracies* (Sage; London, 1994); Burchell *The Evolution of Green Politics*

8 Unfortunately, the party archive of the Irish Greens is rather sporadic (which is quite typical for green parties more generally reflecting their – at least initial – opposition to bureaucratisation). For example, old party constitutions have not been collected systematically which emphasises the importance of using a variety of sources to reconstruct the evolution of the organisation

9 McCluskey, F. 'Organisation as Ends: Comhaontas Glas Observed', unpublished MA Thesis, University College Dublin (1992), p. 15

10 Whiteman 'The Progress and Potential of the Green Party in Ireland', p. 51-3

11 McCluskey 'Organisation as Ends', p. 16

12 Boyle, Dan *A Journey to Change: 25 Years of the Green Party in Irish Politics* (Dublin; Nonsuch, 2006), p. 207

13 McCluskey 'Organisation as Ends', p. 38-9

14 Whiteman 'The Progress and Potential of the Green Party in Ireland', p. 52; McCluskey 'Organisation as Ends', p. 16

15 Kitschelt *The Logics of Party Formation*; Burchell *The Evolution of Green Politics*

16 McCluskey 'Organisation as Ends', p. 16

17 Facilitation Guidelines, May 1990. These guidelines laid out in great detail how a meeting should be run in order to facilitate consensus

18 Constitutional Group Report, Meeting of the CP/CG Constitutional Group April 3rd 1990, p. 2. Internal Document.

19 McCluskey 'Organisation as Ends'

20 Minutes of Constitution Group Meeting Held on 30th April 1990. Internal Document

21 Article 6 Green Party Constitution 2008

22 Even in 1997 the Greens had barely £20,000 for its entire national campaign

23 McCluskey 'Organisation as Ends', p. 36-7

24 Memo of Meeting between Roger Garland with the Clerk of the Dail, Sean Ryall on Wednesday, 21 March 1990

25 Burchell *The Evolution of Green Politics*

26 McCluskey 'Organisation as Ends', p. 32-3

27 *ibid.*

28 Boyle *A Journey to Change*, p. 116

29 Mair, Peter *The Changing Irish Party System: Organisation, Ideology and Electoral Competition* (London; Frances Pinter, 1987); Boyle, Dan *A Journey to Change*

30 Boyle *A Journey to Change*, p. 188

31 *ibid.*, p. 94

32 Bolleyer, Nicole and Liam Weeks 'The Puzzle of Non-Party Actors in Party Democracy: Independents in Ireland', *Comparative European Politics*, 7(3), (2009), pp. 299-324

33 Feinstein, Mike, Irish Greens enter coalition government for the first time, http://gp.org/greenpages/content/volume11/issue3/world03.php, accessed: 6 May 2008

34 Rose, Richard and Thomas Mackie 'Incumbency in Government: Asset or Liability?' in H. Daalder and Peter Mair (eds), Western European Party Systems: Continuity and Change (London; Sage, 1983), pp. 115-37; Heinisch, Reinhard 'Success in Opposition – Fáilure in Government: Explaining the Performance of Right-Wing Populist Parties in Public Office', *West European Politics*, 26 (3), (2003), pp. 91-130; Herzog, Hanna 'Minor Parties: The Relevancy Perspective', *Comparative Politics*, 19(3), (1987), pp 317-329

35 Bolleyer, Nicole 'Inside the Cartel Party: Party Organization in Government and Opposition', *Political Studies*, 57(3), (2009), pp. 559-79

36 While local autonomy and participatory modes of decision-making are not necessarily linked, they tend to be closely tied in Green parties, which favour local autonomy as a way to bring decision making closer to the members and to avoid power concentration on a national elite

37 *The Irish Times*, 12 February 2010

38 *The Irish Times*, 'Déirdre de Búrca's letter of resignation', 12 February 2010, accessed: 9 November 2011.

39 It was argued that part of reason for de Burca's resignation was was being denied a position in an EU Commissioner's cabinet. *The Irish Times*, 'Gormley dismisses de Búrca criticisms', 12 February 2010

40 Bolleyer, Nicole 'Small Parties – From Party Pledges to Government Policy', *West European Politics*, 30(1), (2007), pp. 121-47; Deschouwer, Kris (ed.) *New Parties in Government* (London; Routledge, 2008); see also chapter 5

41 Collins, Stephen 'Greens' Bid to Secure Survival is Logical for FF Coalition Partners', *The Irish Times*, 17 May 2009

42 Quinlan, Stephen 'The 2009 European Parliament Election in Ireland', *Irish Political Studies*, 25(2), (2010), pp. 289-301

43 For a detailed analysis see Minihan, Mary *A Deal with the Devil: The Green Party in Government* (Dublin; Maverick House, 2011)

44 On the evolution of other Greens in Europe see Burchell *The Evolution of Green Politics;* Kitschelt *The Logics of Party Formation;* Poguntke 'Green Parties in National Government'

45 Farrell, David 'Ireland: The "Green Alliance"', in Ferdinand Müller Rommel (ed.) *New Politics in Western Europe: the Rise and Success of Green Parties and Alternative Lists* (Boulder; Westview, 1989)

46 Poguntke 'Green Parties in National Government'

47 Bolleyer, Nicole *New Parties in Old Party Systems: Patterns of Persistence and Decline in 17 Democracies* (Oxford; Oxford University Press, forthcoming 2013)

## 7. *The Party That Ran Out of Lives: The Progressive Democrats*

1 The party did not officially cease existence until 20 November 2009

2 Mair, Peter *The Changing Irish Party System: Organisation, Ideology and Electoral Competition* (London; Frances Pinter, 1987), p. 216

3 Farrell, David 'Campaign Strategies: The Selling of the Parties' in Michael Laver, Peter Mair and Richard Sinnott (eds) *How Ireland Voted: The Irish General Election* (Dublin; Poolbeg Press, 1987)

4 Farrell, Brian and David Farrell 'The General Election of 1987' in Howard Rae Penniman and Brian Farrell (eds) *Ireland at the Polls 1981, 1982 and 1987* (Washington DC; Duke University Press, 1987), pp. 236-9

5 O'Malley, Eoin 'Punch Bags for Heavyweights? Minor Parties in Irish Governments', *Irish Political Studies*, 25(4), 2010), p. 554

6 Girvin, Brian 'The Campaign' in Michael Gallagher and Richard Sinnott (eds) *How Ireland Voted 1989?* (Galway; PSAI Press, 1990), p. 11

7 *ibid.*, p. 16

8 *ibid.*, p. 18

9 *ibid.*, p. 76

10 O'Malley 'Punch Bags for Heavyweights?', p. 555

11 Girvin, Brian 'The Road to the Election' in Michael Gallagher and Michael Laver (eds) *How Ireland Voted 1992* (Limerick; PSAI Press, 1993), p. 11

12 Farrell, 'Campaign Strategies', p. 26

13 Girvin 'The Road to the Election', p. 13

14 Gallagher, Michael 'The Election of the 27th Dáil' in Michael Gallagher and Michael Laver (eds) *How Ireland Voted 1992* (Limerick; PSAI Press, 1993), p. 66

15 Gallagher, Michael and Michael Marsh *Days of Blue Loyalty* (Dublin; PSAI Press, 2002), p. 194

16 O'Malley 'Punch Bags for Heavyweights?', p. 555

17 Collins, Stephen *Breaking the Mould: How the PDs Changed Irish Politics* (Dublin; Gill & Macmillan, 2005)

18 O'Malley 'Punch Bags for Heavyweights?', p. 555

19 Murphy, Gary 'Influencing Political Decision Making: Interest Groups and Elections in Independent Ireland', *Irish Political Studies*, 25(4), (2010), pp. 578

20 O'Malley 'Punch Bags for Heavyweights?', p. 555

21 Collins *Breaking the Mould*, p. 239

22 *ibid.*

23 Gallagher, Michael, Michael Laver and Peter Mair, *Representative Government in Modern Europe* (New York; McGraw-Hill, 2011)

24 Collins *Breaking the Mould*, p. 239

25 Mair, Peter 'The Election in Context' in Michael Gallagher and Michael Marsh (eds) *How Ireland Voted 2011: The Full Story of Ireland's Earthquake Election* (Basingstoke; Palgrave Macmillan, 2011), pp. 291

26 Collins *Breaking the Mould*, p. 239

27 O'Malley 'Punch Bags for Heavyweights?', p. 539

28 Weeks, Liam 'Minor Parties: A Schema for Analysis', *Irish Political Studies*, 25 (4), (2010), p. 498

29 Mair, Peter 'Fianna Fáil, Labour and the Irish Party System' in Michael Gallagher and Michael Laver (eds) *How Ireland Voted 1992* (Limerick; PSAI Press, 1993)

30 Marsh, Michael, Richard Sinnott, John Garry and Fiachra Kennedy *The Irish Voter: The Nature of Electoral Competition in the Republic of Ireland* (Manchester; Manchester University Press, 2008), p. 37-8

31 Mair, Peter 'The Electoral Universe of Small Parties in Post-war Western Europe' in Ferdinand Müller-Rommel and Geoffrey Pridham (eds) *Small Parties in Western Europe: Comparative and National Perspectives* (London; Sage, 1991), p. 58

32 Laver, Michael (1998) 'Party Policy in Ireland 1997: Results from an Expert Survey', *Irish Political Studies*, 13, (1998), pp. 159-71

33 Benoit, Kenneth and Michael Laver 'Estimating Irish Party Policy Positions Using Computer Wordscoring: The 2002 Election – A Research Note', *Irish Political Studies*, 18(1), (2003), pp. 97-107

34 Volkens, Andrea, Onawa Lacewell, Pola Lehmann, Sven Regel, Henrike Schultze and Annika Werner *The Manifesto Data Collection: Manifesto Project (MRG/CMP/MARPOR)* (Berlin; Wissenschaftszentrum Berlin für Sozialforschung (WZB), 2011)

35 O'Malley 'Punch Bags for Heavyweights?'

36 Marsh, Michael and Kevin Cunningham 'A Positive Choice, or Anyone but Fianna Fáil?' in Michael Gallagher and Michael Marsh (eds) *How Ireland Voted 2011: The Full Story of Ireland's Earthquake Election* (London; Palgrave, 2011), pp. 180

37 Mair, Peter and Liam Weeks 'The Party System' in John Coakley and Michael Gallagher (eds) *Politics in the Republic of Ireland*, 4th edition (London; Routledge/PSAI Press, 2005), pp. 149

38 Weeks 'Minor Parties'

39 Pedersen, Mogens N. 'Towards a New Typology of Party Lifespans and Minor Parties', *Scandinavian Political Studies*, 5 (1), (1982), pp. 6-9

40 De Bréadún, Déaglán 'Democracy Now Alliance Cancelled Launch Over Timing', *The Irish Times*, 31 January 2011; Reidy, Theresa 'Candidate Selection' in Michael Gallagher and Michael Marsh (eds) *How Ireland Voted 2011: The Full Story of Ireland's Earthquake Election* (London; Palgrave, 2011), p. 47

## 8. *Seeking the Fianna Fáil Vote: Why do Interest Groups Run for Office in Ireland?*

1 A previous version of this chapter was published in 2010 as 'Influencing Political Decision-Making: Interest Groups and Elections in Independent Ireland', *Irish Political Studies*, 25:4, pp. 563-58. This version contains significant new material. I thank Liam Weeks and Kevin Rafter for comments on earlier drafts

2 Schattschneider, Elmer E., *Party Government* (Westport; Greenwood Press, 1942), p. 1

3 Gallagher, Michael 'Parties and Referendums in Ireland 1937-2011', *Irish Political Studies*, 26(4), (2011), p. 536

4 Weeks, Liam 'Parties and the Party System' in John Coakley and Michael Gallagher (eds)
  *Politics in the Republic of Ireland*, 5th edition (London; Routledge, 2009), p. 143

5 Whelan, Noel *Fianna Fáil: A Biography of the Party* (Dublin; Gill & Macmillan, 2011), p. 3

6 Garvin, Tom *The Evolution of Irish Nationalist Politics* (Dublin; Gill & Macmillan, 1981), p. 224

7 For a list of all opinion polls between 2007 and 2011 see: http://www.fairocracy.com/
  general_election_2011/irish_political_opinion_polls_2007_to_2011.html

8 Farrell, Sean, Ciara Meehan, Gary Murphy and Kevin Rafter 'Assessing the Irish General
  Election of 2011: A Roundtable', *New Hibernia Review*, 15(3), (2011), pp. 36-7

9 Beyers, Jan, Rainer Eising and William Maloney 'Researching Interest Group Politics in
  Europe and Elsewhere: Much We Study, Little We Know?', *West European Politics*, 31(6),
  (2008), pp.1,107

10 Murphy, Gary and John Hogan 'Fianna Fáil, the Trade Union Movement and the Politics
   of Macroeconomic Crises, 1970-82', *Irish Political Studies*, 23(4), (2008), pp. 577-98

11 Allern, Elin H. and Tim Bale 'Political Parties and Interest Groups: Disentangling
   Complex Relationships', *Party Politics*, 18(1), (2012), pp. 9

12 Wilson, Graham K. *Interest Groups* (Oxford; Basil Blackwell, 1991), p. 8

13 Beyers *et al.* 'Researching Interest Group Politics in Europe and Elsewhere', p. 1,106-7

14 Sartori, Giovanni *Parties and Party Systems: A Framework for Analysis*, vol. 1 (Cambridge;
   Cambridge University Press, 1976); Panebianco, Angelo *Political Parties: Organization and
   Power* (Cambridge; Cambridge University Press, 1988)

15 Katz, Richard S. 'Party Government and its Alternatives' in Richard S. Katz (ed.) *Party
   Government: European and American Experiences* (Berlin and New York; Walter de Gruyter,
   1987), p. 4

16 Puirséil, Niamh *The Irish Labour Party, 1922-73* (Dublin; University College Dublin Press,
   2007), p. 6

17 Murphy, Gary 'Interest Groups in the Policy Making Process' in John Coakley and
   Michael Gallagher *Politics in the Republic of Ireland*, 4th edition (Abingdon; Routledge,
   2005), p. 333

18 Coakley, John 'The Rise and Fall of Minor Parties in Ireland', *Irish Political Studies*, 25(4),
   (2010), p. 527; Murphy, Gary 'Influencing Political Decision Making: Interest Groups and
   Elections in Independent Ireland', *Irish Political Studies*, 25(4), (2010), p. 570

19 Mair, Peter and Ingrid van Biezen 'Party Membership in Twenty European Democracies,
   1980-2000', *Party Politics*, 7(1), (2001), pp.5-21

20 Beyers *et al.* 'Researching Interest Group Politics in Europe and Elsewhere', p. 1,111-2;
   Jordan, Grant and William A. Maloney *Democracy and Interest Groups* (Basingstoke;
   Palgrave, 2007)

21 McGraw, Seán 'Managing Changes: Party Competition in the New Ireland', Irish
   Political Studies, 23(4), pp. 631

22 Marsh, Michael 'Parties and Society' in John Coakley and Michael Gallagher (eds), *Politics
   in the Republic of Ireland*, 4th edition (Abingdon; Routledge, 2005), pp.170

23 Mair and van Biezen 'Party Membership in Twenty European Democracies, 1980-2000', p.
   9

24 Gallagher 'Parties and Referendums in Ireland 1937-2011', p. 538

25 Weeks 'Parties and the Party System', p. 155

26 Gallagher 'Parties and Referendums in Ireland 1937-2011', p. 539

27 Murphy 'Interest Groups in the Policy Making Process', p. 340

28 Therborn, Goran *European Modernity and Beyond: The Trajectory of European Societies
   1945-2000* (London; Sage, 1995), p. 307

29 Irish Social and Political Attitudes Survey, cited in Garry, John, Niamh Hardiman,
   Diane Payne (eds) *Irish Social and Political Attitudes* (Liverpool; Liverpool University
   Press, 2006)

30 Central Statistics Office, 'Community Involvement and Social Networks 2006', July 2009, available at: http://www.cso.ie/releasespublications/documents/labour_market/2006/comsoc06.pdf, pp. 5-9

31 Mair, Peter and Liam Weeks 'The Party System' in John Coakley and Michael Gallagher (eds) *Politics in the Republic of Ireland*, 4th edition (London; Routledge/PSAI Press, 2005), p. 156

32 Weeks, Liam 'We Don't Like (To) Party: A Typology of Independents in Irish Political Life, 1922-2007', *Irish Political Studies*, 24(1), (2009), pp. 1-2

33 Bolleyer, Nicole and Liam Weeks 'The Puzzle of Non-Party Actors in Party Democracy: Independents in Ireland', *Comparative European Politics*, 7(3), (2009), pp. 299-324

34 Lee, John J. *Ireland 1912-1985: Politics and Society* (Cambridge; Cambridge University Press, 1989), p. 271

35 McGarry, Fearghal *Eoin O'Duffy: A Self-Made Hero* (Oxford; Oxford University Press, 2005), p. 280

36 Coakley, John 'Minor Parties in Irish Political Life, 1922-89', *Economic and Social Review*, 21(3), (1990), p. 289

37 Ní Lochlainn, Aoife 'Ailtirí na hAiseirge: A Party of its Time' in Dermot Keogh and Mervyn O'Driscoll (eds) *Ireland in World War Two: Neutrality and Survival* (Cork; Mercier Press, 2004), p. 210

38 Coakley, John 'The Rise and Fall of Minor Parties in Ireland', *Irish Political Studies*, 25(4), (2010), pp. 503-58

39 Murphy 'Interest Groups in the Policy Making Process', p. 343

40 *ibid.*, p. 371

41 Millward Brown IMS, 'Post Lisbon Treaty Referendum Research Findings', September 2008, available at: www.dfa.ie; Sinnott, Richard *et al.* 'Attitudes and Behaviour in the referendum on the Treaty of Lisbon', report prepared for the Department of Foreign Affairs, 2009, available at http://www.dfa.ie/uploads/documents/ucd per cent20geary per cent20institute per cent20report.pdf

42 Galligan, Yvonne *Women and Politics in Contemporary Ireland: From the Margins to the Mainstream* (London; Pinter, 1998)

43 Girvin, Brian 'Social Change and Moral Politics: The Irish Constitutional Referendum 1983', *Political Studies*, 34(1), (1986), pp. 61-81

44 Quinlan, Stephen 'The Lisbon Treaty Referendum 2008', *Irish Political Studies*, 24(1), (2009), pp. 109, 111-12

45 Ward, Margaret *Unmanageable Revolutionaries: Women and Irish Nationalism* (Dingle: Brandon, 1983), p. 239

46 *The Irish Times*, 27 November 1995

47 *The Irish Times*, 16 July 2008; *The Sunday Times*, 22 June 2008

48 Rafter, Kevin 'Wanted: A Champion of Public-sector Cuts', *The Sunday Times*, 19 April 2009

49 Katz 'Party Government and its Alternatives', p. 4

50 Mair, Peter 'The Election in Context' in *How Ireland Voted 2011: The Full Story of Ireland's Earthquake Election* (Basingstoke; Palgrave Macmillan, 2011), p. 291; Marsh, Michael and Kevin Cunningham 'A Positive Choice, or Anyone but Fianna Fáil?' in Michael Gallagher and Michael Marsh (eds) *How Ireland Voted 2011: The Full Story of Ireland's Earthquake Election* (London; Palgrave, 2011), pp. 185

51 Gallagher, Michael 'The Earthquake that Never Happened: Analysis of the Results' in Michael Gallagher and Michael Marsh (eds) *How Ireland Voted 2007: The Full Story of Ireland's General Election* (Basingstoke; Palgrave Macmilan, 2008), pp. 91-2

52 O'Malley, Eoin 'Government Formation in 2007' in Michael Gallagher and Michael Marsh (eds) *How Ireland Voted 2007: The Story of Ireland's General Election* (Basingstoke; Palgrave, 2008), p. 211

53 Gallagher, Michael 'Ireland's Earthquake Election: Analysis of the Results' in Michael Gallagher and Michael Marsh (eds) *How Ireland Voted 2011: The Full Story of Ireland's Earthquake Election* (Basingstoke; Palgrave Macmillan, 2011), p. 151

54 Mair and Weeks 'The Party System', p. 156

55 Reidy, Theresa 'Candidate Selection' in Michael Gallagher and Michael Marsh (eds) *How Ireland Voted 2011: The Full Story of Ireland's Earthquake Election* (London; Palgrave, 2011), p. 47

56 *ibid.*; Leahy, Pat 'Campaign Strategies and Political Marketing'in Michael Gallagher and Michael Marsh (eds) *How Ireland Voted 2011: The Full Story of Ireland's Earthquake Election* (Basingstoke; Palgrave), p. 77

57 I am paraphrasing Donnelly here as he made this observation on the RTÉ election program on Sunday 27 February 2011. The author was on the same panel as Donnelly and vividly recalls this politically astute observation as to why the Irish electorate in rejecting Fianna Fáil so vehemently decided to go with the established alternative coalition of Fine Gael and Labour

58 Mair, Peter 'The Election in Context' in *How Ireland Voted 2011: The Full Story of Ireland's Earthquake Election* (Basingstoke; Palgrave Macmillan, 2011), p. 296

59 Murphy 'Interest Groups in the Policy Making Process'; Reidy 'Candidate Selection'

60 McGraw 'Managing Changes', p. 630

## 9. *Irish Farmers' Parties, Nationalism and Class Politics in the Twentieth Century*

1 Lee, John J. *Ireland 1912-1985: Politics and Society* (Cambridge; Cambridge University Press, 1989), pp. 72-3

2 *ibid.*, pp 70-2; Contrastingly, Lipset and Rokkan view relations formed between 'landed and urban interests' around commodity markets as generating conflicts that could but 'did not invariably prove party-forming'. See Lipset, Seymour Martin and Stein Rokkan, 'Cleavage Structures, Party Systems and Voter Alignments: An Introduction' in Seymour Martin Lipset and Stein Rokkan (eds) *Party Systems and Voter Alignments: Cross-National Perspectives* (New York; The Free Press, 1967), p. 21

3 Duverger, Maurice *Political Parties: Their Organisation and Activity in the Modern State*, 3rd edition (London; Methuen, 1969), p. 236

4 Larkin, Emmet 'Foreword' in William L. Feingold (ed.) *The Revolt of the Tenantry: The Transformation of Local Government in Ireland 1872-1886* (Boston; Northeastern University Press, 1984), pp.xiv–xv

5 *ibid.*, p. xv; Bew, Paul *Ireland: The Politics of Enmity 1789-2006* (Oxford; Oxford University Press, 2007), p. 568; Nor did agricultural labourers, an agrarian class in steep decline, seriously threaten the power of the strong farmers (Lee *Ireland 1912-1985*, p. 71-2; Hoppen, K. Theodore *Elections, Politics, and Society in Ireland 1832-1885* (Oxford; Oxford University Press, 1984) p. 103

6 Campbell, Fergus *Land and Revolution: Nationalist Politics in the West of Ireland 1891-1921* (Oxford; Oxford University Press, 2005), pp. 303-4

7 Jordan, Donald 'Merchants, "Strong Farmers" and Fenians: The Post-Famine Political Élite and the Irish Land War' in C.H.E. Philpin (ed.) *Nationalism and Popular Protest in Ireland* (Cambridge; Cambridge University Press, 1987), pp. 347-8

8 Campbell *Land and Revolution*, pp. 149-51

9 Murphy, John A. *Ireland in the Twentieth Century* (Dublin; Gill & Macmillan, 1975), p. 115; Dunphy, Richard *The Making of Fianna Fáil Power in Ireland 1923-1948* (Oxford; Oxford University Press, 1995), p. 286

10 Mitchell, Arthur *Labour in Irish Politics 1890-1930: The Irish Labour Movement in an Age of Revolution* (Dublin; Irish University Press, 1974), p. 192

11 Manning, Maurice 'The Farmers' in John J. Lee (ed.) *Ireland 1945-70* (Dublin; Gill & Macmillan, 1979), p. 51

12 Gallagher, Michael *Political Parties in the Republic of Ireland* (Dublin; Gill & Macmillan, 1985), p. 98

13 Manning, Maurice *James Dillon: A Biography* (Dublin; Wolfhound Press, 1999), p. 79; The two men in question were Frank MacDermot and James Dillon

14 Garvin, Tom *The Evolution of Irish Nationalist Politics* (Dublin; Gill & Macmillan, 1981), p. 166

15 Manning *James Dillon*, p. 188

16 Murphy *Ireland in the Twentieth Century*, pp. 115-16

17 *ibid.*

18 O'Connor, Emmet *Syndicalism in Ireland* (Cork; Cork University Press, 1988)

19 Gallagher *Political Parties in the Republic of Ireland*, p. 102

20 O'Sullivan, Donal *The Irish Free State and its Senate: A Study in Contemporary Politics* (London; Faber and Faber, 1940), p. 299; Gallagher *Political Parties in the Republic of Ireland*, p. 103

21 Such relations had already been institutionalised in Northern Ireland (Greer, Alan *Rural Politics in Northern Ireland: Policy Networks and Agricultural Development Since Partition* (Aldershot; Avebury, 1996), pp. 3, 123-4)

22 Bradley, Dan *Farm Labourers: Irish Struggle 1900-1976* (Belfast; Athol Books, 1988), pp. 31-72; O'Connor *Syndicalism in Ireland*, pp. 74-6, 33-53; Fitzpatrick, David *Politics and Irish Life 1913-21: Provincial Experience of War and Revolution* (Cork; Cork University Press, 1998), pp. 223-5

23 *The Irish Times*, 16 March 1923; Gallagher, Michael 'The Pact General Election of 1922', *Irish Historical Studies*, 21(4), (1979), pp. 408-9

24 *The Irish Times*, 16 March 1923

25 Gallagher *Political Parties in the Republic of Ireland*, p. 104; In 1933 elements in Cumann na nGaedheal portrayed 'the government's modest land redistribution bill as the "first step in an Irish anti-Kulak campaign"' (McGarry, Fearghal *Eoin O'Duffy: A Self-Made Hero* (Oxford; Oxford University Press, 2005), p. 203)

26 Moss, Warner *Political Parties in the Irish Free State* (New York: Columbia University Press, 1933), pp. 186, 193

27 Gallagher *Political Parties in the Republic of Ireland*, p. 104

28 M. Donnellan, Commission on Vocational Organisation. Minutes of Evidence, National Library of Ireland (NLI), MS 931, 18 April, 1941, p. 3,190

29 Moss *Political Parties in the Irish Free State*, p. 57

30 O'Connor *Syndicalism in Ireland*, p. 74; Fitzpatrick *Politics and Irish Life 1913-21*, p. 229

31 Fitzpatrick *Politics and Irish Life 1913-21*, p. 229

32 *ibid.*, p. 225

33 *ibid.*, p. 226

34 *Connacht Tribune*, 31 August 1918

35 Gallagher *Political Parties in the Republic of Ireland*, p. 104

36 *The Irish Times*, 30 March 1932, 13 October 1932

37 *The Irish Times*, 13 December 1932

38 *The Irish Times*, 6 January 1933

39 *Roscommon Herald*, 13 February 1932

40 *Irish Farmers' Paper*, July 1942. By 1940 the IFF was claiming to have a membership of about 14,500, of which 13,500 were farmers and the balance agricultural labourers (Commission on Vocational Organisation. Minutes of Evidence, NLI, MS 929, 24 October 1940, pp. 2,635, 2,649)

41 Gallagher, Michael *Irish Elections 1922-44: Results and Analysis* (Limerick PSAI Press, 1993), p. 46

42 In 1923 the Farmers' Party also faced competition from some other aspiring (but electorally unsuccessful) farmers' parties professing to speak for small farmers. See John

Coakley 'Minor Parties in Irish Political Life, 1922-89', *Economical and Social Review*, 21(3), (1990), p. 282

43  Gallagher *Irish Elections 1922-44*, pp. 87, 118

44  *ibid.*, p. 148

45  Gallagher *Political Parties in the Republic of Ireland*, p. 104; Seven of the party's twenty-six candidates in 1933 (and three of those elected) were either outgoing or former Farmers' Party TDs (Gallagher *Irish Elections 1922-44*)

46  Sinnott, Richard *Irish Voters Decide: Voting Behaviour in Elections and Referendums Since 1918* (Manchester; Manchester University Press, 1995), p. 62

47  McCracken, J.L. *Representative Government in Ireland: A Study of Dáil Éireann 1919-48* (London; Oxford University Press, 1958), pp. 77, 105

48  Varley, Tony 'Farmers Against Nationalists: The Rise and Fall of Clann na Talmhan in Galway' in Gerard Moran and Raymond Gillespie (eds) *Galway: History and Society* (Dublin; Geography Publications, 1996), p. 601

49  McCracken *Representative Government in Ireland*, p. 116

50  *ibid.*, p. 115; In the current 31st Dáil, the product of the highly exceptional 2011 election, farmers account for 7 (9.2%) of Fine Gael's 76 TDs and for 5 (25 per cent) of Fianna Fáil's 20 TDs (Courtney, M. 'Appendix 2: Members of the 31st Dáil' in Michael Gallagher and Michael Marsh (eds) *How Ireland Voted 2011: The Full Story of Ireland's Earthquake Election* (Houndmills, Basingstoke; Palgrave Macmillan, 2011), pp. 304-9)

51  Gallagher, Michael 'The Pact General Election of 1922', *Irish Historical Studies*, 21(4), (1979), p. 407

52  Gallagher *Political Parties in the Republic of Ireland*, p. 102; Regan, John M. *The Irish Counter-Revolution 1921-1936: Treatyite Politics and Settlement in Independent Ireland* (Dublin; Gill & Macmillan, 1999), pp. 320, 341-2

53  *The Irish Times*, 6 January 1933; Varley 'Farmers Against Nationalists', p. 602

54  Gallagher, Michael *Electoral Support for Irish Political Parties 1927-1973* (London; Sage Publications, 1976), pp. 9, 19, 30-2

55  Rumpf, Erhard and A.C. Hepburn *Nationalism and Socialism in Twentieth-Century Ireland* (Liverpool; Liverpool University Press, 1977), pp. 73-4, 103, 143; Mair, Peter *The Changing Irish Party System: Organisation, Ideology and Electoral Competition* (London; Frances Pinter, 1987), pp. 25, 51; Bew *Ireland*, p. 452

56  Gallagher, Michael 'Party Solidarity, Exclusivity and Inter-Party Relationships in Ireland, 1922-1977: The Evidence of Transfers', *Economic and Social Review*, 10(1), (1978), pp. 13-15, 18-22

57  Regan *The Irish Counter-Revolution 1921-1936*, p. 241

58  Cumann na nGaedheal had earlier captured Farmers' Party seats and support in the September 1927 election (Meehan, Ciara *The Cosgrave Party: A History of Cumann na nGaedheal* (Dublin; Prism, 2010), pp. 125-7)

59  Lee *Ireland 1912-1985*, p. 73

60  *ibid.*, pp. 72-3

61  'Clann na Talmhan has not many landlords to drive', Donnellan pointed out in 1942, 'but it has landlordism No. 2, namely, politicians, and they must go' (*Irish Farmers' Paper*, April 1942)

62  Fitzpatrick *Politics and Irish Life 1913-21*, p. 223

63  Coakley 'Minor Parties in Irish Political Life, 1922-89', p. 282

64  See *Dáil Debates* 4: 289, 5 July, 1923; Col. George O'Callaghan-Westropp to R.A. Butler, 19 April 1927 (O'Callaghan-Westropp papers, P38/4, UCD Archives)

65  Varley, Tony 'On the Road to Extinction: Agrarian Parties in Twentieth-Century Ireland' *Irish Political Studies* 25(4), (2010), p. 593

66  Fitzpatrick *Politics and Irish Life 1913-21*, p. 223

67  *The Irish Times*, 27 September 1932, 12 January 1933

68 *Roscommon Herald*, 21 January 1933

69 Varley 'Farmers Against Nationalists', pp. 600, 617

70 *ibid.*, p. 602

71 Subsequently Cogan briefly returned to the fold before leaving the party for good

72 McCullagh, David *A Makeshift Majority: The First Inter-party Government, 1948-51* (Dublin; Institute of Public Administration, 1998), pp. 238-40; Manning *James Dillon*, pp. 265, 272

73 Manning 'The Farmers', p.51

74 Weeks estimates that independent farmers, 'regularly gained between one-quarter and one-third of the Independent vote from the 1920 to the 1960s ...' (Weeks, Liam 'We Don't Like (To) Party: A Typology of Independents in Irish Political Life, 1922-2007', *Irish Political Studies*, 24(1), (2009), p.15

75 *The Irish Times*, 11 November 1927. The Farmers' Party leadership had advised its supporters to give their lower preference votes to Cumann na nGaedheal candidates in the September election (Meehan *The Cosgrave Party*, pp. 125-7)

76 McCracken *Representative Government in Ireland*, pp. 104-5; Regan *The Irish Counter-Revolution 1921-1936*, p. 265

77 Moss *Political Parties in the Irish Free State*, p. 7; Ryan, Raymond 'The National Farmers' and Ratepayers' League', *Studia Hibernica*, 34, (2007), pp. 184, 187-9

78 Varley 'Farmers Against Nationalists', pp. 601-3

79 Sinnott *Irish Voters Decide*, p. 62

80 Urwin, Derek W. *From Ploughshare to Ballotbox: The Politics of Agrarian Defence in Europe* (Oslo; Universitetsforlaget, 1980), pp. 237-41

81 Micheletti, Michele *The Swedish Farmers' Movement and Government Agricultural Policy* (New York; Praeger, 1990), p. 48; Christensen, Dag Arne 'The Norwegian Agrarian-Centre Party: Class, Rural or Catchall Party?' in David Arter (ed.) *From Farmyard to City Square? The Electoral Adaptation of the Nordic Agrarian Parties* (Aldershot; Ashgate, 2001), p. 37; Urwin *From Ploughshare to Ballotbox*, pp. 237, 251-2

82 Widfeldt, Anders 'The Swedish Centre Party: The Poor Relation of the Family?' in David Arter (ed.) *From Farmyard to City Square? The Electoral Adaptation of the Nordic Agrarian Parties* (Aldershot; Ashgate, 2001), p. 12; Christensen 'The Norwegian Agrarian-Centre Party', p. 39; Arter, David 'The Finnish Centre Party: A Case of Successful Transformation?' in David Arter (ed.) *From Farmyard to City Square? The Electoral Adaptation of the Nordic Agrarian Parties* (Aldershot; Ashgate, 2001), p. 82

83 Widfeldt 'The Swedish Centre Party', p. 23; Christensen 'The Norwegian Agrarian-Centre Party, p. 46; Arter 'The Finnish Centre Party', pp. 86-92

84 Gallagher, Michael *Irish Elections 1922-44*, p. 157; Murphy, Gary 'The Irish Government, the National Farmers Association, and the European Economic Community, 1955-1964', *New Hibernia Review*, 6(4), (2002), p. 84

85 Gallagher *Political Parties in the Republic of Ireland*, p. 98

86 Urwin *From Ploughshare to Ballotbox*, p. 237

87 Micheletti *The Swedish Farmers' Movement and Government Agricultural Policy*, pp. 50-2

88 McGuire, Charlie *Roddy Connolly and the Struggle for Socialism in Ireland* (Cork; Cork University Press, 2008), pp. 187, 193-6

89 *The Irish Times*, 2-3 March 1981

90 For accounts of these interest groups, see Collins, Neil 'Still Recognisably Pluralist? State-Farmer Relations in Ireland' in R.J. Hill and Michael Marsh (eds) *Modern Irish Democracy: Essays in of Basil Chubb* (Dublin; Irish Academic Press, 1993), pp. 104-22; Adshead, Maura 'Beyond Clientelism: Agricultural Networks in Ireland and the EU', *West European Politics*, 19(3), (1996), pp. 583-608; and Murphy, Gary *In Search of the Promised Land* (Cork; Mercier Press, 2009), pp. 204-35

## 10. *To the Left of Labour: The Workers' Party and Democratic Left,* 1982-97

1 Copus, Colin, Alistair Clark, Herwig Reynaert and Kristof Steyvers 'Minor Party and Independent Politics Beyond the Mainstream: Fluctuating Fortunes but a Permanent Presence', *Parliamentary Affairs*, 62(1), (2009), p. 4

2 Chubb, Basil *The Government and Politics of Ireland* (London; Oxford University Press, 1974), p. 91

3 Mair, Peter 'Fianna Fáil, Labour and the Irish Party System' in Michael Gallagher and Michael Laver (eds) *How Ireland Voted 1992* (Limerick; PSAI Press, 1993)

4 Farrell, David 'Ireland: The "Green Alliance"', in Ferdinand Müller-Rommel (ed.) *New Politics in Western Europe: the Rise and Success of Green Parties and Alternative Lists* (Boulder; Westview, 1989)

5 Hanley, Brian, and Scott Millar *The Lost Revolution: the Story of the Official IRA and the Workers' Party* (Dublin; Penguin Ireland, 2009), p. 591

6 Coakley, John 'The Rise and Fall of Minor Parties in Ireland', *Irish Political Studies*, 25(4), (2010), pp. 510

7 Spring, Dick *Examiner* 6 November 1997

8 Rooney, Eddie 'From Republican Movement to Workers' Party: An Ideological Analysis' in Chris Curtin, Mary Kelly and Liam O'Dowd (eds) *Culture and Ideology in Ireland* (Galway; Galway University Press, 1984), pp. 79-98

9 Dunphy Richard and S. Hopkins 'The Organisational and Political Evolution of the Workers' Party of Ireland', *Journal of Communist Studies*, 8(3), (1992), p. 91

10 Girvin, Brian 'The Campaign' in Michael Gallagher and Richard Sinnott (eds) *How Ireland Voted 1989?* (Galway; PSAI Press, 1990), p. 32

11 Gallagher, Michael 'The Earthquake that Never Happened: Analysis of the Results' in Michael Gallagher and Michael Marsh (eds) *How Ireland Voted 2007: The Full Story of Ireland's General Election* (Basingstoke; Palgrave Macmilan, 2008), p. 80

12 *ibid.*, p. 77

13 Interview with Eric Byrne, 29 August 2006

14 Kavanagh, Ray *Spring, Summer and Fall: The Rise and Fall of the Labour Party* (Dublin; Blackwater Press, 2001), p. 214

15 Finlay, Fergus *Snakes and Ladders* (Dublin; New Island Books, 1997), p. 129

16 Kavanagh *Spring, Summer and Fall*, p. 90

17 Rabbitte, Pat. Quoted in *Dungarvan Observer*, 4 April 1992

18 Rafter, Kevin *Democratic Left the Life and Death of an Irish Political Party* (Dublin; Irish Academic Press, 2011), p. 143

19 Interview with Eamon Gilmore, 11 September 2006

20 *ibid.*

21 Dunphy, Richard 'From Eurocommunism to Eurosocialism: The Search for a Post-Communist European Left', *Occasional Papers*, 1(7) (Dundee; University of Dundee, 1993), 29

22 Gottfried, Paul *The Strange Death of Marxism: The European Left in the New Millennium* (Columbia; University of Missouri, 2005), p. 2

23 Interview with Eamon Gilmore, 11 September 2006

24 Interview with Proinsias De Rossa, 7 September 2007

25 Bull, Martin J. 'The West European Communist Movement in the Late Twentieth Century', *West European Politics*, 18(1), (1995), p. 79

26 Dunphy 'From Eurocommunism to Eurosocialism'

27 Kindersley, Richard 'In Lieu of a Conclusion: Eurocommunism and 'the Crisis of Capitalism' in Richard Kindersley (ed.) *In Search of Eurocommunism* (London; Macmillan, 1981), p. 186

28 Patterson, Henry *The Politics of Illusion: A Political History of the IRA* (London; Penguin, 1997), pp. 257-8

29 Interview with Tony Heffernan, 13 September 2006

30 Dunphy and Hopkins 'The Organisational and Political Evolution of the Workers' Party of Ireland', p. 92

31 Interview with Eric Byrne, 29 August 2006

32 Interview with Tomás MacGiolla, 30 November 2006

33 Interview with Proinsias De Rossa, 7 September 2007

34 Interview with Des Geraghty, 9 May 2006

35 Interview with Proinsias De Rossa, 7 September 2007

36 Sassoon, Donald *One Hundred Years of Socialism: The West European Left in the Twentieth Century* (New York; New Press, 1996), p. 733

37 Rafter *Democratic Left the Life and Death of an Irish Political Party*, p. 43

38 Walsh, Dick *The Irish Times*, 20 March 1992

39 Arter, David 'Scandinavia: What's Left Is the Social Democratic Consensus', *Parliamentary Affairs*, 36(1), (2003), p. 76

40 Democratic Left Secretary's Report, Annual Conference (1993)

41 Democratic Left Youth Report to Executive, unpublished (1994)

42 *ibid.*

43 Interview with Tony Heffernan, 13 September 2006

44 Interview with John Gallagher, 15 June 2007

45 Rafter *Democratic Left the Life and Death of an Irish Political Party*

46 Democratic Left Task Force Report, unpublished draft (1997)

47 *ibid.*

48 *ibid.*

49 O'Malley, Eoin 'Punch Bags for Heavyweights? Minor Parties in Irish Governments', *Irish Political Studies*, 25(4), 2010), pp. 539-62

50 Interview with Des Geraghty, 9 May 2006

51 Interview with Eamon Gilmore, 11 September 2006

52 Correspondence from Dick Spring to Proinsias De Rossa, unpublished 27 March 1992

53 Interview with John Gallagher, 15 June 2007

54 Coakley 'The Rise and Fall of Minor Parties in Ireland'

55 McGraw, Seán 'Managing Changes: Party Competition in the New Ireland', *Irish Political Studies*, 23(4), (2008), pp. 627-48

56 Interview with Pat Rabbitte, 9 January 2007

11. *Major Breakthrough or 'Temporary Little Arrangement?' The Labour Party's 2011 Electoral Success in Historical Perspective*

1 Hazelkorn, Ellen 'Why is There No Socialism in Ireland? Theoretical Problems of Irish Marxism', *Science & Society*, 2, Summer (1989), pp. 137

2 Against this, Alan Siaroff has argued that 'the late 1980s and early 1990s saw two-and-a-half partyism cease to exist in Ireland', Siaroff, Alan 'Two-and-a-half Party Systems and the Comparative Role of the "Half"', *Party Politics*, 9(3), (2003), pp. 267-90

3 Horgan, John *Labour: The Price of Power* (Dublin; Gill & Macmillan, 1986), p. 164

4 Figures compiled from data on electionsireland.org, 2011

5 McDaid, Shaun and Kacper Rekawek 'From Mainstream to Minor and Back – The Irish Labour Party, 1987-1992', *Irish Political Studies*, 25(4), (2010), pp. 628

6 Weeks, Liam 'Parties and the Party System' in John Coakley and Michael Gallagher (eds) *Politics in the Republic of Ireland*, 5th edition (London; Routledge, 2009) pp. 140

7 ElectionsIreland.org, 2011

8 Coakley, John and Michael Gallagher *Politics in the Republic of Ireland*, 5th edition (London; Routledge, 2009), p. 28.

9 McDaid and Rekawek 'From Mainstream to Minor and Back'

10 Albert Reynolds used this phrase to refer to his hope that the FF-PD coalition of 1989-1992 would soon be replaced by single-party FF government (Reynolds, Albert, *Albert Reynolds: My Autobiography* (Dublin; Transworld Ireland, 2009), p. 188)

11 See: Gallagher, Michael *The Irish Labour Party in Transition 1957-82* (Manchester; Manchester University Press, 1982); Puirséil, Niamh *The Irish Labour Party, 1922-73* (Dublin; University College Dublin Press, 2007); Horgan, John *Labour: The Price of Power* (Dublin; Gill & Macmillan, 1986); Gallagher, Michael *Political Parties in the Republic of Ireland* (Dublin; Gill & Macmillan, 1985), Bew, Paul, Ellen Hazelkorn and Henry Patterson *The Dynamics of Irish Politics* (London; Lawrence and Wishart, 1989); Collins, Stephen *Spring and the Labour Story* (Dublin; O'Brien, 1993)

12 Mair, Peter 'The Electoral Universe of Small Parties in Post-war Western Europe' in Ferdinand Müller-Rommel and Geoffrey Pridham (eds) *Small Parties in Western Europe: Comparative and National Perspectives* (London; Sage, 1991), pp. 43-4

13 Copus, Colin, Alistair Clark, Herwig Reynaert and Kristof Steyvers (2009) 'Minor Party and Independent Politics Beyond the Mainstream: Fluctuating Fortunes but a Permanent Presence', *Parliamentary Affairs*, 62(1), 2009, p. 6; Sartori, Giovanni *Parties and Party Systems: A Framework for Analysis*, vol. 1 (Cambridge; Cambridge University Press, 1976), p. 122

14 O'Malley, Eoin 'Punch Bags for Heavyweights? Minor Parties in Irish Governments', *Irish Political Studies*, 25(4), 2010), pp. 539-62

15 Herzog, Hanna 'Minor Parties: The Relevancy Perspective', *Comparative Politics*, 19(3), (1987), pp. 317-329

16 Pedersen, Mogens N. 'Consensus and Conflict in the Danish Folketing 1945-1965', *Scandinavian Political Studies*, 2, (1967), pp. 143-66

17 Pedersen's four thresholds are: declaration of a party's intention to contest elections; successfully fulfilling the legal requirements to form a political party in a given jurisdiction (authorisation); gaining representation in a legislature; and relevance

18 Smith, Gordon 'Small Parties: Problems of Definition Classification and Significance' in Ferdinand Müller-Rommel and Geoffrey Pridham (eds) *Small Parties in Western Europe: Comparative and National Perspectives* (London; Sage, 1991)

19 *ibid.*, p 36

20 McDaid and Rekawek 'From Mainstream to Minor and Back'

21 Sartori *Parties and Party Systems*, pp. 122-3

22 The table excludes 1922 which was not a fully competitive election, owing to the pact between Pro-and Anti-Treaty Sinn Féin candidates. Labour did not contest in 29 per cent of constituencies. Sources: Gallagher, Michael *Irish Elections 1948-77: Results and Analysis* (London; Routledge, 2009); *The Irish Times* 7 February 1948, 21 May 1954, 22 February 1987; 26 February 1987. Walker, Brian Mercer *Parliamentary Election Results in Ireland 1918-92*: Irish Elections to Parliaments and Parliamentary assemblies at Westminster, Belfast, Dublin, Strasbourg (Dublin; Royal Irish Academy, 1992), pp. 166-76; electionsIreland.org.

23 *The Irish Times*, 15 November 2011

24 *The Irish Times*, 1 December 2011, 7 December 2011

25 Interview with Ruairi Quinn, TD, 12 December 2011

26 Interview with Eric Byrne, 9 December 2011

27 Interview with Ruairi Quinn, 12 December 2011

28 Interview with Patrick Nulty, TD, 21 December 2011

29 Interview with Ruairi Quinn, 12 December 2011

30 *Phoenix Magazine*, 2 December 2011

31 Interview with Ray Kavanagh, 2 December 2011

32 Interview with Patrick Nulty, 21 December 2011

33 *ibid.*

34 *ibid.*

35 *ibid.*

36 Dillon, Paul 'Explaining the Emergence, Political Impact and Decline of Labour Left, 1983-1992' (MsocSc Thesis, University College Dublin, 2007), p. 10

37 Interview with Emmet Stagg, TD, Dublin, 4 December 2008

38 Kavanagh, Ray *Spring, Summer and Fall: The Rise and Fall of the Labour Party* (Dublin; Blackwater Press, 2001), pp. 37, 41

39 *The Irish Times*, 28 September 1987

40 Interview with Ruairi Quinn, 17 November 2008

41 Interview with Emmet Stagg, 4 December 2008

42 Interview with Ruairi Quinn, 17 November 2008

43 Interview with Ray Kavanagh, 23 October 2008

44 Interview with Emmet Stagg, 4 December 2008

45 Interview with Joe Costello, TD, 16 October 2008

46 *Belfast Telegraph*, 6 October 2010

47 O'Hare, Edward 'Getting to know Gilmore', (2011), available at: http://politico.ie/irish-politics/7462-getting-to-know-gilmore.html (accessed 28 December 2011)

48 Labour comments by Eamon Gilmore TD following declaration of his election as leader of the Labour Party, (2007), available at: http://www.labour.ie/press/listing/11890762431926105.html (accessed 28 December 2011)

49 Labour 'Report of the 21st Century Commission', (2009), available at: http://www.labour.ie/download/pdf/21stcenturycommission.pdf (accessed 28 December 2011)

50 Interview with Ruairi Quinn, 12 December 2011)

51 Interview with Patrick Nulty, 21 December 2011

52 Dáil Debates, vol. 726, col. 28, 12 January 2011

53 *The Irish Times*, 6 June 2010; Electionsireland.org 2011; *The Irish Times*, 6 January 2011

54 *Phoenix Annual*, 1998

55 Interview with Joe Costello, 16 October 2008

56 Interview with Ray Kavanagh, 23 October 2008

57 Interview with Brendan Howlin, TD, 23 October 2008

58 Labour 'Report of the Commission on Electoral Strategy' (Dublin; Labour Party, 1986), p. 32

59 Interview with Ray Kavanagh, 23 October 2008

60 Dáil Debates, vol. 391 col. 171, 12 July 1989

61 Interview with Ruairi Quinn, 17 November 2008

62 Quinn, Ruairi *Straight Left: A Journey in Politics* (London; Hodder Headline Ireland, 2005), pp. 262-3

63 Labour 'Never Again: Labour's Plan to Improve Standards in Business and Public Life', (2009), available at: http://www.labour.ie/download/pdf/never_again.pdf (accessed 2 January 2012)

64 Interview with Ruairi Quinn, 12 December 2011

65 Interview with Patrick Nulty, 21 December 2011

66 Interview with Eric Byrne, TD, 9 December 2011

67 Interview with Ray Kavanagh, 2 December 2011

68 Interview with Ruairi Quinn, 12 December 2011

69 Interview with Eric Byrne, 9 December 2011

70 Interview with Patrick Nulty, 21 December 2011

71 Labour 'Report of the Commission on Electoral Strategy', p. 24

72 Collins *Spring and the Labour Story*, p. 99

73 Puirséil *The Irish Labour Party, 1922-73*, p. 309; Gallagher *The Irish Labour Party in Transition*, pp. 253-4

74 Interview with Ruairi Quinn, TD, 17 November 2008

75 Interview with Brendan Howlin, 23 October 2008

76 *Magill*, October 1987

77 Kavanagh *Spring, Summer and Fall*, p. 52

78 PLP Minutes, 23 September 1987

79 Interview with Joe Costello, TD, 16 October 2008

80 Administrative Council (AC) Minutes, 28 September 1988

81 Interview with Ray Kavanagh, 23 October 2008

82 Interview with Ruairi Quinn, 17 November 2008

83 Finlay, Fergus *Snakes and Ladders* (Dublin; New Island Books, 1997), p. 61

84 Kavanagh *Spring, Summer and Fall*

85 PLP Minutes, 7 February 1990

86 Labour 'Report to the National Conference 1991-1993' (Dublin; Labour Party, 1993)

87 Farrell, David M. 'Campaign Strategies' in Michael Gallagher and Michael Laver (eds) *How Ireland Voted 1992* (Dublin; Folens and PSAI Press, 1993), p. 26

88 Interview with Brendan Howlin, TD, Dublin, 23 October 2008

89 McGee, Harry 'Technical Group Makes Voice Hard and Gives Bigger Parties Run For Their Money, *The Irish Times* (2011)

90 Electionsireland.org, 2011

91 Interview with Eric Byrne, TD, 9 December 2011

92 Ó Broin, E. 'Time for Sinn Féin to Work Out What it Stands for Now the Armed Struggle is over…', (2008), available at: http://sluggerotoole.com/2008/11/27/time-for-sinn-fein-to-work-out-what-it-stands-for-now-the-armed-struggle-is (accessed 28 December 2011)

93 Adams, G. 'A Sense of Hope and Purpose', (2009), available at: http://www.sinnfein.ie/contents/15516 (accessed 28 December 2011)

94 Ó Culain, C. 'Sinn Féin – Moving to the Centre', (2011), available at: http://politico.ie/irish-politics/fair-comment/7626-sinn-fein-moving-to-the-centre.html (accessed 28 December 2011)

95 Ó Broin, E. *Sinn Féin and the Politics of Left Republicanism* (London; Pluto Press, 2009)

96 Interview with Patrick Nulty, 21 December 2011

97 Coakley, John and Michael Gallagher *Politics in the Republic of Ireland*, 4th edition (London; PSAI Press/Routledge, 2005); Electionsireland.org, 1998-2008

98 Labour 'Report to the National Conference 1989-1991' (Dublin; Labour Party, 1991); Labour 'Report to the National Conference 1991-1993' (Dublin; Labour Party, 1993)

99 Interview with Brendan Howlin, 23 October 2008

100 Gallagher, Michael and Richard Sinnott (eds) *How Ireland Voted 1989* (Galway; University College Galway, 1990), 68-70

101 PLP Minutes, 19 June 1991

102 *Phoenix Annual*, 1989

103 Rekawek, Kacper *Irish Republican Terrorism and Politics: A Comparative Study of the Official and the Provisional IRA* (Abingdon; Routledge, 2011), p. 87-97

104 *Magill*, October 1988

105 Interview with Ray Kavanagh, 2 December 2011

106 *ibid.*

107 McDaid and Rekawek 'From Mainstream to Minor and Back'

108 O'Malley, Eoin 'Punch Bags for Heavyweights? Minor Parties in Irish Governments', *Irish Political Studies*, 25(4), 2010), pp. 539-62

109 RTÉ News, 2011

110 thejournal.ie, 2011

111 Interview with Eric Byrne, 9 December 2011

112 Interview with Ray Kavanagh, 2 December 2011

113 Gallagher *The Irish Labour Party in Transition*, pp. 253-4

114 Barberis, Peter, John McHugh and Mike Tyldesley *Encyclopedia of British and Irish Political Organisations* (London; Pinter, 2000), p. 217

115 Interview with Joe Costello, 16 October 2008

116 Interview with Ruairi Quinn, 17 November 2008

117 Interview with Eric Byrne, 9 December 2011; interview with Ruairi Quinn, 12 December 2011

118 Interview with Patrick Nulty, 21 December 2011

119 Interview with Ray Kavanagh, 2 December 2011

120 Brennan, Joe 'Irish Ruling Coalition Support Falls in Poll, Sunday Times Says' (2011), available at http://www.bloomberg.com/news/2011-12-18/irish-ruling-coalition-support-falls-in-poll-sunday-times-says.html (accessed 28 December 2011)

121 Red, C. 'Vote Intention Opinion Poll', 12 Jan 2012, (2012), available at: http://redcresearch.ie/wp-content/uploads/2012/01/Paddy-Power-12th-Jan-Political-Poll-2012-Vote-Intention-Report2.pdf (accessed 29 January 2012)

122 *Sunday Business Post*, 4 December 2011; *The Sunday Times*, 18 December 2011; Red, C. 'Vote Intention Opinion Poll', 12 January 2012

## 12. The Slow Growth of Sinn Féin: From Minor Player to Centre Stage?

1 Murray, Gerald and Jonathan Tonge *Sin Féin and the SDLP: From Alienation to Participation* (London; Hurst & Co., 2005)

2 Mailot, Agnés *New Sinn Féin: Irish Republicanism in the Twenty-first Century* (London; Routledge, 2005)

3 Doyle, John 'Republican Policies in Practical Politics: Placing Contemporary Sinn Féin in a European Context', working papers in *British-Irish Studies*, 13, (2005), p. 7

4 Coakley, John 'The Election that Made the First Dáil' in Brian Farrell (ed.) *The Creation of the Dáil* (Blackwater Press, 1994)

5 Taylor, Peter *Provos: The IRA and Sinn Féin* (London; Bloomsbury, 1998), p. 24

6 *ibid.*

7 Moloney, Ed *A Secret History of the IRA* (London; Allen Lane, 2002), p. 75

8 *ibid.*

9 English, Richard *Armed Struggle: The History of the IRA* (London; Macmillan, 2003), p. 112

10 Murray and Tonge *Sinn Féin and the SDLP*, p. 152

11 Mailot, Agnés *New Sinn Féin*, p. 104

12 Gallagher, Michael 'The Election Results and the New Dáil' in Michael Gallagher and Richard Sinnott *How Ireland Voted 1989?* (Galway; PSAI Press, 1990), p. 77

13 Ó Broin, E. 'Time for Sinn Féin to Work Out What it Stands for Now the Armed Struggle is over...', (2008), available at: http://sluggerotoole.com/2008/11/27/time-for-sinn-fein-to-work-out-what-it-stands-for-now-the-armed-struggle-is (accessed 28 December 2011)

14 Doyle 'Republican Policies in Practical Politics', p. 9

15 Interview with Daithí McKay, 14 December 2011

16 Ó Broin, E. 'Time for Sinn Féin to Work Out What it Stands for Now the Armed Struggle is over...', (2008), available at: http://sluggerotoole.com/2008/11/27/time-for-sinn-fein-to-work-out-what-it-stands-for-now-the-armed-struggle-is (accessed 28 December 2011)

17 Arnold, Bruce and Jason O'Tool *The End of the Party: How Fianna Fáil Lost its Grip on Power* (Dublin: Gill & Macmillan, 2011), pp. 50-4

18 O'Malley, Eoin 'Why is there no Radical Right Party in Ireland?', *West European Politics*, 31(5), (2008), pp. 960-77

19 Rabbitte, Pat 'Talks Offer Chance to Deal with "Race to the Bottom" Issue' (2006), available at http://www.labour.ie/press/listings/20060112154651.html

20 Sinn Féin 'Sinn Féin General Election Manifesto 2002: Building an Ireland of Equals' from http://www.sinnfein.ie/pdf/GeneralElection02.pdf, p. 16

21 Adam 1988 cited in Whyte, John H. *Interpreting Northern Ireland* (Oxford; Clarendon Press, 1990), p. 134

22 Murray and Tonge *Sinn Féin and the SDLP*, p. 165

23 Adams, Gerry *The New Ireland: A Vision for the Future* (Dingle; Brandon, 2006)

24 Sinn Féin 'Sinn Féin General Election Manifesto 2002', p. 22

25 Sinn Féin, General Election Manifesto, 2011

26 Curry, Phillip and Michael O'Connell 'Post-materialist Values and Political Preferences: Some Unlikely Findings from Northern Ireland', *European Journal of Political Research*, 35, (2000), pp 19-30

27 Moloney *A Secret History of the IRA*, p. 197

28 Sinn Féin 'Sinn Féin General Election Manifesto 2002', p. 7

29 Benoit, Kenneth and Michael Laver *Party Policy in Modern Democracy* (London; Routledge, 2006), p. 104

30 Suiter, Jane and David M. Farrell 'The Parties' Manifestos' in Michael Gallagher and Michael Marsh (eds) *How Ireland Voted 2011: The Full Story of Ireland's Earthquake Election* (London; Palgrave, 2011), pp. 29-46

31 Benoit and Laver *Party Policy in Modern Democracy*, see Appendix D

32 Gilland Lutz, Karin and Christopher Farrington 'Alternative Ulster? Political Parties and the Non-constitutional Policy Space in Northern Ierland', *Political Studies*, 54, (2006), pp. 715-42

33 Garry, John 'Consociationalism and its Critics: Evidence from the Historic Northern Ireland Assembly Election 2007', Electoral Studies, 28, (2009), pp. 458-66

34 Collins, Stephen 'Campaign Strategies', in Michael Gallagher, Michael Marsh and Paul Mitchell (eds) *How Ireland Voted 2002* (Basingstoke; Palgrave, 2003), p. 34

35 Weeks, Liam 'We Don't Like (To) Party: A Typology of Independents in Irish Political Life, 1922-2007', *Irish Political Studies*, 24(1), (2009), pp. 1-28

36 Marsh, Michael and Kevin Cunningham 'A Positive Choice, or Anyone but Fianna Fáil?' in Michael Gallagher and Michael Marsh (eds) *How Ireland Voted 2011: The Full Story of Ireland's Earthquake Election* (London; Palgrave, 2011), p. 177

37 O'Malley, Eoin 'The 2011 Irish Presidential Election: Culture, Valence, Loyalty or Punishment?', *Irish Political Studies*, 27(4), (2012)

38 *The Irish Times*, 21 March 2012

39 Interview with Daithí McKay, 14 December 2011

40 Taylor *Provos*; Moloney *A Secret History of the IRA*

41 Moloney *A Secret History of the IRA*

42 Rafter, Kevin *Sinn Féin 1905-2005; In the Shadow of Gunmen* (Dublin; Gill & Macmillan, 2005), p. 6

43 *ibid.*, p. 8, 10

44 Maillot, Agnés *New Sinn Féin: Irish Republicanism in the Twenty-first Century* (London; Routledge, 2005), p. 98

45 Interview with Daithí McKay, 14 December 2011

46 *ibid.*

47 *The Irish Times*, 21 March 2012

48 Moloney *A Secret History of the IRA*

49 Ó Broin, E. 'Time for Sinn Féin to Work Out What it Stands for Now the Armed Struggle is over...', (2008), available at: http://sluggerotoole.com/2008/11/27/time-for-

sinn-fein-to-work-out-what-it-stands-for-now-the-armed-struggle-is (accessed 28 December 2011)

### 13. *Voting in Dáil Éireann: The Changing Roles of Minor Parties and Independents, 1937-2011*

1 For example, Weeks, Liam 'We Don't Like (To) Party: A Typology of Independents in Irish Political Life, 1922-2007', *Irish Political Studies*, 24(1), (2009), pp.1-28; Weeks, Liam 'Minor Parties: A Schema for Analysis', *Irish Political Studies*, 25 (4), (2010), pp. 481-501; Coakley, John 'The Rise and Fall of Minor Parties in Ireland', *Irish Political Studies*, 25(4), (2010), pp. 503-58; O'Malley, Eoin 'Punch Bags for Heavyweights? Minor Parties in Irish Governments', *Irish Political Studies*, 25(4), 2010), pp. 539-62; Hansen, Martin E. 'The Parliamentary Behaviour of Minor Parties and Independents in Dáil Éireann', *Irish Political Studies*, 25(4), (2010), pp. 643-660; Clark, Alistair 'Breaking the Mould or Fiddling at the Edges? Ireland's Minor Parties in Comparative and Systemic Perspective', *Irish Political Studies*, 25(4), (2010), pp. 661-80

2 Hansen, Martin E. 'The Positions of Irish Parliamentary Actors', *Irish Political Studies*, 24 (1), (2009), pp. 29-44; Hansen. 'The Parliamentary Behaviour of Minor Parties and Independents in Dáil Éireann'; Sircar, I. and B. Høyland 'Get the Party Started: The Development of Political Party Legislative Dynamics in the Irish Free State Seanad' (1922-1936), *Party Politics*, 16, (2010), pp. 89-110

3 Hansen 'The Positions of Irish Parliamentary Actors'

4 Weeks 'We Don't Like (To) Party'

5 Weeks, Liam 'Parties and the Party System' in John Coakley and Michael Gallagher (eds) *Politics in the Republic of Ireland*, 5th edition (London; Routledge, 2009) pp. 137-67

6 Gallagher, Michael *Political Parties in the Republic of Ireland* (Dublin; Gill & Macmillan, 1985); Mair, Peter 'Explaining the Absence of Class Politics in Ireland' in John T. Goldthorpe and Christopher T. Whelan (eds) *The Development of Industrial Society in Ireland* (Oxford; Oxford University Press, 1992), pp. 383-410

7 Laver, Michael 'Are Irish Parties Peculiar?' in John T. Goldthorpe and Christopher T. Whelan (eds) *The Development of Industrial Society in Ireland* (Oxford; Oxford University Press, 1992), pp. 359-82

8 Weeks 'Parties and the Party System'

9 Gallagher *Political Parties in the Republic of Ireland*, p. 140; Gallagher, Michael and Michael Marsh *Days of Blue Loyalty: The Politics and Membership of Fine Gael* (Dublin; PSAI Press, 2002); Weeks 'Parties and the Party System'

10 Hansen 'The Positions of Irish Parliamentary Actors'

11 Mair, Peter *The Changing Irish Party System: Organisation, Ideology and Electoral Competition* (London; Frances Pinter, 1987)

12 Mitchell, Paul 'Ireland: From Single-Party to Coalition Rule', in Wolfgan Müller and Kaare Strøm (eds) *Coalition Governments in Western Europe* (Oxford; Oxford University Press, 2000)

13 Hansen 'The Positions of Irish Parliamentary Actors'

14 Mair *The Changing Irish Party System*; O'Malley, Eoin and Matthew Kerby 'Chronicle of a Death Foretold? Understanding the Decline of Fine Gael', *Irish Political Studies*, 19, (2004), pp. 39-58; Weeks 'Parties and the Party System'

15 Pedersen, Mogens N. 'Towards a New Typology of Party Lifespans and Minor Parties', *Scandinavian Political Studies*, 5 (1), (1982), pp. 1-16

16 *ibid.*

17 Hansen 'The Positions of Irish Parliamentary Actors'

18 The study of coalitions and coalitional behaviour is too comprehensive to go into detail here, but elements of these arguments can be found in, for instance Laver, Michael and

Norman Schofield *Multiparty Government: The Politics of Coalition in Europe* (Ann Arbor;
University of Michigan Press, 1990); Laver, Michael and Kenneth Shepsle *Making and
Breaking Governments: Cabinets and Legislatures in Parliamentary Democracies* (Cambridge;
Cambridge University Press, 1996)

19 Bolleyer, Nicole and Liam Weeks 'The Puzzle of Non-Party Actors in Party Democracy:
Independents in Ireland', *Comparative European Politics*, 7(3), (2009), pp. 299-324;
Weeks 'We Don't Like (To) Party'; Weeks, Liam 'Crashing the Party: Does STV Help
Independents?', *Party Politics* (published online, 2012)

20 Gallagher *Political Parties in the Republic of Ireland*, p. 119

21 Carty argues that members representing Clann na Poblachta and Clann na Talmhan
were to all intents and purposes independents after 1957 (Carty, R.K. *Party and Parish
Pump: Electoral Politics in Ireland* (Ontario; Wilfred Laurier Press, 1981), p. 30). However,
they are in Walker registered as running under their respective party labels, though it
should be noted that no official register of parties existed until 1963 (Walker, Brian
Mercer (ed.) *Parliamentary Election Results in Ireland: 1918-92: Irish Elections to Parliaments
and Parliamentary Assemblies at Westminster, Belfast, Dublin, Strasbourg* (Dublin; Royal Irish
Academy, 1992)

22 Weeks 'We Don't Like (To) Party'

23 *ibid.*

24 Another often used word for this type of independents would be 'gene-pool'
independents, though as argued and demonstrated by Hansen 'gene-pool' independents
are a more inclusive group than apostate independents (Hansen 'The Parliamentary
Behaviour of Minor Parties and Independents in Dáil Éireann')

25 Weeks 'We Don't Like (To) Party', p. 9-20

26 *ibid.*

27 *ibid.*, p. 7

28 Cowley, Philip and Mark Stuart 'There was a Doctor, a Journalist and Two Welshmen: the
Voting Behaviour of Independent MPs in the United Kingdom House of Commons,
1997-2007', *Parliamentary Affairs*, 62(1), (2009), p. 28

29 Thomas Burke who sat as an independent in the 13th Dáil cast only one vote as an
independent. Sources disagree on whether Burke was a representative for the Farmers'
Party (1937-1948) or only from 1937-43 and an independent from 1943-44 and from
1944-48. However, in the Dáil from 1944-48 he cast no votes either as independent or
Farmers' Party TD. In the Dáil of 1943-44 he cast three votes, one on 2 July 1943 and
two on 9 July 1943

30 Pedersen, Mogens N. 'Consensus and Conflict in the Danish Folketing 1945-1965',
*Scandinavian Political Studies*, 2, (1967), pp. 143-66; Hansen, Martin E. 'Reconsidering the
Party Distances and Dimensionality of the Danish Folketing' *Journal of Legislative Studies*,
14, (2008), pp. 264-278

31 Cowley and Stuart 'There was a Doctor, a Journalist and Two Welshmen'

32 Hansen 'The Positions of Irish Parliamentary Actors'; Hansen 'The Parliamentary
Behaviour of Minor Parties and Independents in Dáil Éireann'

33 Walker *Parliamentary Election Results in Ireland: 1918-92*

34 Weeks 'We Don't Like (To) Party'

35 I am grateful to Liam Weeks for supplying me with detailed data on the Irish
independents

36 The case of the Progressive Democrats officially disbanding in November 2009 has meant that
for the 30th Dáil the party has been coded up until November 2009. Mary Harney and Noel
Grealish have not been included as independents as they did not get elected as such

37 Hansen, in 'The Parliamentary Behaviour of Minor Parties and Independents in Dáil
Éireann', presents a similar analysis which also includes Labour. The omission of Labour

here does not change the results in any way. Indeed, the correlation between Labour and Fine Gael is around .90

38 The observant reader might notice that one minor party who entered government is missing from the table. Democratic Left entered the Fine Gael–Labour coalition in December 1994, but in the preceding Dáil Democratic Left was still a breakaway from the Workers' Party, and thus not having presented themselves to the electorate are not counted in this chapter

39 Weeks 'We Don't Like (To) Party'

40 *ibid.*, p. 19

41 *ibid.*

42 *ibid.*, p. 19

43 Hansen 'The Parliamentary Behaviour of Minor Parties and Independents in Dáil Éireann'

44 Weeks 'We Don't Like (To) Party', p. 15

45 Weeks 'We Don't Like (To) Party', p. 6-7

46 Hansen 'The Positions of Irish Parliamentary Actors'

## 14. *Radical, Redundant or Relevant? Minor Parties in Comparative and Systemic Perspective*

1 Laver, Michael 'Voting Behaviour', in John Coakley and Michael Gallagher (eds) *Politics in the Republic of Ireland*, 4th edition( London; Routledge/PSAI Press, 2005), pp. 202-9

2 Müller-Rommel, Ferdinand 'Small Parties in Comparative Perspective: The State of the Art', in Ferdinand Müller-Rommel and Geoffrey Pridham (eds) *Small Parties in Western Europe: Comparative and National Perspectives* (London; Sage, 1991), p. 14

3 Collins, Stephen *Breaking the Mould: How the PDs Changed Irish Politics* (Dublin; Gill & Macmillan, 2005)

4 The main source of data was the website: 'Election Resources on the Internet: Western Europe' (http://electionresources.org/western.europe.html) [November 2008 and November 2011]. Additional sources are listed under table 1. It is unfortunately not possible to be precise about the number of organisations falling under the 'others' category because of the tendency for small results to be combined in a catch-all 'others' category. Individual party results down to the 0.1 level contributed to the analysis because, as Gallagher notes, this allows more accurate calculation of electoral indices such as ENP (Gallagher, Michael 'Election Indices', (2008), available at: www.tcd.ie/PoliticalScience/staff/michael_gallagher/ElSystems/Docts/ElectionIndices.pdf, [22/10/08]). Figures for Germany are based on the second, list, vote of the country's MMP system. They are also based on West Germany pre-unification, and Germany as a whole post-unification. Italian figures between 1994-2001 are also based on the proportional element of the MMP system used in that period. As with all these data, the interpretation is however the author's own. Further details on the classification of parties are not reported here because of the limitations of space.

5 Mair, Peter 'The Electoral Universe of Small Parties in Post-war Western Europe' in Ferdinand Müller-Rommel and Geoffrey Pridham (eds) *Small Parties in Western Europe: Comparative and National Perspectives* (London; Sage, 1991)

6 Mair's analysis covered the period between 1947-87. This analysis overlaps with and extends that to the current period in which minor parties are seemingly more in evidence both electorally and in government across Europe

7 Lijphart, Arend *Patterns of Democracy: Government Forms and Performance in Thirty-Six Countries* (New Haven; Yale University Press, 1999), p. 67-9

8 Weeks, Liam 'We Don't Like (To) Party: A Typology of Independents in Irish Political Life, 1922-2007', *Irish Political Studies*, 24(1), (2009), pp.1-28

9 Weeks, Liam 'Parties and the Party System' in John Coakley and Michael Gallagher (eds) *Politics in the Republic of Ireland*, 5th edition (London; Routledge, 2009) pp. 137-67

10 Mair 'The Electoral Universe of Small Parties in Post-war Western Europe'

11 The clustering method used was between-groups linkage, while the cluster measure utilized was squared Euclidean distance

12 Mair 'The Electoral Universe of Small Parties in Post-war Western Europe'

13 Clark, Alistair 'Breaking the Mould or Fiddling at the Edges? Ireland's Minor Parties in Comparative and Systemic Perspective', *Irish Political Studies*, 25(4), (2010), pp. 661-80

14 Mair 'The Electoral Universe of Small Parties in Post-war Western Europe'

15 Herzog, Hanna 'Minor Parties: The Relevancy Perspective', *Comparative Politics*, 19(3), (1987), p. 318

16 Lawson, Kay 'When Linkage Fails' in Kay Lawson and Peter H. Merkl (eds) *When Parties Fail: Emerging Alternative Organisations* (Princeton, N.J.; Princeton University Press, 1988), pp. 13-38; Katz, Richard S. and Peter Mair 'Changing Models of Party Organization and Party Democracy: The Emergence of the Cartel Party', *Party Politics*, 1(1), (1995), pp. 5-28

17 Copus, Colin, Alistair Clark and K. Bottom 'Multi-Party Politics in England? Small Parties, Independents and Political Associations in English Local Politics', in Marion Reiser and Everhard Holtmann (eds) *Farewell to the Party Model? Independent Local Lists in Eastern and Western European Countries* (Wiesbaden; VS Verlag, 2008), pp. 254

18 Gallagher, Michael and Michael Marsh (eds) *How Ireland Voted 2011: The Full Story of Ireland's Earthquake Election* (London; Palgrave, 2011)

19 Weeks 'Parties and the Party System'; Coakley, John 'The Rise and Fall of Minor Parties in Ireland', *Irish Political Studies*, 25(4), (2010), pp. 503-58

20 Weeks, Liam 'Independents in Government: A Sui Gereris Model' in Kris Deschouwer (ed.) *Newly Governing Parties: In Power for the First Time* (London; Routledge, 2008), pp. 136-56; Weeks 'We Don't Like (To) Party'; Gallagher, Michael 'Ireland's Earthquake Election: Analysis of the Results' in Michael Gallagher and Michael Marsh (eds) *How Ireland Voted 2011: The Full Story of Ireland's Earthquake Election* (Basingstoke; Palgrave Macmillan, 2011), pp. 139-71

21 Mair, Peter and Liam Weeks 'The Party System' in John Coakley and Michael Gallagher (eds) *Politics in the Republic of Ireland*, 4th edition (London; Routledge/PSAI Press, 2005), pp. 153; O'Malley, E. and Kerby, M. 'Chronicle of a Death Foretold? Understanding the Decline of Fine Gael', *Irish Political Studies*, 19, (2004), pp. 39-58

22 Marsh, Michael, Richard Sinnott, John Garry and Fiachra Kennedy *The Irish Voter: The Nature of Electoral Competition in the Republic of Ireland* (Manchester; Manchester University Press, 2008)

23 Pedersen index figures for net volatility are the author's own calculations from the data in Coakley, John 'Appendix 2 Electoral Data', in John Coakley and Michael Gallagher (eds) *Politics in the Republic of Ireland*, 4th edition (London; Routledge/PSAI Press, 2005), p. 466; Gallagher, Michael 'The Earthquake that Never Happened: Analysis of the Results' in Michael Gallagher and Michael Marsh (eds) *How Ireland Voted 2007: The Full Story of Ireland's General Election* (Basingstoke; Palgrave Macmilan, 2008), p. 82; and Gallagher, Michael 'Ireland's Earthquake Election: Analysis of the Results' in Michael Gallagher and Michael Marsh (eds) *How Ireland Voted 2011: The Full Story of Ireland's Earthquake Election* (Basingstoke; Palgrave Macmillan, 2011), pp. 139-71

24 Run as bivariate regressions with volatility as the independent variable, the adjusted $R^2$ for 'Others' including independents was .738, while for the small party share only the adjusted $R^2$ was .781.

25 Gallagher 'The Earthquake that Never Happened', p. 89

26 Marsh *et al.* *The Irish Voter*, p. 17, 68

27 O'Malley, Eoin 'Punch Bags for Heavyweights? Minor Parties in Irish Governments', *Irish Political Studies*, 25(4), 2010), pp. 539-62

28 Marsh *et al. The Irish Voter*, p. 193; Gallagher 'Ireland's Earthquake Election'

29 ENEP measures were sourced from Gallagher 'Election Indices' and author's calculations. The adjusted R² for the bivariate regression of ENEP on turnout was .570.

30 The Pearson correlation was -.846 which was significant at the p<0.01 level. The bivariate adjusted R² was .687

31 Kavanagh, Adrian 'The 2004 Local Elections in the Republic of Ireland', *Irish Political Studies*, 19(2), (2004), pp. 69

32 Marsh *et al. The Irish Voter*, p. 17

33 Marsh, Michael and Kevin Cunningham 'A Positive Choice, or Anyone but Fianna Fáil?' in Michael Gallagher and Michael Marsh (eds) *How Ireland Voted 2011: The Full Story of Ireland's Earthquake Election* (London; Palgrave, 2011), pp. 182

34 Marsh *et al. The Irish Voter*, pp. 199-200

35 *ibid.*, p. 37-8

36 *ibid.*, pp. 38, 73-5

37 Marsh and Cunningham 'A Positive Choice, or Anyone but Fianna Fáil?', p. 183

38 Marsh *et al. The Irish Voter*, pp. 173-7

39 Marsh, Michael 'Parties and Society' in John Coakley and Michael Gallagher (eds), *Politics in the Republic of Ireland*, 4th edition (Abingdon; Routledge, 2005), pp.169-70; Weeks 'Parties and the Party System', p. 155

40 Estimated from the party voters figure in table 6.2 in Marsh 'Parties and Society', p. 169 and table 5.1 in Weeks 'Parties and the Party System', p. 155

41 Unfortunately no such study has yet been carried out. Nevertheless, for an insight into members' views of minor party strategy and health, see Dunphy, Richard '"A Group of Individuals Trying To Do Their Best': The Dilemmas of Democratic Left", *Irish Political Studies*, 13(1), (1998) pp. 50-75

42 Scarrow, Susan E. *Parties and Their Members: Organizing for Victory in Britain and Germany* (Oxford; Oxford University Press, 1996)

43 Laver, Michael (1998) 'Party Policy in Ireland 1997: Results from an Expert Survey', *Irish Political Studies*, 13, (1998), pp. 159-71

44 Benoit, Kenneth and Michael Laver 'Estimating Irish Party Policy Positions Using Computer Wordscoring: The 2002 Election – A Research Note', *Irish Political Studies*, 18(1), (2003), pp. 97-107

45 Marsh *et al. The Irish Voter*, pp. 50-2

46 Sudulich, Maria L. and Matthew Wall 'Rewarding the Wealthy Versus Looking After The Poor: Affective Perception of Right and Left by Candidates in the 2007 Irish General Elections', *Irish Political Studies*, 25(1), (2010), pp. 95-106; Suiter, Jane and David M. Farrell 'The Parties' Manifestos' in Michael Gallagher and Michael Marsh (eds) *How Ireland Voted 2011: The Full Story of Ireland's Earthquake Election* (London; Palgrave, 2011), pp. 29-46

47 Benoit and Laver 'Estimating Irish Party Policy Positions Using Computer Wordscoring'

48 See also Gilland Lutz, K. 'Irish Party Competition in the New Millennium: Change or Plus Ca Change?' *Irish Political Studies*, 18(2), (2003), pp. 40-59. He argues that it is in their long-term policy priorities that the parties have the most distinct policy profiles

49 McDonnell, Daniel 'The Republic of Ireland: The Dog That Hasn't Barked in the Night', in D. Albertazzi and Daniel McDonnell (eds) *Twenty-First Century Populism: The Spectre of Western Democracy* (Basingstoke; Palgrave, 2008), p. 201

50 Marsh *et al. The Irish Voter*, chapter 3

51 *ibid.*

52 Kitschelt, Herbert *The Radical Right in Western Europe: A Comparative Analysis* (Ann Arbor; Michigan University Press, 1997); Mudde, Cas *Populist Radical Right Parties in Europe* (Cambridge; Cambridge University Press, 2007)

53 Garner, S. 'Ireland and Immigration: Explaining the Absence of the Far Right', *Patterns of Prejudice*, 41(2), (2007), pp. 109-30

54 O'Malley, Eoin 'Why is there no Radical Right Party in Ireland?', *West European Politics*, 31(5), (2008), pp. 960-77

55 Both terms are regularly used in explaining the appeal of the radical right. See Kitschelt *The Radical Right in Western Europe* and Mudde *Populist Radical Right Parties in Europe*

56 McDonnell 'The Republic of Ireland', p. 204

57 *ibid.*, p. 204-5

58 Costello, Rory and Robert Thomson 'The Fulfilment of Election Pledges' in Michael Gallagher and Michael Marsh (eds) *How Ireland Voted 2007: The Full Story of Ireland's General Election* (Basingstoke; Palgrave Macmillan, 2008), p. 25

59 *ibid.*, p. 24-6

60 Coakley, John 'The Rise and Fall of Minor Parties in Ireland', *Irish Political Studies*, 25(4), (2010), pp. 503-58; see also chapter 3

61 Varley, Tony 'On the Road to Extinction: Agrarian Parties in Twentieth Century Ireland', *Irish Political Studies*, 25(4), (2010), pp. 581-602

62 Murphy, Gary 'Influencing Political Decision Making: Interest Groups and Elections in Independent Ireland', *Irish Political Studies*, 25(4), (2010), pp. 563-80; see also chapter 8

63 McDaid, Shaun and Kacper Rekawek 'From Mainstream to Minor and Back – The Irish Labour Party, 1987-1992', *Irish Political Studies*, 25(4), (2010), pp. 625-42; see also chapter 11

64 O'Malley, Eoin 'Punch Bags for Heavyweights? Minor Parties in Irish Governments', *Irish Political Studies*, 25(4), 2010), pp. 539-62

65 Bolleyer, Nicole 'The Irish Green Party: From Protest to Mainstream Party?', *Irish Political Studies*, 25(4), (2010), pp. 603-23; see also chapter 6

66 Harmel, Robert and John D. Robertson 'Formation and Success of New Parties', *International Political Science Review*, 6(4), (1985), pp. 501-23

67 Murphy 'Influencing Political Decision Making: Interest Groups and Elections in Independent Ireland'; see also chapter 8

68 Smith, Gordon 'In Search of Small Parties: Problems of Definition, Classification and Significance' in Ferdinand Müller-Rommel and Geoffrey Pridham (eds) *Small Parties in Western Europe: Comparative and National Perspectives* (London; Sage, 1991), pp. 23-40

69 Coakley, John 'The Rise and Fall of Minor Parties in Ireland'; see also chapter 3

70 Weeks 'We Don't Like (To) Party'

71 Mair 'The Electoral Universe of Small Parties in Post-war Western Europe', p. 44

72 McDaid and Rekawek 'From Mainstream to Minor and Back'; Weeks 'Parties and the Party System'; Coakley 'The Rise and Fall of Minor Parties in Ireland'; Weeks, Liam 'Minor Parties: A Schema for Analysis', *Irish Political Studies*, 25 (4), (2010), pp. 481-501

73 Smith 'In Search of Small Parties', p. 25

74 O'Malley 'Punch Bags for Heavyweights?'

75 Mair 'The Electoral Universe of Small Parties in Post-war Western Europe'

76 Deschouwer, Kris 'Comparing Newly Governing Parties' in Kris Deschouwer (ed.) *New Parties in Government: In Power for the First Time* (London; Routledge, 2008), pp. 1-16; Müller-Rommel 'Small Parties in Comparative Perspective'; Müller-Rommel, Ferdinand 'The Lifespan and Political Performance of Green Parties in Western Europe' in Ferdinand Müller-Rommel and Thomas Poguntke (eds) *Green Parties in National Governments* (London; Cass, 2002), pp. 1-16; Pedersen, Mogens N. 'Towards a New Typology of Party Lifespans and Minor Parties', *Scandinavian Political Studies*, 5 (1), (1982), pp. 1-16

77 Pedersen 'Towards a New Typology of Party Lifespans and Minor Parties'

78 Hug, Simon 'Studying the Electoral Success of New Political Parties', *Party Politics*, 6(2), (2000), pp. 187-97; Pedersen 'Towards a New Typology of Party Lifespans and Minor Parties'; Rochon, Thomas R. 'Mobilizers and Challengers: Towards a Theory of New

Party Success', *International Political Science Review*, 6(4), (1985), pp. 419-39; Tavits, Margit 'Party System Change: Testing a Model of New Party Entry', *Party Politics*, 12(1), (2006), pp. 99-119

79 Deschouwer 'Comparing Newly Governing Parties'

80 O'Malley 'Punch Bags for Heavyweights?'

81 McDaid and Rekawek 'From Mainstream to Minor and Back'

82 Bolleyer 'The Irish Green Party'

83 Aars, J. and H.E. Ringkjob 'Party Politicisation Reversed? Non-Partisan Alternatives in Norwegian Local Politics', *Scandinavian Political Studies*, 28(2), (2005), pp. 161-81; Reiser, Marion and Holtmann, Everhard (eds) *Farewell to the Party Model? Independent Local Lists in Eastern and Western European Countries* (Wiesbaden; VS Verlag)

84 Berry, R. *Independent: The Rise of the Non-Aligned Politician* (Exeter; Imprint Academic, 2008)

85 Weeks 'We Don't Like (To) Party'

86 Copus *et al.* 'Multi-Party Politics in England?'

87 Bolleyer, Nicole and Liam Weeks 'The Puzzle of Non-Party Actors in Party Democracy: Independents in Ireland', *Comparative European Politics*, 7(3), (2009), pp. 299-324

88 Cowley, P. and M. Stuart 'There was a Doctor, a Journalist and Two Welshmen: The Voting Behaviour of Independent MPs in the United Kingdom House of Commons, 1997-2007', *Parliamentary Affairs*, 62(1), pp. 18-31

89 Russell, Meg and Sciara. Maria 'Independent Parliamentarians En Masse: The Changing Nature and Role of the 'Crossbenchers' in the House of Lords', *Parliamentary Affairs*, 62(1), (2009), pp. 32-52

90 Hansen, Martin E. 'The Parliamentary Behaviour of Minor Parties and Independents in Dáil Éireann', *Irish Political Studies*, 25(4), (2010), pp. 643-660

91 Mair 'The Electoral Universe of Small Parties in Post-war Western Europe'

# Notes on Contributors

**Nicole Bolleyer** is a Senior Lecturer in Politics at the University of Exeter. Her research focuses on comparative federalism and party politics in advanced democracies. She is the author of *Intergovernmental Cooperation – Rational Choices in Federal Systems and Beyond* (Oxford University Press, 2009) and recently completed her second research monograph *New Parties in Old Party Systems*, forthcoming with Oxford University Press. Her articles on party politics have appeared in journals such as *Governance, Political Studies* and *Party Politics* and are forthcoming with the *European Journal of Political Research*.

**Alistair Clark** is Lecturer in Politics in the School of Geography, Politics and Sociology at Newcastle University. His research interests include political parties, party organisation, small party challenges and party system change. His work has appeared in journals such as *Party Politics, Parliamentary Affairs* and *Irish Political Studies*. He has recently published *Political Parties in the UK* (Palgrave, 2012).

**John Coakley** is a professor in the School of Politics and International Relations at University College Dublin. He has published extensively on Irish politics, comparative politics and nationalism. His publications include *Politics in the Republic of Ireland* (5th edn, Routledge, 2010; edited with Michael Gallagher) and *Making and Breaking Nations: Nationalism, Ethnic Conflict and the State* (Sage, 2012).

**Martin Ejnar Hansen** is Lecturer in Politics at the Department of Politics and History, School of Social Sciences, Brunel University. His primary research interests lie in legislative studies and comparative politics. Among his publications are a number of articles on Irish politics in *Irish Political Studies*.

**Shaun McDaid** is a Research Fellow at the School of Human and Health Sciences, University of Huddersfield. His primary research interests are in the fields of British and Irish politics and history. His first book entitled *Template for Peace: Northern Ireland, 1972-75* will be published by Manchester University Press in 2013.

**Gary Murphy** is Associate Professor of Government in the School of Law and Government at Dublin City University. He has written extensively on Irish politics. Recent publications include *In Search of the Promised Land: Politics in Postwar Ireland* (Mercier Press,

2009); *Continuity, Change and Crisis in Contemporary Ireland* (Routledge, 2010; co-edited with Brian Girvin); and *Regulating Lobbying: A global Comparison* (Manchester University Press, 2010) with Raj Chari and John Hogan. He was a visiting Fulbright Professor of Politics at the University of North Carolina, Chapel Hill, in 2011–12.

**Kacper Rekawek** is an analyst at the Polish Institute of International Affairs (PISM) and Adjunct Professor of Politics at the Warsaw School of Humanities and Social Sciences (SWPS). He is the author of *Irish Republican Terrorism and Politics. A Comparative Study of the Official and the Provisional IRA* (Routledge, 2011) and his research interests are in both Irish politics and international terrorism.

**Séin Ó Muineacháin** holds a PhD from Trinity College Dublin, which investigates the reasons for the persistence of factions in political parties. His research interests include electoral systems, political parties, political reform and Irish politics. He previously worked for the Joint Oireachtas Committee on the Constitution during its work module on electoral reform. He currently works as a policy analyst in London.

**Eoin O'Malley** is a lecturer in political science at the School of Law and Government, Dublin City University. He is the author of over thirty journal articles or book chapters, mainly on Irish politics, and author of *Contemporary Ireland* (Palgrave, 2011) and co-editor of *Governing Ireland: From Cabinet Government to Delegated Governance* (IPA, 2012). He is currently working on a book on leadership and political power in Ireland.

**Kevin Rafter** is a senior lecturer in political communication and journalism at Dublin City University. He worked previously as a political journalist with *The Irish Times, The Sunday Times*, the *Sunday Tribune*, and with RTÉ as a presenter of the *This Week* radio programme and as a correspondent with *Prime Time*. He has published widely on media and politics. Recent publications include *Democratic Left: The Life and Death of an Irish Political Party* (Irish Academic Press, 2011) and *Road to Power: How Fine Gael Made History* (New Island, 2011). He is also editor of *Irish Journalism Before Independence: More a Disease than a Profession* (Manchester UP, 2011) and co-editor of *Independent Newspapers: A History* (Four Courts, 2012).

**Tony Varley** lectures in Political Science and Sociology at the National University of Ireland, Galway. He has recently co-edited *A Living Countryside? The Politics of Sustainable Development in Rural Ireland* (Ashgate, 2009) and *Integration through Subordination: The Politics of Agricultural Modernisation in Industrial Europe* (Brepols, 2012).

**Dawn Walsh** is a PhD candidate at the School of Law and Government, Dublin City University. She previously worked in the Houses of the Oireachtas and has an M.Phil in International Peace Studies from Trinity College Dublin. Her main research interests centre on the Northern Ireland peace process, and her PhD focuses on the use of independent commissions in Northern Ireland, for which she was the recipient of the 2010-2011 Paddy Moriarty Postgraduate Fellowship.

**Liam Weeks** is a lecturer in politics at the Department of Government, University College Cork. He is on an Irish Research Council CARA postdoctoral fellowship (co-funded by the European Commission) from 2010 to 2013, on which he was a Visiting Fellow at Sydney Macquarie University and the University of Sydney. He has published on Irish politics in *Party Politics, Irish Political Studies, Parliamentary Affairs* and *Comparative European Politics*. His first book, *All Politics is Local* (Collins Press, 2009), was co-authored with Aodh Quinlivan.

# Acknowledgements

This book has its origins in a special issue of *Irish Political Studies*, following which we felt there was a lot more to be said about the topic of minor parties, particularly given the ongoing political turmoil at home and abroad.

We are extremely grateful to The History Press Ireland for the opportunity to express our thoughts on this matter. In particular, we would like to thank the enthusiasm of Ronan Colgan to our initial proposal and the work of Beth Amphlett in the production process.

Although our names adorn the cover, this book is a joint effort by all involved and we thank the input of all the contributors, who responded to our many demands with patience and efficiency.

We thank the Political Studies Association of Ireland for sponsoring a collaborative workshop of the authors and supporting the development of this book project.

Liam thanks the Irish Research Council for its support during the time he served on its CARA postdoctoral fellowship scheme, which was co-funded by the European Commission.

Finally, we thank the support, as always, of our loved ones. They know who they are.